Theorizing Legal Punishment

This book systematically defends an account of the institution of legal punishment that draws on both retributive and crime-prevention thinking.

The work argues that legal punishment censures convicted offenders and thus morally communicates with them, any victims, and the broader community, while also serving to reduce future crime. The expressive or retributive element is assigned the lead role in this mixed account because it better captures the notion that members of society are to be held morally accountable for their failures to abide by defensible criminal prohibitions of various kinds. Despite this, it is conceded that the reduction of crime plays a vital role in justifying the institution of legal punishment and the book contains extended discussion of how and why this is so. Beyond its explication of the aims of legal punishment and their respective roles within a mixed theory, the study devotes separate chapters to sentencing, criminal procedure, and the imposition of fees and collateral legal consequences on individuals who have been convicted of crimes and fully served their sentences. In these ways, the work moves beyond discussion of the abstract aims of legal punishment to details of the institution's internal structure and operations. The many historical deficiencies and failures of the institution are duly noted and the challenges they pose for punishment theorizing are examined.

The book closes with discussion of the limited success of punishment institutions in apprehending, convicting, and punishing those who violate the law, including many who do so in serious ways. Alternatives to reliance on legal punishment institutions are briefly examined. In the end, retention of such institutions is urged although it is suggested that we ought to have modest expectations about their ultimate success. The work will be of interest to those working in the areas of Legal Philosophy and Criminology.

Richard L. Lippke is emeritus professor of criminal justice at Indiana University-Bloomington. He is the author of four books and 75 published articles or book chapters.

Routledge Research in Legal Philosophy

The Origin of Copyright
Expression as Knowing in Being and Copyright Onto-Epistemology
Wenwei GUAN

Constitutional Imaginaries
A Theory of European Societal Constitutionalism
Jiří Přibáň

Human Dignity and the Law
A Personalist Theory
Michał Rupniewski

Legal Ethics for Lawyers
A New Model
Barbara Mescher

Moral Pluralism and the Complexity of Punishment
The Penal Philosophy of H.L.A. Hart
Nicolas Nayfeld

Sport, Law and Philosophy
The Jurisprudence of Sport
Miroslav Imbrisevic

Cosmopolitanism, State Sovereignty and International Law and Politics
A Theory
Jorge E. Núñez

Theorizing Legal Punishment
Richard L. Lippke

For more information about this series, please visit: www.routledge.com/Routledge-Research-in-Legal-Philosophy/book-series/RRLP

Theorizing Legal Punishment

Richard L. Lippke

Routledge
Taylor & Francis Group
LONDON AND NEW YORK

Acknowledgments

Some of the work on this book was undertaken while I was on sabbatical leave from my teaching and other responsibilities at Indiana University-Bloomington. I am grateful to the university for the opportunity furnished by the leave.

Several of the chapters of this book incorporate some of my previously published work. Part of Chapter 2 draws on "Two Ways of Thinking About the Value of Deserved Punishment," Richard L. Lippke, *The Journal of Ethics* 23 (2019): 387–406, Springer Nature, https://doi.org/10.1007/s10892-019-09301-6, as well as "The Nature of Retributive Justice and Its Demands on the State," Richard L. Lippke, *Law and Philosophy* 38 (2019): 58–77, Springer Nature, https://doi.org/10.1007/s10982-018-9336-6. Parts of Chapters 3 and 8 draw on "Retributivism and Victim Compensation," *Social Theory and Practice* 46 (2020): 317–38. Part of Chapter 7 incorporates material from "Punishment, Public Safety, and Collateral Legal Consequences," *Journal of Applied Philosophy* 2023 at https://doi.org/10.1111/japp.12653. The lattermost article was improved by various comments I received about an earlier draft from the participants in a Zoom conference sponsored by the University of Nottingham. The conference was organized by Zach Hoskins and William Bülow.

The manuscript was also improved substantially by various reviewer comments and suggestions. I wish to thank all of them for their efforts.

Thanks also to Alison Kirk, at Routledge, who was unfailingly helpful and encouraging in seeing the book through to completion.

Finally, I want to thank my wife, Theresa Brezina, for her patience while I toiled through the latter stages of the book's completion and especially for keeping me sane and happy.

Introduction

The extant literature on the justification of legal punishment at times reads a bit like a partisan brawl. Those who support retributive theories of the institution's justification often seem to have little use for approaches that emphasize the reduction of crime. Although retributivists might concede that preventing or reducing crime is an effect of the institution, they mostly seem to treat this as a fortunate side effect, one to be noted and then mostly relegated to the sidelines. Those who favor crime reduction approaches to the institution's justification at times edge toward scornfulness in their assessments of theories offered by their retributive counterparts. Lots of ink is spilled in efforts to demonstrate the questionable or worrisome features of retributivism. Less is spilled, it seems to me, on carefully spelling out, in some detail, how the aim of reducing crime would have us structure the institution or in responding to the empirical evidence that has emerged over the last 50 years that casts doubt on punishment's crime reduction credentials.

For some time, my sense has been that both of the main theoretical approaches to the justification of legal punishment have something important to offer and that the sensible thing to do is to find some way of combining them. The first step toward doing so is to identify plausible interpretations of each of the main theoretical elements. The first four chapters of this book work toward doing so. I urge a view according to which moral communication with offenders, victims, and the public should occupy the lead role in justifying the institution. I assign it this role because, like others, I believe that doing so is most consistent with an understanding of legal punishment as an institution that holds those who commit crimes morally accountable for their acts. Notoriously, not all of the individuals convicted of crimes, or tempted to commit them, are sufficiently responsive to the moral reasons they have against doing so. They might be somewhat more amenable to deterrent threats; failing that, they might be incapacitated for some period of time in order to protect the public, perhaps with the hope that they will, during their stints in confinement, mature a bit or rekindle their moral bearings. These might be vain hopes in relation to many offenders, for reasons with which penal theorists and social scientists are well familiar. Still, I embrace the notion that the reduction of

DOI: 10.4324/9781032661667-1

crime is an important purpose of legal punishment and attempt to show how it can be integrated into an overall account of the institution that assigns moral communication the lead role. One of the signal contributions of the book is, I believe, the close attention I pay to explaining how the moral communication and crime reduction elements of my theory are to be combined into a unified account. In doing so, I seek to move beyond gestures toward a mixed theory of punishment that have too often been the norm in the field.

Further, I contend that other values should guide and constrain the criminal law and the institutions we devise to enforce it. That the criminal law should at least partly consist of prohibitions on actions that violate the basic moral rights of individuals will not be terribly controversial position. There is, of course, considerable debate about which basic moral rights individuals have, a point of controversy that I will deal with by suggesting that there is likely to be considerable overlap among competing accounts, at least with respect to many familiar *mala in se* provisions of the criminal law. In this way, the concept of basic moral rights offers important insights into the content of the criminal law. But the concept will also be invaluable in shaping and constraining criminal procedure and sentencing. If basic moral rights are to be given their due, they should not be easily set aside or overridden by state officials as they perform the vital tasks of investigating crimes, prosecuting those they have accused of them, and punishing those who they convict. The value of parsimony in state action will often be invoked in my account of legal punishment. As I construe that value, we should insist that state officials act cautiously and move incrementally in infringing rights—always being prepared to infringe them less rather more—as they enforce the criminal law and punish those convicted of violating it. Although the concepts of basic moral rights and the parsimony in state action they demand might not tell us much about why we punish, they should be understood to play significant roles in shaping the institutions of criminal justice.

It is one thing to specify and defend abstract justifying aims of legal punishment, including a mixed one of the sort I defend. It is another to spell out, in some detail, the implications of such a theory for the design of a formidable and complex institution like that of legal punishment. My sense is that penal theorists have too often focused on the former while devoting insufficient attention to the latter. In particular, how criminal procedure and sentencing should be structured to accomplish whatever purposes it is believed justify the institution are not matters that should be relegated to the sidelines of penal theorizing, treated as mere technical details of secondary importance. Presumably, no penal theorist wants to set up an institution that routinely fails to separate the guilty from innocents wrongly accused or tends to convict the guilty of greater or lesser crimes than they committed. Likewise, no penal theorist desires a sentencing regime that predictably fails to match crimes to appropriate sanctions or utilizes sanctions that degrade offenders or make them more crime-prone. But specifying, in some detail, how we should proceed with the complex tasks of criminal procedure and sentencing in ways that avoid or minimize the likelihood of such undesirable outcomes are matters that have received less attention in the penal theory literature.

Three themes of considerable importance recur throughout the book. One of them is the fraught character of legal punishment institutions. Not only have such institutions often failed to reliably restrict the imposition of penal sanctions to those provably guilty of crimes, they have employed sanctions that degrade those convicted of crimes, caused them needless and damaging suffering, and likely made reoffending by many of them more likely. Second, there has also been a marked tendency of legal authorities to target the poor and racial or ethnic minorities in their efforts to control crime. Sadly, when these same individuals are victimized by crimes, legal authorities seem to neglect them. Penal theorists must grapple with these salient defects of past and present criminal justice systems and contrive solutions that offer us some hope of rectifying or at least minimizing them. Third, there is some tendency for penal theorists to focus too much attention on more serious crimes and their punishment. This is understandable, perhaps, since it is such crimes that most frighten us and thus undermine the perceived safety and stability of our rights. However, modern criminal justice systems are often inundated with minor offenders and their crimes.[1] No doubt there are some minor criminal prohibitions that we should strongly consider eliminating. Many of them aim at discouraging self-harm or actions that violate widely held moral beliefs without really harming anyone.[2] That being said, I will assume that many of the kinds of minor criminal prohibitions that are routinely violated are ones that we ought to retain. Not only is incarceration unlikely to be a defensible sanction for such crimes, but we should strive to hold those who violate such prohibitions accountable for doing so in ways that shore up, or at least do not diminish, their capacities for responsible conduct.

A More Detailed Overview

Let me turn, then, to a more elaborate overview of the arguments of the book. In Chapter 1, I examine legal punishment's role in the reduction of crime. Legal punishment is supposed to prevent or reduce crime through the familiar mechanisms of deterrence (both general and specific), incapacitation, and rehabilitation. Some have also suggested that it prevents crime by reinforcing moral norms against offending. Instead of emphasizing the ways in which the logic of crime reduction might countenance punishment of the innocent or over- or underpunishment of the guilty, I focus on the ways in which legal punishment, as an institution, does not appear to be a very impressive force for the reduction of crime. There are well-known limitations with each of the standard modes of crime reduction and, in particular, the effectiveness of legal punishment in deterring crime. Many of the mostly young (predominately male) individuals inclined to commit crimes are not all that amenable to legal punishment's deterrent threats. The rest of us rarely need such threats to dissuade us from committing crimes, and especially serious ones. Moreover, it is increasingly clear that involvement with the criminal justice system is far from a positive force in offenders' lives, such that it will make some of them more apt to continue offending than desist from it. My conclusion is that legal punishment, at most, works to tamp down crime, although to what extent it does so is unclear. If that is correct, we are not left with a rousing defense of the institution.

In the second chapter, I examine two well-known versions of positive retributivism. According to the first version, legal punishment is justified because it aims at giving those (appropriately) convicted of crimes the punishment they deserve. According to the second version, it is justified because it censures offenders for their crimes, thus morally communicating with them, their victims (when there are any), and other members of society about the public wrongs of which their crimes consist. With regard to desert retributivism, I raise a number of concerns. First, I note that extreme cases of criminal wrongdoing that desert retributivists often invoke to convince us that wrongdoers deserve to suffer are unlike many of the criminal acts that society must address. Crimes that consist of violations of *mala prohibita* or that result from interpersonal disputes or desperate poverty are commonplace. Yet we might hesitate to say that their perpetrators "deserve to suffer," although we might agree that their wrongs need to be censured as violations of the governing rules of the society. Second, I question the plausibility of the contention by some desert retributivists that the punishment of convicted offenders is an intrinsic good. Some crimes leave victims dead, profoundly injured, or emotionally debilitated for years to come. It is hard to see how punishing the perpetrators of such crimes transforms what is bad or ugly into something noble or good. I contend that we need an account of legal punishment that explains why there is something valuable that comes from punishment even in the face of substantial and enduring harm to victims. Third, I note the ways in which investigating crimes, apprehending likely offenders, convicting, and punishing them are costly endeavors. Desert retributivism, I contend, struggles to explain how far society should go in investing its limited resources in capturing and punishing offenders, many of whom will have committed relatively minor offenses. Should we focus as many of our limited resources on punishing minor offenses as major ones? If punishment of the deserving is an intrinsic good, it might make sense to do so, yet that is a conclusion we should be reluctant to accept.

I then attempt to show how expressivist accounts of retributivism fare better in addressing the problems I pose for desert versions of the theory. After sketching such an account, I contend that it does not construe the punishment of convicted offenders as an intrinsic good, and especially not a good that supports a duty on the part of the state to punish offenders. Instead, effecting moral communication through punishment provides a reason for the state to pursue punishment of the guilty the strength of which varies depending on the severity of the crimes in question. We should, as a society, be prepared to invest more of our limited resources in capturing, convicting, and punishing those whose crimes violate basic rights of individuals in egregious ways that are prohibited by the criminal law. It is vitally important for the state to stand by and for the victims of crimes, to affirm, emphatically, that their lives and vital interests are not to be destroyed or damaged with impunity by those who commit crimes against them. The good consequences of such communication are numerous and not reducible, simply, to the prevention of future crimes. The victims of crime (and those who care about them) are often traumatized by what others illicitly do to them, profoundly so when the crimes in question are grave. Arguably, they look to the state to reaffirm the value and legitimacy of their violated interests even if they are not convinced of or concerned about whether state efforts to hold their victimizers accountable will reduce future crimes. Indeed, persistent state failures to capture, convict, and punish the individuals who wronged them will leave victims (and members of the general public) demoralized, with various collateral effects on their abilities or willingness to exercise and enjoy their most basic rights.

In the third chapter, I more fully develop and defend the moral communication version of retributivism, drawing heavily on the work of other theorists who have advanced such an approach.[3] Moral communication versions of retributivism have numerous critics, whose doubts about the approach must be addressed. I cast punishment's communicative aims widely, arguing that it is directed not only to those convicted of crimes, but also to the victims of their crimes (if there are victims), and to the broader public. My account prioritizes the importance of accurate communication, and thus an appropriate valuing of any victims' violated interests through both the language and burdens of punishment. Alternatives to the imposition of penal burdens on offenders as forms of moral communication are examined and rejected. These include proposals to celebrate victims' lives and interests or to compensate them, at state expense, for the harms they have suffered. They also include proposals to "merely censure" criminal acts without imposing hard treatment on offenders.

In the fourth chapter, I elaborate my mixed theory of legal punishment, contrasting it with other mixed theories, and show how the two elements of moral communication and crime reduction are to be combined into a unified account. Again, it is an account that puts moral communication in the lead role because doing so better coheres with our understanding of legal punishment as an institution that holds individuals accountable for the public wrongs they have committed. The crime reduction element, by contrast, tends to emphasize threats, restraint, or the alteration of offenders so that they are less crime-prone. Such modes of attempting to influence individuals make sense in a back-up role, but fail to fully acknowledge the moral infractions of which many crimes consist. Still, I cast the lead role of moral communication as presumptive. There are circumstances in which the crime reduction benefits of departures from accurate moral communication with offenders, victims, and the public might be substantial. However, we should be cautious about embracing such departures and so I discuss the conditions under which they might defensibly be made. I also spend time discussing the significant roles that general deterrence and incapacitation play in my mixed theory.

Beginning in the fifth chapter, I elaborate the implications of my mixed theory of legal punishment for the complex process whereby individuals suspected of crimes are investigated, arrested, charged, and convicted (if they are convicted). I first argue that the dignity of persons requires state officials to be parsimonious in the deployment of their coercive powers. Parsimony requires those officials to surmount progressive justificatory barriers as they work toward the conviction of those they suspect of crimes. At the limit, the state should have to demonstrate the guilt of the accused to a high standard of proof. In cases in which charges are resolved through guilty pleas, limits on the kinds of pressures that prosecutors can exert to induce such pleas should be in place. Second, if state officials are to effect moral communication with those convicted of crimes, they must take steps to ensure that they occupy the moral high ground while and when they do so. This entails that they must seek assiduously to get at the truth of the charges against those whom they suspect of crimes. They must be understanding of and committed to avoiding the kinds of errors that often plague criminal investigations and charge adjudication and they must embrace checks and balances on their powers to move the criminal process along. Third, state officials must be committed to treating all members of society as equals before the law. Historically, criminal justice systems have often fallen well short of this ideal. They have subjected some individuals in society to closer official scrutiny of their conduct and what comes with that—arrest, charges, and convictions. Or they have failed to police and prosecute crimes against some members of society. What emerges from these official missteps and shortcomings is a distorted picture of who commits crimes and who suffers from them, contrary to what should be the veridical moral communication aims of state officials. Worse than this, the neglected victims of crime will likely despair at the recognition that the state, and the larger social order on whose behalf it is supposed to act, does not appear to value their lives and interests.

In Chapter 6, I explore the implications of my mixed theory for the sentencing of those convicted of crimes. The value of parsimony, understood in this context as requiring state officials to justify employing more rather than less burdensome penal measures, plays a vital role in my account. So does the value of proportionality, although I concede to its critics that its relative (or ordinal) and absolute (or cardinal) constraints are unlikely to yield precise guidance in setting up a defensible sentencing regime and administering it. What seems more likely is that considerations of proportionality will leave us with a range of defensible sentencing regimes, with some employing harsher penal measures than others across the range of offenses. I suggest that parsimony might help us to pare down the number of defensible regimes if the harsher ones are not needed to communicate the wrongs done by crimes, and especially the wrongs done by the most serious crimes. Further, although I express skepticism about the prospects of crime reduction considerations yielding precise sentencing guidance, I contend that we have useful information from the study of crime prevention about the kinds and durations of criminal sanctions that tend to exacerbate, rather than reduce, offending. We should not want criminal sanctions to be self-defeating. This means that if considerations of proportionality leave us with a range of defensible sentencing regimes, we might, with a view to not making continued offending more likely, opt for sentencing regimes that are milder or more constructive in the array of sanctions employed for moral communication purposes.

In the seventh chapter, I turn my attention to what we might think of as forms of "post" or "side" punishment. The former encompasses what have come to be termed the "collateral legal consequences" attendant to conviction, most of which are imposed on those convicted of crimes after they have served whatever sentences are assigned to them by the courts. The latter consist of the fees of various kinds assessed to the individuals charged with and convicted of crimes. Such fees, which some have termed "legal financial obligations" (LFOs), are premised on the notion that those who commit crimes unjustifiably drive up the costs of the criminal justice system and should therefore be made to pay some of those costs. I argue that biased enforcement of the criminal law, along with underenforcement of it in poor or socially marginalized communities, undermine the case for the imposition of LFOs. Biased enforcement entails that a skewed sample of those who are raising the costs of law enforcement are assessed such costs; underenforcement entails that poor or socially marginalized individuals are not receiving the benefits of law enforcement, and this despite the fact that they likely will have paid for such benefits through tax assessments of a various kinds. Even those who are guilty of offending will have prepaid for the operations of the criminal justice system in many cases.

Turning then to collateral legal consequences (CLCs), I note that these have been defended in numerous ways, the most common and persuasive of which invoke public safety. Measures such as prohibitions on driving, denials of licenses to perform jobs of various kinds, and residency restrictions have all been deemed useful or necessary to keep ex-offenders from committing further crimes. I limit my focus to the defense of CLCs on public safety grounds. I consider one recent attempt to defend them as such, contending that more conditions would have to be satisfied by state officials if public safety based CLCs are to be justified. I also suggest that governments in liberal democratic societies not only have neglected to satisfy the relevant conditions but will find it challenging to do so.

The final chapter sounds something of a desultory note about state punishment institutions, especially after I have spent the previous seven chapters defending them (albeit in highly modified forms in some cases). Unlike others who express skepticism about such institutions due to the biases, errors, and cruelties marking their operations—all of which deficiencies I acknowledge throughout the book—the grounds for skepticism I invoke in Chapter 8 are different. It appears that contemporary criminal justice systems are not very successful at capturing, convicting, and punishing individuals for most of the crimes they commit. In the United States, for instance, it is estimated that fewer than 5 percent of major crimes are resolved via convictions of those who perpetrated them.[4] This means that the criminal justice system does not very often morally communicate with offenders about their crimes, nor with their victims or the public about them. And given the apparently limited crime reduction effects of legal punishment outlined in Chapter 1, it seems that the institution does not very often do what we want (or our best theories tell us we should want) it to do.

In light of this, it might seem that we should consider options other than state punishment for securing or standing for the most basic rights of persons, if they exist. The remainder of the chapter briefly surveys some of these options. I suggest that self-enforcement of our rights, or private security enforcement of them, are not viable alternatives. Substituting restitution requirements or restorative justice conferences for traditional state penal measures will not fare much better. Both approaches presuppose the existence of state criminal justice agencies to identify, capture, and convict offenders, or at least to turn them over to restorative justice proceedings and to serve as back-ups should such proceedings fail to produce agreements or if offenders neglect to live up to them. As such, the deficiencies of the state in capturing and convicting offenders will plague these alternatives. This leads me to consider two nonpenal supplements to reducing crime or standing by and for the victims of crime. The first involves providing a substantial welfare floor and access to decently-paying jobs in order to reduce the desperation and alienation that appears to fuel some criminal offending. The second involves state-supplied compensation to the victims of crimes, whether or not those who wrong them are ever convicted of having done so. Although these alternatives to state penal institutions have considerable merit, both will be controversial and will not eliminate the need for such institutions. We should therefore insist that state penal institutions strive for accurate moral communication and the reduction of crime, or at least not the worsening of it. But we should have modest expectations about what the institution is likely to achieve.

Notes

1 See Alexandra Natapoff, "Misdemeanors," *Southern California Law Review* 85 (2012): 1313–75; Jenny Roberts, "Why Misdemeanors Matter: Defining Effective Advocacy in the Lower Criminal Courts," *University of California-Davis Law Review* 45 (2011): 277–372; and Alice Ristroph, "Criminal Law as Public Ordering," *University of Toronto Law Journal* 70 (2020): 64–83.

2 For the more or less definitive treatment of such issues, see Joel Feinberg's four-volume set on the limits of the criminal law: *Harm to Others* (New York: Oxford University Press, 1984); *Harm to Self* (New York: Oxford University Press, 1986); *Harmless Wrongdoing* (New York: Oxford University Press, 1990); and *Offense to Others* (New York: Oxford University Press, 1985).

3 Joel Feinberg, "The Expressive Function of Punishment," *The Monist* 49 (1965): 397–423; R. A. Duff, *Trials and Punishments* (Cambridge: Cambridge University Press, 1986); John Kleinig, "Punishment and Moral Seriousness," *Israel Law Review*

25 (1991): 401–21; Igor Primoratz, "Punishment as Language," *Philosophy* 64 (1989): 187–205; Jean Hampton, "An Expressive Theory of Retribution," in Wesley Craig (ed.), *Retributivism and Its Critics* (Stuttgart: V. Steiner Verlag, 1992): 1–21; Andrew von Hirsch, *Censure and Sanctions* (Oxford: Clarendon Press, 1993); Uma Narayan, "Appropriate Responses and Preventive Benefits: Justifying Censure and Hard Treatment in Legal Punishment," *Oxford Journal of Legal Studies* 13 (1993): 166–82; Thaddeus Metz, "Censure Theory and Intuitions about Punishment," *Law & Philosophy* 19 (2000): 491–512; and Bill Wringe, *An Expressive Theory of Punishment* (London: Palgrave Macmillan, 2016).

4 See Shima Baughman, "How Effective Are Police? The Problem of Clearance Rates and Criminal Accountability," *Alabama Law Review* 72 (2020): 48–130 and Andrew D. Leipold, "The Puzzle of Clearance Rates, and What They Can Tell Us about Crime, Police Reform, and Criminal Justice," *Wake Forest Law Review* 56 (2021): 47–95.

1 Legal Punishment and Crime Reduction

A Reassessment

In the past half-century, retributive theorists of legal punishment have labored long and hard to develop and defend their views about the justifying aim of legal punishment.[1] These labors have resulted in a somewhat bewildering assortment of retributive theories, or, perhaps, near-retributive theories. Critics of retributivism have also labored long and hard to discredit these "varieties" of retributivism, to demonstrate how they are either incoherent or unappealing.[2] In all of this, it is often assumed that the primary alternative to retributivism, according to which legal punishment is justified by its crime reduction effects, is sufficient to justify it, even if that alternative suffers from some well-known defects. Surprisingly, not much ink has been spilled by penal theorists carefully exploring how and whether general and special deterrence, incapacitation, rehabilitation, and moral reinforcement actually work, in effective and coherent ways, to reduce crime. Criminologists have posed challenges to legal punishment's deterrence credentials, as well as to its prospects for rehabilitation.[3] Nevertheless, my sense is that it is too often assumed that the crime reduction approach to legal punishment's justification is ready and available in the event that all of the versions of retributivism are shown to be untenable. Part of my aim in this chapter is to call that assumption into question.

To be clear, my intention is not to argue that legal punishment plays no role in the reduction of crime. It is, instead, the more modest one of showing how that role seems a limited one, such that the reduction of crime is unlikely to provide a robust justification, all by itself, for erecting and maintaining the institution of legal punishment. Even many retributivists appear to take the crime reduction credentials of legal punishment for granted, only to emphasize what they believe are the moral problems with relying on them to justify the complex practices that comprise legal punishment. My strategy will be to downplay the moral problems, though I believe that some of them are worrisome, and to play up what might be termed "efficacy" problems with the crime reduction approach. I contend that crime reductionists have considerably more work to do to convince us that the threat and actuality of legal punishment play vital roles in keeping criminal offending in check. Indeed, there is

DOI: 10.4324/9781032661667-2

a plausible case to be made for the claim that legal punishment, if not carefully structured and administered, actually produces a fair amount of crime.

Some Preliminary Points

How is it possible to contest the crime reduction credentials of legal punishment? It will be tempting to exaggerate those credentials if we make certain assumptions about human beings and the social orders that they inhabit. First, suppose that most individuals are rational and self-interested. They are primarily motivated to focus on and pursue what they take to be in their self-interest and disposed to act on the outcomes of their deliberations. The need for deterrent threats, and for incapacitation when those threats fail, will seem heightened if it is supposed that most individuals are on the lookout for opportunities to advance their own interests, even at the expense of their fellow human beings and their interests. Second, suppose that state authorities have the resources and expertise to monitor communities for crime, and to track down, arrest, and prosecute many, if not most, of the individuals who engage in it. When the threats such authorities pose to the wayward are not sufficient to generally deter, suppose further that arrest, conviction, and punishment either incapacitates individuals from further crime for some substantial period of time, convinces them to avoid future legal wrongdoing, or transforms them into citizens who are more apt to respect the law. Finally, suppose that there is little reason to believe that legal punishment worsens most offenders, making them more hostile toward the constraints of the social and legal order, or more desperate to commit crimes because they have fewer opportunities to satisfy their needs and wants within the limits of the criminal law.

If all of the preceding assumptions were plausible, then the crime prevention credentials of the criminal justice system would appear formidable, and the case for believing that the reduction of crime was a persuasive justification for such a system would be powerful. The problem is that none of the assumptions stand up to close scrutiny, some for reasons of logic and others based on what the study of offenders and the criminal justice system reveals.

Start with the notion that most individuals are primarily self-interested in their outlook on the world and the options that the social orders they inhabit present to them. If to this is added the assumption that most individuals are avidly searching for opportunities to advance their interests, at the expense of others and their interests, then a strong case for institutionalizing the deterrent threats of the criminal law would appear to exist. However, although rule by assertive self-interest no doubt characterizes some human beings in modern social orders, it is doubtful that it aptly characterizes most of them.

First, humans are an incredibly diverse lot. It is a mistake to conceive of most of them as young, capable males who are actively searching for ways to advance their interests at the expense of others and their interests. It seems highly unlikely, for instance, that elderly people, living in nursing homes or assisted living facilities, need the threat of the criminal law to keep them from committing crimes, including serious crimes. But equally, it seems doubtful that most females, and many middle-aged males, require the deterrent threats of the criminal law to dissuade them from stealing, assaulting, and rampaging against their fellow citizens. Throw in the very young, the sick or disabled, the timid or physically unimposing—and more than a few of us are timid or physically unimposing—and the picture that emerges of human beings and their criminal predilections becomes more complex and significantly less threatening. The less threatening the overall population is conceived to be, the less urgent are the deterrent threats needed to keep its members in check.

Second, setting to one side the myriad ways in which age, ability, and temperament distinguish the inhabitants of modern societies, most individuals are not rational egoists, or not simply or solely rational egoists. Most of us have internalized moral norms against preying on our fellow human beings. We need not oversimplify this. Obviously, some of us have internalized such norms more fully and deeply than others. Responsiveness to moral considerations that counsel against violence, predation, theft, and dishonesty will always be matters of degree across a sufficiently wide sample of individuals.[4] Notoriously, as well, individuals can be somewhat moved by moral considerations without being continually or reliably moved by them. But it nonetheless remains true that many of us, much of the time, do not contemplate committing criminal offenses, and especially not serious ones.[5] Grandma is not only too weak or timid, perhaps, to rob banks or assault her neighbor whose dog barks all hours of the day and night, she would be aghast at the prospect of doing so. In the words of some contemporary criminologists, moral beliefs and commitments function like a "filter," screening out criminal misconduct as live options for many people most of the time.[6] Because preying upon others is not an attractive option for many of us, we do not need deterrent threats or incapacitating force to keep our criminal proclivities in check.

Crime reduction theorists would likely concede that many of us do not actively contemplate serious forms of criminal offending most of the time. Yet minor forms of offending might seem tempting options, even to those whose moral filters do not permit them to consider rape, murder, or armed robbery. Those reliably responsive to moral considerations against serious crimes might be tempted to cheat on their taxes, drive under the influence of alcohol or drugs, or speed recklessly down highways. Especially where misconduct seems more or less victimless, more than a few of us might engage in it were it not for the risk of incurring legal sanctions. And some of us might be drawn toward more serious crimes were it not for the "background threat" of eventual legal unpleasantness, especially in circumstances in which we are enraged, provoked, or desperate. Happily, I can admit all of this without budging much on my central claim, which is that the criminal law's crime reduction influence is residual and modest for many people. My position is not that such influence is nonexistent, only that it may not be impressive enough to warrant the costs and dangers of erecting and maintaining a criminal justice system.

Also, it is not solely moral beliefs and commitments that screen out offending for many individuals. As Tom Tyler has argued, some role in reducing crime is played by the sense many of us have that the demands of the criminal law and its enforcing authorities are "legitimate."[7] Even if individuals' moral beliefs and commitments are weak or nonexistent with respect to some provisions of the criminal law, the belief that those provisions were enacted by democratically elected legislators and enforced by officials who are either directly elected or appointed by individuals who are elected may have some, and perhaps considerable, motivational force in their lives. The notion that we should abide by certain requirements on our conduct "because it's the law" is not an unfamiliar one; such a notion makes sense independently of the sanctions that attach to violations of the law's various provisions. In short, some of us obey the law's edicts more or less out of habitual deference to what we deem to be its legitimate authority.

Beyond this, we are social creatures and many of us care deeply about what others in our families, workplaces, and broader communities think of us. There is a social cost to being perceived as violent, abusive, predatory, dishonest, or shirkers of our fair share in shouldering the burdens of communal living. What John Stuart Mill termed the "inconveniences which are strictly inseparable from the judgment of others" will often be sufficient to dissuade many of us from the more serious forms of wrongdoing, even if that wrongdoing would never come to the attention of police or prosecutors.[8] These inconveniences include the loss of the esteem and respect of others—or worse—the painful knowledge that one is the subject of public or private derision by others. They also include the withholding by others of various and diverse opportunities, as well as their reluctance to offer help or solace in times of need.

In summary, it seems a mistake to believe that, were it not for the existence of the criminal law and its allied institutions, many of us, most of the time, would be sorely tempted to engage in criminal misconduct, especially of the more egregious kinds. Many of us refrain from offending for reasons that have relatively little to do with the threat of legal punishment, which is not to say that the threat has no effect on us whatsoever. My contention is that the threat resides mostly in the background for many members of contemporary societies.[9]

By contrast, it makes more sense to suggest that legal punishment has a significant crime reduction impact in relation to what I will term the "target audience" of criminal offenders. Who is this target audience? Those who study offending concur that 16 to 35 year-old males are the dominant perpetrators of crimes.[10] Many of these young males are also socially and economically disadvantaged.[11] Importantly, many of them will be arrested and convicted of mostly minor forms of criminal offending. Also, some of them will be punished for criminal offenses whose moral foundations are insecure.[12] But set these latter two points to one side for the moment. The question I now wish to raise is to what extent the criminal justice system is a powerful crime reduction force in relation to this target audience. The answer to this question, surprisingly, is that it may not be.

Limitations with General Deterrence

The individuals in the target audience will be a diverse lot, with some of them at least partially responsive to the moral considerations that counsel against the more serious forms of offending. Many of them will also be somewhat receptive to the social costs of offending or perceived offending, or moved by the notion that they ought to obey the law simply because it is the law. Yet, notoriously, the younger members of the target audience, those 16–25 years old, are moral works in progress.[13] Though they will not usually be wholly unresponsive to moral considerations, their responsiveness might be weaker or more unreliable. Also, to the extent that some of them believe that the social and economic system is indifferent to their needs, or worse, hostile to their interests, the alienation this breeds might predictably and effectively counter whatever moral norms against offending they have imbibed or weaken their sense of the legitimacy of the state and its various institutions. Making matters worse, among socially marginalized youths, encounters with criminal justice officials might take on a normatively positive stamp, such that incurring convictions and spending time in prison are understood and accepted as part of the normal life cycle.[14] Also, if large numbers of individuals in poor communities come to have criminal records, then the stigmatizing effects of such records will be diminished in ways that could reduce general deterrence.[15]

Consider also some of the limitations in legal punishment's general deterrent effects on the target audience, even if that audience is conceived to be responsive primarily to self-interested reasons. To begin with, individuals in their teens and early twenties are, on average, more impulsive than mature adults.[16] They are therefore less prone to thinking about the long-term costs of conviction and punishment or giving those costs sufficient weight. They also seek excitement or risk in more active ways, to stimulate themselves and those around them. Yet such behavior does not bode well for their susceptibility to the criminal law's deterrent threats. Further, younger members of the target audience are more susceptible to peer pressure or to efforts to win the respect or esteem of their peers.[17] This makes them more inclined to engage in misconduct that older, more mature individuals will eschew, such that they ignore or downplay the personal costs that involvement with the criminal justice system might exact from them.

If the agents of criminal law enforcement were usually at hand to act quickly and decisively in order to counter the impulsive or thrill-seeking conduct of the target audience, then the crime reduction effects of legal punishment might remain robust. As numerous studies of the criminal justice system's deterrent effects suggest, it is the certainty of punishment that deters more reliably than its severity.[18] Certainty of punishment has to do with the likelihood of arrest for crimes. Putting more police on the streets, especially in areas where crime is apt to be more frequent, or having them utilize surveillance technologies that increase the scope or accuracy of what Daniel Nagin has termed their "sentinel" activities, are the kinds of things that enhance the certainty of punishment.[19] The reality, however, is that the certainty of punishment is often low because clearance rates for many types of crimes are surprisingly modest.[20] Clearance rates measure the percentage of reported crimes of a given type for which an arrest is made. However, not all crimes are "reported"; indeed, estimates are that only about half of all actual crimes are reported.[21] This means that the perpetrators of many crimes face little risk of arrest. Also, even for many serious crimes, clearance rates fall well below the 50 percent rate. For many of the less-than-serious offenses that are much more common, clearance rates often fall below 10 percent.[22] What this means is that, realistically, lots of offenders face, at most, only some modest risk of being apprehended for their crimes.

Granted, the reality of low clearance rates might not matter, especially if members of the target audience falsely believe them to be higher than they, in fact, are. It is, after all, the perception of the risk of arrest that matters with regard to punishment's deterrent effects. Novices to offending might worry unreasonably about the chances of getting arrested. The problem is that "veteran" offenders probably come to understand the low risks of their criminal enterprises. Add to this the tendency of many criminal offenders to overestimate their proficiency at evading arrest for their crimes and the general deterrent effect of legal punishment in relation to the target audience is further weakened.[23] Notice that this tendency will make more sense in some contexts or with regard to certain crimes than others. For instance, so long as societies criminalize vice, it will be relatively easy for those determined to evade punishment to do so, since they are engaged in crime whose "victims" are disinclined to complain to the authorities.[24]

To the preceding we must add the tendency of most persons to discount future costs.[25] Although all of us display this tendency to some extent, it is likely heightened in young and more impulsive offenders. The legal punishment of offenses, if it occurs at all, will take place sometime off in the future. First there has to be an arrest, followed by the filing of charges by police or prosecutors. Add to this the possibility of pretrial detention in some cases, along with various kinds of delays in the ultimate adjudication of charges, not to mention the sentencing of offenders, and the reality of punishment is pushed further into the future. There is also the possibility, probably not unknown to veterans of the criminal justice system, that all charges will at some point be dropped. Not only does all of this take time, but the outcomes are uncertain. Admittedly, in the world of misdemeanor offending that dominates the criminal justice system, overall case processing is relatively quick (to the point of being brusquely indifferent to norms of due process, or so some would argue).[26] Nonetheless, even in that world some time elapses between the commission of offenses and the (far less than certain) advent of legal punishment. This means that the immediate gains of offending, whatever they might be, will sometimes be weighed too heavily by offenders, and especially young offenders, compared with the costs they might incur sometime off in the future.

It might be thought, or perhaps hoped, that the problems posed by legal punishment's uncertainty and lack of immediacy, as well as the impulsiveness and peer-influence susceptibility of its target audience, can be countered by upping the penal ante for offending. If many of the individuals who are most in need of deterrence are not prime candidates for its successfully working its effects on them, then perhaps the thing to do is to raise the stakes by threatening them with significantly harsher penal outcomes—more use of imprisonment, longer prison sentences, and austere, if not cruel, prison conditions of various kinds. Here we run up against one of the seeming "hard truths" of the empirical study of general deterrence: The link between harsher punishment and marginal deterrence seems weak if not nonexistent. Economists might believe that if we increase the "price" of crime, then fewer individuals will be willing to pay it. However, there is not much evidence, despite years of study, to support the claim that longer and harsher sentences increase legal punishment's general deterrence effects.[27] Add to this the fact that interviews with imprisoned offenders reveal that they are overconfident about avoiding arrest, or that they are mostly thinking about how to commit their crimes when and as they commit them. Rarely are they thinking about the penal outcomes they face if they are apprehended and convicted, if they even know them with any degree of precision.[28] Yet it makes no sense, from a consequentialist crime-reduction perspective, to increase the use or length of prison sentences, with their steep economic, personal, and social costs, if we are unlikely to see substantial or even modest gains in crime reduction through general deterrence.

The solution, it might seem, is to instead expend more of society's scarce resources in efforts to increase the certainty of punishment. We can do this by putting more police on the streets or by adopting technologies of various kinds that will better enable the authorities to monitor the places where crimes are mostly likely to be committed. There is some evidence that the use of CCTV, for instance, has some effect on reducing crime when employed in certain areas.[29] What is less clear is whether the effects will persist and whether determined offenders will find ways to commit crimes by evading stepped-up detection strategies. Also, the costs of the cameras, of installing them, and of monitoring them must be factored into any consequentialist analysis of their deployment.

In bringing this section to a close, it should be noted that imprudent behavior is hardly the exclusive domain of youthful members of society. Individuals of all ages are prone to ignoring the advice of experts on such things as diet and exercise, the use of certain kinds of drugs, smoking, drinking too much alcohol, or going too far into debt. Many of us, much of the time, fail to do what is in our best interests, though we are continually reminded of the negative consequences of doing so by the media, our friends and relatives, and our physicians and financial advisors. It might be tempting to think that although our responsivity to moral considerations is tenuous or inconsistent, our responsivity to our own interests, and especially our longer-term ones, is relatively unproblematic. I suspect that we ought to be much more cautious about assuming any such thing. And this might be true before we factor in other things that likely erode our willingness or ability to apprehend or act in our long-term self-interest: mental illness, addiction, or difficult, if not desperate, economic straits. Notably, these obstacles to prudent behavior are not uncommon among those most prone to offending.

Special Deterrence

To this point, we have been focusing on general deterrence—the alleged sobering effect of the prospect of incurring legal punishment on individuals in the population who have not experienced it first-hand, but who can appreciate its stigmatizing impact and other hardships enough to dissuade them from offending. Oversimplifying a bit, my argument in the previous section comes to this: On the one hand, many in society do not really need the threat of legal punishment to keep them from committing crimes, and, in particular, serious crimes. They have moral beliefs and commitments that make doing so largely unthinkable. Also, many are invested in their social reputations enough to not want to risk them. Further, some will see the state's criminal prohibitions as comprising legitimate rules that citizens in democratic societies ought to abide by, even where their moral beliefs might not align with all of those rules. On the other hand, those individuals most in need of the criminal law's deterrent effects—what I have termed the "target audience" for its threats—might be significantly unresponsive to them, for a variety of reasons.

Nevertheless, once individuals have been arrested, convicted, and punished, their beliefs and attitudes about incurring further punishment might shift, hopefully in the direction of making them less inclined to risk incurring it again. This, at least, is the premise on which special deterrence builds. Special deterrence is the idea that the experience of legal punishment, if unpleasant enough, will convince the previously wayward to abandon their offending ways. It seems fair to say that special deterrence has not been as extensively studied by social scientists as has general deterrence.[30] What have been studied are the various criminogenic effects of legal punishment, and here the conclusions toward which the evidence points are not encouraging.

Before we consider that evidence, two preliminary points should be made. The first is this: Again, most of the crimes processed by criminal justice systems are not the ones that we most fear. The mostly minor offenses which occupy the time and energy of criminal justice officials might be punished with short jail or prison terms, but most criminal justice systems have evolved a wide variety of lesser sanctions to address them. Incarceration for any period of time is costly to society, appears disproportionately severe in relation to many offenses, and has the potential to damage the persons made to endure it. These points are widely recognized and accepted. Thus, minor offenders are instead fined, required to pay restitution to victims, put on probation, sentenced to community service, diverted to alcohol or drug treatment programs, or assigned to home confinement. Admittedly, the threat of custodial sentences will often loom in the background as back-ups in the event that offenders fail to satisfy the conditions of their noncustodial sentences. But lots of offenders are punished in ways that fall well short of imprisonment, with all of its real and imagined terrors. Imprisonment is reserved for more serious offenses, or for repeat minor offenders. This means that many offenders will not suffer the extensive loss of their liberty of which penal custody consists, with all of its accompanying effects on their lives. Instead, they will experience impositions and burdens of various kinds, some that they can endure without much impact on their activities, projects, or relationships with others. This is not to deny, as critics of misdemeanor case processing have noted, that there can be many enduring negative effects of diverse kinds to such convictions.[31]

A second preliminary point is related to the first one. To the mostly law-abiding, the many unpleasant aspects of legal punishment will likely appear to be well worth avoiding. Having had no or little experience of arrest, pretrial detention, court appearances, and the burdens imposed by criminal sanctions, many citizens will regard entanglement with the criminal justice system with concern and perhaps dread. Again, this is consistent with many of them not really needing the threat of legal punishment to keep them in conformity with what the law requires. Surprisingly, though, individuals who have endured such entanglement, perhaps on more than one occasion, may come to view further entanglement with something less than dread. Noncustodial sanctions, as we have just seen, impose burdens of various kinds, but offenders remain mostly free to go on about their lives. And once individuals have one or more criminal convictions on their records, further ones have fewer costs in terms of damage to their reputations. Equanimity about enduring criminal sanctions also extends to the experience of custodial sanctions. Jail or prison might be difficult, even terrifying, for those encountering it for the first time. However, "veterans" of custody, of which there are quite a few, come to realize that they can "do the time," as it were.[32] This realization dilutes the special deterrent effects of legal punishment. Worse than this, time spent in jail or prison might lead offenders to establish connections with other individuals committed to deviant careers and lifestyles. A most worrisome form of this in recent years involves the increase in prison gangs, many of which retain their hold on inmates after they are released, thus encouraging, or perhaps demanding further offending of them.[33]

The theoretical and empirical literature on the criminogenic impact of both noncustodial and custodial sentences is impressive in scope and variety. Individuals labelled as "criminals" or "deviants" in society sometimes come to embrace the identities that society foists upon them.[34] As we have seen, individuals who are alienated from society, because they are members of socially or economically marginalized groups, may be especially susceptible to embracing such defiance. Those convicted of felonies or multiple misdemeanors will find their job prospects bleak. At best, they will be, in the words of Bruce Western, "restricted to the secondary sector, where employment is precarious and wages are stagnant."[35] At worst, they will substitute illegal work for legal work, or supplement legal work with illegal work.[36] Employers are understandably leery of hiring individuals with substantial criminal records, even if those records have receded into the past and the individuals involved have remained law-abiding for many years.[37] The economic marginalization of persons with criminal records is exacerbated by the variety of collateral legal consequences they are made to endure. Restrictions on where ex-offenders can live, denials of access to low-interest student loans, and bans on employment of certain kinds, push those who have served their official sentences further to the social and economic margins.[38] Those so pushed will sometimes resort to further offending, despite its known risks and costs to them.

The empirical literature on imprisonment's effects on persons is especially concerning. The prison environment tends to produce profound changes in the habits and ways of thinking of its inhabitants. While such changes may help prisoners to cope with the ardors and humiliations of prison life, they do not set offenders up for success once they emerge from prisons. As Craig Haney vividly demonstrates, prisons encourage inmates to adopt a mantle of toughness, shut down any emotions that hint at vulnerability, and develop hair-trigger responses to signs of aggression or disrespect.[39] Such learned dispositions do not immediately disappear once individuals are released from prisons. Prospective employers, family members, and others in the community will be understandably wary of individuals who exhibit this complex of characteristics. Also, as Western argues, time spent in prisons is time away from the world of education, job-training, and the development of work habits and responsibility.[40] Prison consists, at best, of a void in the lives of many offenders, one that is particularly damaging to teens and young adults who should be acquiring work skills and experience. Many offenders emerge from prisons in their late twenties or early thirties with few skills attractive to employers and little understanding of what steady work means or requires of them. Not surprisingly, perhaps, more than a few drift back toward the only lifestyle they know, which consists of further offending.[41]

As if to provide something of an exclamation point to the preceding discussion, estimates of recidivism rates in the United States and elsewhere place them at well over 60 percent.[42] Such figures are usually based on re-arrest rates of individuals with criminal records over some specified period of time. Thus, it probably underestimates the actual occurrence of reoffending, since, as we have seen, clearance rates for many crimes are low. These figures on recidivism should give pause to anyone inclined to taut the special deterrence effects of legal punishment. We need not hold that legal punishment never or rarely convinces individuals to refrain from further offending; no doubt some, perhaps many, individuals find the experience of legal punishment unpleasant enough to convince them to desist from offending, if not after their first conviction, then after several of them.

That being conceded, we should be cautious in estimating the impact of special deterrence. It would be a mistake, for instance, to infer from high recidivism rates that, say, 30 percent of offenders are specially deterred.

Individuals might refrain from further offending for reasons largely unrelated to their experience of legal punishment. As we will see in the next section, there is the well-established if not well-understood phenomenon of offenders "aging out" once they reach their late twenties or early thirties.[43] Whether or to what extent such age-based desistance from crime is related to the experience of legal punishment is unclear. Many criminologists attempt to account for it in other ways. My sense, again, is that while legal punishment might play some role in reducing crime via special deterrence, that role is more modest and complex than is often recognized. Just as people might refrain from committing crimes for lots of reasons that have little to do with the punishment threats they face, many who have committed crimes might desist from further offending at some point for reasons that have little to do with their experience of legal punishment. And some will persist in offending partly because of the many damaging effects of legal punishment on their lives.

Indeed, whether more special deterrence benefits than criminogenic costs result from the institution of legal punishment is, I would submit, a question the answer to which is not obvious.[44] Of course, those who favor a crime reduction approach to justifying legal punishment have other cards to play. Importantly, among them might be the options of reducing the harmful effects of criminal sanctions and the collateral consequences that are often imposed on offenders consequent to their having served their sentences. These are points that we will come back to.

Incapacitation

Unlike general and special deterrence, incapacitation as a mode of crime prevention does not depend on the perceptions and motivations of individuals. Incapacitation is a blunter instrument because it works by reducing or eliminating the abilities of persons to engage in crime. This is most vivid when incarceration is utilized as the form of penal hard treatment. Whether they are inclined to commit further crimes or not, individuals locked in prisons have considerably reduced abilities to do so, though short of extreme measures such as execution or drug-induced stupors, prison inmates will retain some limited capacities to engage in legally prohibited acts.[45] Have we therefore arrived at a mode of crime reduction that supplies powerful support for erecting and maintaining the institutions of criminal justice?

The first point to make in response to this question is the obvious one that many criminal sanctions commonly employed have, at best, modest incapacitation effects. Most people convicted of minor crimes are not imprisoned; they are fined, put on probation, required to perform community service or pay restitution to victims, or required to attend drug or alcohol treatment programs. These sanctions impose various burdens or requirements on offenders but leave them otherwise free to go on about their lives. If those enduring such sanctions are determined to commit further crimes, as some of them will be, noncustodial sanctions will do little to impede them.

The second point to make in response to the question of whether incapacitation can serve as a convincing justification of the institutions of legal punishment is one we have already made: Though custodial sanctions, through their restriction of liberty, significantly reduce the abilities of persons to commit crimes for the period of their duration, such sanctions may stimulate more or worse offending in some individuals who experience it. Imprisonment is far from a benign "time out" from ordinary social life. Instead, it is often a damaging stretch of time for many offenders. Some, perhaps many, emerge from it changed psychologically for the worse, further marginalized from productive social and economic lives, attached to gangs or other criminal associates, and facing a host of collateral legal consequences that will make their re-entry into society more difficult than it already is. Those offenders who struggled with mental illness before their imprisonment, which a significant number do, will likely emerge worse off if prisons offer substandard medical care.[46] Or they will emerge in poorer shape since the mentally ill find it harder to cope with prison confinement than other inmates.[47] None of this bodes well for the readjustment of mentally ill inmates to civil society and to lives of work and responsibility.

Other limitations on incapacitation as a crime reduction tactic are well-known. Some crimes are committed in or by groups. If the authorities do not capture all or most of the group members, those who are not apprehended might continue to commit crimes.[48] Perhaps there will be some reduction in the frequency with which they do so, but not invariably. That partly depends on whether the remaining members of the group recruit replacements and how skillful or motivated those replacements turn out to be. The addition of an energetic new recruit might enable the group to commit more or more sophisticated crimes. Society is thus, in this narrow way, worse off for having arrested and incapacitated one or more members of the group. Even if the authorities manage to capture and imprison all of the individuals engaged in some type of crime in a community, if the crimes they were involved in are lucrative enough, other criminal entrepreneurs might emerge to replace the imprisoned.[49] Again, if the new kids on the criminal block are more energetic or innovative, offenses of the kind in question might increase.

The preceding points about the effectiveness of incapacitation in some cases should not be taken to show that apprehending and imprisoning offenders does nothing to reduce crime. It will certainly do so in some cases. If we arrest and imprison serial rapists or murderers, for instance, the community is clearly better off, since it is unlikely that the problems posed by co-offenders, new recruits, or criminal entrepreneurs will exist in such cases. The lesson here is the more limited one that whether imprisonment reduces crime via incapacitation must be viewed with caution. Sometimes it will, sometimes, and perhaps more often, it is unlikely to do so.

This brings us to the aforementioned "aging out" phenomenon. It is tempting to think that if individuals are engaged in violence or predation, and especially if they have been repeatedly convicted of doing so, that they are apt to continue offending so long as they live as free citizens in society. If that were true, then lengthy prison sentences for offenders of certain kinds might make eminent good sense on grounds of incapacitation. Such sentences would be most defensible if the crimes being committed were serious enough to outweigh the significant financial and other costs of imprisoning those who commit them. However, the fact is that most offenders desist from offending in their late twenties or early thirties. There is considerable debate about why this is, and it is a fascinating debate.[50] But that it is true is not much in dispute. One eminent criminologist described aged-based desistance from crime as "the best documented empirical regularity in criminology."[51] Again, we must be careful about how we understand the phenomenon. Some offenders will persist in offending, even into old age. Incapacitating them might be socially beneficial, despite its formidable costs to them and to society, especially if their crimes are likely to be serious. But incapacitating many other offenders into middle or old age makes little sense for penal theorists committed to weighing the bad consequences of legal punishment against its good ones. Imprisoning individuals for ten, twenty, or thirty years who would have ceased offending on their own is enormously costly to them and larger society and achieves little of value.

Rehabilitation

Let me start with a bold claim about rehabilitation: It seems doubtful that we erect and maintain the institutions of legal punishment in order to rehabilitate those who commit crimes. Instead, a rehabilitation focus makes sense once we have decided to hold offenders accountable for their crimes for other reasons, whatever those might turn out to be. When the state has wayward citizens in its control—as it most decisively does when it assigns them to jails or prisons—then it may be sound public policy to attempt to address some of the well-known factors that lead individuals to offend. Further, a rehabilitative purpose appears to make sense primarily for more serious offenders. It seems doubtful that many of the kinds of noncustodial sanctions commonly in use have much utility as rehabilitative measures. We might tell ourselves that fines, required community service, or probation teach offenders needed lessons or reorient their outlooks on their lives and the communities in which they live. However, such penal measures seem poorly conceived and fitted to the wide variety of minor offenders and the features of their lives that incline them to commit crimes. Again, however, the majority of offenders will be assigned sentences of just these kinds. Or they will be assigned brief stints in custody that more or less preclude their meaningful participation in rehabilitation programs. Granted, forms of noncustodial sanctions aimed at addressing offenders' criminogenic needs have emerged in recent years, administered by drug and mental health courts.[52] These more targeted forms of state intrusion into the lives of offenders have plausible rehabilitative purposes compared with more traditional noncustodial sanctions.

If we are concerned primarily with reducing crime, then once we have offenders in our grips, so to speak, we ought to design our penal institutions so that they do two things: First, we should see to it that they avoid making offenders more crime-prone in the variety of ways that many existing penal institutions have been shown to do.[53] Clearly, locking prisoners in cells with little to do for months or years on end undermines their capacities for responsible conduct. Also, isolating them from their families, through the imposition of restrictive or onerous visiting requirements, deprives them of pro-social relationships that can bolster them during the difficult period of incarceration and give them something to look forward to, and rely upon, when they are released. Worse, depriving prisoners of all privacy and dignity, subjecting them to harassment or violence by guards, or looking the other way when other inmates prey upon them, are all recipes for turning out broken or dysfunctional human beings who are less likely to do well upon their return to civil society.

Second, beyond being made more humane, our penal institutions should adopt rehabilitative measures that have been shown to reduce recidivism.[54] Among such programs, drug addiction treatment, education, job training, and cognitive-behavioral modification programs seem especially promising. Further, facilitating the successful re-entry of prisoners back into society also seems imperative, though doing so might seem to take us somewhat beyond a focus on rehabilitation in the usual sense.[55]

Presumably, crime reduction theorists would support all of these ways of reducing the misery and damage wrought by prisons. Yet such an emphasis on making criminal sanctions more helpful and humane exposes a tension in crime reduction thinking about legal punishment. It might seem that keeping criminal sanctions onerous or severe comports better with the approach's general and special deterrence modes of reducing crime. It is, after all, the perceived unpleasantness of entanglement with the criminal justice system that supposedly convinces would-be offenders to refrain from acting on their criminal impulses. The question is whether a kinder and gentler system will work as well to make penal confinement sufficiently "less eligible."[56] What will be the message sent to members of what I have termed the "target audience" if they come to realize that the worst that will happen to them if they commit serious crimes is that they will be confined in humane facilities for a period of time and offered education, job training, and help re-entering society once they have served their sentences? It might be claimed that no penal facility can be made so hospitable as to not be feared or loathed. That might be correct, although I am not sure that the case for believing it is as obvious as supporters of an enlightened crime reduction approach might hope it is. That there is some tension between "softening" legal punishment's hard edges and maintaining its deterrent functions seems an issue that crime reductionists will have to confront.

The more sobering fact is that even the best-designed rehabilitative programs are rather far from being fully effective in reducing recidivism. Even the notoriously humane and dignified Scandinavian penal institutions turn out individuals who revert to crime in significant numbers.[57] This should lead even the most ardent crime reductionist to question how much weight the rehabilitation mode of their theory can bear in providing an overall justification of the institution of legal punishment.

Moral Reinforcement

Occasionally, in discussions of legal punishment's justification, a further mode of crime prevention is noted, although I think it is fair to say that it receives considerably less attention than the other modes.[58] It involves the idea that by emphatically communicating the appropriate illegality of certain acts, legal punishment reinforces commitments to refraining from them, especially in members of the broader community. Put differently, legal punishment is held by some crime reductionists to strengthen or deepen the internalization of moral norms against offending. Importantly, if legal punishment is successful in this role, more members of the community will have the kinds of moral filters referred to earlier in this chapter. That, in turn, means that fewer of them will seriously contemplate committing crimes. Given the uncertainties and limitations that exist with the other modes of crime reduction, it is encouraging to think that there might be a back-up mode of crime reduction that actually precludes the need for the others to operate as often.

Importantly, the notion of moral reinforcement acknowledges, to some extent, the kind of responsiveness to moral considerations among persons that the crime reduction theory has been criticized for ignoring. G. W. F. Hegel famously wrote that "to base a justification of punishment on threat is to liken it to the act of a man who lifts his stick to a dog."[59] Hegel's concern has usually been interpreted as one according to which the use of deterrent threats is degrading to our status as moral beings. Neither general nor specific deterrence require would-be or convicted offenders to be anything other than narrowly self-interested. The thoroughly amoral can be generally deterred from offending if legal punishment is certain or perhaps severe enough. And though special deterrence might be understood to have a moral dimension to it, as when offenders who have been punished learn or more deeply absorb the message that their conduct is prohibited because wrongful, it need not and is typically not so interpreted. Special deterrence will work if offenders find the experience of punishment unpleasant enough that they desist from further offending purely out of self-interest. Further, incapacitation can work to reduce offending even among individuals who chronically fall short of being rationally self-interested. We cage wild animals and can lock up, and thereby incapacitate, the violently insane or radically impulsive, which is not to say that we should do so. Nothing in the logic of incapacitation precludes it, however.

As with special deterrence, rehabilitation might be understood to include efforts to induce some heightened responsivity to moral considerations. It seems doubtful that we can impart such beliefs and dispositions to those who altogether lack them for some reason, but perhaps we can bolster them in individuals who exhibit them weakly or unreliably. Yet rehabilitation also can be understood more narrowly, in terms of removing obstacles (such as drug addiction or inability to control or manage violent or predatory impulses) to the successful functioning of rational self-interest in offenders. All we might be trying to do with rehabilitation measures is to make it more feasible for offenders to anticipate and act in their own interests, broadly conceived.

With the moral reinforcement mode of the crime reduction approach, the notion that humans are moral beings seems to assume more significance. If the workings of the criminal justice system strengthen preexisting moral beliefs and commitments in ways that make crime unthinkable or unattractive to most persons, then they will refrain from offending for moral reasons. Of course, whether the criminal justice system will have this effect likely depends on how it is structured and how it operates. If it continually reveals itself to be substantially indifferent about the guilt or innocence of those who fall under its purview, or if it routinely employs sanctions that seem unrelated to the seriousness of crimes or that leave offenders damaged, alienated, or more crime-prone, then its credentials as a moral reinforcement mechanism likely will be weakened.[60] Legal punishment probably cannot be cast as an upholder of moral norms if it is widely perceived as running roughshod over them.

Although it sounds plausible to say that legal punishment, and more broadly, the operations of the criminal justice system, reinforces moral beliefs and commitments against certain kinds of wrongdoing, it is important to consider whether or to what extent this is true. Again, many in the population might not need such reinforcement. They have already sufficiently internalized moral norms against offending. Or even if they haven't, they are unlikely, for a wide variety of reasons, including age, disability, temperament, and vulnerability to harassment or harsh treatment from police or immigration officials, to risk offending. Those who most need their moral beliefs and commitments reinforced if crime is to be averted—many of them youthful, poor or otherwise socially marginalized—are apt to be poor candidates for such reinforcement, especially at the hands of the state, which is likely too impersonal, bureaucratic, or regarded with suspicion or contempt to be an effective moral teacher.

Also, the state is hardly the only agent of moral norm cultivation in persons and may be rather far down the list of the most effective ones. Parents, other family members, churches, the schools, and civic organizations of various kinds all play vital roles in inculcating moral values and commitments in us. In fact, if we are concerned about the moral development of persons, a strong case can be made for the state's acting sooner and in different ways than through legal punishment. For instance, the state might do more to strengthen families, by providing an array of social welfare services to the poor. These services could include providing funds for childcare for single parents or for parents who struggle to make ends meet. They could also include requiring workers to be paid decent, living wages that keep them (and their children) out of poverty, helping the unemployed find work, and retraining or moving workers, along with their families, when work is no longer available in their communities. Further, the state could ensure that all children and young adults have access to adequate schools, particularly children in poor and immigrant communities. Arguably, these kinds of measures, and others like them, would enable families and communities to more effectively transmit appropriate moral values to children and young people. Such values would, in turn, better insulate young people from forms of deviance that are apt to bring them into contact with the criminal justice system. But notice, such proposed state welfare or social justice measures have little to do with legal punishment per se. They are, in fact, efforts to preclude or at least limit the need for it. This is a point I will come back to in the final chapter.

My position is not that the institution of legal punishment plays no role whatsoever in morally educating people or reinforcing the moral values that families and other institutions attempt to inculcate in us. It is, instead, that legal punishment is simply one of several "agents" of moral norm teaching and reinforcement, and probably not the most direct or effective one, compared with parents, schools, and churches. The state might play a more substantial, if nonetheless indirect, role in the enterprise of crafting morally responsible citizens if it were to act more decisively to support the families, schools, and communities that shape the lives of many of the poor or socially excluded individuals who are disproportionately represented in the criminal justice system.

Summing Up

My remarks toward the end of the preceding section about the other measures that the state might employ to secure and stabilize the basic moral rights of all members of society bear emphasizing. I would not want what I have claimed throughout this chapter to be misunderstood. There are things that the state can do to prevent or reduce crime—lots of them, in fact. However, imposing punishment on individuals found guilty of violating the criminal law does not seem to be one of the more impressive ways in which the state acts to secure and stabilize a defensible scheme of basic moral rights.

In response, it might be conceded that each of the crime reduction modes is less than impressive on its own, especially when examined carefully in light of what we know about individuals living in modern, pluralistic, democratic societies. However, it might be argued that, when combined, they make a sufficiently strong case for setting up and operating institutions of legal punishment. Set to one side the question whether a collection of weak rationales for having some institution can, when joined, produce something more robust, as opposed to a collectively weak rationale. I am not sure how to answer that question in the abstract, though I would admit that the answer might be "yes, they can."

The more significant problems with this suggestion have already been signaled. First, as we have seen, some tensions exist among the various modes of crime reduction. Legal sanctions that would be much more humane and rehabilitative than many current ones might lose some of their penal bite, and thus their deterrent effect. Likewise, sanctions that might be defended on incapacitation grounds, because some offenders are deemed likely to continue committing serious crimes, will be apt to undermine the rehabilitation prospects of those offenders. Long stints in custody might damage offenders in ways and to a degree that even more humane prisons will be hard-pressed to effectively counter.

Second, whatever aggregate crime reduction impact the various modes have will need to be weighed against the criminogenic effects of legal punishment. Suppose that, collectively, the crime reductive effects of the various modes is substantial—more so than any of the modes, taken individually, appears to be. Still, if exposure to legal punishment, even more constructive legal punishment than is often the norm in modern societies, produces some further offending, then the case made by aggregating the modes will be subverted to some extent. Where that would leave us depends on both how crime reductive the various modes are when combined and how criminogenic legal punishment, in any form, turns out to be. I would submit that it is not clear that we are left with a strongly persuasive overall case, based on the reduction of future crime, for setting up and operating institutions of legal punishment.

In spite of these doubts, I would concede that the institution does have a significant crime reduction role to play, although it is probably one that mostly operates in the background to tamp down offending. What do I mean by this? Daniel Nagin draws a distinction between the "absolute" and "marginal" deterrence of crime by legal punishment.[61] He is skeptical about the latter, by which he refers to the link between increases in sentence severity and deterrent effects. But he does not question the former, which concerns the overall impact of the institution of legal punishment on the prevention of crime. He, like others, is confident that if the entire criminal justice system were to disappear, we would likely see an increase in offending. Perhaps the increase would not occur immediately, since members of society likely would persist in believing that untoward legal consequences await them if they offend and are caught. Also, as we have seen, many members of society do not really need the deterrent threat of punishment to dissuade them from committing crimes, especially the more serious kinds of them. And many would simply not have the stomach to engage in offending or would be too young or old or disabled to do so. Nonetheless, we might plausibly expect that among some of the younger members of the population, we would gradually see an uptick in offending. We might also see a shift from less serious to more serious crimes. Not all in society are as responsive to the moral considerations against offending as we would like them to be, and some will not be much moved by the social costs of being perceived as offenders. Further, as other members of society became aware of increases in crime and the reduced costs of engaging in it, some of them might be more tempted to resort to offending, or more disposed to take measures to prevent it that might spur more aggression or violence.

All of this convinces me that legal punishment very likely does work to tamp down crime, or perhaps to simply "keep a lid" on it. What is the difference? Crime is, as we have seen, far from uncommon. It occurs despite the existence of legal punishment, and in some countries despite vast resources being poured into capturing, convicting, and punishing individuals who engage in it. It seems hard to tell whether such efforts actually reduce offending, or by how much. They might simply keep crime from becoming worse than it already is. In that sense, they keep a lid on it without much reducing it.

Still, even if we admit that the criminal justice system works to keep down the overall level of offending in society, this does not get us very far by way of helping us to determine in what ways and to what extent to punish those convicted of crimes. In fact, our knowledge of how much and in what ways to punish the various kinds of criminal offenses to reduce them effectively, that is, at minimal cost and without actually making future offending more likely, is quite limited. I will have more to say about this in Chapter 6. More to the point, my sense is that the crime prevention rationale for legal punishment should be viewed with more caution than it often is. It might play some role in providing a full justification for the institution of legal punishment, but I believe that we have reason to doubt that its role is robust or sufficient, all by itself.

In the next two chapters, I examine retributive justifications for the institution. As noted at the beginning of this chapter, there is considerable dissensus among penal theorists about what a defensible account of the retributive element consists of. In Chapter 2, I examine two competing conceptions of the retributive justification. As against desert versions of retributivism, I argue that the moral communication versions of the theory are more plausible. In Chapter 3, I clarify the moral communication approach, respond to various objections to it, and begin the task of considering how robust of a defense of legal punishment it provides. The lattermost is an undertaking that, in various ways, continues throughout the remainder of the book.

Notes

1 Prominent retributive theorists include Michael Moore, *Placing Blame: A General Theory of the Criminal Law* (Oxford: Clarendon Press, 1997); R. A. Duff, *Trials and Punishments* (Cambridge: Cambridge University Press, 1986); George Sher, *Desert* (Princeton, NJ: Princeton University Press, 1987); Wojciech Sadurski, *Giving Desert Its Due* (Dordrecht, Netherlands: D. Reidel, 1985); Jean Hampton, "A New Theory of Retribution," in R. G. Frey and C. W. Morris (eds.), *Liability and Responsibility: Essays in Law and Morals* (Cambridge: Cambridge University Press, 1991); Herbert Morris, "Persons and Punishment," *The Monist* 52 (1968): 475–501; and Jeffrie G. Murphy, "Marxism and Retribution," *Philosophy and Public Affairs* 2 (1973): 217–43.

2 The phrase "varieties of retributivism" comes from John Cottingham, "Varieties of Retributivism," *Philosophical Quarterly* 29 (1979): 238–46. The critics include David Dolinko, "Some Thoughts about Retributivism," *Ethics* 101 (1991): 537–59, and "Retributivism, Consequentialism, and the Intrinsic Goodness of

Punishment," *Law and Philosophy* 16 (1997): 507–28; Richard Burgh, "Do the Guilty Deserve Punishment?" *Journal of Philosophy* 79 (1982): 193–210; C. L. Ten, *Crime, Guilt, and Punishment: A Philosophical Introduction* (Oxford: Clarendon Press, 1987); and David Boonin, *The Problem of Punishment* (Cambridge: Cambridge University Press, 2008).

3 Daniel S. Nagin, "Criminal Deterrence: Research at the Outset of the Twenty-First Century," *Crime and Justice: A Review of Research* 23 (1998): 1–42, and "Deterrence in the Twenty-First Century," *Crime and Justice: A Review of Research* 42 (2013): 199–263; Anthony N. Doob and Cheryl Marie Webster, "Sentence Severity and Crime: Accepting the Null Hypothesis," *Crime and Justice: A Review of Research* 30 (2003): 143–95. On the effectiveness of rehabilitation, see Gerald G. Gaes, Timothy J. Flanagan, Laurence L. Motiuk, and Lynn Stewart, "Adult Correctional Treatment," *Crime and Justice: A Review of Research* 26 (1999): 361–426; Paul Gendreau, "Offender Rehabilitation: What We Know and What Needs to Be Done," *Criminal Justice and Behavior* 23 (1996): 144–61; and Mark W. Lipsey and Frances T. Cullen, "The Effectiveness of Correctional Rehabilitation: A Review of Systematic Reviews," *Annual Review of Law and Social Science* 3 (2007): 297–320.

4 The notion of responsivity to moral considerations is developed in J. Martin Fischer and Mark Ravizza, *Responsibility and Control: A Theory of Moral Responsibility* (Cambridge: Cambridge University Press, 1998) and R. Jay Wallace, *Responsibility and the Moral Sentiments* (Cambridge, MA: Harvard University Press, 1998).

5 John Braithwaite and Philip Pettit emphasize this point in various places in *Not Just Deserts: A Republican Theory of Criminal Justice* (Oxford: Clarendon Press, 1990): 89, 142.

6 Per-Olof H. Wikström, "Explaining Crime as Moral Actions," in Steven Hitlin and Stephen Vaisey (eds.), *Handbook of the Sociology of Morality* (New York: Springer, 2010): 211–39.

7 Tom R. Tyler, *Why People Obey the Law* (Princeton, NJ: Princeton University Press, 2006).

8 John Stuart Mill, *On Liberty* (Indianapolis, IN: Hackett Publishing, 1978): 76.

9 Granted, in times of social unrest or chaos, threats of state sanctions for prohibited conduct might need to play a more prominent role in keeping violent or predatory conduct in check. Whether such threats will be effective in these circumstances is, one suspects, a highly contingent matter.

10 Jeffrey T. Ulmer and Darrell Steffensmeier, "The Age and Crime Relationship: Social Variation, Social Explanations," in Kevin M. Beaver, J. C. Barnes, and Brian B. Boutwell (eds.), *The Nurture Versus Biosocial Debate in Criminology: On the Origins of Criminal Behavior and Criminality* (Thousand Oaks, CA: Sage, 2015): 377–96.

11 Loïc Wacquant, *Prisons of Poverty* (Minneapolis, MN: University of Minnesota Press, 2009) and Bruce Western and Becky Pettit, "Incarceration and Social Inequality," *Daedelus* (Summer 2010): 8–19. That prisons are disproportionately populated by the poor is not much in doubt. However, a note of caution: There is considerable debate about whether or at what rates the poor and socially marginalized commit more crimes than other members of society or are policed and prosecuted more intensely than other members of society.

12 This will be especially true for the many offenders convicted in response to the "war on drugs." See Douglas Husak, *Drugs and Rights* (Cambridge: Cambridge University Press, 1992) and Michael Tonry, *Punishing Race: A Continuing American Dilemma* (Oxford: Oxford University Press, 2011).

13 For a useful overview of the development of youths and their responsivity to both prudential and moral considerations, see Barry C. Feld, "A Slower Form of Death:

Implications of *Roper v. Simmons* for Juveniles Sentenced to Life without Parole," *Notre Dame Journal of Law, Ethics, and Public Policy* 9 (2008): 9–65. For a somewhat contrasting view, with more of a focus on moral development, see Stephen J. Morse, "Delinquency and Desert," *The Annals of the American Academy of Political and Social Science* 564 (1999): 56–80.

14 Dorothy E. Roberts, "The Social and Moral Costs of Mass Incarceration in African-American Communities," *Stanford Law Review* 56 (2004): 1272–305.

15 Daniel S. Nagin, "Deterrence and Incapacitation," in Michael Tonry (ed.), *The Handbook of Crime and Punishment* (New York: Oxford University Press, 1998): 345–68, at 361.

16 Feld, "Slower Form of Death," 26–43.

17 Feld, "Slower Form of Death," 26–43.

18 Nagin, "Deterrence in the Twenty-First Century," 201.

19 Nagin, "Deterrence in the Twenty-First Century," 207.

20 Paul H. Robinson and John M. Darley, "The Utility of Desert," *Northwestern University Law Review* 91 (1997): 453–99, at 458–64.

21 Andrew D. Leipold, "The Puzzle of Clearance Rates, and What They Can Tell Us About Crime, Police Reform, and Criminal Justice," *Wake Forest Law Review* 56 (2021): 47–95, at 62–63.

22 Robinson and Darley, "Utility of Desert," 459.

23 Doob and Webster, "Null Hypothesis," 183.

24 A point made by numerous scholars of the criminal justice system, among them, William J. Stuntz, in "Race, Class, and Drugs," *Columbia Law Review* 98 (1998): 1795–842, at 1799.

25 Robinson and Darley, "Utility of Desert," 460.

26 Alexandra Natapoff, "Misdemeanors," *Southern California Law Review* 85 (2012): 1313–75.

27 Doob and Webster, "Null Hypothesis," and Nagin, "Deterrence in the Twenty-First Century."

28 Doob and Webster, "Null Hypothesis," 182.

29 Jerry A. Ratcliffe, Travis Taniguchi, and Ralph B. Taylor, "The Crime Reduction Effects of CCTV Cameras: A Multi-Method Spatial Approach," *Justice Quarterly* 26 (2009): 746–70, and Brandon C. Welsh and David P. Farrington, "Public Area CCTV and Crime Prevention: An Updated and Systematic Review and Meta-Analysis," *Justice Quarterly* 26 (2009): 716–45.

30 Daniel S. Nagin, Frances T. Cullen, and Cheryl Lero Jonson, "Imprisonment and Reoffending," *Crime and Justice: A Review of Research* 38 (2009): 115–200, at 116.

31 Natapoff, "Misdemeanors," 1323–27. See also Jenny Roberts, "Why Misdemeanors Matter: Defining Effective Advocacy in the Lower Criminal Courts," *University of California-Davis Law Review* 45 (2011): 277–372.

32 John Bronsteen, Christopher Buccafusco, and Jonathan S. Masur, "Happiness and Punishment," *University of Chicago Law Review* 76 (2009): 1037–81.

33 David Pyrooz, Scott H. Decker, and Mark Fleisher, "From the Street to the Prison, from the Prison to the Street: Understanding and Responding to Prison Gangs," *Journal of Aggression, Conflict, and Peace Research* 3 (2011): 12–24.

34 Jön Gunnar Bernburg, Marvin D. Krohn, and Craig J. Rivera, "Official Labeling, Criminal Embeddedness, and Subsequent Delinquency: A Longitudinal Test of Labeling Theory," *Journal of Research in Crime and Delinquency* 43 (2006): 67–88.

35 Bruce Western, *Punishment and Inequality in America* (New York: Russell Sage Foundation, 2006): 121.

36 Richard Freeman, "Why Do So Many Young American Men Commit Crimes and What Might We Do about It?" *Journal of Economic Perspectives* 10 (1996): 25–42.

37 Western, *Punishment and Inequality*, 112. See also Devah Pager, "The Mark of a Criminal Record," *American Journal of Sociology* 108 (2003): 937–75.

38 See Gabriel J. Chin, "The New Civil Death: Rethinking Punishment in the Era of Mass Conviction," *University of Pennsylvania Law Review* 160 (2012): 1789–833 and Zachary Hoskins, *Beyond Punishment? A Normative Account of the Collateral Consequences of Conviction* (New York: Oxford University Press, 2019).
39 Craig Haney, *Reforming Punishment: Psychological Limits to the Pains of Imprisonment* (Washington, DC: American Psychological Association, 2006).
40 Western, *Punishment and Inequality*, 109–15.
41 Ros Burnett and Shadd Maruna, "So 'Prison Works', Does It? The Criminal Careers of 130 Men Under Release from Prison under Home Secretary, Michael Howard," *The Howard Journal* 43 (2004): 390–404.
42 "Recidivism," National Institute of Justice, U. S. Department of Justice, 2008, at https://nij.ojp.gov/topics/articles/recidivism-core-criminal-justice-concern (accessed June 2, 2023).
43 Ulmer and Steffensmeier, "Age and Crime Relationship."
44 See Nagin, Cullen, and Jonson, in "Imprisonment and Reoffending," who write that "compared with noncustodial sanctions, incarceration appears to have a null or mildly criminogenic effect on future criminal behavior" (115). This concedes that custodial sanctions might not have such effects at all or to the same extent. See also Lipsey and Cullen, who reach similar conclusions in their "The Effectiveness of Correctional Rehabilitation," 302.
45 If prisoners can run criminal organizations from within prisons, as appears to be the case, then their abilities to commit crimes is much less constrained by imprisonment than we would ordinarily imagine.
46 "Indicators of Mental Health Problems Reported by Prisoners and Jail Inmates," Bureau of Justice, U. S. Department of Justice, at www.bjs.gov/index.cfm?ty=pbdetail&iid=5946 (accessed January 29, 2022). Estimates put the proportion of jail or prison inmates suffering with serious mental health problems at one in six or one in five. Higher estimates put the proportion as over one in two. For the latter, see "Incarceration Nation," American Psychological Association, at www.apa.org/monitor/2014/10/incarceration (accessed January 29, 2022).
47 Haney, *Reforming Punishment*, 241–67.
48 Franklin E. Zimring and Gordon Hawkins, *Incapacitation: Penal Confinement and the Restraint of Crime* (New York: Oxford University Press, 1995): 53–55.
49 Zimring and Hawkins, *Incapacitation*, 55–56.
50 Ulmer and Steffensmeier, "Age and Crime Relationship;" John H. Laub, Daniel S. Nagin, and Robert J. Sampson, "Trajectories of Change in Criminal Offending: Good Marriages and the Desistance Process," *American Sociological Review* 63 (1998): 225–38; Travis Hirschi and Michael Gottfredson, "Age and the Explanation of Crime," *American Journal of Sociology* 89 (1983): 552–84; and Christopher Uggen, "Work As a Turning Point in the Life Course of Criminals: A Duration Model of Age, Employment, and Recidivism," *American Sociological Review* 65 (2000): 529–46.
51 Nagin, "Deterrence and Incapacitation," 364.
52 Ojmarrh Mitchell, David B. Wilson, Amy Eggers, and Doris L. MacKenzie, "Assessing the Effectiveness of Drug Courts on Recidivism: A Meta-Analytical Review of Traditional and Non-Traditional Drug Courts," *Journal of Criminal Justice* 40 (2012): 60–71 and Christine M. Sarteschi, Michael G. Vaughn, and Kevin Kim, "Assessing the Effectiveness of Mental Health Courts: A Quantitative Review," *Journal of Criminal Justice* 39 (2011): 12–20.
53 Haney, *Reforming Punishment* and Nagin, Cullen, and Lero, "Imprisonment and Reoffending."
54 Gaes, Flanagan, Motiuk, and Stewart, "Adult Correctional Treatment," Gendreau, "Offender Rehabilitation" and Francis T. Cullen, "Rehabilitation: Beyond Nothing Works," *Crime and Justice: A Review of Research* 42 (2013): 299–376.

55 Richard P. Seiter and Karen R. Kadela, "Prisoner Reentry: What Works, What Does Not, and What Is Promising," *Crime & Delinquency* 49 (2003): 360–88.

56 Jeremy Bentham, *The Works of Jeremy Bentham,* Vol IV, J. Bowring (ed.) (London: Edinburgh, Simpkin, and Marshall, 1843): 122–23. See also Edward W. Sieh, "Less Eligibility: The Upper Limits of Penal Policy," *Criminal Justice Policy Review* 3 (1989): 159–83.

57 Seena Fazel and Achim Wolf, "A Systematic Review of Criminal Recidivism Rates Worldwide: Current Difficulties and Recommendations for Best Practices," *PloS One* (2015), at https://doi.org/10.1371/journal.pone.0130390. As Fazel and Wolf show, there is little consistency across countries in how they interpret recidivism rates. Still, even in the Scandinavian countries, rates often exceed 40 percent.

58 Johannes Andenaes, "The General Preventive Effects of Punishment," *University of Pennsylvania Law Review* 114 (1966): 949–83, and Richard S. Frase, "Punishment Purposes," *Stanford Law Review* 58 (2005): 67–83.

59 G. W. F. Hegel, *Philosophy of Right*, T. M. Knox (trans.) (Oxford: Oxford University Press, 1965): 246.

60 See Paul H. Robinson, Geoffrey P. Goodwin, and Michael Reisig, "The Disutility of Injustice," *New York University Law Review* 85 (2010): 1940–2033.

61 Nagin, "Deterrence in the 21st Century," 3.

2 In Search of the Retributive Element

In the previous chapter, I discussed the familiar proposition that part of what justifies having the institution of legal punishment is its instrumental role in the prevention of crime, especially through the familiar mechanisms of deterrence, incapacitation, and rehabilitation. Although I conceded that legal punishment's role in preventing crime is part of what justifies having the institution in society, I urged caution regarding how significant we should conceive that role to be. As I noted, many of the individuals most in need of deterrence will be poor candidates for it, while many individuals who are more susceptible to deterrence will be in less need of it, because they have other significant reasons to refrain from legal wrongdoing. Also, there is concerning evidence that some of the most commonly employed penal sanctions might actually increase crime by encouraging recidivism, rather than reduce it. Still, that legal punishment works to tamp down criminal offending to some extent or in some ways are claims that I accept. How much it does so seems harder to gauge.

In this chapter, my aim is to identify the most plausible version of the retributive element in the mixed theory of legal punishment that I defend in subsequent chapters. Anyone familiar with the history of punishment theory will know that numerous versions of the retributive element, or near relatives of it, have been advanced.[1] My aim is not to discuss all or most of them. Instead, it will be to identify two of what I believe are the most prominent and plausible versions and then to spend the bulk of the chapter explaining why one of them seems more defensible and thus eligible for a prominent role in a mixed theory of punishment.

The first account holds that the primary justifying aim of the institution of legal punishment is to give those who have committed culpable wrongs prohibited by the criminal law the punishment they deserve.[2] The view to be discussed is not, simply, that the negative deserts of criminal offenders supply us with a reason to punish in particular cases (or weaker still, a reason to do so if no other reasons suffice).[3] It is rather that the negative deserts of offenders provide a powerful reason (or on some accounts, a duty) to set up institutions of legal punishment to see to it that criminal wrongdoers are given what they deserve.[4] Elaborating this a bit further, desert retributivists tend to claim that

DOI: 10.4324/9781032661667-3

the punishment of culpable wrongdoers has intrinsic value. What this means and the problems it presents will be examined at length. What is clear is that for standard desert retributivists, whatever crime reduction benefits the institution of legal punishment provides are incidental, neither necessary nor sufficient for its defense.

The second account of the retributive element discussed is expressivist in character. It holds that the institution of legal punishment serves the important purpose of forcefully censuring those convicted of violating the criminal law.[5] The "hard treatment" aspect of legal punishment is crucial to this, as it makes clear to offenders and to others (including victims, if there are any) that the conduct in question was a public wrong, one justifiably prohibited by the criminal law. Importantly, as I shall interpret expressive retributivism, what justifies legal punishment is the instrumental role in plays in emphatically affirming and upholding what I term the "public rights and responsibility narrative." That narrative is an account of the legally enforced rights and responsibilities that individuals in liberal, democratic societies have.[6] How this instrumental value is to be understood and how it is distinct from the reduction of crime are matters addressed in this and subsequent chapters.

Much of my analysis in this chapter of the competing retributive elements is shaped by the challenges posed to retributive accounts of legal punishment by the limited resources that liberal democratic societies have on hand to identify, capture, convict, and punish those who violate provisions of the criminal law.[7] As numerous penal theorists have noted, the institution of legal punishment will be in competition with other state institutions and practices that require resources for their operations. These institutions and practices include national defense, infrastructure, market regulation, and social welfare programs. While more public resources can be collected through taxation or other means, and more might be provided to the criminal justice system relative to other state institutions and practices, there will inevitably be some upper limit to the resources that state officials can call upon to catch, convict, and punish legal wrongdoers. What seems clear is that there will be more, and perhaps many more, crimes committed than state officials can manage to punish fairly and appropriately. These crimes will vary considerably in their seriousness, from grave to relatively minor. Also, new crimes will continually be committed as older ones that state officials have failed to resolve through legal punishment recede into the past.

My contention will be that an expressivist account of the retributive element provides more compelling answers to the problems posed by limited state resources than does desert retributivism. Not only does the intrinsic value claim of desert retributivism seem a dubious basis for justifying the institution of legal punishment, its implications for the resource-constraint problem are either unclear or worrisome. By contrast, expressivist accounts can claim that the instrumental purposes served by legal punishment are especially significant when crimes are more serious. Also, while those instrumental purposes might weaken considerably in their force as unresolved minor offenses recede into the past, expressivists can plausibly maintain that those purposes retain at least some of their significance when the crimes in question are more serious.

I begin the chapter with brief characterizations of the competing retributive elements. My purpose in doing so is not to defend either one of them at length, but simply to lay out plausible versions of them for the discussion that follows. A more elaborate defense of the expressivist version of the retributive element will be provided in Chapters 3 and 4. Once I have identified the two versions of the retributive element that will be the focus of this chapter, I examine the intrinsic value claim often advanced by desert retributivists and discuss its plausibility and force. I then take up the issues posed by society's limited resources.

Desert Retributivism Defined

Again, according to desert retributivism, the primary reason why we should set up and operate institutions of legal punishment in society is to see to that those who are convicted of violating defensible criminal prohibitions receive the punishment that they deserve. As Mitchell Berman has shown, it is possible to water down the retributive element so that it plays only a modest justificatory role.[8] On such an account, the negative deserts of individuals convicted of crimes give us reason to inflict sanctions on them if no other purposes are served by doing so. However, my sense is that most penal theorists who defend desert retributivism have something more robust in mind—namely, that giving those convicted of crimes the punishment they deserve is a reason, and usually a strong reason, for setting up and administering institutions of legal punishment, not simply a residual reason for punishing the deserving in particular cases. Indeed, Michael Moore has suggested that the strength of the reasons negative desert provides is such that we have a duty to do see to it that the deserving are punished.[9] Yet, even if we do not go this far, I think it is fair to say that most desert retributivists are "immodest," in that they interpret negative deserts as supplying necessary and sufficient reasons for having and operating institutions of legal punishment. Pursuant to this, societies should make concerted efforts both to avoid punishment of the nondeserving and to see to it that the deserving are visited with sanctions proportional with the seriousness of their crimes. Crime seriousness is standardly understood in terms of the harms done, risked, or threatened by the various types of offenses and the culpability with which those who inflict, risk, or threaten such harms acted.

When asked why we should see to it that the deserving are punished appropriately (that is, proportionally) for their crimes, desert retributivists do not invoke the instrumental goods served by doing so. Instead, they maintain that offenders "deserve to suffer," or, following Berman, that "a wrongdoer's life should go less well."[10] These propositions are often supported with thought experiments about particularly awful crimes and the allegedly happy prospect of those who committed them receiving their deserved punishments.[11] If pressed a bit further, desert retributivists suggest that deserved punishment is an intrinsic good.[12] As such, its goodness is inherent, in the ways in which the goodness of beauty, love, or friendship is supposed to be. Desert retributivists will admit that legal punishment has instrumental value, typically in the form of the reduction of future crime. But this instrumental good typically plays no significant justificatory role in desert retributivism; it is simply an additional benefit of deserved punishment.

Importantly, although desert retributivists might believe that many of the *mala in se* provisions of the criminal law concern "prelegal" wrongs, they can endorse the notion that such wrongs should not be visited with state punishment unless or until they are adopted by (presumably democratic) legislators concerned with securing the basic moral rights of individuals in civil societies. Such actions by elected officials designate these wrongs as more than private or prelegal, but as "public."[13] Desert retributivists could also admit that there is room for debate about what basic moral rights individuals have such that actions in violation of those rights should be legally prohibited and punished.[14] In this way, desert retributivism could be melded together with different political theories about the basic rights of all persons. Also, given the need for stable and predictable social orders in which individuals can meaningfully exercise their basic rights, desert retributivists can support the adoption and enforcement of various *mala prohibita*. Again, once they are enshrined in the law, violations of such provisions become "public" in ways that make them fit subjects of deserved state punishment.

Expressivist Retributivism Briefly Characterized

Expressive retributivist theories hold that what justifies institutions of state punishment is the vital role they play in emphatically communicating censure, and thus official disapproval, of proven violations of the provisions of the criminal law. This censure is communicated both verbally and through the use of various forms of penal deprivation or infringement, ranging from fines at one end of the hard treatment spectrum, to imprisonment (although perhaps only relatively humane forms of it) at the other end. Here, I set to one side whether death can ever be a defensible form of penal hard treatment. As with desert retributivism, expressivists will sensibly restrict state censure to public wrongs, that is to violations of criminal prohibitions, of various kinds, that have been adopted by (presumably) democratic legislatures concerned to secure the basic rights of all members of society. Again, there is considerable debate among political theorists about what basic moral rights all individuals have and which violations of them merit state penal sanctions. There are also tensions that exist between the provisions of the criminal law adopted by particular democratic legislators and those implied or supported by the most defensible theory of basic moral rights. I set these controversies aside for the purposes of this chapter.

As most expressivists conceive it, the moral communication of which legal punishment consists is directed first and foremost at convicted wrongdoers.[15]

They presumably already know or sense that their actions were violations of the law, ones of which society disapproves. Although some offenders will take to heart the official disapproval of the conduct conveyed by their punishment, some might choose simply to ignore or dismiss it. Their doing so does not make that censure irrelevant or unimportant. The state, as the official spokesperson for the polity, has the responsibility to uphold and remind all citizens of what I term the "public rights and responsibilities narrative." This narrative consists of an account of the most basic, publicly stated and enforced, rights of all members of society under the criminal law, along with the responsibilities attendant to honoring those rights. Even if offenders choose to ignore what their legal punishment "says," their punishment vividly reminds all citizens of the rights they have in society and the responsibilities that go with them. Importantly, in cases in which crimes have one or more direct victims, the censure of offenders "stands by" them by communicating that the state (acting on behalf of the polity) will not permit others to wrong them with impunity. This serves to reassure victims, or those who survive them or care deeply about them, that the polity is "on their side," that they are not alone, and that the wrongs done to them will be taken seriously and dealt with forcefully.

Expressive forms of retributivism are not plausibly interpreted as holding that the punishment of convicted offenders has intrinsic value. Instead, expressivism holds that punishment serves a variety of instrumental purposes, ones that while not inconsistent with the reduction of crime, are not wholly or substantially reducible to it. Legal punishment of the convicted continuously reaffirms the public rights and responsibility narrative. This not only reminds offenders and the public of that narrative, it demonstrates that the state, acting on behalf of the polity, takes that narrative seriously. In so acting, state officials do not simply threaten wrongdoers or potential ones, they appeal to their sense of moral responsibility in supporting and abiding by the values of the polity. This is the sense in which, on expressivist accounts, legal punishment is a form of moral communication. Also, and importantly, when there are direct victims of crimes, those victims (or their partisans) will want to know that the state is prepared to address, in forceful ways, the wrongs done to them. Failure or neglect to do so will be a significant source of discouragement or despair to victims and those who care about them, as if the state is saying to them that their lives and vital interests do not matter, or do not matter much. And notice, victims and their partisans might reasonably want the state to address the wrongs done to them even if they are unsure about whether doing so will have general deterrent effects or they doubt that it is needed to further restrain those who have attacked or exploited them. More than this, all of us want assurance that if we undertake projects of various kinds, ones in which we invest our time, energy, and resources, we cannot be attacked or have things taken from us without real consequences being visited by the polity upon those who do so. Indeed, the prospect that wrongdoers, and especially serious ones, will not be convicted and punished will likely stifle our energy and enthusiasm for living our lives as we see fit. The result will be lives that are more cramped or anxious than they should be, ones that are far from those we want and expect free persons living in organized civil societies to have and enjoy.

There is, it must be admitted, much that can be said against expressive forms of retributivism.[16] In the next two chapters, I take up and respond to objections to it. In this chapter, my aim is the more limited one of outlining the ways in which I think it yields a more plausible version of the retributive element, at least compared with desert versions of retributivism.

The Intrinsic Value of Deserved Punishment: Some Doubts

Because desert retributivists do not believe that legal punishment's justification is grounded in its production of instrumental goods, such as the reduction of crime, they typically endorse the notion that punishment of the deserving is good in itself or intrinsically good. They attempt to convince us of this claim with thought experiments involving particularly heinous criminal wrongdoers. Some of these thought experiments are third-person ones: We are presented with the horrific details of the crimes of individuals and encouraged to believe that a natural or at least highly plausible response to such acts is that the individuals in question "deserve to suffer," or on Berman's less dramatic account, that they "deserve to have their lives go less well." Moore adds a first-person example of an individual who commits an awful deed and then contemplates his or her act.[17] Moore tells us that if he were to have committed such an act, he would believe that he deserved to suffer some appropriate punishment for having done so. Such a response is, we are told, the appropriate one of individuals who have moral beliefs and commitments of the kinds to which most of us aspire.

Two initial problems with this intrinsic value claim might be noted. First, if the idea is simply that heinous wrongdoers deserve to suffer or have their lives go worse in certain respects, it does not follow that it must be state institutions of legal punishment that effect this. The friends or relatives of crime victims might track down those who committed wrongs and inflict the appropriate amount of suffering on them. Alternatively, in some cases, perpetrators might, shortly after their criminal acts, contract debilitating illnesses or accidentally suffer injuries that "make their lives go appropriately worse" and no one, it seems, would have to see to it that these things happened to them.[18] Desert retributivists might respond to the first possibility with a plausible list of contingent reasons why it would be better for deserved suffering to be meted out by state officials. I am less certain how they could respond to the second possibility. What both of these possibilities suggest is that there seems no necessary link between wrongdoers experiencing their deserved suffering or life-worsening and the state being the agent which effects them. Expressive retributive accounts, by contrast, hold that it is the state, not private individuals, who are appropriately charged with backing and asserting the public rights and responsibilities narrative. It is the state that "speaks" on behalf of the polity, not private individuals.[19] Also, expressivists could plausibly argue that naturally occurring diseases or accidentally incurred injuries do not express anything about the previous wrongs committed by individuals. Legal punishment does so and does so authoritatively.

Second, the intrinsic value claim will seem more convincing in some cases of criminal wrongdoing than others. We might all "cheer" when horrific wrongdoers suffer their appropriate penal fates. But the world of criminal wrongdoing is vast and, more importantly, highly varied in the severity of the wrongs it contains and in the quality or character of those wrongs. Recall the fact that the majority of crimes punished in at least some legal jurisdictions are relatively minor—misdemeanors in the language of the US legal system.[20] Many of these criminal offenses will involve violations of *mala prohibita*, crimes for which there will often be few if any direct victims. If we contemplate those who violate *mala prohibita*, or ourselves having done so, I doubt that we will be quite as strongly struck by the notion that they (or we) "deserve to suffer." However, assuming that many of these provisions are defensible, there does seem some point to censuring violations of them, to remind violators (and others) of their responsibilities under the law, and perhaps also to reassure the law-abiding that they are not being "played for fools" by continuing to observe such legal requirements while others decline to do so with relative impunity.

As for what I termed the "quality and character" of the wrongs done by some criminal acts, consider not the egregious wrongs that are the stock and trade of desert retributivism, but the more fraught ones that are not uncommon in many societies. For instance, there are assaults that occur as a result of interpersonal disputes that have gotten out of hand. The perpetrator might not be able to mount a convincing defense of provocation under the law, but he or she may have acted in the heat of the moment in reaction to a series of taunts or demeaning remarks by the person assaulted. Also, consider crimes committed by those who struggle with mental illness or homelessness or desperate poverty.[21] Again, when individuals facing these kinds of difficulties commit crimes, and especially serious ones, it may well be necessary to hold them accountable, to censure their breaches of the rules of civil society and thereby make clear that their conduct is unacceptable under the public rights and responsibilities narrative. Yet I suspect that our intuitions about their deserving to suffer or about their lives being made to go worse will be more tentative or qualified. We will and arguably should be more hesitate to "cheer" when they are punished.

This brings me to a third point. If deserved punishment is an intrinsic good, it is something of an unusual one. Why do I say this? Imagine a world in which there is no wrongdoing—or no wrongdoing of the kind that the criminal law is concerned to prohibit. Such a world, while perhaps scarcely imaginable, would seemingly be a far better one than the world we inhabit, at least on the assumption that it lacked none of the other intrinsic goods that our world has, or even if it had them in somewhat less abundance. Indeed, a world in which no one was cruelly victimized by anyone else, while retaining most of the other intrinsic goods that our world enjoys, would be a kind of paradise, though it would lack all deserved punishment. Yet if we imagine our world without one or more of the other goods typically denominated "intrinsic"—pleasure, beauty, love, or friendship—then surely we would have a difficult time conceiving of it as a better world. Perhaps we could be convinced that the absence of one or more such goods is made up for by the greater abundance of others of them.[22] But we would have to be convinced of this and would probably be warranted in doubting that such an argument could be made persuasive.

In response to this, it might be argued that all intrinsic goods are "relational" in the sense that their goodness depends on overcoming or improving upon something lacking in the world, some deficit in it.[23] Beauty is an intrinsic good because of the ugliness or featurelessness of the natural or humanly-made world; love is an intrinsic good because there is hatred or indifference or alienation among persons in the world; and knowledge or wisdom is an intrinsic good because the world is rife with ignorance or the misevaluation or misunderstanding of things. Deserved punishment is thus likewise an intrinsic good because of the "deficit" caused by wrongdoing of certain kinds.

However, the deficits that deserved punishment fills or makes up for are normatively defined. It is wrongdoing of (appropriately, let us assume) legally proscribed kinds to which punishment is a valuable response. With more standard intrinsic goods, the deficits are part of the natural world or, if caused by the actions of humans, need not involve proscribed wrongs. Further, it is not clear that standard intrinsic goods require deficits of any kind. Imagine a canyon made lovely by brightly colored rocks carved into magnificent shapes by the erosion caused by wind and water. It rains and flowers bloom, further enhancing the beauty of the canyon. There seems no deficit made up for, just more beauty added. Or imagine a person with numerous caring friends who makes an acquaintance from which a new friendship is born. Again, there was nothing missing in or inadequate about the person's life before this happy occurrence, friendship wise. This shows how standard intrinsic goods can simply add to already good states of affairs. However, deserved punishment, as an intrinsic good, requires not only a deficit, but a wrong. That is what makes it possible to conceive of a world that is wholly lacking in deserved punishment and yet much better—because there is no wrongdoing—than one that has lots of it. Yet paradise with respect to more standard intrinsic goods is not a state of affairs in which there is none of them; it is one in which there is an abundance of them.

Further, the appropriate punishment of crimes does not appear to somehow vanquish or eliminate the seeming disvalue created by crimes, especially ones that inflict significant harms upon victims. This invites the question of how the world is, overall, a better place when those who commit crimes are punished. One possibility is suggested by Leo Zaibert.[24] Zaibert claims that deserved punishment produces an "organic whole" that is superior to, or as least "less bad" than that which we would have if wrongdoers went unpunished.[25] Taken in isolation, both the wrongs committed by offenders, and the proportional punishment meted out to them by the state, appear to be evils. Zaibert then argues that insofar as deserved punishment is a response to criminal wrongdoing, the result is a whole which is "less evil than the sum of the value of the parts."[26] Zaibert's depiction of the ultimate value outcome of deserved punishment's infliction is revealing. The relationship he describes is not one that comes to "cancellation" or "annulment," let alone something more positive. "Neutralization," or something like it, seems closer to the mark. Imagine that there are two caustic chemicals such that each, by itself, is dangerous or even deadly, but that when combined, they interact chemically in ways that produce something less bad. This analogy, or something like it, seems to capture the kind of organic whole to which Zaibert points.

Whether other retributivists who endorse the intrinsic value claim would go along with Zaibert's characterization of the relationship between crime and deserved punishment is uncertain. Yet something about it seems fundamentally correct. Deserved punishment, no matter how well or swiftly executed, cannot always (or perhaps ever) fully make up for the wrongs suffered by the victims of crime. There is some residual loss or badness that deserved punishment cannot fully extirpate. And this seems especially true when the crimes being punished are horrific. Consider, once again, the extreme cases retributivists put forward to convince us that deserved punishment is an intrinsic good. These are cases in which numerous innocent people have been cruelly victimized. The "moral monsters" who commit such heinous acts surely deserve to suffer penal losses, desert retributivists would have us believe, whether or not inflicting them will produce any further instrumental goods. Perhaps so, except that there seems no clear sense in which the deserved punishment of such monsters fully counteracts the disvalue of their many crimes. We might cheer when the perpetrators of great evils are punished but it is hard to do so with much enthusiasm if we contemplate the awfulness and permanence of what they have done. If deserved punishment is an intrinsic good, it is one that is often tinged with sorrow or tragedy.

Moreover, if deserved punishment did wholly counter the disvalue of crimes—or worse, if it created some positive good that overshadowed the disvalue of crimes—then desert retributivists would have a hard time explaining how a world in which in which horrific crimes did not occur in the first place would be better than one in which they occurred but were met with proportional punishment. Neutralization would leave us with a world that was no worse than the one which existed before crimes occurred. And if the intrinsic value of deserved punishment exceeded the disvalue produced by crimes, we would find ourselves in the awkward position of not abhorring—or worse, applauding—the occurrence of crimes because they provide us with opportunities to produce a better world. No one would sensibly do such a thing.

Perhaps desert retributivists need not claim that the intrinsic value of deserved punishment somehow creates greater value out of the disvalue created by crimes. Their view might simply be that the infliction of deserved punishment is intrinsically valuable because it conforms with our settled beliefs that wrongdoers' lives cannot be allowed to go on as before, that they must be made to endure penal losses or deprivations of more or less burdensome kinds. On this approach, punishment's value need not exceed or somehow transform the disvalue produced by the harms of criminal misconduct. Neither must it produce any other goods for it to be sufficiently justified as an institution, although desert retributivists could concede that it will often do so. If this is correct, we might reasonably worry that this is a too spartan rationale for the institution of legal punishment. Are we really prepared to say that all that is needed to fully justify the institution of legal punishment is that it serves the purpose of making criminal wrongdoers' lives go appropriately worse, such that no other goods need be promoted or attained by it?[27] That seems a dubious proposition to defend, especially given the other goods it arguably does provide according to crime reduction and expressivist accounts of the institution. It seems more plausible to hold that a more complex array of goods is needed to justify the institution, even if we then must face difficult questions about the priorities among them.

One further point might be made about the central task that desert retributivists seem prepared to assign to state agents. I would concede that when others wrong us in ways that are not prohibited by the criminal law, we might wish them some misfortune. If someone is unfaithful to us in a relationship after making a commitment to fidelity, or if a family member siphons off more than his or her fair share of an inherited family estate, we might hope that those who act in these ways encounter a few emotional or financial bumps and bruises in the near future as a kind of payback for what they have done. But we might hesitate to ourselves inflict those bumps and bruises, worrying that we might have misunderstood, or worse, somehow spurred their actions. Or we might believe that it is simply not our role to determine how their lives will go in terms of their subjective experience of it, that it is arrogant or even dangerous to think that we should try to make them suffer. All of this is consistent, arguably, with our hoping that they do suffer a bit.

The question is whether we should have any similar qualms about having state agents dedicated to the task of making criminal offenders lives go worse. Is this the kind of thing that, although we might hesitate to do it ourselves, we can feel confident that state officials are better qualified or more able to do and do well? Such confidence should be hard to come by, it seems to me, given the history of mistakes, overreach, corruption, and brutality that have, at times, marked penal institutions.[28] At the very least, if we are willing to admit that purposes of other kinds are vital in justifying the institution of legal punishment, there is more at stake in taking on the risks that the institution poses. We do not have to put all of our eggs in the dubious basket of having state officials attempt to do what many of us might be wary of doing ourselves.

One of the reasons for preferring expressive versions of retributivism is that they are not so spartan in their accounts of the purposes served by legal punishment. Expressive retributivism, as I have indicated, claims that by holding legal wrongdoers accountable for their crimes, punishment forcefully stands for and reinforces the public rights and responsibilities narrative. In doing so, it reminds wrongdoers and the public of the importance of that narrative and stands for the victims of crimes, when there are victims, assuring them that individuals who have wronged them will not be permitted to do so with impunity. This, in turn, has numerous laudatory effects on victims' (and others') beliefs that their lives are theirs to determine and lead without interferences of various kinds. Still, when the harms done to victims are grave, there might be little legal punishment, by itself, can do to make good such losses beyond holding accountable those who committed them. That accountability holding is a good—one with a variety of consequences in the real world—but not one that transforms a bad thing into a good one. Instead, by holding wrongdoers accountable, punishment marks and condemns their actions as ones that the polity will not abide. Sadly, the damage such crimes have done will often persist.

Deserved Punishment and Limited State Resources

Not surprisingly, those who deserve legal punishment are often reluctant to come forward and receive it. To identify, arrest, convict, and assign them sanctions, not to mention carry out those sanctions, requires the expenditure of substantial state resources. Inevitably, there will be competition for those resources, as the state is deemed to have costly and complex responsibilities of other kinds to its citizens. However, the resource demands of desert retributivism have not often been noted or systematically addressed by the theorists who support it.[29]

Start with the plausible assumption that there is some limit to the resources that the state can call upon to fulfill its various functions, including its retributive punishment function. Consider, first, what might be termed the "stringency" of the demand to mete out to criminal offenders the punishments that they deserve. The stringency of negative desert-claims has two dimensions. First, there is what we might term the "absolute" stringency of such claims: Should state officials be prepared to invest so many resources in the pursuit of deserved punishment claims that they thereby siphon off resources that the state would otherwise utilize to accomplish its other significant tasks? In other words, should we be prepared to think that state officials should spend less on external defense of the country, infrastructure, or education and healthcare for its citizens if doing so is necessary to achieve retributive justice?

Second, even if we assume some upper limit on the resources that criminal justice officials can call upon, there is also the "relative" stringency of negative desert claims: Should criminal justice officials be prepared to expend more resources on some deserved punishment claims than others? Specifically, should they use more of their limited resources to apprehend, convict, and punish the perpetrators of more serious crimes than less serious ones? We might term their being prepared to do so a "variable stringency" approach.

Alternatively, it might be suggested that all deserved punishment claims have the same weight or urgency, such that an "invariant stringency" approach is preferable. According to the latter, the authorities should act to pursue and sanction offenders of all kinds, rather than focus their resources on the punishment of some crimes (presumably the more serious ones) at the cost of punishing other (presumably less serious) crimes.[30]

Let us set to one side the issues raised by "absolute" stringency, although I revisit them in subsequent chapters. There are enough puzzles with "relative" stringency to give pause to anyone attracted to desert retributivism. It seems fair to say, at the outset, that the most plausible position on relative stringency is one that involves variable stringency. It seems doubtful that most retributivists would have us invest as many of society's limited resources in capturing and punishing bicycle thieves as in capturing and punishing murderers or rapists. The question is how theorists who justify state punishment by saying that it gives individuals what they deserve for their crimes can defend such a position. Guilty petty offenders deserve punishment, as do guilty serious ones. More to the point, if deserved punishment has intrinsic value in both kinds of cases, how can desert retributivists account for the seeming rationality of the preference for pursuing more rather than less serious offenders? Is it that the deserved punishment of more serious offenses has more intrinsic value than the deserved punishment of less serious offenses? Perhaps, although a case might be made that the intrinsic value of deserved punishment is binary in character—either wrongdoers get their just deserts and thus their punishment has intrinsic value or they do not and no intrinsic value is produced. In the former case, they suffer as they deserve or their lives go appropriately worse; in the latter case, they neither suffer as they deserve nor do their lives go appropriately worse. If we keep to the bare bones account of desert-retributivism identified at the end of the previous section, there is not much more to be said and so it is not apparent how the theory's proponents could account for the notion that the deserved punishment of some offenders has more intrinsic value than the deserved punishment of others.

In response, it might be argued that desert retributivists can easily maintain that the state ought to give priority in its expenditure of limited resources to more serious offenders. More serious offenders, it might be claimed, are more deserving of punishment, because the kinds of crimes they commit tend (culpably) do more harm. Less serious offenders commit crimes that produce moderate to minor harms, if they cause any harm at all. Or, perhaps, they commit moderately harmful crimes with low levels of culpability.[31] However, this response, although initially plausible, appears to rest on a conflation of two claims. It is one thing to say that those who commit more serious crimes deserve more punishment. Standard proportionality doctrine supports such a view, whether we are talking about ordinal or cardinal proportionality.[32] It is another thing to say that more serious offenders *deserve* punishment more than less serious ones. They all deserve punishment; the differences among them concern how much punishment they deserve. Yet if they all deserve punishment, then how exactly are we to make sense of the notion of variable stringency, that is, of differences in how many resources state officials should be prepared to invest in seeing to it that they get what they deserve?

A further puzzle for desert-minded retributivists is posed by the fact that criminal offenses occur at a given moment in time and then gradually recede into the past. In other words, state officials are not confronted by a fixed pool of offenses among which they must make decisions about which ones to pursue and with how much vigor. Instead, the pool is continually growing, with unresolved cases receding into the past. Many crimes are never solved and those who commit them are never punished, including many who commit serious crimes. Is there some point at which, once an unsolved crime recedes into the past, it no longer ought to command the resources of state officials? Or do the deserved punishment claims of offenders persist and retain their "full strength" indefinitely over time, no matter how far they occurred in the past? We might refer to this tendency for crimes to recede into the past as the phenomenon of "decay."

Three possible positions on decay can be identified. The first, which we might term "nondecay," holds that deserved punishment claims retain their full force no matter how far they recede into the past. Accordingly, unpunished crimes committed five, ten, or twenty years ago ought to continue to receive the full attention of state officials. Obviously, such a position would be strongly resource-consumptive. It would require a substantial influx of societal resources from other sources (thus leaving other state responsibilities unmet) or would leave the state officials tasked with meting out deserved punishment with their available resources stretched pretty thin.

A second position on decay is one we might term "gradual decay." According to it, as unsolved crimes recede into the past, they slowly lose their strength to command the investment of societal resources to ensure their deserved punishment. This position would be considerably less resource-demanding. The question is whether it seems credible, especially when the crimes that recede into the past are serious ones. Would we be comfortable saying that heinous murders from five or ten or twenty years ago should receive little (and declining) attention from state officials? I doubt it.

The preceding remarks suggest a third position, which we might term "variable decay." According to it, past crimes vary in the demands they make upon state authorities, with more serious crimes continuing to exert a substantial call upon state officials to act to resolve them, even as they recede into the past. My sense is that the "variable decay" position is probably the most sensible one. It seems to fit best with existing criminal justice practices, wherein officials tend to ignore minor to moderately serious offenses once they recede into the past. By contrast, such officials often continue to try to identify, track down, and punish the perpetrators of more serious crimes, even after many years have passed since those crimes were committed. The question is how an account of legal punishment focused on giving offenders the punishments they deserve for their crimes can make sense of "variable decay." Those who committed minor offenses years ago do not, it would seem, gradually become less deserving of punishment, though saying so is consistent with acknowledging the ways in which it might become more and more difficult to track down and convict them.

Despite the qualms noted previously, let us suppose that the most plausible approach that desert retributivists can take to addressing the resource-allocation questions raised by stringency and decay is to suggest that the punishment of serious offenders has more intrinsic value than the punishment of lesser offenders.[33] It seems natural to wed such a variable intrinsic value approach to some form of consequentialism about desert, according to which state officials should strive to maximize the intrinsic value produced by their criminal justice undertakings. Michael Moore briefly discussed such a consequentialist version of desert retributivism in his work, but opted, instead, for a position that he termed "threshold deontology."[34] According to his preferred position, state officials have a duty to effect deserved punishment, though he admits that the duty might be presumptive, rather than absolute, thus permitting officials to ignore it if the consequences of fulfilling it would, in some cases, prove "disastrous."

The problem with Moore's threshold deontology is that it leaves us guessing about how state officials should resolve the resource-allocation issues raised by stringency and decay. It might be plausible to say that the duty to punish is weightier when crimes are more serious, because punishment in such cases produces more intrinsic value. However, if all offenses ground a duty to punish the deserving, as it seems that Moore will have to concede, how are state officials to determine the mix of more and less serious crimes to pursue, not to mention the mix of recent and past crimes which they have duties to pursue? In the absence of a consequentialist maximizing strategy, the answers to these questions are difficult to discern from what Moore says. The "avoiding disaster" constraint would seem to apply in relatively rare cases, but state officials will continually face decisions about how to invest their limited resources.

Also, even if Moore argued that state duties to punish more serious offenders have priority over state duties to punish less serious ones, such a priority cannot plausibly be absolute. Duties are duties, after all, and so ones to punish lesser offenders remain and their fulfillment will, in various more or less subtle ways, conflict with the fulfillment of duties to punish more serious offenders, including those who acted recently and those whose crimes have receded into the past. How would state officials determine which duties to fulfill and which to set aside? Moore might weaken his position a bit and maintain that deserved punishment only gives state officials reason to act rather than a duty to do so.[35] And he might then claim that their reasons to act are stronger in cases of more serious, recent crimes than in cases of minor, past crimes. Perhaps punishment of the former makes the world a better place, intrinsic value-wise than punishment of the latter. Yet, how Moore could adopt such a view without signing onto consequentialism about negative desert claims is, I would suggest, a bit unclear.

Michael Cahill has done more than most retributivists to raise and address the resource-limitation issues I have identified. He embraces desert-consequentialism, according to which deserved punishment is an intrinsic good that the state ought to pursue with an aim of maximizing the overall quantity of it.[36] He is clear that the state has no deontological duty to punish the deserving, whether such a duty is interpreted as absolute or presumptive. On his account, the state's meting out of deserved punishment is a goal, not a duty. Cahill readily embraces a form of variable stringency. He admits that the authorities might spend more resources pursuing the punishment of more serious crimes than less serious ones, because doing so might yield more intrinsic value.

However, the view that punishment of more serious crimes yields more intrinsic value will not, on a consequentialist approach, yield a straightforward argument for devoting more of the state's limited resources to catching, convicting, and punishing the perpetrators of such crimes. The reason for this is that, quite often, achieving the just punishment of more serious offenders will prove very resource-demanding. Again, many serious crimes go unpunished.[37] It seems doubtful that this is because the authorities do not care about them or want to capture and convict those who committed them. It is rather that the perpetrators of such crimes are often clever enough about committing them, or evasive in admitting guilt about having done so, that the authorities are frustrated in their efforts to bring them to justice. Even those serious offenders who are ham-fisted in their commission of crimes get lucky and evade identification or capture simply because there were no witnesses to their acts or ones willing to testify against them. Also, the punishment of serious offenders when they are caught and convicted is itself more resource-demanding since it will typically require the use of imprisonment, the most costly of penal sanctions. What all of this means is that, arguably, the authorities might produce more overall intrinsic value by focusing their limited resources on the punishment of a larger number of lesser offenses, which while they are lower in intrinsic value, are often easier to police and prosecute and less resource-consuming to punish. If state officials can round up and punish a substantial quantity of such offenders, this might more than make up for the lost value of opting not to pursue the punishment of more serious offenders. If this is correct, consequentialism about deserved punishment does not appear to sit well with the seeming greater urgency of punishing the more serious kinds of legally proscribed wrongdoing.

Cahill does not discuss the possibility of decay, but a sympathetic reading of his position suggests that he would admit some form of it. After all, the authorities might best deploy their limited resources in pursuing the punishment of more recent offenses, ones for which the evidence is fresher or for which witnesses are still available or their memories more reliable. But again, such an approach does not seem to capture the urgency of the punishment of past serious offenses, ones which might have killed victims or ruined their lives. Official persistence in efforts to identify, arrest, and convict the perpetrators of such crimes—a persistence which, I suspect, many of us would deem signally important—seems, in some ways, inconsistent with a maximizing consequentialist approach to such matters. The investigation and prosecution of past serious offenses will not only be resource drains, they will be less likely to yield convictions and punishment of the deserving and thus any intrinsic value. Thus, a maximizing approach to the variable intrinsic value of deserved punishment seems to support not only more official focus on minor offenses but also more official focus on current offenses or quite recent ones. Yet, all of this appears to sit uneasily with the sense we are likely to have that the punishment of serious crimes, even ones that have receded into the past, ought to retain some urgency for state officials.

In response, Cahill might argue that meting out deserved punishment to serious offenders will be very high in intrinsic value, enough so that the resource demands of doing so will be more than offset in many if not most cases. Admittedly, if we focus on the gravest criminal acts—the kinds committed by the "moral monsters" featured in desert retributivists' thought experiments—we might be moved by this argument. However, there are two problems with it that should be noted. First, many serious crimes are dissimilar to those committed by moral monsters. Routine armed robberies, thefts of substantial amounts of property, even aggravated assaults, are crimes that we reasonably believe it important for state authorities to catch, convict, and punish the perpetrators of. But is the intrinsic value of accomplishing this so substantial that the drain on public resources comes to little or nothing by comparison? I doubt it. Second, as we have seen, the gravest criminal offenses are typically awful in their consequences for victims, their survivors, and larger communities whose members must cope with the despair, fear, and trauma they cause. If, somehow, the punishment of those who commit such atrocities wiped clean all of the suffering they caused, it might be convincing to argue that the intrinsic value of deserved punishment, alone, clearly exceeds the substantial resource costs of inflicting it. Yet as we have seen, the deserved punishment of the worst crimes does not seem to produce so much unalloyed intrinsic good that it somehow renders the resource costs of achieving it insignificant.

Expressive Retributivism and Limited Resources

My contention is that the seeming urgency of having state officials focus more rather than fewer of their limited resources on serious criminal offenses, including ones that occurred in the past, has more to do with efforts to counter what those crimes communicate than with producing or maximizing intrinsic value in the world. The punishment of such crimes censures wrongdoers emphatically and thereby assures victims, which their often will be in such cases, that the polity, acting through its officials, will not stand by and let their lives be damaged or destroyed without serious consequences for those who harmed them. The punishment of serious crimes also assures other members of society that the state takes seriously one of the most powerful reasons for its existence, namely, securing the most basic legally protected moral rights of its members. Indeed, if state officials do not act with considerable urgency and determination when persons are murdered, viciously attacked, threatened with death or serious injury, or have the property on which they depend to meet their needs stolen or destroyed, it will not be clear why we invest the state with as much power and authority as we do.

Again, I grant that part of what the institution of legal punishment does is prevent crimes, and especially serious crimes, through various mechanisms. But it does more than this, which becomes apparent once crimes, and especially serious crimes, are committed and the prevention of harms to the victims of such acts is no longer an option. Arguably, then what we want and expect the state to do is to symbolically validate the important interests that have been attacked by identifying, arresting, convicting, and punishing transgressors. Its doing so not only rebukes the offenders, it constitutes an affirmation, or reaffirmation of the significance of victims' lives and fundamental interests. Punishment thereby communicates not only with offenders but with victims, their partisans, and members of the observant public.

Minor criminal offenses implicitly if not explicitly communicate some level of offender indifference to the equal worth of their fellow citizens, including some willingness to use them as mere means to their ends. But such crimes are not plausibly interpreted as communicating the same level or kinds of offender disregard for victim interests that serious crimes communicate, a disregard which says that victims can be destroyed or used in ways that trample under their most elemental interests in their bodies, minds, and property. Also, the harms wrought by minor offenses tend to fade or wear off over time, often quickly. Minor property thefts will be inconvenient and perhaps temporarily disturbing or disorienting. Simple assaults by acquaintances or family members, or even strangers, may cause some bodily injury and trauma, but these effects are generally short-lived so long as the harms inflicted are modest. Also, many victims will have insurance on their property that helps them recoup their losses or health insurance that enables them to have their minor injuries treated. There are also, in many legal jurisdictions, state-sponsored victim compensation programs that help to make crime victims whole again.[38] None of this should be taken to is suggest that minor crimes are ones that state officials ought to ignore. When they can identify, arrest, convict, and punish those who committed them without too much time or effort, they obviously should do so, to censure the conduct in question proportionally with its seriousness and thereby reaffirm the rules of the civil order. Also, even minor offenses, if left largely unchecked, will erode the faith that victims have that violations of their rights will be taken seriously by state officials. More generally, even when minor crimes are victimless, which many of them will be, official neglect of such offenses seems likely to undermine the confidence of the public that the state is committed to maintaining a predictable and stable social order.

Crimes that cause death, grave and permanent injuries, or that assault the basic dignity of persons (including the rightful control they have over their bodies and minds) are different. In much more profound ways, such crimes implicitly if not explicitly communicate that the lives and fundamental interests of victims (or potential victims) can be taken or damaged as if the victims do not matter. In this way, such crimes constitute grave assaults on one of the foundational value premises of liberal democratic societies—that the lives and basic rights of all persons have equal moral worth.[39] Official failures to take such crimes seriously by assiduously seeking out their perpetrators will reasonably be interpreted by victims or their allies as communicating state (and thus societal) indifference toward the lives and basic interests of at least some of its citizens. Granted, even assiduous efforts to identify, capture, and convict the perpetrators of such crimes might not produce convictions. Victims or their allies cannot reasonably demand that much, but they (and other concerned citizens) can insist on persistent and diligent efforts to attain justice for victims, even in the face of other demands on official time and energy stemming from efforts to solve other serious crimes. Even as serious crimes recede into the past, and sometimes the distant past, we might reasonably expect state officials to devote some resources to their resolution, so that the substantial affronts to the lives and dignity of their victims are marked and condemned by state punishment.

Expressive retributivism can accommodate the resource limitations on state punishment because it construes punishment of the provably guilty as a giving state officials reasons to pursue their punishment, which reasons vary in their strength depending on the gravity of the crimes in question. Arguably, the weighty reasons serious crimes furnish state officials to act do not fade entirely as those crimes recede into the past and even the distant past. There might always be some call on state officials to try to arrest, convict, and punish the perpetrators of serious crimes if they can do so because of what such crimes symbolically conveyed—an arrogance, we might say, according to which their perpetrators placed their own desires, no matter how trivial, above the fundamental interests of their victims. Nonetheless, it must be acknowledged that the longer such crimes go unpunished, the less likely it is that they will be. Also, it must also be admitted that the crush of more recent cases, including ones involving other serious offenses, will demand the attention and efforts of state officials—and not unreasonably so, given the greater likelihood of their being resolved through the punishment of perpetrators. Despite all of this, it is not uncommon to find investigators who persist in their efforts to identify, arrest, and convict criminal actors whose grave offenses occurred long in the past.[40] They devote whatever time or energy they can to such cases, refusing to let them fade away entirely. On an expressive retributivist account, such efforts make sense because the weight of reasons that officials have to hold perpetrators accountable and rebuke their actions remains formidable, even if the prospects for success at doing so are bleak.

I would concede that the expressivist approach I am defending, with its contention that the strength of the reasons state officials have for pursuing crimes varies with the seriousness of those crimes, might plausibly be interpreted as a kind of consequentialism about legal punishment. It will be difficult to resist the proposition that state officials should attempt to maximize the deployment of their limited resources to achieve more rather than fewer convictions of those who have committed crimes. Indeed, it seems hard to deny the power of such thinking about any of the major institutions in society. However, I would argue that my account does not support a simple kind of consequentialism, one that might, for instance, countenance ignoring serious crimes if many less serious ones can be resolved by officials through arrests, prosecutions, convictions, and punishment of those who perpetrated them. The resolution of serious criminal cases (in the form of punishment of those who committed them) should be allotted a larger share of the limited resources that state officials have at their disposal. And this is true even if such cases pose unique challenges to state officials and thus are more difficult to make headway with. Complicating things further, even serious crimes that have receded into the past, and perhaps the distant past, should, in my view, continue to exert some "pull" on state officials in their decisions about how to allocate their resources. Of course, the reasons such crimes provide officials to act might be conceived as gradually diminishing in strength since the passage of time will likely, in various ways, reduce the prospects for their successful prosecution and punishment. Still, unlike the vast array of more minor offenses that continually recede into the past and which we should be willing to have state officials mostly ignore, the resolution of serious crimes might be deemed to lose their urgency only gradually.

Hence, if expressivist forms of retributivism must embrace some form of consequentialism in the design and operations of criminal justice institutions, my sense is that it should be conceived as a weighted and complex form of it, the latter because the weights must be understood to change as crimes recede into the past. But even this oversimplifies matters, because, arguably, it should be conceived as a consequentialism that is constrained by the basic rights of suspects and members of the public more generally. On such an approach, state officials must, as they detect, investigate, prosecute, and punish crimes do so in ways that respect the basic rights of persons. Even if such rights should not be conceived as having absolute or overriding weight, they should be regarded as requiring state officials to avoid certain kinds of crime-resolution strategies altogether while employing others parsimoniously.

I will not attempt to spell out such a weighted and constrained consequentialist approach in more detail. Like others who have examined and thought about consequentialism, I suspect that we should be wary of assigning individual actors, including state officials, the complex tasks of figuring out which of the many choices available to them would maximize the good that their actions will do, subject to certain constraints. They, like all of us, will likely lack the information needed to perform such deliberative tasks reliably and well. And they, like all of us, are apt to lack the cognitive abilities needed to competently process that information and to do so in ways that are unaffected by biases of various kinds.[41] To this I would add that a weighted consequentialist approach will be more demanding still, as there will be debate about "how much" weight to assign to resolution of the many different kinds of criminal offenses, including serious ones, and how to channel resources accordingly. It is one thing to examine a set of decisions made by state officials after the fact, so to speak, and raise questions about whether their choices and actions produced the best consequences, taking everything, including the differing weights of their reasons for acting with respect to the different kinds of crimes, into account. It is another to task those officials with figuring out what will produce the best consequences on an ongoing basis, given the crush of competing considerations they must weigh and balance. We might usefully do what many police departments already do—divide the detection and investigation of crimes up into separate units, with some focused on less serious offenses and others focused on more serious ones. A weighted consequentialist approach would plausibly assign more resources to the latter units. Perhaps within those units, some sort of maximizing approach to the deployment of resources will make sense, although, again, it will have to be one that is constrained and gives at least some (although likely diminishing) weight to the resolution of past crimes. Thus, even within such units, no simple maximizing strategy likely will be feasible.

Concluding Remarks

My aim in this chapter has been the limited one of identifying, distinguishing, and supporting what I believe is the most defensible retributive element for a mixed theory of legal punishment. Instead of holding that we design and fund state penal institutions with a view, simply, to making the lives of individuals who are convicted of crimes go appropriately worse, I have argued that it is more plausible to believe that we craft such institutions in order to censure offenders for their crimes, and thereby symbolically affirm the public rights and responsibility narrative. By doing so, we assure the victims of crimes, if they exist, that their lives and vital interests cannot be interfered with or damaged without those who have harmed them suffering appropriate penal consequences. Even where there are no direct victims of crime, the censure of convicted wrongdoers reminds the public of their responsibilities under the criminal law and assures it that the state will act forcefully to maintain the kind of civil order to which the polity is committed. In these ways, legal punishment is instrumentally important, although the goods it achieves are arguably distinct from the prevention of crime. These instrumental goods furnish state officials with reasons to act which reasons vary in their weight depending on the seriousness of the crimes to be addressed. More of the limited resources state official command should be devoted to the identification, arrest, conviction, and punishment of serious legal wrongdoers. I have argued that expressivist theories can better account for this than desert versions of retributivism. Also, expressivist theories do not have to explain how punishment is good-in-itself, even when the criminal harms to which it is a response are awful and enduring. Nor do they have to rest content with the bare claim that making offenders lives go worse is sufficient to justify the social costs and risks of penal institutions.

Significant challenges to penal expressivism remain, however, ones which will be the subjects of succeeding chapters. Among these, doubts about whether penal loss or deprivation is necessary to express censure, whether the goods censure are alleged to create are really distinguishable from the reduction of crime, whether expressivist theories are genuinely retributive in nature, and how significant penal censure is or can be in the justification of legal punishment, loom the largest. Assuming that they can be addressed, I will then have to detail how the retributive and crime reduction elements of my mixed theory can be coherently combined and what such a mixed theory implies about the sentencing of convicted offenders.

Notes

1 See John Cottingham, "Varieties of Retributivism," *Philosophical Quarterly* 29 (1979): 238–46. See also Nigel Walker, "Even More Varieties of Retributivism," *Philosophy* 74 (1999): 595–605.

2 The most prominent defender of this view is Michael S. Moore, *Placing Blame: A Theory of the Criminal Law* (Oxford: Oxford University Press, 1997), especially Chapters 2, 3, and 4. See also John Kleinig, *Punishment and Desert* (The Hague: Martinus Nijhoff, 1973) and Lawrence Davis, "They Deserve to Suffer," *Analysis* 32 (1972): 136–40.

3 See Mitchell N. Berman, "Modest Retributivism," in Kimberly Kessler Ferzan and Stephen J. Morse (eds.), *Legal, Moral, and Metaphysical Truths: The Philosophy of M. S. Moore* (Oxford: Oxford University Press, 2016): 35–47, at 43.

4 Moore defends the "duty" account of desert retributivism, in *Placing Blame*, at 91. For useful discussion of this claim, see Berman, "Modest Retributivism," and Douglas Husak, "What Do Criminals Deserve?" in Ferzan and Morse, *Legal, Moral, and Metaphysical Truths*, 49–62. Moore responds to Berman and Husak in "Responses and Appreciations," in Ferzan and Morse, *Legal, Moral, and Metaphysical Truths*, 323–425, at 344–48.

5 The idea that legal punishment expresses censure or condemnation has been defended by many penal theorists, among them Joel Feinberg, "The Expressive Function of Punishment," *The Monist* 49 (1965): 397–423; R. A. Duff, *Trials and Punishments* (Cambridge: Cambridge University Press, 1986) and *Punishment, Communication, and Community* (Oxford: Oxford University Press, 2001); John Kleinig, "Punishment and Moral Seriousness," *Israel Law Review* 25 (1991): 401–21; Igor Primoratz, "Punishment as Language," *Philosophy* 64 (1989): 187–205; Jean Hampton, "An Expressive Theory of Retribution," in Wesley Craig (ed.), *Retributivism and Its Critics* (Stuttgart: V. Steiner Verlag, 1992): 1–21; Andrew von Hirsch, *Censure and Sanctions* (Oxford: Clarendon Press, 1993); Uma Narayan, "Appropriate Responses and Preventive Benefits: Justifying Censure and Hard Treatment in Legal Punishment," *Oxford Journal of Legal Studies* 13 (1993): 166–82; Thaddeus Metz, "Censure Theory and Intuitions about Punishment," *Law & Philosophy* 19 (2000): 491–512; and Bill Wringe, *An Expressive Theory of Punishment* (London: Palgrave Macmillan, 2016).

6 Obviously, there is considerable room for disagreement among penal, and more broadly, political theorists regarding the details of this narrative. I set this controversy aside for the purposes of this chapter. Expressivist accounts of legal punishment

are consistent with a variety of views about what basic moral rights individuals have and which should be backed by the various provisions of the criminal law.

7 See especially, Michael Cahill, "Retributive Justice in the Real World," *Washington University Law Review* 85 (2007): 815–70 and "Punishment Pluralism," in Mark D. White (ed.), *Retributivism: Essays on Theory and Practice* (New York: Oxford University Press, 2011): 25–48. Others who note the issues raised by the implementation of retributive punishment in a world of limited resources include Douglas N. Husak, "Why Punish the Deserving?" *Noûs* 26 (1992): 447–64; John Braithwaite and Philip Pettit, *Not Just Deserts: A Republican Theory of Criminal Justice* (Oxford: Clarendon Press, 1990): 106–8 and Vincent Chiao, *Criminal Law in the Age of the Administrative State* (Oxford: Oxford University Press, 2018).

8 Berman, "Modest Retributivism," 43.

9 Moore, *Placing Blame*, 91.

10 Mitchell N. Berman, "Rehabilitating Retributivism," *Law and Philosophy* 32 (2013): 83–108, at 88.

11 Kleinig, *Punishment and Desert*, 67 and Moore, *Placing Blame*, 98.

12 Moore, *Placing Blame*, 160. For doubts about the intrinsic value claim, see Douglas Husak, "Retributivism *in Extremis*," *Law and Philosophy* 32 (2013): 3–31, at 7–11.

13 See R. A. Duff and S. E. Marshall, "Crimes, Public Wrongs, and Civil Order," *Criminal Law and Philosophy* 13 (2019): 27–48.

14 See, for instance, the essays in Rowan Cruft, S. Matthew Liao, and Massimo Renzo (eds.), *Philosophical Foundations of Human Rights* (Oxford: Oxford University Press, 2015).

15 See Feinberg, "Expressive Function," 401–2; von Hirsch, *Censure and Sanctions*, 10; and Duff, *Trials and Punishments*, 235 and *Punishment, Communication, and Community*, 79.

16 See, for instance, Victor Tadros, *The Ends of Harm: The Moral Foundations of Criminal Law* (Oxford: Oxford University Press, 2011): 99–110; David Boonin, *The Problem of Punishment* (Cambridge: Cambridge University Press, 2008): 172–79; and Nathan Hanna, "Say What? A Critique of Expressive Retributivism," *Law & Philosophy* 27 (2008): 123–50.

17 Moore, *Placing Blame*, 145.

18 For useful discussion of the possibility that wrongdoers who have already suffered extensively should not be punished further, see Douglas N. Husak, "Already Punished Enough," *Philosophical Topics* 18 (1990): 79–99.

19 This might be the beginning of a response to the questions posed by Malcolm Thorburn concerning why the state has the exclusive authority to punish. See his "Criminal Punishment and the Right to Rule," *University of Toronto Law Journal* 70, Supplement 1 (2020): 44–63.

20 Alexandra Natapoff, "Misdemeanors," *Southern California Law Review* 85 (2012): 1313–75 and Jenny Roberts, "Why Misdemeanors Matter: Defining Effective Advocacy in the Lower Criminal Courts," *University of California-Davis Law Review* 45 (2011): 277–372.

Andrew von Hirsch, *Censure and Sanctions* (Oxford: Clarendon Press, 1993): 18–19.

21 See Erin Kelly, *The Limits of Blame: Rethinking Punishment and Responsibility* (Cambridge, MA: Harvard University Press, 2018). Kelly raises doubts similar to my own about how responsible many offenders are for their crimes. However, she is more concerned to argue that we should be less inclined to blame offenders than that they are not strongly deserving to suffer.

22 Granted, talk about the loss of some intrinsic goods being "made up for" by the greater abundance of others might seem to suggest that these good are somehow fungible, such that they can be measured along some common dimension (say,

their tendency to produce pleasure or happiness in those who experience them). However, it might be possible to make rough comparative judgments about two worlds with distinct intrinsic goods such that we can say that one of them is better than another of them. For instance, if two worlds have roughly the same amount of intrinsic value of one kind, but one of the worlds also has quite a bit of intrinsic value of another kind, it seems plausible to say that the second world is better, and this in spite of the fact that the two goods are not fungible.

23 This might raise problems for value theorists who hold that intrinsic value or goodness is essentially non-relational, something that things have "in isolation" from other things or states of affairs. For discussion of such accounts, see Ben Bradley, "Two Concepts of Intrinsic Value," *Ethical Theory and Moral Practice* 9 (2006): 111–30, at 112–13. Since such a view is contested, I will not pursue it further in this context.

24 Leo Zaibert, *Punishment and Retribution* (Hants, England: Ashgate, 2006).

25 Zaibert, *Punishment and Retribution*, 206.

26 Zaibert, *Punishment and Retribution*, 210.

27 Douglas Husak makes a point similar in several of his articles. See, for instance, his "Retribution in Criminal Theory," *San Diego Law Review* 37 (2000): 959–86, at 975–76.

28 Husak, "Why Punish the Deserving?" 450–51.

29 Again, Cahill is the clearest exception to this claim. See his "Retributive Justice in the Real World," and "Punishment Pluralism." Moore has recently noted the issue, but without elaborating his position on it. See his "Responses and Appreciations," 348.

30 The stringency of deserved punishment claims should be distinguished from a different question, whether those claims should ever yield or be overridden by other considerations. Moore permits the duty to punish the deserving to be set aside in cases in which "disastrous consequences" would ensue. See his *Placing Blame*, 158 and 719–24. Stringency concerns the quantity of resources that state officials should be prepared to invest in pursuing and convicting offenders, even if disastrous consequences would not result from their investing more rather than fewer resources in this endeavor.

31 See von Hirsch's classic discussion of ordinal proportionality in *Censure and Sanctions*, 18–19 and 29–33.

32 von Hirsch, *Censure and Sanctions*, 18–19.

33 Moore, *Placing Blame*, 160, although it is less than clear from the text whether Moore subscribes to variation in the intrinsic value of the deserved punishment of more and less serious crimes.

34 Moore, *Placing Blame*, 158 and 719–24.

35 See Berman, "Modest Retributivism," 43.

36 Cahill, "Retributive Justice in the Real World," 850–53.

37 See Shima Baughman, "How Effective Are Police? The Problem of Clearance Rates and Criminal Accountability," *Alabama Law Review* 72 (2020): 48–130 and Andrew D. Leipold, "The Puzzle of Clearance Rates, and What They Can Tell Us about Crime, Police Reform, and Criminal Justice," *Wake Forest Law Review* 56 (2021): 47–95.

38 Even in the United States, which has a harshly punitive criminal justice system and meager social welfare provisions, most states have some kind of state-sponsored victim compensation. See *U. S. Resource Map of Crime Victim Services and Information*, Office for Victims of Crime, at www.ovc.gov/map.html (accessed November 11, 2022).

39 On the implied premise of equal moral worth in expressivist theories, see Jean Hampton, "An Expressive Theory of Retribution," in Wesley Craig (ed.), *Retributivism*

and Its Critics (Stuttgart: V. Steiner Verlag, 1992): 1–21 and "A New Theory of Retribution," in R. G. Frey and Christopher Morris (eds.), *Liability and Responsibility: Essays in Law and Morals* (Cambridge: Cambridge University Press, 1991): 377–414.

40 See, for instance, Cheryl Allsop, *Cold Case Reviews: DNA, Detective Work, and Unsolved Major Crimes* (New York: Oxford University Press, 2018).

41 Richard Hare made both of these points in his *Moral Thinking: Its Methods, Level, and Point* (Oxford: Clarendon Press, 1981): 44–47.

3 Punishment and Moral Communication

Discontent with desert forms of retributivism has led some penal theorists to develop accounts of legal punishment that cast it as serving valuable purposes that they conceive to be distinct from the reduction of crime. Prominent among these proposed alternatives to the crime-reduction approach are those holding that legal punishment communicates censure to offenders for their criminal misdeeds.[1] Some theorists add that this moral communication speaks to and stands for the victims of crime, when there are victims, as well as serving to remind the public of the important moral values embodied in defensible legal prohibitions.[2] Further, some argue that this moral communication should be crafted in ways to encourage, but not compel, offenders to feel remorse for their crimes, repent of their wrongs, and seek to reform themselves so as to avoid further criminal misconduct.[3] Those who emphasize the morally communicative aspects of legal punishment need not deny that criminal sanctions deter offenders or incapacitate them. But they insist that the moral communication aspect of the institution is distinctive in its assumptions about criminal offending and the appropriate response of the community, acting through the state, to such offending. Those who commit crimes are not simply imprudent beings who are insufficiently responsive to legal punishment's threats, or wild animals who must be corralled until they no longer pose dangers to others. Instead, or in addition, they are moral beings who are presumed to be responsive to the moral considerations backing significant aspects of the criminal law but who have failed to abide by those considerations for one reason or another.

In this chapter, I elaborate and defend further one version of an expressive approach to the justification of legal punishment. It is an approach that draws heavily on the work of others who emphasize punishment's morally communicative role, although I part ways with some or all of them in certain respects. Moral communication approaches face numerous challenges. First, they must specify the audience to whom such communication is to be addressed. Is it simply or primarily the offender who is the target for moral communication, or is it also the victims of crimes or the general public? Second, to what extent, if any, should we care about whether offenders who are on the receiving end

DOI: 10.4324/9781032661667-4

of such communication listen, take it seriously, seek to make amends for their wrongs, or strive to make themselves more responsible beings in the future?

Third, proponents of moral communication approaches must explain why standard forms of penal hard treatment—the impositions, losses, or burdens of criminal sanctions—are needed to morally communicate with the intended audience. This challenge has been seen by many opponents as the Achilles heel of the approach.[4] Even if we grant that those who violate the criminal law should be condemned for their actions, critics wonder why hard treatment—or some say "suffering"—must be employed to effect such communication. Why should we not instead be content with the state verbally reprimanding individuals for the crimes of which they have been convicted and leave it at that? Why deprive offenders of their property or liberty or inflict other unpleasant things upon them? Also, if we wish to symbolically stand by and for victims, why not publicly celebrate them by throwing them parades or, more concretely, by providing them with compensation for whatever harms the crimes committed against them may have caused? Why go further and imposes losses or deprivations on those who wronged them in ways prohibited by the criminal law?

Fourth, some penal theorists have worried that many of the standard forms of hard treatment, prisons foremost among them, if used to censure offenders, might be so difficult or cause so much suffering that their capacities for receiving the moral messages punishment is supposed to communicate will be overwhelmed or undermined.[5]

Fifth, advocates of a moral communication approach must explain whether censuring those convicted of crimes is significant enough, all by itself, to justify the institution. Some critics admit that legal punishment has an important morally communicative function. Yet they question whether that function is sufficient to justify it, especially in light of that institution's substantial demands on scarce societal resources and its well-documented tendencies toward cruelty and excess.[6]

In addition to addressing the challenges that a moral communication approach to justifying legal punishment faces, I contrast my own account with those developed and defended by others. I do this throughout the chapter but most explicitly in the final section, where I clarify my version of the theory by contrasting it with prominent ones advocated by Andreas von Hirsch, Jean Hampton, and Antony Duff.

The Audience with Whom Legal Punishment Communicates

In the debate about legal punishment's communicative aims, it is common to focus primarily on sentencing and, in particular, on the hearings at which judges announce the sentences of individuals who have either been found guilty after trials or agreed to plead guilty without trials (or with abbreviated ones, in some instances). I will, shortly, question that focus, but even if we stick with it, for the time being, my view is that the audience with whom communication occurs should be conceived as multi-faceted.[7]

Before I elaborate and defend that point, I need to say something about the background against which I am assuming that legal punishment operates. Throughout my discussion, I will assume that we are concerned with the operation of such an institution in the context of liberal, democratic societies, ones that take seriously the notion that all members of society have certain basic moral rights that its institutions and practices must respect and, in certain ways, seek to actively promote. It is well-known that there are deep divides among political theorists about which basic moral rights individuals possess.[8] I acknowledge such dissensus but suggest that in thinking about the criminal law and its allied institutions, it is reasonable to operate with a "consensus account" of those rights. All plausible accounts of our basic moral rights presume that we have rights to life, liberty, and some property, although such accounts differ, mostly at the margins, about what those rights encompass or how far they extend. This consensus arguably explains why all modern, democratic societies adopt and enforce prohibitions on certain kinds of conduct, ones designed to shield their members from death, violence, theft, and other acts that interfere with the abilities of individuals to have and live decent lives on their own terms. In this way, the concept of basic moral rights shapes the content of the criminal law. Granted, liberal democratic societies diverge about such things as the required provision of social welfare, the extent to which inequalities in property ought to be tolerated, or the ways in which democratic participation in their institutions and practices is required. But they all have many similar criminal prohibitions and take serious steps to enforce them, albeit not all of them do so as fully or fairly as we might like. It is against such a conceptual and normative backdrop that my defense of a moral communication approach should be read and interpreted. Whether such an approach can be defended in autocratic societies, or ones in which the basic rights of some or most citizens are not enforced or taken at all seriously by officials in positions of power, is a further question about which I will not have much to say in this chapter. In subsequent chapters, I explore some of the deficiencies of legal punishment institutions in modern, democratic societies and consider to what extent they undermine the state's moral authority to communicate about the polity's public rights and responsibility narrative.

When it comes to the audience for moral communication, there is, first and foremost, the individual being sentenced by the judge for his or her crimes. Judges will typically identify the crime or crimes of which the convicted person has either been found or agreed to plead guilty before announcing the applicable sentence. Judges might also make reference to the victims of the crimes involved, if there are any, including the harms that they suffered. Further, judges might note any aggravating and mitigating factors considered in determining the sentence, thereby weighing, in a public manner, the convicted person's culpability for his or her crime (or crimes). All of this, it seems fair to say, will be conducted in language steeped in terms that highlight the convicted person's responsibility for his or her conduct and thus his or her appropriate liability for the sanctions to be imposed. Moral failings or deficits on the part of the convicted person might be identified explicitly or simply implied. The announced sentence will then serve as a kind of exclamation point to this process of moral communication with the convicted person.

As I conceive it, the essential point of this moral communication with the convicted person is to indicate, in clear and forceful terms, that he or she has violated a standard of conduct which all members of society must observe because it embodies a level of required respect or concern for the basic rights of other persons. At least, this way of characterizing things will be true when the convicted person has violated one of the familiar *mala in se* provisions of the criminal law. With violations of *mala prohibita*, the communication will have a slightly different focus. All societies have and enforce a variety of conduct requirements aimed at such things as coordinating the actions of its members, limiting the risks posed by otherwise legitimate activities, and requiring members to contribute to the financial support of state institutions.[9] Together, these conduct requirements attempt to create a safe and predictable framework in which the members of society can enjoy and exercise their basic rights. Violations of *mala prohibita* are thus failures to do one's required part in maintaining this legal and social framework. Punishment of them should reflect and communicate this.[10]

Importantly, whether those convicted of crimes and sentenced for them accept such moral assessments of their conduct, or more, take them to heart in some way that might lead to personal change, are further matters, ones that I contend lie outside the formal moral communication process.[11] Some persons convicted of crimes will be indifferent to what authorized state officials, acting on behalf of the larger public, have to say about their conduct. Others will be defiant in the face of the state's moral communication efforts. I believe that we must be prepared to live with such responses, although we might try to understand why they occur and whether they reflect some failure of state institutions and practices, or a failure on the part of the person convicted to satisfy the liability conditions of legal punishment.[12] Also, and importantly, I would not deny that the courts, legislative bodies, and the larger public on whose behalf they act should take seriously the adoption and employment of sanctions that work to encourage greater responsibility on the part of those convicted of crimes. Even if modern secular states must respect the autonomy of those convicted of crimes, in the sense of respecting their decisions to reject the moral communication inherent in the sanctioning process, it makes sense for such states to assiduously avoid the use of sanctions that damage the moral capacities of the convicted. More than this, they should employ ones that will nourish those capacities. I will have more to say about all of this in Chapter 5.

Second, I contend that crime victims, where they exist, should be conceived as co-equal recipients of the moral communication involved in sentencing. It is possible to resist this claim, to focus narrowly on the individuals being sentenced as the ones to whom the state must justify its actions, as it is their basic rights that will be abridged by the imposition of criminal sanctions. Yet even if we cast victims as members of a "secondary" audience for legal punishment's moral communication aims, that should not be understood to relegate them to some insignificant status. Again, the harms done to victims will often be implicitly if not explicitly acknowledged during the sentencing process, and one suspects more so the more serious the wrongs committed against them.[13] Even if explicit mention of victims and their injuries or losses is not made, it will be natural for victims to interpret the court's findings and sentence as public affirmations of their value as equal citizens in society—at least so long as the sentence assigned reflects, in some appropriate way, the magnitude of the losses or injuries they suffered due to the convicted person's crime or crimes. I will have more to say about this latter point in a moment. Granted, there will be cases in which the victim is deceased or so profoundly disabled so as not to be able to grasp the court's affirmation of his or her standing as an equal citizen who has been wronged. In such cases, partisans of the victim (or victims)—spouses, family members, friends, co-workers—can be plausibly understood to be the significant secondary recipients of the state's condemnation of the wrong or wrongs done to victims.

Also, there will be cases in which there will be no direct victims of the crimes of which individuals have been convicted. This will most commonly be true when individuals violate *mala prohibita*, but it will also be true when they violate legal provisions designed to shield other people from the risks of harms. In the former kinds of cases, legal punishment of individuals can be plausibly interpreted as affirming to the law-abiding that those who defy the relevant legal prohibitions or requirements will be held accountable. In this way, legal requirements that serve to uphold socially beneficial cooperative or resource-allocating schemes are validated and reinforced by state authorities. In cases in which harm is merely (although unjustifiably) risked, the courts can be interpreted as validating the important interests of those who stood in harm's way. This too affirms the worth of all citizens and their right to go on about their lives free from the unreasonable risk of harms that might injure or kill them.

Still, criminal sanctions will not back or stand for victims, in the sense of legally recognizing and condemning the wrongful losses, injuries, or deaths they suffered at the hands of others, if those being sentenced are not convicted of crimes that correspond with the harmful acts they committed or are sentenced inappropriately in light of those harmful acts. The former might occur if individuals are acquitted of some veridical charges, due to lack of evidence or jury error, while convicted of lesser charges. Or more typically, at least in some jurisdictions, plea bargaining practices might enable accused persons to plead guilty to less serious charges in exchange for prosecutors dropping more serious, albeit veridical, ones. For instance, prosecutors might agree to forego charges of rape or sexual assault in some cases in exchange for guilty pleas to simple assault. Admittedly, they might do so if they perceive there to be problems with the evidence such that acquittals at trial are likely.[14]

Inappropriate sentences for crimes, ones that fail to capture the gravity of the wrongs done to victims, can also be imposed by the courts. A legal jurisdiction might adopt sentence ranges for a given crime type, or perhaps for all crime types, that are so mild that they appear to most observers to radically undervalue the violated interests of victims. Alternatively, when it comes to sentencing instances of a crime type, prosecutors making sentencing recommendations, or judges making final sentencing determinations, might regard some convicted persons in ways that are too sympathetic, or some victims in ways that are too unsympathetic.[15] The result in either case could be indefensibly mild sentences for those who perpetrated serious criminal wrongs. There is reason to believe that class, gender, ethnic, or sexual preference biases have infected the sentencing of crime tokens in ways that leave many victims feeling, with some reason, undervalued by the operations of criminal justice systems.[16]

To put it mildly, the claim that sentences must be calibrated to "appropriately value" victim interests encounters a number of challenges. There is little agreement on a precise metric of victim harms or losses, although some rough ranking of them may be possible.[17] Even if there were such a metric, there is deep and abiding controversy about how to link it up appropriately with the variety and duration of penal sanctions available in modern democratic societies. In particular, although moral communication accounts, such as my own, seem most congenial with approaches to sentencing that emphasize proportionality, there is reason to doubt that the concept of proportionality in sentencing can provide us with more than somewhat vague guidance in setting up and operating a sentencing scheme.[18] It may be possible to achieve some rough consensus on the ranking of the various crime types according to their seriousness.[19] We also might find some consensus on the severity of sanction types and durations across a fairly wide range of individuals. It seems apparent, for instance that sentences involving fines, community service, or even probation are less severe in their impact upon offenders than ones involving imprisonment, and that shorter prison sentences should be judged less severe than longer ones. However, there seems little consensus across sentencing theorists, elected legislators, judges, or members of the public about how to link up the crime seriousness and sanction severity scales in some principled fashion. Solutions to what Andreas von Hirsch referred to as the "anchoring problem" in sentencing have proven to be elusive.[20]

Acknowledging this, which I do, is consistent with saying that in certain cases, the sentences which might be attached to crimes clearly undervalue victim interests (or might overvalue them, although that possibility seems rarer). Fines or brief stints of probation for crimes like homicide or aggravated assault resulting in grave bodily injury arguably fail to properly value the interests of victims in some absolute sense (or in cardinal proportionality terms, to use von Hirsch's terminology).[21] There seems, in such cases, little commensurability between the harms the victims suffered and the burdens or impositions that those who culpably harmed them are made to endure. Even brief prison sentences in such cases might be plausibly criticized for their failure to take an emphatic public stand against losses or injuries to victims that are grave or life-altering. Nonetheless, I concede that my claim that sentences for the various crime types ought to be crafted to reflect the seriousness of crimes is not without its difficulties. I will address these further in Chapter 5, where I take up the moral issues raised by sentencing. For now, I simply stipulate that that sentences for crimes must be devised so as to appropriately value the violated interests of victims, or else they will not properly convey to offenders and their victims the gravity of the wrongs involved.

It is not solely victims who have a vital interest in the "accuracy" of the moral communication effected by the legal punishment of offenders. Those arrested for, accused of, and convicted of crimes also have much at stake in the criminal justice system communicating truthfully with them and others about the crimes they have purportedly committed. When it comes to sentencing those convicted of crimes, I shall assume that moral communication ought to be guided by a fundamental principle of accuracy in sentencing. Those who commit crimes cannot reasonably complain if they are held accountable for them, but they can reasonably complain if the sentences imposed on them suggest that they have committed much more serious offenses than they, in fact, have committed (or been convicted of). Again, I concede that "accuracy" in this complex endeavor is not likely to be wholly precise or beyond controversy. Nonetheless, it is not hard to imagine jurisdictions adopting long or harsh sentence ranges for certain types of crimes, perhaps with the hope (whether well-founded or not) of enhancing general deterrence, which sentence ranges distort the public's perceptions about the gravity of the public wrongs committed by the individuals convicted of such crimes. For instance, some scholars have argued that sentence ranges for the sale of illegal drugs adopted by state and federal jurisdictions in the United States in the 1980s resulted in sentences for dealers that effectively treated them as akin to much more serious offenders.[22] Whatever we think or say about the morality of drug dealing, this seems a distortion of its character as a socially harmful act. A coherent moral communication account of legal punishment will insist upon efforts to ensure that what we "say" through the imposition of criminal sanctions bears some plausible—or, if possible, close—relationship to moral reality, both for victims and offenders.

It might be objected that what sentences communicate to offenders and what they communicate to their victims can diverge in an important way in some instances. If sentences should generally reflect both the harm done to victims (if there are any) and offender culpability in producing (or threatening or attempting) those harms, then cases will arise in which victims who are significantly harmed might not see the sentences assigned to those who broke the law as appropriately valuing their interests. For instance, there will be cases in which individuals engage in reckless acts that injure others and cases in which they engage in deliberate acts which do so. If the victims in these two kinds of cases are harmed to the same extent, they might expect the courts to assign the offenders similar sentences, despite differences between the offenders in their culpability. More precisely, the recklessly harmed might believe that their victimizers got off too easy given the extent of their injuries or losses. In response to this I would argue that the courts in both kinds of cases should seek to convey accurately the gravity of the prohibited wrongs, even if this means that deliberate and reckless harmers are sentenced differently. Victims in both kinds of cases might resent the harms done to them, however they were done, but they should also be able to countenance the differences between those who acted deliberately to harm them and those whose reckless actions resulted in harm.

Beyond crime victims and their partisans, the general public is a third audience for legal punishment's communicative efforts. Granted, lots of crimes and the sentences handed out to those who commit them go largely unnoticed by the public. Little of import might seem to be communicated by the punishment of those who commit the mostly minor offenses that clog many criminal justice systems, although even the knowledge that such cases are being addressed by state officials serves as a reminder that certain conduct standards matter and will be enforced.[23] Crime reduction theorists have sometimes acknowledged this moral reinforcement effect of legal punishment, although they tend to view it as simply a means to the prevention of crime.[24] But we can also view the operations of the criminal justice system as part of a vast "morality play," one that continually reminds citizens that certain ways of acting are morally off limits. Also, when crimes are more serious, it is plausible to believe that the public pays more attention, watching to see how the criminal justice system deals with them. The public, through social or more traditional media, might also engage in commentary, in such cases, on the "morality play" of which arrests, charges, and charge adjudication (sometimes in the form of public trials) consists. When legal wrongdoers are eventually convicted and sentenced, hopefully correctly so, this reaffirms to members of the public that certain kinds of conduct are out of bounds in civilized societies. It typically will not be the case that members of the public need to be convinced that the standards of conduct enforced by the criminal law are important or to be honored. Instead, they mostly accept such standards already, especially the ones given voice to by its *mala in se* provisions. Despite this, they might very much want to see the criminal justice system reaffirm such standards, which it will do if it holds those who appear to have violated them accountable.

To this point, I have mostly focused on the sentencing process in laying out the kind of moral communicative approach that I hope to defend. But it is apparent that moral communication with the public, including with those inclined to offend, begins much earlier, arguably with the adoption of provisions of the criminal law that lay out in clear, understandable terms the standards of conduct that all members of society are expected to observe. The provisions of the criminal law identify some wrongs as "public," as Antony Duff has so elegantly shown, in the sense that they constitute wrongs that are of sufficient import that state officials are tasked with addressing them.[25] There is, as Duff readily acknowledges, considerable room for debate about which wrongs deserve this designation; not all do, although those covered by the traditional *mala in se* provisions of the criminal law are among the most plausible candidates for state attention and action. That the state (and the public on whose behalf it acts) takes such wrongs seriously is shown in a multitude of ways: in the considerable resources that are devoted to their detection, as well as to arrests, the levying of charges, and the adjudication of charges. It is also shown by the various impositions and requirements that those suspected or formally accused of crimes are made to endure: stoppages, searches, arrests, detention, mandated attendance at preliminary hearings, and presence at trials or in plea negotiations. Notably, even before individuals are sentenced for crimes of which they have been convicted, the state imposes things on them which they might not wish to endure or with which they might not want to cooperate. Surely, the state must be permitted to do so if it is to advance its defensible criminal justice aims. These impositions or requirements communicate the seriousness with which officials, and the public on whose behalf it acts, view the alleged misconduct of the individuals in question. It will be difficult for criminal suspects, or anyone for that matter, to avoid viewing the process as steeped in moral seriousness. Of course, some accused persons will be so jaded by or alienated from the criminal law and its enforcement mechanisms that they will view the process with cynicism. To be fair, there might be instances in which such a perspective on the workings of the system is understandable, if not defensible. But for the most part, that society takes certain standards of conduct seriously and expects all citizens to observe them is shown in numerous subtle and not-so-subtle ways well before the sentencing of convicted offenders.

It is possible, of course, to cast the various requirements and impositions to which those suspected of violating the criminal law are subjected as nothing more than embodiments of the criminal justice system's crime reduction aims. If those tempted to commit crimes become aware of what they will be subject to if they fall under official suspicion of having offended, they will be provided with powerful reasons to refrain from offending.[26] No doubt arrest, confinement for brief periods in holding cells, searches of homes or vehicles, requirements to appear before judges at preliminary hearings, and possible pretrial detention are all things that most of us will find unpleasant. But I doubt that we subject suspects to all of this solely in order to amplify the deterrent effects of criminal sanctions. Instead, these impositions and requirements seem to exemplify the seriousness with which we take the conduct norms embodied in the criminal law. This will especially be true when there are victims whose lives have been adversely impacted, sometimes devastatingly so, by criminal offenses.

Moral Communication and the Imposition of Penal Burdens or Losses

The second challenge posed by critics of moral communication accounts of legal punishment is a formidable one. Even if it is conceded that legal punishment communicates censure or condemnation of the crimes committed by individuals, a proposition which it seems difficult to deny, many penal theorists question why such communication must include "hard treatment." Critics of the approach can admit that the imposition of penal burdens or losses is a conventional way of expressing disapproval for the public wrongs in which those convicted of crimes appear to have engaged.[27] They might even concede that such impositions are an effective way of communicating censure. But they employ a variety of arguments aimed at convincing us that penal hard treatment is neither necessary in order to morally communicate about offenders' acts nor the most effective way of doing so. My aim in this section is to respond to these arguments to show that they are unconvincing.

One preliminary point is worth making: Critics of the moral communication approach are surely correct in noting that simply because some convention exists, it does not follow that it is a good or defensible way of doing things or the only way of doing things. There may well be other ways of morally communicating the wrongs done by persons convicted of having committed crimes. Still, if it is conceded that the imposition of losses or burdens is an effective form of such communication, as it likely must be, it behooves the critics of that convention to spell out, in some detail, alternative ways of morally communicating with offenders. We might even think that the burden of proof is on critics to demonstrate that the alternatives they propose are close or equivalent to the conventional means employed if not superior to them. As we will see, some of the critics of the moral communication approach do little more than gesture at alternatives, without developing them in the detail that would be needed to demonstrate their equivalence with penal losses or impositions as communicative measures, let alone their superiority to such measures.

Let me start with one proposal that some critics of the moral communication have floated, although it is not clear how serious most of them are about it.[28] Instead of imposing penal burdens of various kinds on those convicted of crimes in order to censure their conduct and to demonstrate society's solidarity with the victims of their crimes, some suggest that we might instead hold ticker-tape parades for the victims in which the value of their violated lives or interests are publicly celebrated. Indeed, Jean Hampton, one of the most prominent early supporters of the moral communication approach, once briefly entertained this suggestion.[29] The idea, I take it, is that by positively celebrating the value of victims' lives and interests, we stand for and by them in the ways that are as, if not more, effective than the imposition of penal burdens on offenders.

I believe it is fair to say that advocates of this alternative do not develop it carefully, consider its implications, or respond to concerns we might have about it. First, how exactly would such parades (or perhaps other victim celebratory events) work? Are we to imagine, for instance, that the quality or extravagance of the parades should be made to vary with the seriousness of the crimes committed? Would the victims of minor thefts, on such an approach, get smallish parades "celebrating" their interests—ones involving a few marchers and maybe a small musical ensemble and a banner or two—whereas the victims of grievous aggravated assaults or homicides would get elaborate, long-lasting parades, complete with marching bands, floats, and fireworks? Surely, we would expect to see some variation in the types of parades to mark the significant differences in what victims lost due to the crimes against them. More to the point, the death of a victim hardly seems to be appropriately marked by an elaborate celebratory event. Instead, it seems better marked by a solemn memorial service, one at which the victim's life is remembered with speeches and public expressions of grief or mourning. Parades in such instances would, it seems, strike the wrong note. Large, elaborate ones would do so in ways that are, arguably, obscene.

Second, would the victims of crimes be required or encouraged to attend such parades? And what if they did not want to attend them or have them at all, perhaps because they are embarrassed about what has befallen them or still recovering from whatever losses or traumas they suffered? It is not hard to imagine that the victims of stigmatized crimes like rape, for instance, would have decidedly mixed feelings about attending parades in their honor, perhaps preferring to cope with the shock and injuries of their victimization on their own or in the company of relatives and friends. Similarly, individuals who have been defrauded or swindled might be chagrined at what happened to them and so not in the mood to "celebrate" their victimhood. Forcing or even strongly encouraging victims like these to attend parades in their honor seems insensitive. But holding the parades without them, and perhaps even in defiance of their wishes, seems useless or counter-productive.

Third, it seems that quite a large number of parades, of the various kinds, some larger and more elaborate, some smaller and less conspicuous, would have to be conducted, at public expense presumably, in order to "stand for" the numerous victims of crimes. In large urban areas, where crime is often more prevalent, one wonders whether parade "burn out" might not occur among citizens. Might not the attitudes among citizens become "oh no, not another one" after some period of time? By contrast, in sparsely populated rural areas, we might wonder whether there would be many witnesses to or participants in the parades. Further, where would the parades for rural victims of crimes be held—near victims' residences or in nearby small towns? And if the latter, would the residents of those small towns tire of the frequent parades or wonder what their point was (the latter especially if the victim him or herself declined to attend)?

Granted, moral communication approaches that favor the use of punitive impositions will also support frequent use of such sanctions and this will constitute a drain on public resources. But unlike victim-celebration parades, standard penal sanctions do not require or presuppose that ordinary citizens should have some role in participating in or witnessing them. Also, penal sanctions do not require the approval or participation of victims, although the hope is that if the sanctions are appropriately calibrated, they will be seen by victims as symbolically backing their vital interests in their lives, liberty, and property. Reluctant or embarrassed victims will not be required to participate in the sanctioning process, although they might have to take part in the trials of those who preyed upon them. Also, penal impositions of various kinds are specifically designed to capture and hold the attention of offenders in ways that it will be difficult for them to ignore. Celebratory parades might go on without their taking notice or caring. Worse, they might roll their eyes at such events. True, the public "rights and responsibility narrative," which the wrongs committed by offenders have defied, might be affirmed by such celebratory events. But offenders will not have much, if any, direct stake or participation in the affirmation of that narrative—no "skin in the game," as we might say. Worse than this, what would we think if offenders, or their supporters, showed up at such parades and mocked its participants and the victims for whom they were being held? Would we prohibit such actions, and on what grounds, exactly? And if we did prohibit them, and individuals were subsequently arrested, charged, and convicted of violating parade protocols, would we hold further parades for the wrongly mocked victims (at which, we might fondly hope, the mockers will not appear to mock them some more)?

A second, seemingly more serious line of argument advanced by critics of moral communication approaches involves suggesting that criminal convictions might merit public censure but not any of the traditional forms of penal hard treatment.[30] The idea seems to be that, upon conviction, the courts (or perhaps some other public agency) would solemnly verbally censure those who were found or pled guilty, but not impose any burdens on them which were expressive of that censure. We might wonder whether the "mere censure" would be more vehement, somehow, in cases of more serious crimes so as to distinguish them from the many less serious crimes that tend to predominate in criminal justice systems. But louder or more harshly condemnatory speech would seem to be the only things that serious offenders, on this alternative approach, would have to endure.

At least one theorist who suggests this possibility, David Boonin, seems prepared to rely on the ways in which such public communications will likely generate stigma and shame on the part of offenders, along with public aversion to the individuals identified as offenders.[31] Boonin admits the various informal social costs of being so identified and condemned might be substantial. Individuals marked out as lawbreakers might be shunned by others, publicly ridiculed, denied jobs, housing, and other goods. Also, and perhaps more disturbingly, their families and loved ones might suffer along with them. To escape some of these costs, offenders might have to move to another part of the country, although their criminal records will continue to dog them if those records are publicly accessible. It is not clear whether Boonin would have them remain accessible, although it is unclear how he could argue against it. The important point, for Boonin, is that since all such informal social costs are not "intended" by state officials, only foreseeable, they are not, on his account of punishment, penal impositions proper.

It is difficult to escape the conclusion that Boonin seems prepared to let someone else, besides the state, do the dirty work of imposing hard treatment on offenders. His claim that while such informal costs are foreseeable, they are not necessarily intended by state authorities, seems unconvincing, as it stands. The main reason this is so is because it is possible to imagine forms of mere censure that do not involve the *public* identification of the individuals being condemned for their crimes. In some European countries, the "right to privacy" is increasing invoked to rule out the public identification of the individuals convicted of crimes, though such practices typically build in limited exceptions to offender anonymity.[32] Thus, there will be, in such societies, fewer informal social costs of criminal conviction, and perhaps substantially fewer such costs.

Boonin might question whether censure without public identification of offenders is consistent with legal punishment as we usually understand it. How can we meaningfully be said to censure someone for his or her crimes if we refuse to disclose his or her identity to the general public? In response to this, note that most, if not all of the other things that we associate with the criminal justice system will presumably be present in penal regimes that shield the identities of those convicted of crimes: police to detect crimes, investigate them, and arrest suspects, prosecutors to charge them, courts to process those charges, judges to sentence those convicted, and, while they are at it, to admonish offenders for their crimes. Also, whatever burdens or impositions judges assign to those convicted will, arguably, express the official public condemnation of the crimes they have committed. The identities of offenders are withheld from the public in order to promote what is termed the "right to be forgotten," that is, the right to get on with their lives despite their convictions and the sentences assigned for them.[33] In light of all of this, it would seem difficult to defend the proposition that such societies lack institutions of legal punishment.

If it is possible to censure offenders without publicly identifying them, the problem that this poses for Boonin's argument is that it will be more difficult for him to argue that a criminal justice system that merely censures offenders, and then lets them bear the informal social costs of their public identification, does not intend the burdens of those costs. Such societies could, after all, eliminate, or at least reduce substantially those costs to offenders by declining to publicly identify them. Perhaps Boonin would embrace such an approach, agreeing that those convicted of crimes should be censured but not publicly identified. Then the question is whether we would see such censure as adequate or meaningful in the complete absence of the official imposition of any forms of penal hard treatment on offenders. It is hard to see how victims and their partisans could see such nonpublic censure as standing effectively for their interests, especially in cases of serious crimes. Those who preyed upon them or attacked them would escape both hard treatment and public ignominy. On the other hand, if Boonin insists on public identification of wrongdoers, then it seems he is willing to let the social costs of such disclosures do something like the work of hard treatment.

Another point to make about a "mere censure" approach is this: There will be significant and predictable variations in the ways and extent to which offenders, including like offenders, are affected by the social costs of offending. Some offenders will be embedded in social networks that they value and which provide them with employment and social goods the loss or diminution of which, upon their public identification as offenders, will more or less inevitably follow. Also, their loved ones might be adversely impacted by the social stigma of such disclosures. Other offenders might simply go back to the gangs or other criminal organizations whose bidding they were doing when they were arrested and convicted, with little change in their income-earning capabilities or their social status. Some offenders might even be celebrated by their communities if it is believed that they violated dubious legal prohibitions. Others might be tolerated within their communities if it is widely believed that the violated provisions, while legitimate, are enforced in a biased fashion by the authorities. Further, some offenders will simply be indifferent to the social costs of the disclosure of their crimes, or they will relocate so as to minimize them.

In response to the preceding objection to "mere censure" approaches, it will be objected that it is well-known that more traditional criminal sanctions of all kinds likewise affect those on whom they are imposed in different ways.[34] Imprisonment surely does so, depending on things like individuals' prior experiences with it or their physical or psychological attributes. Similar things will be true for fines, terms of probation, or required restitution payments to victims. However, one signal advantage of some of these more traditional forms of hard treatment is that if they are meted out consistently (and I need not defend state failures to treat like cases alike), they at least function to signal to offenders and the wider community the comparative and absolute severity of the crimes of which individuals have been convicted. There seem to be clear differences, for instance, between short prison sentences and longer ones, or between short periods of probation and longer periods, in terms of what these communicate about the seriousness of crimes. If hard treatment consists solely of informal social costs of being identified as an offender, it cannot realistically hope to communicate in similarly consistent ways, since there will be so much predictable variation in its impact on offenders. Such costs cannot be "metered" to reflect the absolute or comparative seriousness of crimes.

Other critics of moral communication approaches take a different tack. They argue that various alternatives to traditional forms of penal hard treatment might be used to convey censure to offenders. We need not resort to imprisonment, which often is taken by these critics to be the paradigm of penal hard treatment, to censure offenders. Instead, we could require offenders to pay restitution to their victims, or require them to participate in restorative justice conferences in which, together with their victims, they work out forms of reparations or amends for their crimes while also, hopefully, coming to apologize to those they wronged.[35] Nathan Hanna, for instance, suggests that we might use probation as an alternative to penal hard treatment, or substitute some form of nonpenal confinement for punitive forms of it. However, Hanna does not elaborate what such nonpenal confinement would look like other than gesturing toward the quarantine used in cases in which individuals have infectious diseases and the nonpunitive confinement of the seriously mentally ill.[36] What we should not do in morally communicating with offenders (along with their victims and the larger public), Hanna argues, is impose suffering upon them, which he takes to be essential to traditional forms of penal hard treatment.

I would agree with those who suggest that requiring offenders to pay restitution to their victims or requiring them to participate in restorative justice conferences in lieu of having to endure more traditional forms of penal hard treatment might be sensible things to do in some cases. I am not convinced that either makes sense for all kinds of crimes, no matter their severity or character. But set those reservations aside for the time being. What is puzzling about these proposals is that those who advance them do not seem to see them as forms of state imposition of burdens or requirements on offenders of the kinds of which legal punishment essentially consists. Modern democratic societies have long utilized a wide variety of penal sanctions, ranging from fines to restitution to community service, to probation of both mild and intense forms, to home confinement, and yes, to confinement in local or regional jails or prisons. But lots of crimes are punished without the use of imprisonment; probably the majority are. In the United States, approximately 80 percent of the crimes that are dealt with by the criminal justice system are classified as misdemeanors.[37] Although misdemeanors can be punished with short stints of penal confinement, they are very often punished in a variety of other ways.

All of these standard state-imposed burdens or conduct requirements on individuals in response to their convictions constitute abridgements of what would ordinarily be their rights to go on about their lives. Probation is a very commonly utilized sanction.[38] In its milder forms, it involves various reporting obligations as well as mandated efforts on the part of offenders to find gainful, legal employment. In its more intense forms, there are further conduct requirements, sometimes lots of them, although the convicted otherwise remain free to live and move about in civil society. Required restitution is also an imposition on offenders, one that they might rather avoid and might try to shirk. The state not only requires them to compensate their victims, it must be prepared to act to enforce that obligation if offenders neglect to do so or disappear so that they do not have to do so. Likewise, restorative justice conferences are, I would concede, a valuable alternative to other forms of state-imposed hard treatment on offenders. But it is usually an option offered to some offenders in lieu of their having to endure other forms of state-determined hard treatment. If offenders refuse that option, then what? Surely, the state will have to employ one or more of the traditional forms of penal hard treatment. And the same is true if accused persons agree to participate in restorative justice conferences but refuse to accept reasonable requests from their victims about appropriate amends, or blame the victims for what occurred, or agree to reparative tasks but never complete them. It has long been understood that the state "stands in the background," so to speak, of most plausible restorative justice schemes and, as such, must be prepared to deal with uncooperative offenders or offenders who fail to live up to their agreements.[39] In this way, those charged with or convicted of crimes are not treated by the state in the ways that law-abiding citizens are treated. The basic rights to liberty of the former are subject to abridgement in ways that those of the latter are not.

In response to this, Hanna argues that a defining feature of legal punishment is that it aims to inflict suffering or unpleasantness on offenders.[40] He cites a range of penal theorists who concur with him on this point.[41] He also notes that, unlike things like involuntary quarantine or psychiatric commitment and treatment, we do not take steps to ameliorate the unpleasantness of penal confinement. This suggests to him that such unpleasantness is fully intended and, as such, is part of what essentially characterizes the use of penal sanctions. I would admit that, in the not-too-distant past, we employed forms of penal hard treatment that were intentionally aimed at causing the convicted enormous suffering. It is hard to contemplate things like the rack, burning at the stake, flogging, dismemberment, and the like without concluding that "making them suffer" was indeed part and parcel of punishing offenders (or perceived offenders, in some cases). Also, many countries still employ penal measures that seem aimed at causing pain or suffering to those convicted of crimes. The excessive use of solitary confinement in the United States and elsewhere might seem to constitute such treatment, not to mention the neglect of prisoners' physical and mental health, the intense idleness that characterizes many prisons, and the brutality suffered by prisoners at the hands of guards or other inmates in many prisons. However, such appeals to past and contemporary penal practices are both too selective, on the one hand, and inconclusive as grounds for a normative account of penal hard treatment, on the other.

With regard to the former, it should be pointed out that there are countries in the world, northern European and Scandinavian ones foremost among them, that take seriously the proposition that imprisonment must be kept clear of brutality and degradation.[42] As the official aim of legal punishment in such countries is often the "resocialization" of offenders, they are committed to taking steps to ameliorate the kinds of suffering and loss that imprisonment inflicts on individuals. True, the imprisonment of offenders substantially curtails their rights to liberty and likely impacts the enjoyment and exercise of other of their basic rights. But steps are taken in these countries to lessen those associated impacts. And there is a much greater commitment in them to structuring confinement so that it is consistent, as far as it can be, with respecting the dignity of inmates. Also, it bears repeating that imprisonment is the sanction of last resort in these and other countries, reserved for those who commit serious crimes. Other sanctions that much less extensively curtail or impose upon the basic rights of offenders are used to punish a wide array of less serious criminal offenses.

The more important point to make in response to Hanna, however, is that we arguably need not conceive of defensible penal sanctions as aimed at "causing suffering."[43] If we think about the wide variety of sanctions employed in liberal democratic societies, many of them seem instead to be better understood as burdening the rights of those convicted of crimes in ways that it will be difficult for them simply to ignore without being intended to produce suffering.[44] The use of fines, required community service, victim restitution, restorative justice conferences, and probation (in mild or intensive forms) all constitute impositions upon those convicted of crimes. In this way, they mark out such offenders as different from law-abiding citizens, thereby censuring them for their crimes (assuming that the impositions are proportionate or, at least, not disproportionate). But liberal democratic societies do not much trouble themselves with whether such impositions or conduct requirements cause those on whom they fall to suffer. Neither is it an attractive proposition to hold that they should do so. In order for them to do so effectively, such societies would have to find ways to monitor and evaluate the internal psychological states of those being punished to determine whether they were "suffering enough," whatever that means. Also, it is not clear what the point of such monitoring would be unless the state was prepared to undertake measures to adjust the penal losses or deprivations imposed upon offenders, to get them up to (but not past) the "required level" of suffering. Of course, the state could also seek to reduce their suffering if it was determined that it was disproportionate. In any event, we might sensibly prefer the state to keep some distance from the inner lives of its citizens, even those who it appropriately punishes. It can do so by utilizing forms of penal hard treatment that are what Adam Kolber terms "objective," in the sense that they involve external-to-the person impositions or conduct requirements.[45]

Even when it comes to imprisonment, some have argued that it ought to be viewed as justifiably consisting of no more than the substantial curtailment of individual liberty.[46] They argue that the other kinds of losses that more or less inevitably attend the curtailment of liberty should be strictly limited and that state efforts to ameliorate them ought to be undertaken. Prison life, as far as possible, ought to be "normalized" so that it consists of no more than the substantial loss of liberty. Prisoners should (presumptively, we might say) be afforded private cells, provided adequate nutrition and healthcare, guaranteed freedom from violence and degradation, afforded opportunities to work and be paid for their labor, given ready access to visitors (if not occasional furloughs), permitted to exercise civil rights of various kinds, and provided access to recreation and leisure activities and pursuits. The substantial curtailment of their liberty that they are forced to endure censures them and does so sufficiently, especially if we take into account that the duration of such curtailment should vary with the seriousness of the crimes of which they were convicted (which, presumably, should be fairly serious ones to begin with).[47]

Hanna appears to accept impositions such as victim restitution requirements and probation as nonpunitively censuring criminal offenses because he does not see them as necessarily aimed at making offenders suffer. But I would argue that defensible sanctions of many kinds need not aim at causing suffering, although they might be intended to curtail rights or impose burdens on offenders. Also, Hanna accepts the confinement of offenders if it could be structured more like quarantine or civil commitment, where the aim is not to make those subject to such confinement suffer. Yet confinement of any kind likely will be seen as a burden by those on whom it is imposed. Moreover, it is hard to see how confinement for crimes could be shorn of its penal hard treatment aspects. We cannot plausibly say to those confined for their crimes that we are depriving them of their liberty for their own good or because they pose nonresponsible threats to others (as psychiatric confinement can be defended). Neither can we say to those confined for their crimes that we are depriving them of their liberty for the good of others because they probably cannot help but harm them (as quarantine is standardly defended). Further, we might wonder how such nonpenal offender confinement facilities would be organized and structured differently than prisons, and especially humane and nondegrading prisons of the kinds found in some parts of the world. Again, nothing in the moral communication approach requires penal losses or impositions to be of the dreadful kinds that have too often been the norm in many countries past and present.

This brings us to a further alternative to penal hard treatment as a communicative measure. It might be proposed that we could combine "mere censure" with forms of state-supplied victim compensation. By the former, I mean state condemnation of the crimes committed by individuals in the absence of penal hard treatment of any kind. Instead, the state would back victim interests by vigorous efforts to compensate them for whatever losses they endured at the hands of the individuals convicted and verbally censured for their crimes. Set to one side the problems raised by victims who, for one reason or another, cannot be adequately compensated for their losses, perhaps because they are dead or because their injuries or trauma are so profound that there is little the state can do to try to restore their former lives. The larger problem with this hybrid approach is whether what it communicates is coherent.

Granted, on such an approach, those who commit public wrongs against others, or who fail to observe defensible *mala prohibita*, will be verbally condemned for their crimes. This brings us back to the question of whether these individuals will be publicly identified. Again, it is possible to censure wrongdoers without doing so. If they are identified, then many (although not all) of them likely will suffer a variety of informal social costs and it might be difficult for those who advocate this hybrid approach to argue that such losses are not intended. If they are intended, then the most that can be said on behalf of the hybrid approach is that it "spreads the pain," so to speak, since the larger public will be saddled with the burdens of making victims whole again, at least to the extent that they can be made whole. However, members of the public might reasonably wonder why they, rather than offenders, should be made to bear those burdens. If offenders are not publicly identified, then it might seem that they largely get off the hook on such an approach, while the public picks up the tab for their wrongdoing. As we have seen, while some wrongdoers will be troubled by having been censured, even when their identities are not revealed, others might shrug it off. A few might find it humorous that the public is made to ameliorate the damage they have done to other peoples' lives. In sum, it is hard to see how this hybrid approach produces the kind of clear, emphatic message about the public wrongs of offenders that we want from our criminal justice institutions.

Summarizing, my sense is that the opponents of penal expressivism have yet to articulate and defend adequately a plausible alternative to hard treatment as the vehicle of communication. State-imposed penal losses or deprivations convey censure in ways that send clear messages to offenders, victims, and other citizens about the wrongs offenders have committed. If hard treatment is made to consist of losses, impositions, or conduct requirements of various kinds, the state keeps some distance from offenders and their internal, psychological lives. Also, the kinds and duration of such burdens can be at least roughly quantified and thus applied with some consistency across offenders, including like offenders. In this way state-imposed burdens differ from the informal social costs of being publicly identified as an offender, which costs, as we have seen, will vary considerably. Whether penal expressivists should embrace or reject the public identification of offenders, in addition to official censure of them expressed through the imposition of penal burdens, is a question about which I shall remain neutral at this point. It seems to me possible that moral communication accounts might offer divergent answers to this question.[48]

It might be objected that the imposition of penal burdens on offenders does little for victims, unlike state-supplied compensation to them. To be clear, I have no objection to state efforts to help victims, so long as these are not treated as substitutes for penal hard treatment.[49] There are good reasons to help victims recover from the harms done to them by crimes, although the willingness to impose the burdens of doing so on the wider public might vary with one's views about the nature of the just society. But set that point to one side. The more important point to make here is that we should question the claim that censure communicated through the imposition of penal burdens "does nothing" for victims. Arguably, it demonstrates to victims that the state is prepared to stand by them and emphatically condemn the actions of those who prey upon or do violence to them.

There are numerous contexts in which, as we say, "actions speak louder than words," including ones in which actions demonstrate something of considerable importance to us. Consider the following case. Suppose that a child is being bullied at school by other children. A parent of the child learns of this, perhaps from the child herself, and not only expresses outrage to the child about what the child is experiencing, but takes affirmative steps to contact the school officials and insist that they act to stop the bullying. Further, suppose that the parent keeps up the pressure on school officials to do something, checking in with them from time to time to learn what steps they have taken. From the child's perspective, the actions by the parent, beyond verbally expressing her outrage, are what demonstrate her love and concern. Even if the bullying continues for some period of time, the child is apt to view the parent as standing behind her in ways that are a substantial boost to her morale. The parent's supportive actions might even make the persistence of the bullying somewhat more endurable. By contrast, if the parent does nothing at all or contents herself with simply expressing her disapproval of the bullying to the child, the child is apt to be demoralized by the parent's response.

In a similar way, I believe that those who are victimized by crimes, and especially serious crimes, want to know that the state is there for them, prepared to act to hold their victimizers accountable. Of course, the state is not a parent, but it is the public agent authorized to uphold the provisions of the criminal law. And arguably, the desire of victims (and their partisans and members of the public who are paying attention) to see the state act to censure offenders is not one premised solely on the reduction of future crime.[50] Victims may not care much about whether the punishment of those who commit crimes against them will make some marginal contribution to general deterrence. And they might not fear further victimization by the person who wronged them, especially if the wrong was a likely one-off event committed by a complete stranger. In this way, legal punishment is unlike the actions of the concerned parent of the bullied child. We would be surprised if her contact with school authorities, and her persistence in her efforts to get them to act to stop the bullying of her child, did not have some positive effect in reducing the bullying. But the victims of crime might not expect or care all that much about whether holding those who wronged them accountable contributes to the reduction of crime in society. What they plausibly might want is an official acknowledgement of the wrong done to them in a form that holds the wrongdoer accountable and makes it difficult for him or her to simply ignore the message communicated. Of course, wrongdoers can ignore the message and more than a few will do so. Nonetheless, at least the community, acting through its appointed representatives, will have forcefully communicated with offenders and, through that, with their victims and the public.

Furthermore, and importantly, state failure to punish wrongdoers, especially when this appears to stem from indifference or prejudice on the part of the officials charged with bringing offenders to justice, will send a very different message to victims, one that is apt to be deeply demoralizing. Such failures appear to "say" that state officials do not treat or regard the victims in question as important or as equal members of society. Granted, such failures will no doubt leave the individuals in question more susceptible to further victimization. But again, the devaluing of their lives and vital interests by state failures to act seems to be objectionable in its own right, regardless of whether it precipitates further victimization.

Hard Treatment as Subverting Moral Communication

A further concern about the hard treatment aspects of legal punishment is that they might overwhelm the individuals on whom they are inflicted such that they are left incapable of grasping the moral messages conveyed by punishment. We can imagine the former occurring if offenders are subjected to cruel or degrading forms of legal punishment, ones that turn them, in the memorable words of Jeffrie Murphy, into "terrified, urinating, defecating, screaming animals."[51] Short of such extremes, there might be offenders who, facing very long terms of imprisonment or death sentences, are rendered incapable of focusing on anything but the diminished prospects of their severely constrained or shortened lives. In such cases, the moral message punishment is intended to convey might become lost or drowned out, something which would be less likely to occur if censure was communicated in some other fashion.[52]

In response to these concerns, I would first note that there is nothing in the moral communication approach that requires us to sign onto cruel or degrading forms of penal hard treatment. In fact, in Chapter 5, where I discuss my mixed theory's implications for sentencing, I explicitly reject forms of punishment that leave offenders incapable of grasping the moral communication punishment is meant to convey. Second, as we have already seen, many of the crimes that are processed by contemporary criminal justice systems are relatively minor. They are often punished with a variety of noncustodial sanctions, most of which seem unlikely, if intelligently devised and administered, to degrade offenders or wholly drown out the moral message that punishment conveys. Granted, some of the individuals who commit these kinds of crimes will be disinclined to hear or heed such messages and will view the burdens they are required to bear as little more than hoops through which they must jump. It does not follow from this that they are either incapable of grasping the moral communication involved or that their sanctions have rendered them so.

Setting to one side the death penalty—a sanction which I have no interest in defending—the troubling cases are those posed by serious crimes, ones for which moderate to lengthy terms of imprisonment may be justified. Those assigned such sentences for their crimes will understandably be daunted by them, although some of them will have experienced imprisonment in the past. Should we be concerned that the penal burdens assigned to such offenders are so substantial as to overwhelm or push to the side whatever moral messages they are meant to convey? In thinking about this question, much depends on the kinds of prisons to which we imagine such offenders assigned. Admittedly, all prisons pose challenges to those housed in them, but some are arguably more humane and comport better with the dignity of inmates than others. This certainly seems true of some of the prisons found in Germany and Scandinavia.[53] As I will argue in Chapter 5, we should devise prisons that, while curtailing the liberty of inmates, strive to honor and respect other of their retained rights.[54] Not only should they see to the basic needs of inmates for nutrition, comfort, privacy, recreation, and healthcare, they should provide inmates with opportunities to work, receive visitors on a regular basis, and exercise their civic rights to free speech, political participation, and freedom of religion. The loss of liberty is, on my account, the currency of censure in the case of serious crimes. Other losses that often accompany the curtailment of liberty are arguably not needed to convey to offenders the wrongs they have committed.

Will those facing lengthy prison terms in relatively humane prisons facilities lose or tend to lose their abilities to grasp the moral communication conveyed by their confinement? I am not convinced that they will or must, although I would admit that there is room for debate about this. No doubt most individuals who realize that lengthy terms of confinement lie ahead for them struggle emotionally with the enormity of their fates. Yet the evidence suggests that most prisoners adjust to confinement and many mature or come to regret the wrongs they have committed.[55] This suggests that prisons do not destroy or overwhelm their moral compasses, even prisons that are not as humane as the ones that we might believe are most defensible.

A further point must be reckoned with as well. Legal punishment, on my account, communicates with persons other than those made to endure it. It also communicates with the victims of crimes, and in the cases currently under consideration, the victims of serious crimes (or with their surviving family members). As I note in the next section, many victims' lives are profoundly altered, if not destroyed, by the crimes committed against them. Even the most humane prisons will impose significant losses on offenders, but at least they will be structured to leave other aspects of their lives intact. As such, they seem appropriate forms of censure assigned to individuals who have committed crimes that show little regard for the lives, liberty, or well-being of their fellow human beings. More to the point, it is not clear what other sanctions exist that can appropriately convey to offenders, victims, and the broader community the magnitude of the wrongs done by serious crimes.

Clarifying the Value of Moral Communication

Suppose it is conceded that properly designed and administered state penal institutions morally communicate with offenders, victims (if they exist), and members of the larger community. Will there doing so be enough to justify the institution of legal punishment, especially given its costs, as well as its proneness to error and corruption?[56] Or might we need to supplement whatever communicative purposes its serves with acknowledgement of a crime reduction role for the institution? That leads to a further question about which of the purposes legal punishment serves is more significant, and why.

Again, my approach to justifying the institution of legal punishment is pluralist, in the sense that it draws on both moral communication and crime reduction. Thus, it might seem advisable for me to simply concede that moral communication is not significant enough such that, all by itself, it supplies a convincing justification for the institution. However, there are two reasons to pause and consider the strength of the moral communication branch of the account. First, as we have seen, there are significant questions about whether and to what extent legal punishment is successful at reducing crime. Its various modes of doing so, encompassing general and special deterrence, incapacitation, rehabilitation, and moral reinforcement, are all less than strongly impressive, once the evidence about their impact on crime, both positive and negative, is scrutinized. It therefore makes sense to consider to what extent the moral communication function of legal punishment is capable of bolstering the case to be made for the institution. Second, I believe that there is more to its moral communication function than some critics of the approach seem to think. This seems especially true when we turn our attention to more serious crimes and the state response to them.

It might seem that the value achieved by legal punishment's moral communication is modest. After all, it is "only communication," even if forceful or emphatic communication because given expression by and through various forms of penal burdens. It does not, as communication, prevent much crime, except perhaps by reminding offenders of their responsibilities under the law or by reinforcing the moral norms underlying defensible criminal law provisions in the wider community. Neither does it restore victims in any material way, although it symbolically affirms the value of their violated interests so long as it is calibrated to impose penal losses and deprivations that are commensurate with the wrongs they suffered. Moreover, if we focus on the many minor criminal offenses which tend to predominate in criminal justice systems and the mostly modest ways in which they impact victims, we might conclude that there is not that much to be said on behalf of punishment's communicative contribution to our lives. Many victims of minor offenses manage to go on with their lives in ways that are largely undisturbed by their victimization, whether or not the authorities undertake determined efforts to investigate, track down, arrest, and convict the perpetrators of wrongs against them. And again, private insurance helps the victims of minor crimes to fully recover their property or undo any damage to their persons. So will public victim compensation schemes, which are not uncommon.

Arguably, things are different when we turn to more serious offenses, ones which are what I will refer to as "significantly life-altering." Such crimes are ones that diminish victims' lives by causing them substantial injuries, traumatizing them in ways from which it might take them months or years to recover, or stealing or destroying property on which their lives and futures depend. In extreme cases they leave victims profoundly disabled or dead. The fundamental interests such crimes attack do not seem aptly characterized as things of mere instrumental value to persons. They are not like useful tools, implements or resources. Instead, they are akin to what John Rawls termed "primary social goods" or "things which it is supposed a rational man wants whatever else he wants."[57] Or they are like what Alan Gewirth termed the "generic features of action," in the sense that they are things we require if we are going to be effective agents of any kind.[58] Simply put, serious crimes substantially impede or destroy our abilities to have and live our own lives. When the state fails to prevent such crimes, which it will often do, it matters enormously to us that it does not let them pass by unnoticed. Victims, their families and loved ones, and members of the broader community will very much want the authorities to devote significant resources to their resolution. It would be too much to expect the authorities to successfully track down and prosecute all of the individuals who commit such crimes, but it would be disturbing if they did not make determined efforts to do so. Legal punishment is, in this way, a reactive institution. True, it no doubt prevents some crime. But it also matters enormously what state officials do after crimes are committed, especially when those crimes attack or threaten persons in elemental ways.

It could be argued, of course, that the reason why we so fervently want the authorities to successfully prosecute serious crimes has to do with their prevention. I would not deny that part of what might appropriately motivate investigators is the desire to gain convictions and thereby incapacitate the dangerous or deadly. But again, I contend that things are more complex than a narrow focus on crime reduction suggests. Official persistence in such cases is also motivated by the desire to "give victims justice," as we say, or to provide their loved ones with some closure, in the form of holding wrongdoers accountable when people they care strongly about have been badly victimized. Appropriately so, I would argue. Again, standing for the victims of serious crimes is a significant value in its own right in a crucial subset of cases, one that is not captured by crime reduction logic. Also, it is a value to be pursued despite what cost/benefit analyses of the appropriate use of the resources that officials have at their disposal would likely advise. It might make more sense, if deterrence or incapacitation was their focus, for state authorities to expend fewer resources on the resolution of serious crimes, especially as they recede into the past, and sometimes the distant past, and more on the resolution of less serious and more recent crimes. After all, the latter are often easier for the authorities to identify and convict the perpetrators of. Serious crimes receding into the past seem to be sinkholes into which too many resources might have to be poured, especially if we consider them solely from a perspective according to which we should allocate scarce societal resources in ways that result in the optimal reduction of future crimes. That we do not so regard persistent official efforts to identify, arrest, and hold accountable individuals who have gravely injured or killed their fellow members of society—and indeed might admire and laud such efforts—suggests that crime reduction is not the only or even the most important value served by the efforts of criminal justice officials.

This brings us back to the question of whether the moral communication that legal punishment effects is impressive enough, as a value independent of crime reduction, to justify the institution of legal punishment. I believe that I have shown that the value of such communication is far from insignificant, especially in cases of more serious crimes, such that we might want to see it pursued even if we are unsure that doing so will also reduce future offending. Fortunately, as a proponent of a mixed theory of punishment, I do not have to argue that moral communication is, all by itself, sufficient to justify the institution. Why moral communication should be given the lead role in such a mixed theory, and how to integrate the two values into a coherent account of legal punishment, are matters that I take up in the next chapter.

Contrasts with Other Prominent Moral Communication Approaches

As I indicated at the outset, the version of the moral communication approach that I defend draws on the work of other like-minded theorists. My debts to the work of Jean Hampton, Andreas von Hirsch, and Antony Duff, among others, will be obvious. However, in this section, I draw some contrasts between their accounts and my own to clarify what is and what is not distinctive about the account I have put forward.

Let me begin with Andreas (former Andrew) von Hirsch's hybrid account of legal punishment. Von Hirsch was one of the first to identify "censure" as a crucial component of legal punishment and he is explicit about linking it to the capacity of human beings for responsiveness to moral considerations and our abilities to regulate our conduct by reference to them. As he famously remarked, we are not "tigers," or merely self-interested beings, but moral beings.[59] Von Hirsch also notes that the censure aspect of legal punishment communicates with offenders, victims, and the general public, an important point on which my own account draws, and he links censure to proportionality, distinguishing ordinal and cardinal forms of it.[60] However, when it comes to the justification of what he terms "hard treatment," von Hirsch declines to tie it directly with censure. Instead, he argues that we impose penal losses and deprivations to deter those who are not sufficiently responsive to the moral considerations that ground key aspects of the criminal law. In this, he acknowledges that some or perhaps many of us are tempted, at times, to violate the law and thus ignore the compelling moral reasons we have against doing so. We need the threat of hard treatment as a "prudential disincentive" for engaging in criminal misconduct.[61]

I believe that von Hirsch is too quick to cast the justification of hard treatment as having to do with deterrence, as opposed to emphatically expressing the censure that is inherent to legal punishment. One place in which my own views and von Hirsch's clearly diverge is in his discussion of the appropriate punishment for serious crimes like homicide. Von Hirsch well understands that there is little evidence demonstrating that lengthy prison sentences, let alone the death penalty, are needed to deter would-be murderers. Since his account of hard treatment is entirely deterrence-based, he suggests that prison sentences for homicide should not generally exceed five years in length, as longer sentences are unlikely to have any marginal deterrence impact.[62] If sentences for lesser crimes are appropriately scaled down from there, then the sentencing scheme will satisfy the requirements of ordinal proportionality. Yet I suspect that the partisans of murder victims, as well as members of the public, would generally be dissatisfied with what von Hirsch proposes. Why is this? Suppose that we adopted his proposed maximum presumptive sentence for murder and assigned it to those who deliberately targeted and killed their victims. Presumably, von Hirsch would have us assign such offenders to humane and nondegrading prisons, indeed to ones that offered various rehabilitative opportunities. Murderers would serve their five-year (or perhaps shorter) sentences and then be released back into society to carry on with their lives. I grant that a five-year prison sentence is not nothing—it constitutes a substantial disruption to an offender's life. Nonetheless, the victims of such crimes lose their lives in their entirety and it is hard to see how sentences of "only" five years in prison appropriately value their lost lives. To be clear, my claim here is not that only life sentences, or worse, executions, appropriately do so. It is rather that five-year sentences seem, if not "slaps on the wrist," insufficient to capture the enormity of what is lost by the victims of homicide. Perhaps a 25-year sentence would do so, or even a 15-year one, but five years is fairly brief, all things considered. Von Hirsch is driven to endorsing such sentences by the logic of deterrence. Although I believe that deterrence plays an important back-up role in sentencing (more on that in Chapter 5), I would give censure, with its associated element of valuing victims' lives and interests appropriately in the hard treatment meted out to offenders, a more prominent role in justifying hard treatment than does von Hirsch. I concur with his conjecture concerning how much hard treatment deterrence could justify in this instance; it is his primary and exclusive reliance on deterrence in justifying hard treatment with which I part ways.

Jean Hampton's views about legal punishment evolved over the course of her (sadly, too brief) career.[63] It is in her later writings that her moral communication account emerges, one that emphasizes the ways in which punishment "stands for victims." At times, she casts legal punishment in the role of "annulling" the falsehoods conveyed by crimes.[64] Crimes, she claims, implicitly communicate the superiority of perpetrators over their victims, as if victims can simply be used, and perhaps discarded, as offenders seek, in various ways, to advance their own interests. If we assume a Kantian conception of human worth according to which all persons are equal, crime can be understood to demean victims by falsely communicating their lesser worth relative to that of perpetrators. Hampton urges the punishment of offenders in order to forcefully annul this falsehood.[65] This way of putting things invites the rejoinder made by David Dolinko, who questions whether it is a defensible role for the state, generally speaking, to annul falsehoods.[66] For instance, if I despise certain kinds of people and either say or publish falsehoods of nefarious kinds about them, is it the role of the state to annul the falsehoods I have communicated? One would think not.

In some of her subsequent work on the topic, Hampton retains her emphasis on symbolically "raising victims" and "lowering offenders," but she speaks more often about annulling the "diminishment" of victims than annulling falsehoods.[67] In places, she suggests that crimes furnish evidence of the inferiority of victims, thereby diminishing them. Punishment provides evidence to counter this and thereby stand for the equal worth of victims.[68] Here is how she puts the aim of punishment: "we are morally required to respond to remake the world in a way that denies what the wrongdoer's events have attempted to establish, thereby lowering the wrongdoer, elevating the victim, and annulling the act of diminishment."[69]

On my account, the criminal law consists of a series of provisions that proscribe public wrongs, ones grounded in a conception of persons as having equal moral worth and thus entitled to enjoy and exercise certain basic rights. Many serious crimes consist of violations of these provisions. By arresting, convicting, and appropriately punishing offenders, the state censures them and emphatically reaffirms the standards of conduct described in the criminal law, first and foremost to offenders, but also to victims and members of the public. This is something that I contend victims will want to see. But they might not believe that the crimes against them have somehow diminished their status as equal citizens or worry that others will believe that crimes have done so. Victims might well be angry about the wrongs done to them, and others who learn of what happened to them will often be sympathetic to their plight. What might make victims doubt their worth, in fact, is the failure by state officials to take the crimes against them seriously, by investigating them, arresting suspects, or pursuing vigorously their prosecution. But the crimes themselves will not usually, and perhaps not often, lead victims, or others, to doubt their worth. Or so I would claim.

Also, Hampton's account seems to overdramatize, and thus mischaracterize, what many crimes communicate, including what many who commit them intend or understand them to communicate. Granted, some offenses—hate crimes, for instance—implicitly, if not explicitly communicate contempt for victims, treating them as if their lives and interests are of less worth. Still, it does not follow that the victims of such crimes, or members of the public, will doubt their own worth. In many other kinds of cases, however, the individuals who commit crimes are simply taking shortcuts, often to acquire money or property that they would rather not have to acquire through more honest means. They might, in so acting, put their needs or desires above or before those of their victims, thus failing to show respect for their victims. But does it follow that they believe their victims to be their inferiors, or that victims or others will read off of their criminal acts that they are their inferiors? Again, I doubt this. Moreover, in some cases, those who commit crimes of violence are simply lashing out at others who they believe have wronged or disrespected them, or who, perhaps, have inconvenienced them. In these kinds of cases, it may be the criminal agents who believe that others have somehow denied their worth, which their violent responses are little more than unjustifiably aggressive or destructive efforts at asserting.

My own account is deeply indebted to Antony Duff's moral communication approach.[70] My qualms about his approach stem from two main sources: First, at times he seems to relegate victims to the sidelines while focusing on offenders and their moral agency. Second, I am uneasy about how far he is willing to push what he terms "repentance, reform, and reconciliation" onto offenders.[71] Again, on my account, we must craft penal burdens and impositions with an eye to "appropriately valuing" the losses that victims suffer due to others' crimes against them. I have conceded that there is no precise metric of penal losses; neither is there some simple or agreed upon way in which to link the victim loss and penal burdens scales. I will have more to say about these issues in Chapter 5. What matters for present purposes is that my account would have penal sanctions determined by consideration of the impact of crimes on victims, although we must also factor offender culpability into this. On Duff's account, by contrast, it seems that what should drive sanction forms and duration is their role as penances, and thus as mandated ways in which offenders can be expected to express, and hopefully effect, repentance, reform, and reconciliation. Duff must then explain why sanction severity should correspond, at least roughly, with the harm done to victims by crimes, especially if offenders vary considerably, as they might, in their susceptibility to repentance, reform, and reconciliation. The two—that is, victim harms and improvements in offender moral agency—seem only loosely related.

Duff's critics have questioned whether his focus on tapping into the remorse of offenders and then leveraging it to effect their reform is an appropriate task for the state to undertake.[72] In fairness to Duff, he repeatedly reminds us that we must respect the autonomy of offenders in our efforts to bring them to accept responsibility for their crimes and cultivate greater responsiveness to moral considerations against offending. However, one concern is that the state has the power to coerce and it will be difficult to keep that power from tainting the process of eliciting remorse, fostering reform, and inducing reconciliation with victims. Unless offenders voluntarily embrace the process, it will not be meaningful; that much seems clear. Yet even the most careful or conscientious state agents might, at times, be tempted to push offenders a bit more than they should, and not all state agents will be so careful and conscientious. Also, it arguably makes more sense for people with whom we already have close relationships to be the ones to encourage us to repent our errors and mend our ways. Friends, siblings, parents, or spouses will, more often, have the best interests of the wayward at heart and will be at least somewhat more inclined to support them in loving ways through thick and thin. State penal agents, by contrast, are often strangers to those in whom they must foster change. We might therefore wonder how realistic it is to expect offenders to trust or listen to them, except insofar as state agents have power over them.

A further difficulty Duff's account will have to face is this: For many of those convicted of crimes, this will not be their first rodeo, so to speak. More than a few offenders have substantial criminal histories.[73] Duff's repentance, reform, and reconciliation project will face challenges with such offenders. Of course, he might argue that those histories are partly the products of existing punishment practices that fall short of adhering to the spirit of his approach, and perhaps well short. Too many of those practices will have simply inflicted mindless suffering on offenders for their previous crimes. Fair enough, except that recidivism exists in countries in which penal practices are more enlightened and humane.[74] Some individuals seem unable or unwilling to abandon lives of crime no matter how hard we try to help them as we hold them accountable. And continuing to hold them accountable for their crimes as they persist in offending we surely must. In such cases, it might make sense to impose sanctions on them that appropriately value the harms done to their victims, but without much confidence in effecting their reform.

None of this is meant to suggest that we should not hope that offenders will feel remorse for their crimes, repent their wrongs, apologize to their victims, and undertake reform. Also, it makes eminent good sense, as I will argue in Chapter 5, to devise sanctions that will reduce the impediments to their embrace of responsible lives. My concern is mainly about how far the state should go in plumbing the moral psyches of offenders and inducing them to change their lives. We might reasonably prefer the state to keep some distance from offenders and their inner selves, and thus to rely on other people closer to offenders to push and help them to reform. For the most part, this means that, in the criminal justice context, the state should limit its morally communicative efforts to censuring the wrongs of which individuals have been convicted. This is limited but nonetheless vitally important role for the state. Saying this does not preclude the state undertaking a variety of other vital measures to foster morally responsible conduct, such as ensuring that all members of society have access to adequate housing, nutrition, healthcare, education, and decently paying jobs. These are measures that it seems better suited to undertake than efforts to morally reform the criminally wayward through legal punishment.

Concluding Remarks

My aim in this chapter has been to develop and defend a moral communication approach to justifying legal punishment, one that posits a role for the institution that is distinct from its crime reduction role. The moral communication approach assumes that criminal offenders are beings who are responsive to the moral reasons for action which undergird defensible versions of the criminal law. When they fail to abide by those moral reasons in a given case, state authorities should take the steps necessary to hold them accountable for such public wrongs. In doing so, the state censures offenders through the imposition of penal burdens or losses of various kinds, ones that we have reason to believe most offenders will find it difficult to simply ignore. In forcefully condemning the actions of offenders, the state reaffirms the rights or other legitimate interests of all citizens, including, most directly and pointedly, those of the victims of crimes in cases in which there are victims.

In the next chapter, I take up a number of questions: If both moral communication and the reduction of crime are defensible state penal purposes, are they co-equal purposes, or should one of them be understood to have priority, and why? Is that priority absolute, presumptive, or something else? Also, how might we plausibly integrate the two purposes into a coherent overall account, one that gives each of them a role to play?

Notes

1 Prominent defenders of the view that legal punishment expresses censure or condemnation include Joel Feinberg, "The Expressive Function of Punishment," *The Monist* 49 (1965): 397–423; R. A. Duff, *Trials and Punishments* (Cambridge: Cambridge University Press, 1986) and *Punishment, Communication, and Community* (Oxford: Oxford University Press, 2001); John Kleinig, "Punishment and Moral Seriousness," *Israel Law Review* 25 (1991): 401–21; Igor Primoratz, "Punishment as Language," *Philosophy* 64 (1989): 187–205; Jean Hampton, "An Expressive Theory of Retribution," in Wesley Craig (ed.), *Retributivism and Its Critics* (Stuttgart: V. Steiner Verlag, 1992): 1–21; Andrew von Hirsch, *Censure and Sanctions* (Oxford: Clarendon Press, 1993); Uma Narayan, "Appropriate Responses and Preventive Benefits: Justifying Censure and Hard Treatment in Legal Punishment," *Oxford Journal of Legal Studies* 13 (1993): 166–82; Thaddeus Metz, "Censure Theory and Intuitions about Punishment," *Law & Philosophy* 19 (2000): 491–512; and Bill Wringe, *An Expressive Theory of Punishment* (London: Palgrave Macmillan, 2016).

2 See especially Hampton, "An Expressive Theory of Retribution." She also defends such an account in "A New Theory of Retribution," in R. G. Frey and Christopher Morris (eds.), *Liability and Responsibility: Essays in Law and Morals* (Cambridge: Cambridge University Press, 1991): 377–414, "The Retributive Idea," in Jean Hampton and Jeffrie Murphy, *Forgiveness and Mercy* (Cambridge: Cambridge University Press, 1988), Chapter 4; and "Correcting Harms Versus Righting Wrongs: The Goal of Retribution," *UCLA Law Review* 39 (1992): 1659–702.

3 Duff, *Trials and Punishments* and *Punishment, Communication, and Community.*

4 Victor Tadros, *The Ends of Harm: The Moral Foundations of Criminal Law* (Oxford: Oxford University Press, 2011): 103; David Boonin, *The Problem of Punishment* (Cambridge: Cambridge University Press, 2008): 172–79; and Nathan Hanna, "Say What? A Critique of Expressive Retributivism," *Law & Philosophy* 27 (2008): 123–50.

5 Duff, *Punishment, Communication, and Community*, 88. See also his "Penal Communications: Recent Work on the Philosophy of Punishment," *Crime and Justice: A Review of Research* 20 (1996): 1–96, at 45.

6 H. L. A. Hart, *Law, Liberty, and Morality* (Stanford: Stanford University Press, 1963): 65–66 and Tadros, *The Ends of Harm*, 99.

7 That the audience for punishment's censure is multi-faceted is a claim defended by von Hirsch in *Censure and Sanctions*, 10.

8 See, for instance, the essays in Rowan Cruft, S. Matthew Liao, and Massimo Renzo (eds.), *Philosophical Foundations of Human Rights* (Oxford: Oxford University Press, 2015).

9 For a useful recent discussion of *mala prohibita*, see R. A. Duff, *The Realm of Criminal Law* (Oxford: Oxford University Press, 2018): 313–22.

10 As Duff has argued, unfair advantage forms of retributivism seem to make the most sense in relation to *mala prohibita*. See his *Trials and Punishments*, 211. For a recent defense of this version of retributivism, see Richard Dagger, *Playing Fair: Political Obligation and the Problems of Punishment* (Oxford: Oxford University Press, 2018).

11 Cf. Wringe, *An Expressive Theory of Punishment*, Chapter 3 and Narayan, "Appropriate Responses and Preventive Benefits," 174.

12 Penal theorists have long been concerned about the ways in which social injustices of various kinds might lead members of society to question the rightful authority of the state to punish. See, for instance, Jeffrie G. Murphy, "Marxism and Retribution," *Philosophy and Public Affairs* 2 (1973): 217–34 and Duff, *Trials and Punishments*, 294.

13 Narayan, "Appropriate Responses and Preventive Benefits," 169–70; Hampton, "A New Theory of Retribution," 401; and von Hirsch, *Censure and Sanctions*, 10.
14 For critical discussion of plea bargaining and the ways in which it can distort the conduct of those who have broken the law, see Albert W. Alschuler, "The Prosecutor's Role in Plea Bargaining," *University of Chicago Law Review* 36 (1968): 50–112; Richard L. Lippke, *The Ethics of Plea Bargaining* (Oxford: Oxford University Press, 2011); and Darryl K. Brown, *Free Market Criminal Justice: How Democracy and Laissez Faire Undermine the Rule of Law* (Oxford: Oxford University Press, 2016), especially Chapter 4.
15 See, for instance, David B. Mustard, "Racial, Ethnic, and Gender Disparities in Sentencing: Evidence from the U.S. Federal Courts," *The Journal of Law & Economics* 44 (2001): 285–314.
16 Consider the outrage generated by the lenient sentencing of Brock Turner after his conviction of raping an unconscious woman. See Richard Gonzalez, "Sentence in Stanford Sexual Assault Case Sparks Outrage," at www.npr.org/sections/thetwo-way/2016/06/06/481010919/california-rape-case-sentence-sparks-outrage (accessed October 13, 2021).
17 See Andrew von Hirsch ad Nils Jareborg, "Gauging Criminal Harm: A Living-Standard Analysis," *Oxford Journal of Legal Studies* 11 (1991): 1–38.
18 Andrew von Hirsch, "Proportionality in the Philosophy of Punishment," *Crime and Justice: A Review of Research* 16 (1992): 55–98; Duff, *Punishment, Communication, and Community*, 135–43; Jesper Ryberg, "Retributivism and the (Lack of) Justification of Proportionality," *Criminal Law and Philosophy* 15 (2021): 447–62.
19 Paul H. Robinson has done the most to argue that there are widely shared intuitions of justice, or what he refers to as "empirical deserts," at least about the relative seriousness of criminal offenses. See his *Intuitions of Justice and the Utility of Desert* (Oxford: Oxford University Press, 2013).
20 von Hirsch, "Proportionality in the Philosophy of Punishment," 77.
21 von Hirsch, *Censure and Sanctions*, 18.
22 See Michael Tonry, "Sentencing in America, 1975–2025," *Crime and Justice: A Review of Research* 42 (2013): 141–98. Tonry at one point (p. 169) characterizes the lengthy sentences adopted during what he terms the "Tough on Crime" era in the United States as ones "measured in decades and lifetimes."
23 See Alexandra Natapoff, "Misdemeanors," *Southern California Law Review* 85 (2012): 1313–75. Natapoff notes that roughly 80 percent of the criminal cases that go through the US criminal justice system involve misdemeanors.
24 Johannes Andenaes, "The General Preventive Effects of Punishment," *University of Pennsylvania Law Review* 114 (1966): 949–83.
25 Duff, *The Realm of Criminal Law*, see especially Chapter 2.
26 For a classic discussion of the rigors of criminal procedure, especially in minor criminal cases, see Malcolm M Feeley, *The Process Is the Punishment: Handling Cases in a Lower Criminal Court* (New York: Russell Sage, 1979).
27 Hanna, "Say What?" 130–31. See also Ryberg, "Retributivism and the (Lack of) Justification of Proportionality," 447–62, at 450. But see Christopher Bennett, *The Apology Ritual: A Philosophical Theory of Punishment* (Cambridge: Cambridge University Press, 2008), who suggests (at 37) that we might lack other ways of expressing emotions like anger or resentment towards those who wrong us.
28 Heather Gert, Linda Radzik, and Michael Hand, "Hampton on the Expressive Power of Punishment," *Journal of Social Philosophy* 35 (2004): 79–90, at 83–84.
29 Hampton, "Correcting Harms versus Righting Wrongs," 1695–96.
30 David Boonin, *The Problem of Punishment* (Cambridge: Cambridge University Press, 2008): 177. More recently, Duff has entertained the possibility that wrongdoers could be held to account by subjecting them to public trials such that, if they

are found guilty, we might censure them but without imposing penal hard treatment on them. Duff admits that such a view will be difficult to accept. See his *The Realm of Criminal Law*, 223.

31 Boonin, *The Problem of Punishment*, 178–79.

32 James B. Jacobs and Elena Larrauri, "European Criminal Records and Ex-Offender Employment," *Oxford Handbooks Online*, at https://doi.org/10.1093/oxfordhb/9780199935383.013.157 (accessed October 13, 2012). See also Richard L. Lippke, "Legal Punishment and the Public Identification of Offenders," *Res Publica* 24 (2018): 199–216. In some European countries, prospective employers can inquire of government officials if there are grounds for concern about individuals, based on their criminal pasts. Yet even if employers are told that there are grounds for concern, this is still quite different from the full public identification of offenders.

33 Steven C. Bennett, "The 'Right to Be Forgotten': Reconciling EU and US Perspectives," *Berkeley Journal of International Law* 30 (2012): 161–95.

34 Adam J. Kolber, "The Subjective Experience of Punishment," *Columbia Law Review* 109 (2009): 182–236.

35 Boonin suggests the option of restitution in *The Problem of Punishment*, 178.

36 Hanna, "Say What?" 138.

37 Natapoff, "Misdemeanors," 1320.

38 Duff has argued that probation morally communicates. See his *Punishment, Communication, and Community*, 101.

39 Andrew von Hirsch and Clifford Shearing, "Restorative Justice: A 'Making Amends' Model," in Andrew von Hirsh and Andrew Ashworth (eds.), *Proportionate Sentencing: Exploring the Principles* (Oxford: Oxford University Press, 2005): 110–30, at 125.

40 Hanna, "Say What?" 125–26.

41 Hanna, "Say What?" 126.

42 See Liora Lazarus, *Contrasting Prisoners' Rights: A Comparative Examination of England and Germany* (Oxford: Oxford University Press, 2004) and John Pratt and Anna Eriksson, *Contrasts in Punishment: An Explanation of Anglophone Excess and Nordic Exceptionalism* (New York: Routledge, 2013).

43 See David Gray, "Punishment as Suffering," *Vanderbilt Law Review* 63 (2010): 1617–93.

44 Richard L. Lippke, "Penal Severity and the Modern State," in Michael Tonry (ed.), *Of One-Eyed and Toothless Miscreants: Making the Punishment Fit the Crime* (New York: Oxford University Press, 2020): 127–48.

45 Adam J. Kolber, "The Comparative Nature of Punishment," *Boston University Law Review* 89 (2009): 1565–608, at 1585. See also Kolber, "Subjective Experience," 207. Kolber, it should be noted, rejects such objective accounts of legal punishment. For responses, see Lippke, "Penal Severity and the Modern State," and Dan Markel and Chad Flanders, "Bentham on Stilts: The Bare Relevance of Subjectivity to Retributive Justice," *California Law Review* 98 (2010): 907–88.

46 See Lazarus's discussion of the German Prison Act, which has as one of its guiding principles the claim that "life in prison should, as far as possible, reflect the general relationships of the outside world," in *Contrasting Prisoners' Rights*, 84. See also Michael Tonry, "Has the Prison a Future?" in M. Tonry (ed.), *The Future of Imprisonment* (New York: Oxford University Press, 2004): 3–24 and Richard L. Lippke, *Rethinking Imprisonment* (Oxford: Oxford University Press, 2007).

47 I doubt that we would be troubled if someone confined to a prison reported that it was "the best thing that could have happened to him," or at least an overall good thing for him. He might reflect on how it interrupted a stretch of self- or other destructiveness in his life, forced him to get off of drugs or alcohol, and provided him with opportunities for schooling or work training such that, when he got out, he was better equipped to start living a responsible life. Learning of this, would

we be inclined to send him back to prison, and especially to a cruel or degrading one, to ensure that he suffered enough? I do not think so. If he served his time and made the best of it, that would be viewed as a good thing, the kind of thing we very much want other offenders to emulate.

48 Also, the ways and extent to which those convicted of crimes might be publicly identified can vary. In some countries, offenders are identified as a matter of public record, but they can seek to have their criminal records expunged after some period of time. It might also be possible to publicly identify only those who commit more serious offenses, thereby shielding the identities of minor offenders. For insightful discussion of these matters, see James B. Jacobs, *The Eternal Criminal Record* (Cambridge, MA: Harvard University Press, 2015).

49 Many jurisdictions have government-sponsored victim compensation schemes. Even in the United States, which has a harshly punitive criminal justice system and meager social welfare provisions, most states have victim compensation programs. See *U.S. Resource Map of Crime Victim Services and Information*, Office for Victims of Crime, at www.ovc.gov/map.html (accessed October 14, 2021).

50 See Uli Orth, "Punishment Goals of Crime Victims," *Law and Human Behavior* 27 (2003): 173–86. The victims in Orth's study do identify the reduction of crime as one of the reasons why they seek the punishment of those who criminally wronged them, but they also cite such things as "retaliation," "recognition of victim status," and "confirmation of societal values."

51 Jeffrie G. Murphy, "Cruel and Unusual Punishments," in M. A. Stewart (ed.), *Law, Morality, and Human Rights* (Dordrecht: D. Reidel, 1979): 373–404, at 387.

52 Duff expresses this kind of concern in *Punishment, Communication, and Community*, at 88. See also his "Penal Communications: Recent Work on the Philosophy of Punishment," *Crime and Justice: A Review of Research* 20 (1996): 1–96, at 45.

53 See Lazarus, *Contrasting Prisoners' Rights* and Pratt and Erikson, *Contrasts in Punishment.*

54 See also Lippke, *Rethinking Imprisonment,* and Tonry, "Has the Prison a Future?"

55 See Robert Johnson and Ania Dobrzanska, "Mature Coping among Life-Sentenced Inmates: An Exploratory Study of Adjustment Dynamics," *Corrections Compendium* 30 (2005): 8–9, 36–38 and Margaret E. Leigey, "For the Longest Time: The Adjustment of Inmates to a Sentence of Life Without Parole," *The Prison Journal* 90 (2010): 247–68.

56 Douglas N. Husak, "Why Punish the Deserving?" *Noûs* 26 (1992): 447–64.

57 John Rawls, *A Theory of Justice* (Cambridge, MA: Harvard University Press, 1971): 92.

58 Alan Gewirth, *Reason and Morality* (Chicago: University of Chicago Press, 1978): 25.

59 von Hirsch, *Censure and Sanctions*, 11.

60 von Hirsch, *Censure and Sanctions*, 9–19.

61 von Hirsch, *Censure and Sanctions*, 13.

62 von Hirsch, *Censure and Sanctions*, 43.

63 Earlier in her career, Hampton defended a moral education approach to legal punishment. See her "The Moral Education Theory of Punishment," *Philosophy and Public Affairs* 13 (1984): 208–38.

64 Hampton, "A New Theory of Retribution," 402. Alan Brudner has more recently defended a similar account, according to which those who commit crimes implicitly assert the moral falsehood that they are entitled to "unlimited" freedom. See his *Punishment and Freedom: A Liberal Theory of Penal Justice* (Oxford: Oxford University Press, 2009): 46.

65 Hampton, "A New Theory of Retribution," 402. For a similar account, see Kleinig, "Punishment and Moral Seriousness," 418.

66 David Dolinko, "Some Thoughts about Retributivism," *Ethics* 101 (1991): 537–59, at 551.
67 Hampton, "Correcting Harms," 1686.
68 For useful discussion, see Gert, et al., "Hampton on the Expressive Power of Punishment."
69 Hampton, "Correcting Harms," 1686.
70 Duff, *Trials and Punishments* and *Punishment, Communication, and Community*, among many other publications.
71 Duff, *Punishment, Communication, and Community*, 107.
72 von Hirsch and Ashworth, *Proportionate Sentencing*, 92–109 and Bennett, *The Apology Ritual*, 188–97.
73 See Mariel Alper, Matthew R. Durose, and Joshua Markman, *2018 Update on Prisoner Recidivism: A 9-Year Follow-up Period (2005–2014)*, Bureau of Justice Statistics (2018), at www.bjs.gov/index.cfm?ty=pbdetail&iid=6266 (accessed May 11, 2020).
74 See World Population Review, *Recidivism Rates by Country 2021*, at https://worldpopulationreview.com/country-rankings/recidivism-rates-by-country (accessed October 14, 2021).

4 Merging the Elements

In the previous two chapters, I elaborated and defended a morally communicative approach to justifying legal punishment. Legal punishment, on that approach, censures offenders for the public wrongs they have committed. It also communicates with victims, when there are victims, identifying and standing against the wrongs done to them, and with the broader public, reminding it of the basic responsibilities of citizenship in modern liberal democratic societies insofar as these are codified in the criminal law. Such communication is rendered forceful by its employment of penal losses or impositions of various kinds, ones that should be designed to reflect the gravity of the wrongs committed.

My position is that there is a legitimate purpose to legal punishment that is distinct from its role in reducing future crime through the familiar mechanisms of deterrence, incapacitation, and rehabilitation. However, I embrace the proposition that the reduction of crime plays a significant role in justifying the institution of legal punishment. It should be apparent that if we impose appropriate penal burdens of various kinds on those convicted of crimes to morally communicate with them, there likely will be accompanying deterrent effects borne of those impositions. Of course, whether those deterrent effects will be optimal, in the sense of weighing appropriately their benefits and costs, is a separate question, one to which I return in due course. Also, depending on the seriousness of the crimes being censured, there may be incapacitation of offenders. The punishment of some crimes will only appropriately value the damaged lives or other interests of victims if it includes penal confinement, although I subsequently argue that defensible prisons must be designed to minimize the losses they inflict on offenders and ameliorate ones that cannot be minimized. Finally, censuring burdens and losses should be designed and administered in ways that do not erode offender capacities for responsible citizenship. They also might be supplemented with programs aimed at bolstering those capacities, or perhaps more realistically, removing impediments to their operation.

The suggestion that legal punishment might serve both morally communicative and crime reduction purposes invites the question of how these purposes are to be combined into a single theory.[1] There have been some well-known attempts to develop and defend mixed theories of punishment,

DOI: 10.4324/9781032661667-5

typically ones that combine retributive and crime reduction elements.[2] Two central challenges that such theories face concern their coherence and stability. With respect to the former, the question is whether we will have to intuitively weigh and balance the various elements, if and when they conflict, or is there some convincing account of which element should prevail, and why, when conflicts occur. There is also the question whether that prevalence should be understood as absolute, presumptive, or something else. With regard to stability, the question is whether the two elements can be kept together at all, or whether, when push comes to shove, we will be forced simply to choose one to the exclusion of the other in designing and operating the institution of legal punishment. In the first section of this chapter, I discuss these challenges. I then briefly survey some of the more prominent mixed theories that have been advanced in the literature on penal theory to see how they fare with regard to them.

In the second section, I lay out my own mixed theory. It is one that puts the moral communication element in the lead role, although I construe its priority as presumptive. In designing and administering our legal punishment institutions, we should give priority to communicating with offenders, victims, and the public about the basic rights and responsibilities of citizenship insofar as these are embodied in the criminal law. Importantly, we should strive for accurate moral communication, which entails that we should adopt legal procedures that work reliably to identify and convict those who have violated the law, and to punish them commensurately with the seriousness of their offenses. The prevention of crime will occur as a by-product of so designing and administering the institution of legal punishment, although we will have little reason to believe that the by-product will be optimally crime preventive, assuming that we have the ability to identify with any precision what optimally crime preventive practices would consist in.

In the third section, I discuss the conditions under which punishment's moral communication purpose might be overridden by its crime reduction purpose. I urge a view according to which we should limit the discretion of prosecutors and judges to downplay moral communication in favor of crime reduction. I also suggest that genuine conflicts among the purposes are apt to be relatively rare, more so than critiques of mixed theories sometimes take them to be.

In the fourth section, I consider whether and in what ways a crime reduction account of legal punishment can give moral communication a role, and perhaps a prominent one. It seems fair to say that moral communication has not been assigned a particularly significant part in justifying legal punishment by crime reduction theorists. Both general and special deterrence seem to focus more on addressing potential and convicted offenders as primarily self-interested beings. Incapacitation prioritizes restraint, more than communication, at least with regard to offenders. Depending on whether rehabilitation is understood as aimed at making offenders more prudent about their lives, or more morally responsible in living them, it might create some space for a morally communicative element within crime reduction theory. Last but not least, the claim by some crime reductionists that legal punishment serves to reinforce preexisting moral norms against violent or predatory acts does seem to embrace a form of moral communication. The question I raise is whether the crime reduction approach might be reimagined in ways that would give more emphasis to moral communication. The answer I reach is a skeptical one, since the approach assigns moral communication only an instrumental role in reducing crime, one that must be weighed against other modes of reducing it.

In the fifth section, I address the contention that I have, to too great an extent, sidelined crime prevention in the mixed theory I defend. In response, I outline a number of ways in which crime reduction might figure in our sentencing practices. These include having a more prominent role in the sentencing of *mala prohibita*, supporting higher sentences based on special deterrence or incapacitation in some cases, and helping us to choose among candidate sentencing regimes that all satisfy absolute and relative proportionality constraints.

Several prominent themes of this chapter are worth emphasizing. I distinguish between possible logical tensions in the mixed theory I defend and likely real ones, arguing that theorists who focus on the former do so at the expense of understanding how rare the latter are apt to be. Also, I suggest that it is one thing to imagine conflicts among the aims in highly abstract and hypothetical contexts, but quite another to conceive of them in institutional contexts where officials have limited and defined authority, are required to operate according to certain procedures, and are expected to be transparent about how and why they act as they do.[3] Finally, my position is that legal punishment is a complex undertaking, one not unlike other kinds of complex human undertakings in serving multiple purposes among which there can be tensions. I suggest that we should embrace such tensions where we cannot eliminate them and eschew accounts of legal punishment that seem determined to deny their existence.[4]

The Challenges that Mixed Theories Face

One of the things that seems to unite theorists who put forward mixed theories of legal punishment is the sense that the institution is simply too varied in its purposes and effects to be fully accounted for by a single, unifying value, whether that value is the reduction of crime, moral communication, or something else. It is also a very costly institution, one that citizens as taxpayers are called upon to support. In these ways, legal punishment is like other institutions or practices with which we are familiar. Consider higher education, for instance. It too is an enterprise on which society expends considerable resources, although some of those resources come from private individuals who either pay out of their own pockets for their educations or make charitable contributions to higher education institutions. It seems a dubious enterprise to argue that there is a single purpose to the institution of higher education, even if it might be more plausibly argued that some of the many purposes it serves are more important than others. Among the valuable things that flow from the institution are the social connections and friendships that university attendees make, ones that might benefit them, in a variety of ways, throughout their ensuing lives. Yet few would be inclined to say that these social connections and friendships are the main purpose of higher education, any more than keeping young adults occupied, during a time in their lives when they might be more crime-prone, is a major purpose of it, although it might be a good that flows from it. Among the more plausible central aims of the institution, two stand out. First, higher education prepares individuals for the economic marketplace, and especially for employment that is apt to be better paying and more socially prestigious. Yet many who teach at colleges and universities, and some who attend them, might see this purpose as less important than another one, which we might term that of enlightenment, or, less pretentiously, perhaps, that of cultivating a meaningful understanding, appreciation, and engagement with what the natural and social sciences, the arts, and the humanities have to offer individuals as they contemplate the world and their place in it. I will not pause here to attempt to resolve this controversy. My point in bringing it up is simply to offer one illustration of the ways in which another human institution is complex in its functions and purposes, such that attempts to reduce the role it plays to one of them are apt to be unpersuasive. Nonetheless, some of those purposes or functions seem more important than others.

Unlike those who put forward univocal theories of legal punishment, I believe that we should embrace the complexity of the practice, although we should look for ways to order the purposes it serves. I have identified moral communication and crime reduction as two plausible purposes of legal punishment. They could, of course, be cast as purposes of equal significance. In some contexts, they might point us in roughly the same direction in terms of designing and administering the institution of legal punishment. If and when they conflict in their implications, we could simply operate with intuitive judgments about which purpose to give precedence to and why. However, like most penal theorists who have thought about the matter, I regard such an ad hoc weighing and balancing approach as less than ideal. It makes it seem as if we do not really have a single theory about legal punishment at all, but two distinct ones, such that which one prevails in any given instance is a matter that will depend on judgments that are not only apt to vary among individuals but lack any overarching rationale. Of course, it might be possible to develop and defend some meta-principle that would provide us with a clear basis for determining when to favor the one purpose over the other, and vice versa. But it is difficult to imagine what such a meta-principle would look like given the rather different ways in which the two purposes would have us think about legal punishment. I suspect that a more promising route is to search for convincing reasons for subordinating one of the purposes to the other.

One well-known instance of this kind of subordination occurs in versions of so-called "negative retributivism."[5] According to it, the primary aim of legal punishment is the reduction of crime. However, negative retributivists hold that in setting up the institution of legal punishment, we should constrain its crime reduction operations to ensure that they strictly avoid punishment of the innocent (or, more realistically, those whose legal guilt cannot be established beyond a reasonable doubt) and punish the guilty (or those found guilty beyond a reasonable doubt) proportionally with the seriousness of their crimes. If proportionality is conceded to be a somewhat vague constraint on sentencing, as some argue it inevitably is, the result might be a more dilute form of negative retributivism, known as "limiting retributivism." According to limiting retributivism, those found guilty are to be assigned "not disproportionate" sentences.[6] In either case, the result is a mixed theory with crime reduction in the lead role, albeit one harnessed to recognizable retributive limits.

In contemplating negative retributivism, it is natural to wonder if the merger between the two elements is stable. Why should we stick to retributive limits or constraints on sentencing if sentences exceeding desert limits would better serve punishment's deterrence or incapacitation aims? Also, why not loosen the constraint on not punishing the innocent a bit by weakening the standard of proof required in criminal cases? Doing so would likely ensure that more actually guilty persons were convicted, with attendant salubrious effects on the reduction of crime.[7] Beyond these concerns about stability, there is the question why crime reduction, rather than deserved punishment, is assigned the lead role in the theory. Is it that giving offenders what they deserve just seems too thin a rationale for such a costly and risky institution?[8] Perhaps, but given the various practical problems we saw in Chapter 1 with punishment's crime-reduction tendencies, we should have doubts about whether it constitutes a more substantial justifying aim for the institution. In any case, we might reasonably want to see more by way of a positive defense of putting crime reduction in the lead role within a mixed theory. Too often, doing so seems the unexplained or unexamined default option.

Prominent mixed theories have been put forward by John Rawls, H. L. A. Hart, and Andreas (formerly Andrew) von Hirsch.[9] I discussed von Hirsch's mixed theory in the previous chapter. It combines censure and hard treatment, the latter of which von Hirsch sees as explained narrowly in crime reduction terms. I argued that censure crucially depends on the imposition of penal losses or burdens, the magnitude of which should reflect the seriousness of the crimes involved. Von Hirsch's mixed theory struggles to keep censure and hard treatment in line. If crime reduction purposes would be better served by the imposition of sanctions that are disproportionate, as they might be, then their imposition will not express the appropriate amount of censure.

Rawls distinguishes the justification of legal punishment as an institution from the justification of the sentences assigned to those convicted of crimes.[10] The former is the province of legislators and is forward-looking, focused on the reduction of crime. The latter is the province of judges and is backward-looking, focused on the determination of legal guilt or its absence and the punishment merited by the seriousness of the crime or crimes when guilt has been established. One crucial question Rawls' account must address concerns who determines the sentence ranges for the various different types of crimes. If judges do so, according to their notions of what the various crime types deserve by way of punishment, then the crime-reduction purpose of the institution might be frustrated. There is little guarantee that deserved sentence ranges will coincide with optimal crime-reduction sentence ranges. Alternatively, if legislators set the appropriate sentence ranges within which judges are to assign specific offenders their sentences, there might be little sense to be made of offenders receiving the punishment they merit given their crimes.[11] Optimal crime-reduction sentencing ranges might depart substantially from those that reflect the gravity of offenses, where gravity is measured in standard retributive terms by taking harm and culpability into account. It also is not clear why legislators should not be at all concerned with the proportionality of the sentencing ranges they select—with whether such ranges ordinally rank the seriousness of crimes in appropriate ways or downplay or exaggerate their seriousness in ways at odds with considerations of cardinal proportionality. Likewise, sentencing judges might, within proportionate sentence ranges, let us suppose, take into account considerations of crime reduction, such that offenders who are deemed more dangerous would be assigned longer or more burdensome sentences. In these ways, Rawls' account seems unable to reconcile the two elements which he takes to be central to our understanding of legal punishment.

Hart is explicitly pluralist about legal punishment's justification. He takes the justifying aim of the institution as a whole to be the reduction of crime.[12] When it comes to the distribution of punishment in specific cases, however, he cites several independent principles which limit the institution's crime-reduction aims. First, he argues that sanctions should only be imposed on those found guilty of illegal conduct over which they had voluntary control.[13] Second, in assigning sentences to the convicted, we should abide by the "somewhat hazy requirement" that like cases should be punished alike.[14] Third, he maintains that the severity of sanctions should reflect common beliefs about the seriousness of offenses. If there is too wide a divergence between the two, there is the danger that common moral beliefs will be thrown into confusion and that the sanction scheme will incur contempt.[15]

I think it is fair to say that Hart does not spend much time explaining the two aspects of his account. First, why does he claim that the reduction of crime is the general justifying aim of the institution, a point that many retributivists would, at the very least, dispute? Perhaps he simply takes it to be obvious that the scale and expense of the institution could only be adequately justified if it produced some net good consequences, which he interprets narrowly—too narrowly in my view—as the reduction of crime. Second, given the lead role of crime reduction in his account, why should not it, as opposed to the vaguely retributive principles he invokes, guide the distribution of punishment? Perhaps we should strive to treat like cases alike but only if and when doing so comports with the purpose of reducing crime. Or perhaps we should be willing to assign sentences in conflict with common moral beliefs if doing so will clearly advance the common good of reduced crime. After all, legislators and judges, rather than taking common moral beliefs as fixed points, might seek to convince the public to abandon or modify them when doing so would clearly promote reductions in offending. To his credit, Hart concedes that there might be occasions when the need to reduce crime could override the principles of distribution.[16] This suggests that he views those principles as no more than presumptive. However, his discussion of these tensions is exceedingly brief. My view is that the early proponents of mixed theories needed to address them more systematically to show how they might be resolved.

Recently, Matthew Altman has sought to resurrect and defend, at length, a mixed theory that has close affinities with the theories defended by Rawls and Hart.[17] Altman expends considerably more effort than either of his predecessors in motivating and spelling out his mixed theory. Like Rawls and Hart, he argues that legislators, in setting up the institution of legal punishment, should be focused on the reduction of crime, whereas the judiciary, in meting out punishment to those found guilty of offending, should be focused on deserved punishment.[18] While there is something powerfully attractive about this proposed division of labor, my sense is that it cannot simply be stipulated; it must be shown to be defensible. Even with regard to determinations of guilt or its absence by the courts, some have proposed lowering the standard of proof utilized by the courts in criminal cases for some types of offenses or some types of offenders on the grounds that doing so would produce more convictions and thus crime reduction.[19] We might steadfastly resist such proposals, but more difficult challenges await, especially when we turn to sentencing. In some legal jurisdictions, the sentence ranges for crime types are set by legislative bodies. Should their focus, as Altman's mixed theory proposes, be on the reduction of crime? If so, then the judges who determine sentences for offense tokens will have to work with sentencing schemes that might not comport fully or well with their sense of what offenders deserve for their crimes. Similar problems arise if appointed sentencing commissions determine appropriate sentence ranges for the various types of criminal offenses.[20] What would preclude such commissions, forward-looking as at least some of their members might be, from employing crime reduction logic when it comes to setting up sentencing schemes or modifying existing ones? And again, judges might be tempted to employ crime reduction logic when it comes to the sentencing of certain kinds of offenders. While it might be possible to demonstrate that the deployment of crime reduction logic by sentencing judges is entirely inappropriate in these and other cases, this is something that has to be shown, not stipulated. And my sense is that it will be difficult to altogether resist the deployment of crime-reduction logic in sentencing.

An Overview of the Proposed Mixed Theory

How, then, does the account I propose constitute a new and improved mixed theory? It starts with the notion that moral communication ought to be assigned the lead role in the theory. Again, the kind of moral communication account I defend makes sense only against certain background assumptions: That we live in a stable liberal democratic society whose laws and institutions are concerned to champion and secure certain basic moral rights for all its members; that a substantial portion of the criminal law consists of prohibitions on actions that infringe upon or violate what I have termed a "consensus account" of the basic moral rights of persons; that there are established procedures, which are routinely adhered to by officials, by which allegations of lawbreaking are investigated and adjudicated; and that what I have termed a "rights and responsibility" narrative is routinely invoked by public institutions and accepted by most members of society as a normative standard against which to judge the actions of public officials and private citizens. Again, I concede that there is theoretical dissensus about which basic moral rights individuals possess. However, for the purposes of thinking about the criminal law and the institution aimed at enforcing it, I have suggested that we can reasonably rely on a broad consensus according to which respecting and securing basic rights to life, liberty, privacy, and some personal property are largely uncontroversial features of liberal, democratic social orders of otherwise varying kinds. The criminal law gives voice and effect to the notion that there are certain wrongs that are "public" wrongs, ones that are proper subjects of state investigation and adjudication.[21] In this way, all members of society are put on notice that there are normative standards against which some portion of their conduct will be assessed and to which they will be held accountable.

Against this backdrop, moral communication with those duly convicted of crimes makes sense. Such communication affirms the aspect of the rights and responsibility narrative that the convicted individual's actions have contravened. In cases in which there are victims of the offender's misconduct, appropriately tailored penal burdens or impositions appropriately "value" the victims' violated interests and thereby stand emphatically for them, thus assuring victims that, at least in this instance, the state has their backs. The punishment of offenders also addresses the broader public, assuring it that the state takes seriously and will enforce rules designed to secure all citizens' basic rights. In cases in which there are no direct victims of the crimes of which individuals have been convicted, the imposition of penal burdens reaffirms the public interest in a set of rules (typically in the form of *mala prohibita*) that all members of society are expected to observe, ones that help to produce a stable and predictable social order.

To say that moral communication is assigned the "lead role" in this account entails not only that sentencing ought to be shaped and guided by it, but also that the procedures according to which crimes are detected, investigated, charged, and adjudicated must be carefully designed and administered to ensure that the state's moral communications are, so far as reasonably possible, fair and accurate. Such fairness and accuracy will be the by-products of criminal procedures designed to assiduously "get at the truth" regarding what individuals who fall under the purview of the criminal justice system have or have not done by way of committing criminal offenses. I will have more to say about all of this in Chapter 5. The important take away at this juncture is that the state cannot reasonably claim the authority to morally communicate with offenders, victims, and the public if its officials have not performed careful and impartial investigations of apparent or alleged crimes and seen to it that those accused of crimes have enjoyed full and fair due process. To be blunt, many existing legal orders are deficient in one or more of these respects, thus undermining their authority to morally communicate. Further, only if the penal burdens designed to give effect to such moral communication are calibrated to reflect the seriousness of the crimes of which individuals have been duly convicted will such communication be accurate and warranted.

As I have noted, criminal sanctions that reflect the seriousness of the offenses of which individuals have been convicted, and thus communicate censure to them and moral support to their victims, will also serve to reduce crime. The penal burdens employed to morally communicate will be almost always be unattractive, both in prospect and once directly experienced by individuals. Most members of society will want to avoid them, although many, as we have seen, will have little need of them to keep them from committing crimes, and especially serious crimes. However, some members of society will, for a variety of reasons, be less morally averse to engaging in criminal misconduct. For at least some of them, sanctions will, in addition to morally communicating, provide a "prudential back-up," in the sense that they will supply self-interested reasons to refrain from offending or not repeat it. Of course, more than a few of those who are insufficiently moved by moral considerations to desist from crime will likewise be insufficiently moved by prudential incentives to do so. If and when their crimes are serious enough, sanctions shaped by crime seriousness might incapacitate them for some period of time, by assigning them to terms in state custody. Imprisonment is not a foolproof incapacitation measure, as even jail or prison inmates can commit crimes while in custody. But imprisonment does remove persons from civil society and thus substantially limit the abilities of persons to commit crimes. Further, if we imagine those convicted of crimes assigned to rehabilitation programs—either as conditions of avoiding other or worse sanctions or requirements of their terms in custody—then appropriately morally communicative sanctions might play some role in reducing crime by shoring up (or eliminating obstacles to the effective exercise of) offenders' responsiveness to the moral or prudential considerations that counsel against offending.

Again, although penal sanctions that reflect crime seriousness will have more or less inevitable crime reduction effects, it clearly does not follow that such effects will be optimal, assuming that we can give some precise meaning to what "optimal" effects would come to. That some tension exists between accurate morally communicative sanctions and optimal crime reducing sanctions is something that I will simply concede, at least for the time being. My position on this tension, given the mixed theory I am proposing, is clear: Moral communication has priority over the reduction of crime, at least presumptively. In other words, if we must choose between moral communication and crime reduction in the design and administration of penal sanctions, we should give the former precedence over the latter, in most cases. The same priority will hold for the design and operations of criminal procedure. I will admit some exceptions to the priority of moral communication—more on that subsequently. But even such exceptions should be subject to strict conditions and we should avoid the temptation to think that there are not real dilemmas posed by such exceptional cases, ones that make them unfortunate, if not tragic.

Before turning to the kinds of conditions that must be satisfied, on my account, for crime reduction to override moral communication, let me first explain why the latter should have the presumptive "driver's seat" in our thinking about legal punishment. The account of this priority that I propose rests on the underlying logic of legal punishment and the superior coherence a moral communication approach has with that logic as compared with a crime reduction approach. By the "logic" of legal punishment, I refer to its oft-noted character as a "blaming institution," one that implicitly if not explicitly casts convicted offenders as morally at fault for their refusals to abide by the strictures of the criminal law.[22] Take the *mala in se* provisions of the criminal law. On my account, those provisions are aimed at shielding citizens from wrongful invasions of their basic moral rights. Adult members of society are presumed to be capable of both understanding their responsibilities under the criminal law and conforming their conduct to them. When individuals are found guilty of violating *mala in se* provisions of the law, they are appropriately seen as blameworthy for their acts—they refused to abide by provisions of the law that they had sufficient moral reasons to obey, ones to which they are presumed responsive. Of course, establishing both that individuals have violated provisions of the criminal law and were responsible for doing so are the province of criminal procedure. But on the assumption that both have been proved according to exacting standards (beyond a reasonable doubt in most jurisdictions), the convicted are judged to be "at fault," that is, deficient in their observance of norms of responsible conduct.

To be clear, the norms in question are moral, not prudential ones. We might regard offenders as having acted imprudently by committing crimes—as having taken risks of detection, arrest, and conviction, or as having risked being killed or injured by those they attacked or by the police who come upon them at the scene of their crimes or afterwards as they try to arrest them—but we do not punish them for such failures to act in their own interests. We punish them for their "public wrongs," that is, for their moral failures to abide by rules of conduct that are of sufficient importance as to appropriately receive the state's backing. Obviously, this account makes the most sense in relation to traditional *mala in se* offenses. But it also applies to *mala prohibita*, provisions of the criminal law in accordance with which all persons in society must abide if we are to have stable and predictable social orders in which individuals can live their lives and pursue their chosen interests.

It should be apparent how the moral communication approach to justifying state punishment is directly tied to this understanding of crimes as public wrongs the commission of which renders individuals liable to official opprobrium. Of course, the kind and extent of official censure to which legal wrongdoers should be subjected depends on the seriousness of their infractions, as the moral communication approach also makes clear. Many of the offenders who cycle through contemporary criminal justice systems are convicted of relatively minor offenses. Mild criminal sanctions will effectively communicate with them (and their victims, if there are any), reminding the former of their responsibilities to abide by reasonable limits on their conduct, or of requirements to do their part by way of minimizing risk or supporting public institutions. Yet even less serious criminal infractions are breaches of the public moral order, ones for which individuals ought to be held accountable. The moral communication approach to justifying punishment thus squares comfortably with both the logic of legal punishment as a blaming institution and the variable degrees to which such blame should be assigned to individuals.

Incidentally, there is nothing about the claim that legal punishment is premised on a conception of persons as responsive to moral considerations and required in certain respects to govern their conduct by them that requires us to tie those considerations to any particular moral theory. Despite the affinities between moral communication approaches and more Kantian versions of moral theory, utilitarians could readily embrace the proposition that legal punishment is a blaming institution. Utilitarians will simply cast the moral requirements of the various provisions of the criminal law in terms of their utility-maximizing function.[23] As such, those who violate such provisions fail to act in ways that we have good reason to believe will produce the most good and least bad consequences, the interests of all persons taken impartially into account.

The disconnect between utilitarianism as a moral theory and legal punishment as a blaming institution crops ups when we turn to the utilitarian insistence that the purpose of the institution, and indeed the only defensible purpose of it, is to reduce crime. In particular, claims that we punish in order to deter crime, or to incapacitate offenders, seem to rest uneasily with an understanding of legal punishment as an institution that holds individuals accountable for their moral failures to abide by reasonable constraints on their conduct.[24] We should, it would seem, communicate with offenders first and foremost along moral lines, keeping things like prudential threats and outright restraint in the background. Also, neither deterrence nor incapacitation is as tightly focused on meting out quantities or kinds of blame, through punishment, that are keyed to the magnitude of the public wrongs offenders have committed. Notoriously, deterrence and incapacitation might support sanctions that are either too onerous or not onerous enough to blame offenders appropriately. Indeed, the crime reduction approach seems oddly indifferent to the character of legal punishment as a blaming institution. However, I will have more to say about this in a later section.

In response to this, it might be claimed that we have good reasons to doubt the capacities for moral responsibility of those who have been convicted of criminal offending. They presumably had cogent if not weighty moral reasons against doing what they did and yet chose to ignore them. Also, there will be others in the general population who are similar to such morally unreliable offenders but who have not yet committed or been convicted of crimes. Perhaps it makes sense to provide these kinds of individuals with prudential incentives to refrain from offending. Further, some individuals will engage in repeat offending, sometimes violent repeat offending. Not only will such individuals seem deficiently responsive to the moral considerations against what they do, they might not seem very responsive to the prudential incentives to avoid offending that are, on my account, attendant to censure. For such individuals, restraint might seem to be in order. And while we have such offenders under our control, so to speak, it might make sense to try to reduce their offending proclivities by offering them forms of rehabilitation designed to strengthen their responsiveness to moral and prudential considerations.

The preceding points are all cogent, but they do not show that the individuals threatened with, restrained, or rehabilitated by punishment are unresponsive to moral considerations, at least up to some level of sufficiency. Indeed, if they did show that, we would have to question whether such individuals were appropriately liable to legal punishment for their actions. The criminal law exempts infants, young children, the mentally disabled, and the insane from legal punishment precisely because they do not satisfy the minimum moral reasons responsiveness conditions of punishment.[25] Also, a case can be made that the criminal law should exempt psychopaths from legal punishment, if they are as constitutionally amoral as some believe them to be.[26] All of this makes sense against a backdrop according to which legal punishment is an institution that holds individuals morally responsible for their conduct and censures them appropriately when they fail to abide by the reasonable constraints of the criminal law. It is the moral communication account of legal punishment that builds on and gives expression to this view about individuals living in organized societies, especially ones committed to respecting and securing the basic rights of all of their members. In doing so, it cements its rightful status as the lead purpose in justifying the institution of legal punishment. Saying this is consistent with admitting and welcoming the crime reduction role that legal sanctions also perform. But that role should remain subordinate to a morally communicative one within an account of legal punishment as a blaming institution.

It might be objected that a thinner account of legal punishment as a blaming institution is available, one that is more congenial to the logic of the crime reduction approach. Hart can be seen as giving voice to this account when he notes that individuals are only appropriately liable to legal punishment if two conditions are met. First, they must be shown, in a court of law, to have violated one of more provisions of the criminal law. Second, it must be shown that they did so voluntarily.[27] Hart takes this condition to rule out the legal punishment of infants, the insane, the mentally disabled, and those who, while fully competent adults, have some excuse or justification for having violated the law. To Hart's account, we might add a third condition, one to the effect that individuals are not appropriately punished for their voluntary criminal acts if they lack advance warning of the illegality of their conduct. We should interpret that condition modestly, as one that will be satisfied so long as the various provisions of the criminal law are made public.[28]

If all three of the preceding conditions are satisfied, it can be plausibly argued that individuals who violate the criminal law are appropriately liable to legal punishment. There might even be a dilute sense in which they can be plausibly regarded as "blameworthy" for their misconduct. After all, they had advance warning of what would befall them if they violated the relevant provisions, were (let us assume) shown to have done so, and to have acted voluntarily in doing so. They were competent adults who were not ignorant of the circumstances, under duress, or acting in response to some form of deadly threat. Moreover, even if they were not very responsive to moral considerations, or wholly unresponsive to them, we might hold them accountable for their failures to abide by the announced rules of conduct. Presumably they could understand the threat that failure to abide by the relevant provisions exposed them to and yet went ahead anyway with their crimes. In this way, they are at least beings who can meaningfully be subject to deterrent threats and held to account when they fail to conform their conduct to them.

The problem with this alternative account of the conditions under which persons might be justifiably blamed for their misconduct is that it will not allow us to distinguish the blame to which persons are appropriately liable when they violate defensible provisions of the criminal law from the "blame" to which they are liable to if they ignore the deterrent threats of hoodlums or tyrants. Hoodlums and tyrants might provide those whose conduct they wish to influence advance warning of the "rules" with which they expect those subject to their threats to abide. They might also make allowances for infants, the insane, or mentally disabled, not really expecting or requiring them to do as they are ordered. Yet few of us would be inclined to blame those competent adults who refused to comply with the threats of hoodlums or tyrants, except maybe in the sense of questioning their refusals to act in their own self-interest. Surely, we would not think of those who refused to comply as being morally blameworthy, unless by doing so they put others, besides themselves, at risk. If anyone is to blame in these scenarios, it is the hoodlums and tyrants making the threats to gain the compliance of others. What distinguishes the criminal law in liberal democratic societies from the orders backed by threats of hoodlums and tyrants is that the law's various provisions are aimed at affirming and securing the basic rights of all persons. And the members of such societies are deemed to be bound by the criminal law not simply in the sense that failures to do so will result in bad things predictably happening to them, but because they have moral obligations to comply with it. Those obligations often require that citizens refrain from certain kinds of conduct out of respect for the equal worth of other members of society. Their failures to comply are moral ones for which we are appropriately censured and thereby held accountable.

Again, that institutions or practices sometimes serve dual or even multiple purposes, but with one of them having priority, is not unusual. Consider the practice of instructors grading academic assignments. In performing this important task, instructors should presumably accord the most weight to merit, which in this context has to do with how fully a student's work on an exam, paper, or project meets the relevant standards of excellence in the field. Experienced instructors will know not only that student assignments vary in quality but they will also be adept at distinguishing the highest quality work from lower quality work. Instructors will also recognize that highly motivated students might respond to mediocre to poor grades with more effort. Indeed, instructors might very much hope that they will do so. However, in most cases, the grades they assign should not be based on eliciting such efforts, or else instructors might be tempted to grade down excellent or good work if they believe that a motivated student could do even better work. Granted, there might be cases in which the quality of an assignment is a "close call," as, for instance, between an A- and a B+. If it is early in the term, with other assignments still to come, an instructor might reasonably decide to assign the lower (not undeserved) grade, simply to motivate the student to do a bit better on the next assignment. However, it would seem inappropriate for the instructor to assign the student a substantially lower grade, in order to motivate him or her to do better. The "merit constraint," as we might call it, retains its lead and guiding role, even in the determination of grades in "close call" kinds of cases.

To come closer to the present subject, consider the punishment (or we might prefer, the "disciplining") of young children by parents. Suppose that a young child has, in a moment of frustration, either damaged the toy of a sibling or struck the sibling. The parent who witnesses or hears of this misconduct might respond to it in various ways. She might give the misbehaving child a "time out" in her room, along with a verbal reprimand which aims at conveying to the child why her conduct is unacceptable. Alternatively, the parent might combine the reprimand with the temporary denial of some form of play that she knows the child values, as a way of vividly making the point that the child's behavior is unacceptable. Both the "time out" and the withheld play activity are mild forms of loss or imposition. They might be viewed simply as deterrents, as ways of warning the errant child against further misbehavior. But they also can be plausibly viewed as forms or moral communication, efforts to capture and hold the child's attention and to impress upon her the importance of the conduct norm that she has flouted. A good parent, I would say, should aim at morally educating her child, more than at threatening the child. Yet even a good parent presumably recognizes and accepts that the burdens she imposes to emphatically make her point might also function as deterrents to future misbehavior. The imposed losses thus might be said "to kill two birds with one stone." Still, such losses or impositions ought to reflect the gravity of the misbehavior. A good parent should not be tempted to "go big" with imposed losses to enhance their deterrent effect if doing so distorts the magnitude of the wrong the child committed.

Granted, adults who defy the criminal law are presumed to be unlike children who are, after all, moral works in progress. Also, the state, although a representative of the citizens of liberal, democratic societies, is not like a parent to its wayward members. Nonetheless, penal losses or impositions can, I have argued, constitute effective forms of moral communication, especially if, among other things, they are structured to reflect the gravity of the crimes of which persons have been convicted. Adults convicted of crimes presumably do not need to have their wrongs explained to them in the ways that children might. But they can be usefully reminded, in emphatic ways, of the appropriate limits of their conduct, ones that are grounded in a conception of all members of society as equals entitled to have and live their own lives. Offenders might ignore or dismiss the morally communicative aspects of official censure, as these are expressed through penal loss or imposition. However, they might find the experience of arrest, charge adjudication, conviction, and sanctioning unpleasant enough to convince them to refrain from future misconduct. Unfortunately, as we have seen, many offenders do not respond to punishment's prudential incentives much better than to its morally communication. Again, the evidence concerning harsh legal punishment's marginal deterrence effects is, to say the least, unimpressive.[29] Other members of society might respond to one or both. If so, so much the better. Legal punishment's deterrent (or incapacitation) effects will often supplement its morally communicative effects, even if the former should generally not be allowed to displace or override the latter.

My willingness to admit that where moral communication does not work to dissuade offenders or would-be offenders from committing crimes punishment's deterrent or incapacitation effects should be welcomed might make it seem as if I am implicitly acknowledging that the aim of legal punishment is, ultimately, to reduce future crime. I would admit that it is desirable that legal punishment works to reduce offending, either through moral communication or through its various crime reduction modes. Again, however, it does not follow that reducing future crime is legal punishment's only purpose. What saying so would leave out is how legal punishment morally communicates not only with offenders but also with their victims. It tells victims that the state backs their vital interests, that it will not stand idly by when those interests are attacked but will instead act vigorously to investigate crimes, arrest suspects, charge them, convict them, and impose penal burdens on them that reflect the seriousness of the crimes committed. The assurance to victims that the state takes transgressions against them seriously does not seem equivalent with, or reducible to, the reduction of future crime. Victims might reasonably want those who have violated their basic rights brought to justice whether doing so will prevent future crime or not, and the more so the more serious the harms those violations inflicted. Further, legal punishment communicates with the public, emphatically affirming the rights and responsibility narrative, and thus educating and reminding the public of its importance in a liberal democratic society. It thereby symbolically stands for the fundamental values of the polity in ways that, once again, do not seem reducible to whatever crime reduction effects doing so may or may not produce.[30]

Managing the Tensions

This bring us to the question whether the priority of moral communication in my account is absolute, holding no matter how much departing from it might reduce crime in some general way or in specific cases. Or is the priority presumptive, yielding, at times or in limited ways, to crime reduction purposes, and, if so, under what conditions? My view is that the priority is presumptive, both in general and in specific cases. I also contend that this priority should be delimited by carefully specifying the conditions under which it can be justifiably overridden. Although there might be circumstances in which accurate moral communication ought to yield to the reduction of crime, we should approach permitting it to do so cautiously.

Generally speaking, we should keep moral communication in the lead role in our penal practices unless three conditions are satisfied. First, we should insist that any crime reduction gains to be achieved by sacrificing accurate moral communication with an offender should be substantial, not just in terms of the number of crimes to be prevented but, more importantly, in terms of their seriousness. This means that we should eschew a simple maximizing approach to trading off accurate moral communication for the prevention of crimes. For instance, we should resist trading off accurate moral communication with an offender who committed a serious crime in order to prevent a number of petty offenses. As I have emphasized, serious crimes are often significantly life-altering and we especially look to state authorities to arrest, convict, and censure those who commit them. The punishment of minor offenses does not matter in this way, even the punishment of lots of them. Still, if by sacrificing accurate moral communication with a serious offender we might prevent several serious crimes, or numerous moderately serious ones, that is something to consider. Again, however, we should always approach such possible or proposed trade-offs cautiously.

Second, we should insist on something like a "necessity," or perhaps "near necessity" condition for setting aside the presumption in favor of accurate moral communication. In any given set of circumstances, there might exist ways in which to reduce crime without sacrificing accurate moral communication. If so, those alternative means ought to be preferred. Of course, practically speaking, there will be cases in which it will be difficult to determine if such alternative means exist or what their toll will be on available public resources. The point here is simply that we should be reluctant to treat the sacrifice of accurate moral communication as a readily available shortcut, especially if doing so would distort the character of more serious crimes. We should instead encourage state officials to search for ways to avoid making such sacrifices.

Third, we should require criminal justice officials to demonstrate, preferably at public hearings with specified rules and procedures, that the crime reduction gains they seek by sacrificing accurate moral communication are substantial and likely unavailable otherwise.[31] At the very least, such sacrifices should not be made by officials acting entirely at their own, unchecked discretion. In this way, a broad and serious institutional commitment to accurate moral communication will be sustained and publicly demonstrated.

To illustrate the practical implications of the preceding conditions, let us consider some cases in which tensions appear to exist between moral communication and the reduction of crime. Broadly speaking, punishment's moral communicative and crime reduction purposes might conflict in either the area of criminal procedure or in sentencing. With sentencing, there is the distinction between the assignment of sentence ranges to the various crime types, which will typically be the purview of legislators or special sentencing commissions, and the assignment of sentences in specific cases, which will typically be carried out by criminal court judges. One apparent conflict that has been discussed in the literature involves the proposed extension of confinement for offenders who, having fully served their sentences for their most recent offenses of conviction, appear to be so dangerous that continuing to confine them for some substantially longer period of time seems advisable.[32] Such cases are typically referred to as ones involving the prospect of "preventive detention," where such detention, at least in theory, would be of some nonpunitive kind. The fact that those who support such detention desire to make it "nonpunitive" shows the unease with which they view it.[33] After all, we should assume that appropriate moral communication has been conducted with these offenders for their most recent crimes, in the form of their already assigned and served sentences. Yet their alleged dangerousness raises the prospect of incapacitating them further, to protect the public.

Those who urge us to take such preventive detention seriously make clear that its justifiability depends on a number of conditions.[34] There would have to be a formal hearing at which the state would be required to make a strong case for it. Presumably, the state would have to provide convincing evidence of the almost inevitable dangers posed by a candidate for preventive detention and show that no other reasonable means exist to free the individual from further detention and protect the public from the dangers he or she poses.[35] Such a procedural requirement seems necessary in order to acknowledge and justify the unusual character of the state's move to detain those who have already completed their sentences. Also, the candidates for preventive detention should be permitted not only to attend these hearings, they should be allowed (through their attorneys, perhaps) to offer evidence and arguments in opposition to their further detention. Further, any warranted further detention should not be indefinite. The state should have to renew its requests for preventive detention on a regular basis, each time demonstrating that it is warranted and something of a last resort.[36] Whatever one ultimately thinks about the defensibility of such preventive detention, the proposed resolution of the tension such cases expose between moral communication and prevention seems to me of the right sort if we are to regard moral communication as having the lead role in a mixed theory of punishment.

A similar kind of tension is seen in cases in which judges might be tempted to assign a convicted offender a sentence that is above the statutory or guidelines sentencing range for the type of offense in question.[37] There might be instances in which sentencing judges encounter individuals convicted of crimes who appear to be especially worrisome. Their crimes of conviction might have had unusually disturbing features, ones suggesting that the offenders are much more dangerous than the typical individuals sentenced for the relevant type of offense. Alternatively, the crimes of conviction might have simply been the most recent in what amounts to a long history of criminal convictions, ones which seem to be becoming increasingly more serious. Granted, judges should assign such offenders an appropriately communicative sentence given their most recent crimes of conviction, but judges might, at the same time, reasonably believe that upwards departures from the standard sentencing ranges are warranted on crime reduction grounds.

Again, I concede that we might want to allow crime-reduction considerations to override moral communication in rare cases such as these, but we should, at the very least, subject the judicial discretion to do so to some oversight. For instance, we could make such upward departures automatically subject to appellate review, with the burden being placed on sentencing judges to justify them. Given that judges in such cases could have simply assigned sentences at or near the tops of the relevant sentencing ranges, we might reasonably require judges to show that exceeding the ranges is both justified, given the characteristics of offenders or their crimes, and that no other means exist (e.g., the possibility of specially designed rehabilitation programs) to reduce the risks such offenders seem to pose. To be clear, it should not suffice for sentencing judges simply to argue that such offenders appear to be riskier than other offenders of the relevant kinds, for their greater riskiness could be contained by assigning them sentences higher in the relevant ranges. Judges in such cases should, instead, bear the burden of showing that the offenders in question pose something like "extraordinary" risks that cannot otherwise be managed. If they cannot meet this burden, then the priority of accurate moral communication in our punishment practices should prevail.

Another kind of case that appears to pose conflicts between the moral communication and crime reduction aims of legal punishment involves the plea deals prosecutors might be tempted to extend to criminal defendants in certain kinds of cases. In some instances, those charged with serious crimes might offer to provide the state with compelling evidence about other serious crimes that the state will otherwise encounter significant difficulties in prosecuting.[38] For instance, an underling in a criminal organization might agree to provide information that is likely to produce convictions of those higher up in the organization, individuals who are often insulated from criminal investigations and convictions. If the past crimes that might be successfully prosecuted or the future crimes that might thereby be averted are grave, the benefits afforded by such plea deals with cooperators will be tempting to prosecutors. Yet the plea deals might be plausibly cast as distorting, and thus falsely communicating about, the crimes of the cooperators, typically by making them appear less serious than were. How, then, to manage the tension between moral communication and crime reduction that seems to exist in such cases?

Again, the solution would seem to lie in constraining the authority of prosecutors to make such plea deals. In the United States, prosecutorial authority to engage in plea bargaining is largely unfettered.[39] This means that the public often has little assurance that plea deals with cooperators in these kinds of cases are appropriately conducted, so as to not wholly whitewash the crimes of those supplying vital evidence to the state. Also, there are few constraints on prosecutors extending such plea offers to cooperators in less urgent kinds of cases, or in cases in which more investigative efforts by the authorities would produce the evidence needed for convictions independently of the plea deals. I would urge more judicial oversight of these kinds of plea deals, both to ensure that the authorities are not making them when other means exist to prevent future crimes and to keep plea deals from distorting, too significantly, the crimes committed by those who agree to cooperate.[40] Granted, when the future crimes that might be averted by such plea deals are serious, and the prospects of preventing them are otherwise dim, we might have to accept them. But the authority of prosecutors to enter into them should be subject to appropriate checks and balances, ones that might be supplied by judicial oversight.

Importantly, the kinds of plea deals just described need not be seen as illustrating any tension between legal punishment's moral communication and crime reduction functions. Instead, they might be cast as involving choices between gaining more, or less, moral communication by the state about crimes that have already been committed. If officials offer plea deals to cooperators whose testimony or other tips produce numerous further convictions, ones that might not otherwise be available given the limitations on the evidence that the state is able to gather, then the result will be moral communication with more of the individuals who have committed crimes. And that will be true whether or not the convictions of such individuals prevent future crimes, although one might reasonably assume that it will. This way of looking at things raises the question, once again, whether moral communication is the kind of good that we should seek to maximize, or at least produce more rather than less of.

It seems clear that we should want the authorities to catch and convict more offenders rather than fewer of them, other things beings equal, since by doing so it will back the interests of more rather fewer victims of crimes (where there are victims). However, a simple maximizing approach to doing so might countenance efforts to resolve more minor criminal offenses, which are generally easier to arrest and convict people of, at the expense of resolving serious crimes, which generally require more investment of scarce societal resources. By that logic, the authorities would maximize moral communication by capturing and convicting lots of minor offenders, more serious ones be damned. Again, however, serious crimes not only destroy or significantly alter victims' lives, their occurrence flouts in more elemental ways the values around which liberal democratic societies structure their institutions and practices. Society arguably owes the victims of such crimes more by way of efforts to capture, convict, and censure those who wronged them, even if this comes at the cost of leaving more minor crimes unresolved.

Also, plea deals that significantly distort the public wrongs committed by those who cooperate with the authorities might be so deficient in the censure they communicate that the victims of such crimes will struggle to see how the state has stood by them. Should we attempt to convince the victims that they ought to be satisfied with the outcomes in their cases because other victims will, as a result, have the wrongs done to them more fully censured? Perhaps, although I suspect that it makes more sense to view the compromises we might feel compelled to make in such cases with some regret. One option would be to refuse to allow the cooperator to plead to charges that are significantly less serious than the ones of which he seems guilty. We could then "purchase" his cooperation by assigning him a sentence that was either very low in the relevant range, or even somewhat below that range. At the very least, proceeding in this way would accurately signal the gravity of his crimes to the victim and public, albeit while communicating something different in his sentencing. Perhaps such a mixed approach would make it easier to convince the victim or victims of his crimes that his wrongs were not being whitewashed by his cooperation with state authorities

Skeptics of the hybrid approach I am proposing might argue that there will be significantly more tensions between the two elements than the preceding examples suggest. In particular, it might seem plausible to believe that longer or harsher sentences will better deter crimes, or incapacitate offenders, in lots of cases, even if such sentences thereby distort the seriousness of the crimes committed by overcensuring them. In other cases, sentences that insufficiently convey appropriate censure might be deemed sufficient for deterrence or incapacitation purposes. In response to these conjectures, some of which I address more fully in Chapter 6, I would say two things. First, opponents of a hybrid approach such as mine should be expected to show, in more detail, that such tensions are plausible. In particular, claims that longer or harsher sentences will deter better than shorter or less harsh ones that accurately censure should be subjected to close scrutiny. As we have seen, the empirical evidence for the deterrent properties of harsher punishment is weak. Also, the costs and negative consequences of such punishment must be factored into the analysis. With incapacitation claims, the costs and negative consequences—the former in the form of wasted expenditures of public resources since many offenders age out, the latter in the form of harsh punishment's tendency to produce recidivism—must likewise be fully accounted for before allegations of conflict with punishment's moral communication aims can be convincingly shown.

Second, as I will detail in Chapter 6, we should be rather less confident than many proponents of the crime reduction approach appear to be that it can be made to yield determinate sentence ranges for the full range of criminal offenses. The information we would need to determine optimal crime reductive sentence ranges for the different kinds of criminal offenses is probably not available. The processing capacities that would be required to weigh and balance that empirical information in systematic fashion are likely not available either. The vagueness of proportionality as a guide to sentencing is a recurring theme among its critics, and even among some of its supporters. My contention will be that the prospects of devising an optimal crime reduction sentencing scheme are equally if not more dim. Tensions between the two approaches that amount to anything more than vague conjecture might be difficult to demonstrate, which is not to say that they never exist. If and when they do, my position is clear: Presumptively, sentences should be keyed to crime seriousness, not optimal crime reduction. Again, from the former some of the latter will inevitably follow.

Crime Reduction and Moral Communication

Earlier in the chapter, I noted the ways in which the crime reduction approach to punishment's justification seems to rely more on threats, restraint, and efforts to modify offenders' criminogenic tendencies than on morally communicating with them. I pointed to the ways in which these modes of addressing offenders seem at odds with the blaming aspect of legal punishment, according to which those convicted of violating the criminal law are thought to be deficient in their adherence to moral considerations that should govern their (and everyone's) conduct in liberal democratic societies that place a premium on respect for the basic rights of all persons. I argued that the ground for giving the moral communication priority over crime reduction was precisely that the former more fully embodies a conception of members of society as morally responsible creatures who are obliged to refrain from wrongs of various kinds. Their failures to refrain from such wrongs makes them eligible for censure expressed through the imposition of penal burdens. Offenders or potential offenders are not, in other words, beings who are simply to be threatened or restrained by legal punishment.

That being said, there is a strand of crime reduction thinking about legal punishment that I ignored in the earlier section's analysis. It is a strand according to which one of the ways in which legal punishment reduces crime, in the aggregate, so to speak, is by reinforcing moral norms against offending.[41] When the public witnesses what happens to those caught and convicted of crimes, not only might its members be deterred from committing crimes themselves, they will also see what I have termed the "rights and responsibility narrative" implicitly (if not explicitly) affirmed. Most citizens have been taught by family members, schools, churches, and civic organizations that certain kinds of behavior are not only legally prohibited, but wrongful and to be avoided for that reason. As we saw in Chapter 1, these lessons are important ones, as the internalization of norms against seriously wrongful conduct will presumably reduce it in ways that are much less costly and damaging than employing penal measures to do so. Those never tempted to commit crimes, or those who resist such temptations for moral reasons, do not have to be arrested, investigated, prosecuted, or punished. Although the operations of the criminal justice system might play only a modest role in teaching young members of society such moral norms, they will remind all of us of such norms and thereby reinforce them. Moral communication, of a sort, can thus be cast as one of the modes of crime reduction, albeit one that is aimed more at the law-abiding public than at those convicted and punished for crimes. The latter kinds of individuals, it might seem, have already shown themselves to be deficient in their internalization of the relevant norms, or at least unreliable about heeding them. Resort to other measures to reduce their offending thus seems to be the dominant mode of responding to them, on the crime reduction account.

Nonetheless, we should consider whether the crime reduction approach could be modified so as to give moral communication with offenders, and also with victims, a more significant role. Initially, at least, the prospects of doing so might not seem promising. The sentence ranges for the various offense types, within which the tokens committed by individuals are to be sentenced, should, on crime reduction logic, be determined by some combination of deterrent, incapacitation, and rehabilitation factors. The goal, on such an approach, will be to find sentence ranges that optimally reduce crime, taking into account the costs and negative effects of the various candidate sentence ranges. Standard concerns that optimal crime reductive sentence ranges might not match up well with ones that accurately censure offenses according to their seriousness would quickly emerge, or so it would seem. Likewise, the sentences assigned to individual offenders might not censure them correctly if crime reduction considerations suggest otherwise. Also, crime victims' losses and injuries might by symbolically downplayed by optimal crime reduction sentences, or, alternatively, exaggerated by them. In these familiar ways, crime reduction logic seems in tension with accurate moral communication between the state, the individuals convicted of crimes, and the victims of those crimes.

However, there might be another way for crime reductionists to approach this, one that, at least initially, seems to reflect some closer affinity between the reduction of crime and moral communication. It might be suggested that sentences for offenses that were too out of line with a morally communicative account of crime seriousness would undermine punishment's moral reinforcement effects.[42] If the public perceived optimal crime reduction sentences to be either too harsh or too lenient, then such sentences would not align with its internalized norms regarding crimes and their relative or absolute seriousness. For instance, if crime reduction considerations supported relatively brief terms of imprisonment for serious crimes like homicide, as Andreas (formerly Andrew) von Hirsch at one point suggested they might, such sentences might conflict with the public's belief that homicide is a very serious crime, one meriting rather more lengthy terms of imprisonment.[43] The dissonance this could create might undermine the legitimacy of the criminal justice system in ways that would be worrisome. If the public became disenchanted with what it perceived to be inappropriate sentences for a range of offenses, its members might be less inclined to report crimes or cooperate with the authorities. Or they might be tempted to take matters into their own hands, so to speak, in the form of vigilante action aimed at "properly" addressing serious crimes. Thus, it might seem that there is room within the crime reduction approach to accord some weight to accurate moral communication to maintain the fit between sentencing and the public's internalized norms about crimes and their relative or absolute seriousness.

However, I believe that this apparent reconciliation between moral communication and crime reduction is unlikely to be stable. For one thing, there is no guarantee that the public's internalized norms with respect to wrongdoing will support all and only penal responses to it that are appropriately morally communicative. The public's norms with respect to offending and the appropriate responses to it could call for harsh punishment of relatively minor offenders, lenient punishment for some relatively serious ones, or any number of things in-between. There is no guarantee, in other words, that the public's preexisting views about such matters will match up, in any very reliable way, with a more thoughtful and theoretically well-grounded approach to crime seriousness. Yet it is presumably such an approach to sentencing that moral communication theorists, and perhaps all of us, would endorse. Second, even if the public's norms were consistent with appropriately censuring sentences, or sentence ranges, crime reductionists would be loath to accord those norms much weight if it turned out that sentences at odds with them could be shown to have more optimal crime reduction tendencies. Committed crime reductionists would and should look for ways to move the public away from its suboptimal (from a crime reduction perspective) perceptions of appropriate sentences for some or all of the various crime types. How they might do so without causing too much resistance to or resentment of their efforts is a difficult question to answer, but it does seem like proponents of the approach should push in that direction.

What this shows, I believe, is that it will be difficult to reconcile an emphasis on crime reduction with the priority my mixed theory accords to moral communication with offenders, victims, and the public, communication that aims to characterize appropriately the seriousness of the crimes for which individuals are being sentenced. The root of the problem, not surprisingly, is that crime reduction logic treats such appropriate communication as only a contingent good, one to be supported only insofar as it yields punishment practices that optimally reduce crime.

Clarifying the Role of Crime Reduction

To some it will seem that I have pushed the crime reduction role of legal punishment too much to the margins. I have embraced its role insofar as I admit that some deterrence, incapacitation, and moral reinforcement will likely follow from the use of sanctions that morally communicate in ways that track the seriousness of crimes. Also, although I am not convinced that we punish offenders in order to rehabilitate them, I embrace the notion that while we are sanctioning their crimes with imposed burdens of various kinds, it makes sense to try to strengthen their responsiveness to both moral and prudential considerations, perhaps by offering them access to programs aimed at reducing the criminogenic factors in their lives. But I have made clear that crime reduction takes a back seat to censure and that its doing so entails that our primary focus in sentencing will not be on maximizing the reduction of crime. To some, it will seem that I treat the reduction of crime as a bit of an afterthought.

I have already hinted at one way in which I would concede more of a role for crime reduction in sentencing. At most, we might be able to identify sentence ranges for the various different crime types, ones that roughly track their severity. I will have more to say about this in Chapter 6. However, assuming that we can do that much, the judges who assign sentences in specific cases will have some discretion in determining where within the relevant ranges they should peg an offender's sentence. I concede that crime reduction considerations could play some legitimate role in the thinking of judges as they determine sentences in specific cases.[44] For instance, sentencing judges will often confront individuals who have previous convictions, ones who have apparently not taken to heart either the moral or prudential lessons from their previous convictions. Encountering such offenders, judges might be tempted to assign them sentences somewhat higher in the relevant ranges than the ones they would assign first-time offenders, and this for two identifiable reasons: First, judges might reasonably believe that repeat offenders need to be sent firmer messages about their continued offending. Of course, part of the reason for doing so might be to send a more emphatic moral message that such continued misconduct is unacceptable. Yet given that repeat offenders already seem disinclined to accept or act on such moral messages, judges might hope that a more burdensome sentence will, at the very least, speak to such offenders' self-interest in avoiding further crimes and the increasingly longer sentences that will go with convictions of them. Still, sentencing judges must be alive to the possibility that longer sentences might backfire with respect to crime reduction. As we saw in Chapter 1, there is some reason to believe that more time spent in jails or prisons, for instance, has corrosive effects on the willingness of individuals to refrain from further offending.[45] Nonetheless, within sentence ranges that are shaped by considerations of crime seriousness, sentencing judges might reasonably seek more special deterrence effects in some cases.

A second reason why judges might reasonably assign sentences somewhat higher in the relevant ranges for repeat offenders invokes the incapacitation effects of such sentences. Some repeat offenders might have engaged in violent or predatory conduct, and perhaps in ways that indicate worrisome escalations in these tendencies. Faced with assigning sentences for the most recent convictions involving such misconduct, sentencing judges might reasonably seek to remove such offenders from civil society for somewhat longer periods of time by assigning them sentences higher in the relevant ranges. Again, however, we must urge caution here, as longer sentences might make it harder, once individuals have served them, to readjust to civil society. There is also the "aging out" phenomenon that we noted in Chapter 1.[46] Most offenders gradually begin to desist from further crimes in their late twenties or early thirties. Assigning them longer terms in custody might not only harm them, it might produce little by way of crime reduction and do so at considerable public expense. Still, I admit that sentencing judges act reasonably by considering longer incapacitative sentences within relevant sentencing ranges when they encounter repeat offenders. They might also act reasonably in this way if the evidence concerning a first-time offender's crimes indicate significant indifference to the lives or well-being of other citizens.

To this point, I have focused primarily on *mala in se* offenses, ones that have identifiable victims. I have done so because it is somewhat easier to think about such offenses in terms of their absolute and relative seriousness. Such crimes threaten or impose harms of various kinds and to various degrees on other individuals. Those harms are also inflicted with greater or lesser degrees of culpability by offenders. Things are more complicated when we turn to *mala prohibita*. Such offenses encompass a wide range of prohibited conduct, from violations of public standards that determine acceptable levels of risk, to conduct that involves violations of various reporting or filing requirements. As Antony Duff points out, *mala prohibita* violations will often harm no one, although in some cases they will elevate the risk of harm.[47] As a result of their more tenuous connection to harm, it will be more difficult to gauge their seriousness. Also, culpability in committing them will sometimes be minimal, as when individuals or businesses neglect to report things they are required by law to report or err in believing that they do not have to file a form or pay a tax on some item.

Given these features about violations of *mala prohibita*, it might seem that that sanctions for them will, to a greater extent than with *mala in se*, depend on calculations about how to optimally reduce their occurrence, especially through means of general deterrence. It is important for people to engage in permissible activities in ways that minimize risks to others, or to pay their taxes, or get licenses to drive or operate businesses of various kinds. But the failures to do so are less apt to seem like occasions for official moral communication, especially not beyond modest reminders to individuals to "follow the established rules" or "do their part." Granted, since violations of *mala prohibita* often will not result in harm to identifiable individuals, some rough cap on the severity of sanctions attached to their violation might be suggested by considerations of ordinal and cardinal proportionality. It would be ludicrous to treat those who violate such provisions like murderers or rapists, or to imprison them at all or for more than brief periods of time, at least in the vast majority of cases. But considerations of general deterrence might counsel a range of sanctions varying somewhat in their severity, with more substantial penal burdens imposed in order to deter offenses that risk harm and especially substantial harm. As always, however, the costs and possible negative consequences of such sanctions would have to be countenanced, along with the limited ability of harsher sanctions to marginally deter.

One further possible role that general deterrence might play in the design of a sentencing scheme should be noted. Suppose that the concept of proportionality in sentencing yields no more than vague upper and lower boundaries on sentence ranges for the various crime types. Indeed, some theorists have suggested, and not implausibly, that all we might be able to meaningfully say about proposed sentence ranges for crime types is that some of them are "not disproportionate," that is, are not so out of synch with our vague intuitions about crime seriousness that they are obviously disproportionate.[48] If this is correct, we might find ourselves with a number of possible sentence ranges for any given crime type, or for all crime types, from which to choose, since no one of them can be identified as the most suitable one, based solely on proportionality considerations. It might then be suggested that our choice among "not disproportionate" sentence ranges for crime types could be influenced by considerations of general deterrence. Perhaps a jurisdiction is seeing a somewhat prolonged spike in certain kinds of offenses. In response, a bumping up of the relevant sentence ranges for those kinds of offenses might be urged on grounds of general deterrence. So long as an "enhanced' sentence range fell within the group of "not disproportionate" ranges, there would be no violation of proportionality, and thus no worrisome deviation from accuracy in moral communication. Moral communication would retain its lead role, but its lack of determinacy would allow for some increase in the sentence ranges for certain crime types, if there was a convincing case for such increases based on grounds of general deterrence. Of course, there might not be a convincing case to be made. As we have seen, the link between sentence severity and general deterrence is weak, at best. And again, the costs and negative consequences of such increases would have to be weighed against any likely enhancement of deterrent effects. Finally, just as considerations of general deterrence might support sentence range increases within the range of "not disproportionate" options, so might the absence of any decrease in general deterrence support sentence ranges lower within the group of "not disproportionate" sentencing options.

Concluding Remarks

I have attempted in this chapter to indicate both the underlying rationale for the hybrid theory of punishment I propose and the complications with that theory. It is a theory that gives moral communication the lead role but grants a supplementary role to the reduction of crime. The moral communication aspect of the theory coheres more robustly with our understanding of legal punishment as a blaming institution, one that holds those who violate the criminal law accountable for their public wrongs. Such wrongs are derived from standards of conduct which it is presumed most adult members of society are capable of understanding and complying with. Legal punishment should, in my view, address offenders first and foremost on such terms and it should respond to their demonstrated failures to observe the strictures of the criminal law with sanctions that reflect the seriousness of their prohibited conduct. In doing so, legal punishment will also produce crime reduction effects. It might not produce optimal such effects, assuming that we can identify the criminal justice practices that would do so.

I have cast the moral communication element as presumptively dominant and indicated the conditions under which that presumption might be overcome. I have also argued that we should view the relatively rare occasions on which moral communication's priority might be justifiably set to one side with some ambivalence. Something significant is sacrificed when we fail to censure offenders according to the severity of their actual or provable crimes. Finally, in response to concerns that my account minimizes, to too great an extent, the crime reduction role of legal punishment, I have sought to show how its role in my account remains significant, especially when it comes to the sentencing of crime tokens in some cases as well as in the sentencing of *mala prohibita* more generally.

Notes

1 Two useful overviews of the challenges posed by mixed theories include David Wood, "Retribution, Crime Reduction, and the Justification of Punishment," *Oxford Journal of Legal Studies* 22 (2002): 301–21 and Zachary Hoskins, "Hybrid Theories of Punishment," in Bruce Waller, Elizabeth Shaw, and Farah Focquaert (eds.), *The Routledge Handbook of the Philosophy and Science of Punishment* (New York: Routledge, 2021): 37–48.

2 John Rawls, "Two Concepts of Rules," *The Philosophical Review* 64 (1955): 3–32; H. L. A. Hart, *Punishment and Responsibility: Essays in the Philosophy of Law* (Oxford: Clarendon Press, 1968), especially Chapter 1; Andrew von Hirsch, *Censure and Sanctions* (Oxford: Clarendon Press, 1993); and J. L. Mackie, "Retributivism: A Test Case for Ethical Objectivity" reprinted in J. Feinberg and H. Gross, *Philosophy of Law, Fourth Edition* (Belmont, CA: Wadsworth, 1991): 677–84. More recently, Thom Brooks and Matthew C. Altman have put forward mixed theories. See Brooks' *Punishment, Second Edition* (London: Routledge, 2020) and Altman's *A Theory of Legal Punishment: Deterrence, Retribution, and the Aims of the State* (London: Routledge, 2021).

3 My indebtedness to Rawls's discussion of telishment in "Two Concepts of Rules" (at 11–12) should be evident.

4 In this way, I agree with Hart, who seems to embrace value pluralism in his discussion in *Punishment and Responsibility*, 3.

5 See Mackie, "Retributivism."

6 Such an approach to the justification of legal punishment is found in the writings of Norval Morris, *The Future of Imprisonment* (Chicago: University of Chicago Press, 1974) and *Madness and the Criminal Law* (Chicago: University of Chicago Press, 1982). For a recent discussion, see Richard S. Frase, *Just Sentencing: Principles and Procedures for a Workable System* (New York: Oxford University Press, 2013).

7 See Larry Laudan, "The Rules of Trial, Political Morality, and the Costs of Error: Or, Is Proof beyond a Reasonable Doubt Causing More Harm than Good?" in L. Green and B. Leiter (eds.), *Oxford Studies in Philosophy of Law, Volume 1* (Oxford: Oxford University Press, 2011): 195–223.

8 Douglas N. Husak, "Why Punish the Deserving?" *Noûs* 26 (1992): 447–64.
9 Rawls, "Two Concepts of Rules"; Hart, *Punishment and Responsibility*; von Hirsch, *Censure and Sanctions.*
10 Rawls, "Two Concepts of Rules," 6–7.
11 Granted, judges might assign crime tokens sentences within the relevant ranges based on their sense of what the tokens "merit." But presumably, in doing so, they will mostly be influenced by their sense of how crime-prone individual offenders are, and thus the risks they pose to others. This is a sense of "merit" distinct from standard retributive understandings of deserved punishment.
12 Hart, *Punishment and Responsibility*, 9.
13 Hart, *Punishment and Responsibility*, 14.
14 Hart, *Punishment and Responsibility*, 24.
15 Hart, *Punishment and Responsibility*, 25.
16 Hart, *Punishment and Responsibility*, 12.
17 Altman, *A Theory of Legal Punishment.*
18 See especially Chapter 5 of Altman's *A Theory of Legal Punishment.*
19 See Laudan, "The Rules of Trial" and Erik Lillquist, "Recasting Reasonable Doubt: Decision Theory and the Virtues of Variability," *University of California-Davis Law Review* 36 (2002): 85–197.
20 See, for instance, Michael Tonry, "Sentencing Commissions and Their Guidelines," *Crime and Justice: A Review of Research* 17 (1993): 137–95.
21 R. A. Duff, *The Realm of Criminal Law* (Oxford: Oxford University Press, 2018), especially Chapter 5.
22 See Joel Feinberg, "The Expressive Function of Punishment," *The Monist* 49 (1965): 397–423, at 400 and R. A. Duff, *Punishment, Communication, and Community* (Oxford: Oxford University Press, 2001): 79.
23 See Richard Brandt, "A Utilitarian Theory of Excuses," *The Philosophical Review* 78 (1969): 337–61, in which he argues that those with excuses should not be punished because they have not shown themselves to be unresponsive to the moral considerations underlying the criminal law. However, as a utilitarian, he takes those moral considerations to be grounded in utility.
24 It is tempting to invoke G. W. F. Hegel's quip that "to base a justification of punishment on threat is to liken it to the act of a man who lifts his stick to a dog." See Hegel's *Philosophy of Right*, T. M. Know (trans.) (Oxford: Oxford University Press, 1965): 246. However, in fairness to the crime-reduction approach, deterrence is supposed to work through an appeal to a rational agent's self-interest, and the "threat" is one aimed at inducing such an agent to refrain from conduct that they have some duty to avoid. In these ways it is somewhat unlike the situation of dogs made to cower out of fear.
25 R. Jay Wallace, *Responsibility and the Moral Sentiments* (Cambridge, MA: Harvard University Press, 1996), especially Chapter 6.
26 Stephen J. Morse, "Psychopathy and Criminal Responsibility," *Neuroethics* 1 (2008): 205–12 and Cordelia Fine and Jeanette Kennett, "Mental Impairment, Moral Understanding, and Criminal Responsibility: Psychopathy and the Purposes of Punishment," *International Journal of Law and Psychiatry* 27 (2004): 425–43. More generally, see Peter Arenella, "Convicting the Morally Blameless: Reassessing the Relationship between Legal and Moral Accountability," *UCLA Law Review* 39 (1992): 1511–622. For the view that psychopaths should remain subject to punishment, albeit mitigated punishment, see Adam R. Fox, Trevor H. Kvaran, and Reid Griffith Fontaine, "Psychopathy and Culpability: How Responsible Is the Psychopath for Criminal Wrongdoing?" *Law & Social Inquiry* 38 (2013): 1–26.
27 Hart, *Punishment and Responsibility*, 14 and 23.
28 In fairness, Hart hints strongly at this condition in *Punishment and Responsibility*, 23.

29 Daniel S. Nagin, "Criminal Deterrence: Research at the Outset of the Twenty-First Century," *Crime and Justice: A Review of Research* 23 (1998): 1–42 and "Deterrence in the Twenty-First Century," *Crime and Justice: A Review of Research* 42 (2013): 199–263; Anthony N. Doob and Cheryl Marie Webster, "Sentence Severity and Crime: Accepting the Null Hypothesis," *Crime and Justice: A Review of Research* 30 (2003): 143–95.

30 That the criminal law expresses the fundamental views of the polity concerning the nature and limits of responsible conduct within a civil order is defended by Duff, *Realm of the Criminal Law*, Chapter 5.

31 I would concede that there might be circumstances in which public or press access to such hearings should be restricted. In the plea bargaining case I subsequently discuss, those whose criminal misconduct will be exposed by the cooperating defendant might be tipped off about the legal dangers they face from the cooperator's testimony if the hearings at which state officials seek approval for their actions were open to the public.

32 R. A. Duff, "Dangerousness and Citizenship," in A. Ashworth and M. Wasik (eds.), *Fundamentals of Sentencing Theory: Essays in Honour of Andrew von Hirsch* (Oxford: Clarendon Press, 1998): 173–201 and Stephen J. Morse, "Blame and Danger: An Essay on Preventive Detention," *Boston University Law Review* 76 (1996): 113–55.

33 I have expressed doubts about our ability to practically distinguish preventive detention from legal punishment. See Richard L. Lippke, "No Easy Way Out: Dangerous Offenders and Preventive Detention," *Law and Philosophy* 27 (2008): 383–414. This debate matters in the current context, for if is possible to distinguish them, then there is less of an apparent conflict between penal moral communication and crime reduction. If preventive detention is not punishment, then its use might not constitute a departure from accurate moral communication.

34 Morse is clearer about spelling out these conditions than Duff, although Duff hints at them. See Morse, "Blame and Danger," 152–53, and Duff, "Dangerousness and Citizenship," 161.

35 Morse, in "Blame and Danger," suggests (at 152) that we extend the crime of "reckless endangerment" to cover cases of individuals who know that they pose an extreme risk to others and who have failed to voluntarily take steps to avoid causing future harm. This would presumably require conviction on the charge in a court of law.

36 Morse suggests a maximum one-year term of imprisonment for those convicted of the charge of reckless endangerment, although he allows that the state could re-charge those whom it deemed still dangerous. See "Blame and Danger," 152.

37 Frase takes a firm stand against such upwards departures from established (let us suppose on moral communication grounds) sentencing ranges for the various crime types, even for recidivists. See *Just Sentencing*, 190. I am willing to allow the possibility of such departures, but only under limited conditions.

38 See Daniel C. Richman, "Cooperating Defendants: The Costs and Benefits of Purchasing Information from Scoundrels," *Federal Sentencing Reporter* 8 (1996): 292–95; Ian Weinstein, "Regulating the Market for Snitches," *Buffalo Law Review* 47 (1999): 563–643; and Richard L. Lippke, "Rewarding Cooperation: The Moral Complexities of Procuring Accomplice Testimony," *New Criminal Law Review* 13 (2010): 90–118.

39 Angela J. Davis, *Arbitrary Justice: The Power of the American Prosecutor* (Oxford: Oxford University Press, 2007), especially Chapter 1.

40 More oversight of such agreements seems to be provided in Germany by judges, who have the overriding responsibility to get at the truth. See Màximo Langer, "From Legal Transplants to Legal Translations: The Globalization of Plea Bargaining and the Americanization Thesis in Criminal Procedure," *Harvard International*

Law Journal 45 (2004): 1–64, at 39–46 and Jenia I. Turner, *Plea Bargaining across Borders* (New York: Aspen Publishers, 2009): 109–10 and 114–20.

41 See Johannes Andenaes, "The General Preventive Effects of Punishment," *University of Pennsylvania Law Review* 114 (1966): 949–83, at 950.

42 See Hart, *Punishment and Responsibility*, 25. See also Paul H. Robinson and John M. Darley, "The Utility of Desert," *Northwestern University Law Review* 91 (1997): 453–99.

43 von Hirsch, *Censure and Sanctions*, 43.

44 Here I draw on Frase, *Just Sentencing*, 35–36, although Frase is wary about increasing an offender's sentence based on deterrence considerations, as opposed to considerations involving risk of future offending.

45 See Daniel S. Nagin, Frances T. Cullen, and Cheryl Lero Jonson, "Imprisonment and Reoffending," *Crime and Justice: A Review of Research* 38 (2009): 115–200.

46 Jeffrey T. Ulmer and Darrell Steffensmeier, "The Age and Crime Relationship: Social Variation, Social Explanations," in Kevin M. Beaver, J. C. Barnes, and Brian B. Boutwell (eds.), *The Nurture Versus Biosocial Debate in Criminology: On the Origins of Criminal Behavior and Criminality* (Thousand Oaks, CA: Sage, 2015): 377–96.

47 Duff, *Realm of Criminal Law*, 314.

48 Again, this kind of limiting retributivism is found in Morris, *The Future of Imprisonment* and *Madness and the Criminal Law*.

5 Criminal Procedure and the Moral Authority to Punish

In the previous chapter, I elaborated a mixed theory of legal punishment. It is one that puts moral communication by state officials to offenders, victims, and the broader public in the lead role, while embracing crime reduction as a secondary purpose of the institution. I posited that such a justification of the institution presupposes the backdrop of a society that is both democratic and committed to respecting and securing the equal basic rights of its members. Although I conceded that there is debate about what those rights come to and how far some or all of them must be secured, I suggested that there is sufficient overlap among competing accounts to ground the familiar *mala in se* provisions of the criminal law and some *mala prohibita* provisions. Disagreement will persist about the nature and contours of the criminal law, but a plausible theory of legal punishment can be defended that sidesteps or at least minimizes that dissensus.

Nothing I have said in the preceding chapters should be interpreted as implying that instituting legal punishment in society is anything but a complicated, and indeed deeply fraught, enterprise. It is one thing to articulate and defend an abstract account of legal punishment's justifying aims. It is another to fashion and maintain a complex institutional structure designed to achieve those aims while also adhering to other important moral values.[1] The list of failures or abuses by state officials in their efforts to arrest, investigate, charge, and convict individuals of crimes is long and varied. I will, in this chapter, note and discuss many of them and propose solutions to some of them. I do so because I believe that the approach to justifying legal punishment I have defended puts a substantial burden on state officials to conduct themselves in accordance with demanding standards. Such officials cannot justifiably claim to morally communicate with individuals convicted of crimes about the public wrongs they have committed unless they assiduously seek to reach and remain on the moral high ground, so to speak. Tyrants or bullies might pretend to engage in "moral communication" with those who they dominate or hold accountable to their arbitrary or self-interested demands, but no one should take seriously their claims to merit the respect or loyalty of those they rule by intimidation, force, or cruelty. State officials in liberal,

DOI: 10.4324/9781032661667-6

democratic societies, by contrast, are supposed to behave differently. They are the elected or in some cases appointed representatives of the public. They act on its behalf and enforce provisions of the criminal law that prohibit public wrongs. Those who are duly convicted of crimes and punished for them are forcefully reminded of their moral obligations under the law, obligations that require them to, in various ways, limit the pursuit of their own interests in order to respect and preserve others' vital interests.

My position will be that that state officials can only meaningfully claim the moral authority to censure the misconduct of members of society if they satisfy three broad conditions. First, those officials must respect the dignity of all those who fall under their purview and treat them in ways that uphold it even as they investigate and prosecute their suspected crimes. Official state inquiries into criminal misconduct will more or less inevitably intrude upon the basic rights of individuals. Those individuals will be required to do things that they might not want to or turn over things in their possession that they might not wish to allow state officials to have. While state officials must be permitted to proceed against those they suspect of crimes, they should have to justify intrusions upon the rights of suspects, and the more so the more substantial or enduring those intrusions turn out to be. Also, state officials must not treat accused individuals inhumanely or without the respect they are due as members of society.

Second, state agents must support and abide by the requirements of full and fair due process in investigating and attempting to convict accused persons of criminal misconduct. There is considerable debate about what such due process consists in, especially when it comes to the adjudication of criminal charges. Some view criminal trials as the gold standard and regard other forms of charge adjudication with considerable skepticism. Even with trials, there is controversy about their required features and the parties who should be deemed qualified to render verdicts at their conclusions.[2] Some scholars defend restrained versions of negotiated criminal pleas.[3] Some even defend the kinds of robust plea bargaining practices that exist in countries like the United States.[4] I contend that defensible forms of due process must keep steadfastly in view the aim of getting at the truth concerning what those accused of crimes have or have not done.

The proceeding way of putting things is, admittedly, somewhat vague in its implications. Most legal systems accept some limits on efforts to get at the truth during trials or other forms of charge adjudication, typically in the form of various exclusionary rules.[5] Also, there will inevitably be obstacles to getting at the truth about what those charged with crimes have done no matter how fervently we attempt to do so. Most notably, some persons accused of crimes will seek to thwart truth determination to ward off convictions. Nonetheless, we cannot abide a complete or even substantial divorce between criminal procedure and truth determination if we are to defend legal punishment on morally communicative grounds. As Thomas Weigend has noted, we would not accept a negotiated plea of guilt in which state officials, and the accused who agreed to the plea, openly acknowledge that the plea falsely characterized the crimes the person committed.[6] Such an announced agreement would too blatantly confound our expectations about the process of investigating crimes and adjudicating charges against the accused.

Despite this, it must be admitted that the required link between criminal procedure and truth can be characterized in various ways. We might describe it in fairly modest terms, according to which the state must avoid investigative and adjudication procedures that routinely and predictably produce outcomes in criminal cases that distort the truth about the crimes persons have committed. Or we might opt for something more positive and hopeful, to the effect that the state officials must abide by procedures that, for the most part or in the main, accurately communicate the gravity of the crimes committed by those who are convicted. What we cannot accept, if legal punishment is to morally communicate, is a system that is substantially indifferent to the truth, for then we would be endorsing false moral communication with those convicted, as well as with their victims and the broader public.

Third, it is not enough for state officials to see to it that those suspected or accused of crimes are treated with dignity, and that their alleged misconduct is investigated and adjudicated in ways that preserve some substantial link with the truth about their crimes. Criminal procedure could satisfy these conditions and yet state officials might fail systematically to treat all members of society as equals before the law. Insofar as liberal democratic societies are committed to doing so, such systemic failures should be seen as undermining the moral authority of officials to communicate with offenders about their crimes. Failures to treat all members of society as equals before the law will usually take one of two forms. The first is that of what we might term "selective enforcement," whereby some in society are more often targeted for scrutiny by state officials because of their poverty, race, ethnicity, religion, gender, sexual preference, or some other characteristic unrelated to their conduct. Those targeted might be guilty of crimes; what is unfair is that others, who are equally guilty of the same or similar crimes, are much less often investigated, charged, or convicted of them, and for reasons that few would defend. Second, there is what might be termed "underenforcement," whereby crimes against some members of society are systematically neglected or downplayed by the authorities.[7] In some cases, these neglected crimes will be serious ones. Sadly, sometimes it is the same members of society who state officials focus too much of their criminal justice resources on and too little of them. With selective enforcement, the recipients of state sanctions might reasonably accuse the state of inconsistency—as unjustifiably concerned to censure misconduct only when certain people engage in it.[8] With underenforcement, the neglected victims of crimes can plausibly maintain that the state does not care about or stand by their interests. Worse than this, if the state sees to the punishment of some members of society when they commit crimes, but neglects them when they are victims of crimes, then the inconsistencies in its treatment of these individuals are pernicious. Arguably, the more extensive selective or underenforcement become, the weaker are the state's credentials as a moral authority to whom citizens should look for accurate communication about society's fundamental values.

As should be apparent, criminal justice systems might fall short along one or more of the three dimensions just identified in a variety of ways and to different degrees. There might also be local and regional failures or shortcomings to take into account. We might hope that abject failure along all three dimensions will be rare, but many existing societies exhibit substantial shortcomings with respect to them that should concern us. When carelessly or improperly deployed, state powers to arrest, prosecute, convict, and punish people will obviously do much more than falsely communicate; they will damage or destroy lives and may confound efforts to prevent crime. We should therefore see to it that such powers are exercised in accordance with exacting standards.

Dignity, Rights, and Criminal Procedure

The concept of "human dignity" is contested, at least in the scholarly literature. There is ongoing debate about what it means—in particular, whether it refers to some distinctive nonnatural property of humans or is simply another way of referring to certain natural properties of humans, while exhorting us to respect those properties.[9] I prefer the latter account, although not much turns on which of them is most defensible in the current context. Although some dismiss Immanuel Kant's views about human dignity as being too focused on rationality, the core of Kant's account, with its emphasis on the capacity of most human beings, once they reach a certain age, to reflect on their lives and attempt to shape them in accordance with that reflection, captures something of elemental significance in how human dignity should be understood.[10] Each of us is the subject of a life that typically matters, and matters enormously, to us. Few of us want to be treated as mere objects to be used or trampled upon by others. Instead, we want to have and chart our own lives, although we must accept the limits to doing so entailed by the dignity of others. It is a short step from the fundamental desire to have and live our own lives to a list of basic moral rights designed to secure the things we need to do so: Life, physical and psychological integrity, liberty, privacy, and the resources needed to sustain ourselves. As I have already noted, there is considerable debate about the content and limits of the basic moral rights that individuals possess.[11] But I have suggested that there is consensus on a core set of such rights, ones premised on securing the conditions under which individuals can have and live lives shaped by their own choices. That core set of rights is the basis for many of the familiar *mala in se* provisions of the criminal law.

As previous chapters have indicated, the institution of legal punishment has a vital role to play in backing the basic rights of members of society. We might hope that it will prevent a variety of assaults upon those rights, through its deterrence, incapacitation, or rehabilitation effects. Yet the sad fact is that legal punishment is often a reactive institution, one that comes into play once crimes have occurred. On my account, a significant part of what we want legal punishment to do is stand by and for victims—to detect, investigate, document, and publicly communicate about the wrongs they have suffered. But even if we look for the state to, in these ways, uphold the basic rights of members of society, we should, at the same time, insist that its officials respect the rights of those who come under its purview. Initially, it might seem unclear how state officials can respect the rights of suspects or accused persons as they carry out their important tasks. In the course of detecting and investigating crimes, arresting and charging suspects, and seeing to the adjudication of charges, state officials must, it seems, be permitted to intrude upon the rights of individuals in various ways. They must be able to stop and briefly detain suspects for questioning or pursue them and use force to arrest and question them if they flee. State officials also must be permitted to search the vehicles of persons in certain circumstances and obtain warrants to search their residences. Further, they must be able to require suspects to appear in police line-ups and before judges for initial hearings. If those hearings result in formal charges, officials must be able to compel the accused to appear for the subsequent hearings or trials necessary to adjudicate the charges. To facilitate such appearances, or to protect the public, officials might be justified in holding some individuals in detention until the charges against them are fully adjudicated. All of these infringements are ones that the basic moral rights of individuals would ordinarily seem to prohibit. Thus, how do we square permitting them with the notion that state officials must, as they perform their various important tasks, respect the rights of suspects and the formally accused?

The way forward, I believe, is to grasp how basic moral rights are supposed to constitute weighty considerations in our thinking about how to treat individuals, such that they cannot be easily infringed or overridden.[12] If rights are to be given their due, certain procedures must be followed by the authorities, ones that regulate and constrain their actions. By requiring adherence to such procedures, we ensure that the rights of suspects and accused persons are not infringed without justification. In this way, procedural criminal rights should be understood as second-order rights, ones that suspects and accused individuals have to ensure that their basic moral rights are not run roughshod over by state officials. Also, when the rights of suspect or accused persons are justifiably infringed, we should insist that they are infringed no more than is necessary for the authorities to hold offenders accountable for their crimes.

A useful way to conceptualize such procedural rights is in terms of their constituting normative hurdles that legal officials must successively surmount as they advance suspects through the system, which hurdles should increase in height the more or longer persons' basic rights are infringed. State officials should always be expected to justify their use of power, although sometimes the burdens of doing so will be easily met. For instance, stopping citizens and questioning them about suspected crimes, things that the police must be able to do with relative ease and frequency, constitute minimal and brief infringements on the rights of individuals. To justify them, and thus overcome the presumption that individuals ought to be able to go on about their lives without such interferences, the police should have to have (and be prepared to articulate and defend, in a court of law, if necessary) something like "reasonable suspicion" of criminal activity on the part of those they stop.[13] This is a modest burden of justification for the police to meet, as it should be. Still, in theory, at least, having to meet it would preclude them from stopping or harassing individuals for no reason whatsoever or for the wrong kinds of reasons (e.g., racial animus).

As measures more intrusive into the lives of the individuals they investigate are employed by the authorities, such as searches of suspects' homes or property, the burdens of justification on the authorities ought to increase. At the limit, before legal sanctions are imposed on individuals, which typically infringe upon or curtail their basic rights in more substantial ways, state authorities should be expected to shoulder a strong burden of proof, one captured by the "reasonable doubt" standard of the criminal law.[14] Short of that limit, if pretrial detention is used against persons charged with crimes, the presumption against interference with their basic rights should impose a significant burden on the authorities to justify such intrusive and enduring right-curtailment.[15]

A further point toward which I have already gestured should be made explicit. In sentencing theory, there is what is known as the "principle of parsimony."[16] According to that principle, state officials should not impose criminal sanctions on convicted offenders that are more severe than necessary to serve legitimate penal aims. If less harsh or intrusive sanctions will suffice to serve those aims, then they should be utilized. Something similar seems true in criminal procedure. Even if state officials can justify some infringement upon the basic moral rights of suspects or formally accused persons, the justified infringements should be as narrowly tailored as possible. This means that if state officials can accomplish their various investigatory or adjudicatory tasks with less rather than more intrusion upon basic moral rights, then less intrusion ought to be preferred. If we are to accord basic rights their due, we should be grudging about conceding justified intrusions upon them. For instance, consider the pretrial detention of accused persons who the authorities can demonstrate, to the satisfaction of a court, pose substantial, ongoing threats to the community or who are highly likely to abscond before the charges against them can be adjudicated. Even if such detention can be justified in some instances, it arguably should come to no more than is necessary to restrain the individuals in question from committing further crimes or absconding. Those detained have not yet been convicted of any crimes and arguably retain their other basic rights. The state must not only respect their retained rights, it might be required to take steps to facilitate their continued exercise and enjoyment, to the extent that doing so is possible. Thus, not only are things like squalid and degrading pretrial detention, marked by the absence of proper sanitation, food, and privacy ruled out, but more positive efforts to facilitate visitation, work, or provide basic income to detainees will be required if the state is to be parsimonious in its infringement upon their basic rights.[17]

More complex issues are raised by the vaunted right against self-incrimination, with its prohibition of certain kinds of interrogation techniques by state officials. It is widely accepted that state officials are not justified in employing torture, threats, physical force, or various forms of extended deprivation—of food, drink, sleep, or social interaction—in their efforts to induce suspects to provide incriminating evidence against themselves or others.[18] It might seem that basic moral rights against assault and coercion, or to minima of social welfare, unproblematically rule out such measures by the authorities. But what if such abusive techniques reliably yielded incriminating evidence concerning serious criminal offenses? Why would that possibility not suffice to overcome the strong presumption against their use? Part of the answer to this question will be that if there exist other ways of gathering incriminating evidence, such that the authorities do not need to employ such brusque measures, those measures should be denied them. Another part of the answer will be that such measures tend to produce poor quality evidence. Suspects desperate to ward off further pain or humiliation will say just about anything, whether true or not. Even things like isolation in the hostile environment of a police station will sometimes induce persons to confess crimes they did not actually commit. Add in the youthfulness of many suspects, the presence of things like mental illness in more than a few of them, and the case against allowing officials to employ aggressive or harsh interrogation measures appears almost decisive.

It can be made stronger still by noting the ways in which harsh interrogation measures tend to degrade the individuals who are their targets. We should not, it might be claimed, ever permit the employment of measures that reduce criminal suspects, even guilty ones, to fearful, starving, or humiliated animals.[19] To do so is to deprive them of the modicum of respect they are due as intelligent, sensitive, and reasonable creatures, ones who are presumably at least somewhat responsive to moral considerations. Granted, we do permit the police to use force, even lethal force, against individuals in limited circumstances. But on those occasions, something equivalent or close to a necessity condition must be satisfied, in the sense that state agents act permissibly only if they lack other, less right-infringing alternatives to prevent grave harm to themselves or to capture and detain dangerous, or seemingly dangerous, suspects. Force, and especially deadly force, is recognized to be an extreme option available only as necessity demands. The degradation of suspects or accused persons to extract evidence from them, by contrast, will almost never be justified, at least not on grounds of necessity.[20]

The dignity of persons can be seen as doing more than placing surmountable justificatory hurdles in the paths of the officials who must do the work of the criminal justice system. There is persuasive evidence that in our encounters with other persons we very much want our worth to be recognized and affirmed. We do not want to be ridiculed, ignored, or run roughshod over, but listened to, allowed to explain ourselves and our actions, and be taken seriously as we do so.[21] Put differently, as beings who are capable of rational thought and action, we want to be treated as if we have understandable reasons for acting as we do, reasons that matter to us and ought to be taken into account by others. And this will be true even if some of things we do appear to comport poorly with the rights or well-being of others. This powerful desire to be treated as if our explanations of what we are doing or have done matter and ought to be given a hearing does not disappear when we encounter criminal justice officials. Persons who have broken the law and who understand that the authorities are behaving appropriately by stopping and questioning them might sincerely believe that they have not offended or that they had good reasons for behaving as they did, or at least that their side of the story complicates things in ways that the authorities ought to countenance. Suspects and accused persons who are treated gruffly by the authorities tend to resent it, feeling that their worth as human beings has not been given its proper due. Also, as Tom Tyler has shown, individuals who have committed crimes and who are treated as if they are persons whose accounts of what they have done and why they have done it matter will be more inclined to accept responsibility for their crimes and the sanctions meted out to them.[22]

The preceding brings us to the important role of defense attorneys in ensuring that individuals suspected of or charged with crimes are treated with dignity and subject to no more loss or infringement of their rights than the state can adequately justify.[23] It should be apparent how having competent and motivated defense counsel helps to ensure these things. It will be much easier for state officials to convince the judges who issue warrants, conduct preliminary hearings, or authorize pre-trail detention that they have met the justificatory burdens needed to infringe the basic rights of suspects or formally accused persons if those persons lack knowledge of the law and its workings, which many of them will. Also, some of the suspected or accused will be bewildered or cowed into silence by the intricacies of criminal procedure and the formalities of court appearances. Similarly, accused persons who lack adequate defense counsel will struggle to effectively "tell their stories" at trials or in plea negotiations, or to challenge prosecution accounts of the crimes they are alleged to have committed. Individuals caught up in the criminal justice system often have explanations of or justifications for their actions, or important clarifying bits of information about them. Even if what they offer does not constitute a convincing justification or excuse, or grounds for modifying the charges against them or dropping them altogether, it is important to their dignity to be given a chance to explain themselves and be taken seriously. Competent and motivated defense attorneys play vital roles in facilitating and protecting opportunities for the suspected or accused to tell their stories in the presence of the authorities whose decisions will ultimately determine their fates.[24]

Furthermore, the dignity of accused persons is disrespected by state authorities when they decline to reveal the nature and quality of the evidence they have against the accused. It is natural, in this context, to focus on the ways in which state failures to reveal exculpatory evidence thwarts the search for the truth about what persons accused of crimes have done. However, here I want to focus on the ways in which official reluctance to reveal incriminating evidence against persons impacts their dignity. Conduct of this kind by officials might be rarer when the accused go to trial, although it will still be important for them and their attorneys to have access to the evidence against them in a timely fashion. More troublesome are negotiated pleas that occur without the accused or their attorneys having access to the state's evidence. In the United States, for instance, the accused can seek discovery of the evidence against them, and, by law, prosecutors are supposed to comply with requests for its disclosure.[25] However, the reality is that prosecutors often penalize accused persons whose attorneys make such requests, with the sanction consisting of poorer quality plea proffers.[26] This effectively forces individuals to plead guilty in the absence of knowing what the state has on them and thus without being able (with the help of their attorneys) to challenge its veracity or weigh its probative force. I will have more to say about nontrial adjudication in subsequent sections. But this aspect of it in some jurisdictions comports poorly with ensuring that state officials actually have evidence sufficient to shoulder the burden of proof for conviction. Yet demonstrating that they can shoulder that burden ought to be a prerequisite to the state imposing sanctions that infringe the rights of the convicted. Notably, outside the United States, disclosure of the evidence against accused persons is more often the norm as the state proceeds against them.[27]

As I noted in the introduction, failures by state officials to conduct themselves in ways that comport with the dignity of suspects and accused persons can range from isolated incidents to pervasive patterns of abuse. Where violations of dignity are rare or exceptional, the state's moral authority to censure those whom it convicts of crimes might not be undermined in significant ways. Most officials will demonstrate, through their actions, that they understand and respect how a commitment to basic moral rights requires them to proceed with caution against those suspected of crimes, and in ways that they are prepared to explain and justify. However, as failures by officials to respect the dignity of those who fall under their purview become more frequent or profound, with suspects' rights run roughshod over by state officials in the pursuit of convictions, the moral authority of those officials to censure misconduct is compromised. Such widespread misconduct reveals the ways in which the authorities have insufficient regard for what the very rights they are supposed to champion imply about the ways in which they must conduct themselves in the pursuit of wrongdoers. The hard cases will be those in-between the two extremes of occasional misconduct by a few officials and systematic misconduct by most of them. We will be left, in such middle ground cases, with difficult practical judgments about whether state officials have sufficiently abandoned the moral high ground such that their remit to censure convicted wrongdoers has been fatally compromised.

Keeping the Truth in View

Suppose that we devise a system of crime detection, investigation, and adjudication that respects the dignity of those suspected of or charged with crimes. The authorities accept and honor the burdens of justification that I have argued ought to attend increasing incursions into the lives of those whose apparent misconduct has come to their attention. The authorities also resist the urge to use various coercive or humiliating techniques against suspects to gain evidence about their suspected crimes. More than this, they listen to what the suspects have to say about their actions or motives and make sure that they have competent and motivated attorneys to guide them through the investigation and adjudicative process. Where it is justified, pretrial detention is kept free of the taint of punishment, meaning that it is both humane and no more restrictive than necessary to restrain suspects who the authorities can demonstrate pose dangers to other members of society. If state officials do all of these things, and perhaps more, to demonstrate their fealty to human dignity, what could possibly go wrong? The answer, unfortunately, is that lots of things can. And they can go wrong even if state officials are not corrupt, unnecessarily violent, or devious, and even if they try to act responsibly in their attempts to fulfill the roles assigned to them by the criminal justice system.

In this section, my focus will be on the numerous ways in which the investigation of crimes and the adjudication of criminal charges can fall short of maintaining sufficient contact with the truth about what the individuals who the authorities have incriminating evidence against have or have not done. I use the phrase "sufficient contact" intentionally, to signal some ambiguity about the desirable, or perhaps attainable, level of truth-seeking that we can reasonably expect of the complex process of investigating crimes and adjudicating charges. As we have already seen, most legal systems incorporate some compromises with truth-seeking in the realm of criminal justice, typically in the form of various evidence exclusionary rules. There is debate about the wisdom of such rules, as well as about how extensive they should be.[28] More to the point, knowing that we have found the truth about what those charged with crimes have or have not done is probably an unattainable goal. None of us are creatures with infallible powers of truth discernment. At most, we can attempt to devise rules and procedures that seem well-suited to getting us closer to it, rather than further from it. Of course, what those rules and procedures amount to are matters of considerable controversy. My aim in this section is the modest one of pointing us in the right direction given the account of legal punishment defended in previous chapters.

The value of truth in criminal procedure is more often trumpeted in civil law jurisdictions than common law ones.[29] Indeed, there is some tendency in common law jurisdictions, and especially in the United States, to cast criminal procedure as being primarily concerned with "conflict resolution" rather than with truth.[30] Yet to characterize the detection, investigation, and prosecution of criminal offenses in terms of conflict resolution seems to demean the victims of crimes, when there are victims, and illicitly elevate the interests of those who have wronged them. Victims are not simply participants in a dispute that might seem to have two (or more) sides to it. This is not to deny, of course, that some crimes arise out of conflicts for which all parties involved are somewhat responsible, including those who ultimately become victims. But to cast all crimes in this way is misleading. Many victims of crimes are individuals who have been injured or preyed upon by others who have no plausible excuse or justification for what they did. That is the kind of unvarnished truth that we should want the criminal justice system to investigate and validate, through the process of criminal conviction.

Unfortunately, the ways in which criminal justice systems can fail to get reasonably close to the truth, and thus hold accountable all and only those who have actually committed crimes are many and complex. Let us set to one side state officials who act in ways that utterly defy their responsibilities within the criminal justice system. Police who extort others with threats of criminal prosecution to gain financial or other advantages, or prosecutors who seek to frame their opponents or individuals they dislike act atrociously, but such highly intentional forms of malfeasance are only the tip of the proverbial iceberg. Scholars and observers of criminal justice systems have identified the more common and hidden defects of such systems, ones that are not inevitable but which it will be more challenging to address. Importantly, some of them occur despite the officials involved being trained, competent, and well-meaning.

To begin with, it is apparent that arrests, investigations, and prosecutions are subject to a wide variety of cognitive errors and biases, ones that are often compounded by pressures on police, prosecutors, and the courts to efficiently process high volumes of cases. In this section, I will ignore the kinds of biases—class, gender, racial, ethnic, sexual preference—that influence who gets targeted or investigated by criminal justice officials and who does not. I come back to them in the next section. For now, focus on the kinds of cognitive biases that push police, criminal investigators, and prosecutors toward hasty conclusions about the individuals who they suspect of having committed crimes. It is apparent that things like confirmation and outcome bias are rife among those who investigate and prosecute crimes.[31] Too often, police and criminal investigators jump to premature conclusions about the guilt of suspects and employ dubious methods to prove it, all the while dismissing contradictory or confounding evidence, or twisting it to fit their conclusions. Studies of mistaken convictions repeatedly document these errors, which are often easy for outsiders to diagnose, but harder for those caught up in criminal investigations to perceive or consciously control for. These cognitive biases are compounded by caseload pressures and clamoring by the press or public for convictions, especially in cases of serious crimes.[32] Cognitive biases are essentially shortcuts for thinking about the numerous cases that criminal justice officials confront, ones that are useful in some instances but misleading in others. The errors these biases produce will be exacerbated by the use of coercive or manipulative interrogation techniques, the manipulation of line-ups for purposes of identifying possible perpetrators of criminal acts, and the threatening, cooptation, or coaching of witnesses.[33] Although threats employed by police and investigators in these contexts seem to take us beyond more ordinary kinds of human cognitive biases, keep in mind that they are often employed by officials who are convinced that they have guilty parties in their grips but against whom they need more evidence.

It might be thought, or hoped, that prosecutors will carefully vet the evidence that police and investigators bring to them, thus reducing the errors that are rife in the case files. Yet prosecutors face their own pressures and temptations to keep things moving along through the system with a minimum of delays. Prosecutors rely on police and investigators to bring cases and evidence, or to get more evidence, and thus they are often loath to question the evidence with which they are presented. The value of "comity" as between the police and prosecutorial divisions in the criminal justice system is often remarked upon by observers.[34] Also, the caseload pressures prosecutors encounter can be overwhelming. Often, as we have seen, they result, in part, from the arrests of large numbers of mostly minor offenders. Scholars of the misdemeanor case processing world paint a grim picture of it.[35] Prosecutors are reluctant to dismiss charges once they have been lodged; doing so might incur the disfavor of the police on whom they otherwise rely. Hence, prosecutors are, in this realm, prone to becoming "conviction maximizers," meaning that they care less about what offenders have done or what the evidence shows and more about getting some kind of conviction in the majority of cases.[36]

In more serious cases, prosecutors likely will experience more public scrutiny and what comes with it, pressure to achieve convictions. Such public oversight might be more intense, or might be felt as such, in legal jurisdictions in which prosecutors are subject to popular electoral control. Prosecutorial elections are a distinctly US phenomenon., one the wisdom of which can certainly be questioned.[37] However, even in countries in which prosecutors are members of organized state bureaucracies that insulate them from direct political pressure, public scrutiny of their decisions and actions might still influence the decisions they make about whether and how to pursue cases.

We have already noted that prosecutors will be, at times, reluctant to reveal exculpatory evidence, although in most legal systems, they are legally required to do so.[38] In some cases, they conceal such evidence because they are convinced that the accused are guilty; in others, they might conceal it because they want to win cases and solidify their reputations. Yet this concealment of evidence by prosecutors distorts the search for the truth. Where it occurs, even accused persons who have competent and motivated defense counsel will lack crucial means to fend off convictions or to convince judges or juries that they are guilty of only some of the charges against them.

It is tempting to believe that criminal procedure will be sufficiently evidence-driven so long as it culminates in criminal trials that are appropriately structured. At such trials, there will be a public airing of the charges and evidence against the accused. The accused, presumably aided by competent counsel, will have numerous opportunities to contest the state's case or put forward affirmative defenses. Impartial judges or juries that employ the reasonable doubt standard will then render verdicts. But again, scholars have demonstrated how criminal trials might not be as strongly or reliably evidence-driven as they should be, especially in common law jurisdictions where adversary trials are the norm.

The evidence presented to judges or jurors in common law jurisdictions is typically somewhat "synthesized," meaning that it has been doctored or manipulated in a variety of ways by police, prosecutors, and defense attorneys.[39] Eyewitnesses to crimes, or prosecution witnesses of other kinds, are often coached to appear more confident or consistent than they really are or were in their initial interviews with authorities. The processes by which the police elicit "confessions" from suspects are rarely videotaped, and yet we have good reason to believe that many confessions are gained in ways that stain their credibility.[40] Defense attorneys also coach witnesses, of course. It might be hoped that coaching by both sides will more or less "even things out," but it is difficult to see how pervasive evidence manipulation will enable judges or jurors to arrive, in reliable ways, at sound judgments concerning the validity of the charges against the accused.[41] Importantly, jurors might not be aware of the extent to which the evidence with which they are presented has been shaped by advocates on both sides. They will therefore be in no position to know whether or to what extent it should be discounted.

Jurors in common law systems are probably not helped with the difficult task of evaluating the evidence presented to them by the excesses of adversary process.[42] The hope seems to be that the adversary process will provide jurors with opposing and well-argued viewpoints on the evidence, ones that jurors will then have to sort through to arrive at conclusions about the state's success or failure at having satisfied the reasonable doubt standard. Yet it might be overly optimistic to believe that adversary efforts to (sometimes dishonestly or misleadingly) embellish the evidence in support of one side, while (sometimes dishonestly or misleadingly) discrediting the evidence in support of the other side will put citizen jurors in a position to figure out anything with a high degree of skill or confidence.

To make matters worse, lay jurors in common law countries are, to put it mildly, inexperienced at evaluating and weighing evidence in criminal cases. Many of them will have never served on a jury in a criminal case before and the few who have done so will likely have served in this capacity once or twice. There is reason to believe that lay jurors are more apt to be influenced by their emotions in criminal cases, which encourages prosecutors and defense attorneys to play to them, rather than to dispassionately emphasize what the evidence does or does not show.[43] In recognition of this, there are special evidence exclusionary rules in common law countries that are not typically found in civil law systems, ones that seemingly exclude from juror consideration moderately probative evidence.[44] Further, lay juries are not required to provide reasoned verdicts, that is, ones that detail the grounds for their having reached whatever conclusions they annouce. Lay juries are what some have termed "black boxes" into which evidence is poured and verdicts come out without our having any sense of how or why they were reached.[45] By contrast, judges in civil law systems are not only trained in and experienced at reaching verdicts in criminal cases, they are required to articulate reasons in support of them.[46] If the grounds for their verdicts appear suspect, higher courts can then intervene to correct them. In common law jurisdictions, appellate courts are much less able or inclined to scrutinize juror decision-making. They tend to focus, instead, on the fairness of the trial process rather than the defensibility of the verdict given the evidence.[47] Yet this leaves the courts and the polity on whose behalf they are supposed to operate in a weakened position to determine whether juries have behaved reasonably with respect to the evidence with which they were presented.

Despite their flaws and shortcomings, trials can be at least plausibly construed as consisting of deliberate, although qualified, efforts to get at the truth of what persons accused of crimes have or have not done. The same cannot be said of many nontrial charge adjudication procedures, foremost among them the kinds of free-wheeling plea bargaining practices that exist in the United States and, increasingly, elsewhere.[48] In the United States, prosecutors have been given enormous discretion to "extract" guilty pleas from the accused. They can offer accused persons substantially discounted sentences, although judges must ultimately ratify any sentence agreed to by prosecutors and the accused (or their attorneys). Also, given the ways in which the criminal code has overlapping and redundant prohibitions, prosecutors can stack charges, the cumulative sentences of which might bear little relation to the seriousness of the crimes committed by the accused, if indeed they have committed any.[49] Prosecutors can then offer to reduce the charges in exchange for guilty pleas. Alternatively, prosecutors can make clear through their practices that they will be unsparing in their sentencing recommendations to accused persons who elect trial adjudication and are found guilty. Often, prosecutors are aided in menacing accused persons by the draconian sentences available to them that have been adopted by legislators concerned to appear tough on crime.[50] In short, the tools that prosecutors have to manipulate the "sentencing differential"—that is, the difference in sentences assigned to those who agree to plead guilty versus those found guilty after trials—are prodigious. The problem is that the larger such differentials become, the less assurance we have that it is the evidence the state can muster that convinces accused persons to accede to guilty pleas. Factor in the ways in which the use of pretrial detention puts pressure on accused persons to plead guilty and any confidence that members of the public should have that the system is getting anywhere near the truth about what the accused have or have not done, ought to be shaken. Instead, the main function of such unbridled plea negotiation practices seems to be on the efficient processing of a large volume of cases.

It might be hoped that the judges who oversee guilty pleas will act to check the considerable power that prosecutors have to extract them. Yet in some jurisdictions, judges are effectively kept in the dark about the evidence the state has against the accused and are therefore in no position to challenge prosecutors' recommendations to accept guilty pleas and the sentences that have been worked out in advance between prosecutors and attorneys for the accused, assuming that the accused are competently represented. Scholars of plea bargaining in the United States are skeptical about the proposition that judges do more than "rubber stamp" plea deals in the vast majority of cases.[51] Moreover, once individuals plead guilty, their options for getting their pleas overturned on appellate review are slim. Admissions of guilt made without clear evidence that they were coerced are often treated by appellate courts as final and definitive.[52]

There are legal systems that seem better structured to get at the truth regarding what individuals suspected or accused of crimes have or have not done. Many of these are found in civil law countries that are more committed to truth as a core value of criminal procedure. Accordingly, they more extensively train their police, prosecutors, and judges, and subject them to bureaucratic control measures that monitor and, if necessary, correct their performance of assigned tasks. Such systems also do more to ensure that accused persons are represented by competent and motivated defense attorneys. Further, although negotiated pleas of various kinds are on the increase in such countries, the powers of prosecutors to negotiate are more often constrained and pleas are subjected to more judicial oversight and control.[53] Civil law systems also seek to reduce, if not eliminate, many of the adversary excesses that plague trials in common law countries.[54] Despite these apparently stronger structural commitments to getting at the truth in civil law systems, there might nonetheless be ways in which they could be improved. For instance, some criticize civil law systems for their deficiencies in permitting the accused, though their attorneys, to challenge the state's evidence in criminal cases.[55]

In thinking about how we might generally enhance the abilities of criminal investigations and adjudication procedures to get at the truth more reliably concerning what those suspected or accused of crimes have or have not done, it will be useful to distinguish two broad categories of reform. First, there are structural features of crime investigation and adjudication that need to be established or strengthened if they are to produce more rather than less truthful outcomes. These include seeing to it that crime detection, investigation, and prosecution are set up in ways to require, or at least strongly encourage, criminal justice officials to monitor, check, and, if need be, correct the work of other officials. "Open discovery" would encourage this.[56] So would more stringent appellate review of trial verdicts in cases of convictions and guilty pleas, the latter of which are much more common.[57] And needless to say, insisting that all of those accused of crimes receive timely and effective assistance from defense counsel is crucial in checking the power of state officials to push their accounts of what occurred in disputed criminal cases.[58] Further, strict limits on the magnitude of the charge and sentencing discounts available to persons for pleading guilty should be adopted and enforced.[59]

Second, there are attitudes and dispositions that we must train and encourage the various actors in the system to embrace if truthful outcomes are more often to result. Even if more institutional checks and balances on the various state actors who move cases through the criminal justice system are adopted, adjudicative outcomes might fall short of getting at the truth if those actors are not properly trained and motivated to behave in ways that generate and honor reliable evidence. Police and prosecutors, in particular, must be taught and continuously reminded about such things as how cognitive (and other biases) distort the search for the truth, why conducting line-ups in certain ways undermine their reliability, how individuals held in isolation in police stations might admit to things that they did not actually do, and how suggestion, or worse, witness-coaching, distort the truth-seeking process. More than this, these officials must be encouraged to embrace the value of conducting themselves in ways that are apt to produce veridical criminal justice outcomes. They should not have to be taught about how manufacturing or planting evidence are problematic, or about how withholding exculpatory evidence is. But we need to create cultures in which doing these things is not accepted or subtly encouraged, even if the pressures of heavy caseloads, media attention, or politics, push officials in these directions. Also, officials must be trained and encouraged to not cling to their initial conclusions, or worse, distort or manipulate the evidence to sustain their conclusions, when it becomes apparent that they are mistaken.[60]

Equality before the Law

Suppose that persons suspected of, arrested for, and charged with crimes are treated with dignity. Suppose also that the investigatory and adjudicative procedures to which they are subjected are well-suited to truth-seeking and the officials who move cases forward through the criminal justice system fully embrace the production and rigorous testing of evidence. What could possibly go wrong if all of these conditions are satisfied? Part of the answer to this question can be gleaned by considering how persons are introduced into the system, and thereby become suspects, arrestees, or individuals formally accused of crimes. Police and prosecutors might routinely and systematically focus on some (apparently) non-law-abiding citizens while ignoring others who are equally or more (apparently) non-law-abiding. Historically, the tendency for the authorities to focus their attention on the apparent or real criminal misconduct of the poor, racial or ethnic minorities, or immigrants, while ignoring or not vigorously pursuing the apparent or real criminal misconduct of the wealthy, powerful, or ethnically or culturally dominant majority, is apparent and ought to be deeply troubling.

There are myriad reasons for this skewed focus. They range from overt prejudice to implicit bias to the ease with which marginalized communities can be policed and apparent malefactors arrested and prosecuted.[61] For instance, there is reason to believe that bias against African Americans and other minority members pervades the US criminal justice system. This bias probably affects the ways in which some crimes are policed, prosecuted, and sentenced more than others. African Americans are disproportionately arrested and charged with drug crimes, for instance, although the evidence suggests that they do not use or sell drugs more often than other citizens, and may use or sell them less.[62] Once arrested, African Americans are more often charged and charged with more serious offenses. Given that many of them have criminal records—which records will be, in part, products of their having previously been more often targeted for arrest and prosecution—prosecutors will be reluctant to drop charges against them or offer them attractive plea deals. Once convicted, individuals with criminal records will tend to receive longer sentences and be treated as less eligible candidates for parole, all of this despite their similarities to others in the system who have been convicted of similar crimes or who have similar criminal histories.[63]

As critics of the US system note, its racially, ethnically, and class-skewed "assembly line" approach is especially apparent in misdemeanor cases in which no one—not police, prosecutors, defense attorneys, or judges—have much interest in slowing the process or avoiding mistakes.[64] The unfortunate members of society who find themselves on this assembly line are often so demoralized by the apparent inevitability of its outcomes that they quickly accede to guilty pleas. As Alexandra Natapoff notes, sometimes the only "evidence" against poor persons accused of misdemeanors is the fact that they have been arrested by the police.[65] There are costs to wider society in the perceived unfairness of a criminal justice system that picks on its most vulnerable members and subjects them to investigatory and adjudicative procedures that are not only cavalier about their actual guilt or innocence but ignore the equal or greater criminal misconduct of the privileged.[66] The alienation from the system that this perceived unfairness breeds will make it harder to police and prosecute legitimate crimes in poor communities of color. Individuals who believe themselves to be unfairly targeted by the system, and treated brusquely by it, will be less likely to cooperate with its officials, even when they have information relevant to resolving serious criminal cases. Unfortunately, the United States is not alone in treating some of its citizens less fairly than others in the dispensation of criminal justice. Forms of racial, ethnic, or other bias can be found in the criminal justice systems of numerous countries throughout the world.[67]

It is not that the more favored members of society can get away with all kinds of crimes. There are cases in which wealthy or privileged members of society commit serious crimes of violence or predation and are arrested and prosecuted for them. Of course, the authorities in such cases will often encounter accused persons who have the resources to hire skillful and diligent attorneys. The authorities might also find themselves facing juries who are more reluctant to believe that the famous or well-heeled are guilty of the crimes with which they are charged. Still, the heightened immunity from suspicion, arrest, and prosecution that the affluent enjoy is likely greater when it comes to certain kinds of offenses than others. Notoriously, it is more difficult for the police to detect and investigate crimes involving the use or possession of drugs or sex trafficking in the "suites" versus in the "streets."[68] The "supply lines" for drug and sex trafficking offenses committed by the well-to-do are less vulnerable to official scrutiny; also, the legal barriers to searching homes are higher than those to searching motor vehicles and people congregating on street corners or in back alleys.

Further, the kinds of crimes that wealthier or more powerful members of society commit are different than "street crimes," and that can make them much harder to detect or gather evidence about. In this vein, think about crimes such as insider trading, sophisticated financial fraud, or price-fixing. As scholars of white collar crime have noted, those who have been victimized by such crimes might not realize that they have been harmed, and so will not report anything amiss to the authorities.[69] Also, in some cases, responsibility for crimes committed by businesses or large corporations is quite diffuse, such that it will be difficult to pin down who knew what and who, exactly, did what.[70] It will be possible, in some of these kinds of cases, for those under investigation to claim, with some plausibility, that they did not know what others involved in the complex scheme were doing or that they lacked the ability to control them. All of these factors and others help to explain why the authorities might be more reluctant to invest their scarce resources in detecting and prosecuting the crimes of the affluent or powerful. And this is true despite the fact that the crimes of businesspeople or the wealthy may involve thefts of enormous sums of money or the infliction of substantial harm in ways compared to which the crimes of many poor offenders pale by significance.[71] Finally, as critics of case dispositions in crimes of the affluent point out, those actually found guilty seem to be the recipients of kinder and gentler sentences. Often, restitution to victims is imposed on such offenders by the courts in lieu of imprisonment. As Barbara Hudson has noted, the poor do not have the ability to pay to avoid imprisonment; instead, they are forced to give up their liberty.[72]

A different kind of failure to treat all members of society as equals occurs when criminal justice officials ignore or downplay crimes committed against certain kinds of victims. There is disturbing evidence that police and prosecutors fail in various ways to take female victims of sexual assault or domestic violence seriously and to assiduously pursue those who commit such crimes against them. For instance, scholars have documented the failure by police in the United States to submit tens of thousands of rape kits for testing.[73] A variety of explanations for this conduct have been uncovered, but the fact remains that female rape victims' lives and interest do not appear to be given their full due by predominantly male criminal justice officials. Likewise, domestic violence against females was long treated as a "private matter," ill-suited to official recognition by the criminal justice system.[74] Recently, evidence has emerged of widespread failures by criminal justice officials to take much interest in serious crimes committed against Native American females in the United States and Indigenous women in Canada.[75] Further, as Alexandra Natapoff has persuasively shown, persistent and pervasive "underenforcement" of the criminal law occurs in poor communities of color.[76] Even when crimes are reported, state officials often appear to do little by way of investigating or resolving them. Not surprisingly, this breeds despair and cynicism about the criminal justice system among the denizens of such communities.

In these kinds of cases, the problem is not that criminal justice officials focus too much or too harsh attention on some offenders while ignoring others. It is instead that they fall short, and sometimes well short, of acting in ways that validate some crime victims' lives and interests. The more or less inevitable result of such selective policing and prosecutorial practices will be the profound demoralization of the neglected victims and their survivors. Not only might those denied equal justice under the law be more wary about exercising and enjoying their most basic rights, they likely will be vulnerable to further property loss, injury or death. Worse than this, the individuals whose victimhood is slighted by state officials will often overlap with the individuals whose criminal misconduct is closely policed and reliably prosecuted. Their victimhood does not appear to matter much, even when it is severe. But their criminal misconduct receives lots of official attention, even when it is not very serious.

The problems that biased or selective enforcement of the criminal law pose for the state's moral authority to censure criminal misconduct can be seen most clearly if we focus on the overall picture of criminal wrongdoing that a criminal justice system marked by them will produce. It is one that disproportionately casts poor and minority populations as the perpetrators of crimes in society and thus as the individuals toward whom moral communication should be directed. Yet many members of the majority population commit crimes and escape censure for them. Others in society—often the more affluent or those who occupy positions of power in the business world—commit crimes that have quite severe repercussions for the lives of their fellow citizens. But since such crimes tend to escape detection, prosecution, or conviction, the wrongs involved are not censured. Further, the wrongs suffered by many poor or minority citizens are more often ignored or slighted by the authorities, while those suffered by better off or socially privileged members of society are more likely to officially condemned through arrest and conviction of their perpetrators. The result of all of this is that the moral communication "big picture" produced by state enforcement of the criminal law is skewed, perhaps profoundly so. True, the poor or socially marginalized who commit crimes might be appropriately censured for their acts (although official errors and biases of various kinds will obviously complicate this). However, lots of others who commit similar or worse acts go on about their lives without being condemned for them and the reasons for this are not traceable to state inabilities to detect or prosecute their crimes or resource constraints. Instead, they result from bias, neglect, disinterest, or decisions to direct state criminal justice resources toward the policing and prosecution of more vulnerable populations.

Just how skewed the resulting "big picture" of criminal offending and criminal victimization turns out to be will depend on a number of factors. In some societies, more resources might be devoted to detecting and prosecuting white collar crime. Or there might be less focus on policing and punishing the poor and more on helping the impoverished, mentally ill, or drug or alcohol dependent to gain or regain decent and responsible lives. Still, the more distorted the picture of who commits crimes and who is victimized by them that official arrests, charges, and successful prosecutions turns out to be, the more problematic will be the state's bona fides as the authoritative communicator about public wrongs. Not surprisingly, poor or minority members of society whose misconduct often receives the brunt of official censure, but whose victimization is more often ignored or slighted, tend to resent and mistrust state authorities.[77] Many of them would probably roll their eyes at claims to the effect that the state is a reliable or accurate moral communicator when it comes to the wide range of criminal misconduct in society; reasonably so, I would say.

In civil law systems, the equal treatment of all citizens in the enforcement of the criminal law might seem more likely under long-standing principles of "mandatory prosecution."[78] Such principles are supposed to ensure that prosecutorial charging decisions are rendered according to the facts and the law, exclusive of other factors that might sway prosecutors one way or the other. However, the pressures of case processing seem to have eroded these principles somewhat, especially with respect to less serious criminal offenses. As a result, prosecutorial offers of reduced charges or sentences in exchange for admissions of guilt have emerged.[79] Yet such practices inevitably give prosecutors more discretion and what comes with that discretion—the possibility that it will be exercised on behalf of some accused persons but not others. Moreover, as in common law systems, which crimes are detected and prosecuted depends, in part, on police and investigator decisions about where to look for them and which ones to persist in investigating. It seems likely that such decisions will be influenced to some extent by factors such as class, race, and ethnicity in civil law systems just as they are in common law ones. But this means that the value of equal treatment by and before the law is one that cannot be taken for granted in civil systems simply because they give less discretion to state officials in other respects.

There might be no easy fix for the various forms of unequal treatment found in many if not most criminal justice systems. We might hope that better education or more training for police, prosecutors, and judges about the varied and subtle ways in which forms of implicit bias distort criminal justice outcomes will lead to needed changes. Yet practices of bias or discrimination are often deeply entrenched in ways that will make them nearly intractable, especially if we rely solely on better education or training. One partial solution to this involves taking steps to ensure greater transparency on the part of criminal justice officials regarding the demographic characteristics of the individuals arrested, charged, and convicted, as well as the sentences assigned to them. At times, criminal justice officials have resisted such transparency, thus depriving litigants of the vital evidence they need to pursue claims of systematic discrimination.[80] In addition, the case dispositions of complaints filed by crime victims, along with the reasons for those dispositions, should be compiled and made public.

Still, greater transparency alone might not bring about the changes needed to ensure that all members of society are treated fairly by criminal justice officials. In addition, there must be individuals, organizations, or public bodies prepared to peruse the records compiled and disseminated and demand change if officials are to be held more accountable for their acts. Lawyers who are prepared to file lawsuits on behalf of individuals who believe that they were victims of unfair treatment by officials are one possibility. We might also hope that scholars or public interest groups committed to equal enforcement of the law will examine publicly available records and release their findings. Further, many communities have instituted citizen review boards to investigate police conduct and push for changes in where and how the police concentrate their efforts.[81] We might envision similar boards emerging to investigate the decisions of prosecutors with regard to charging decisions and case dispositions that result from guilty pleas. Still, it seems prudent to admit that the jury is still out about whether and to what extent such public bodies can effect needed reforms.

Concluding Remarks

I have not attempted to address many of the complicated issues with which evidence and criminal procedure scholars wrestle. Instead, my focus in this chapter has been on the ways in which criminal procedure must be broadly structured if it is to cohere with the account of legal punishment defended in previous chapters. I have argued that to have and maintain the moral authority to punish, and thus to censure those convicted of crimes for their public wrongs, several conditions must be satisfied. First, we must see to it that criminal justice officials perform their various tasks in ways that are consistent with the dignity of those who come under their purview. Second, we must make sure that criminal investigations and charge adjudication maintain sufficient and reliable contact with the truth about those suspected or accused of crimes have or have not done. Third, we must ensure that all members of society are treated as equals by and before the law, both insofar as they are or might be guilty of violating it and insofar as they are victims of the misconduct of others. Failures or deficiencies by state officials in any or all of these three areas will undermine their moral authority to effect moral communication with the convicted, with victims, or with members of the public. Still, how far or in what ways such failures or deficiencies weaken that authority will be matters of degree and will inevitably be ones about which there will be contention.

Importantly, I have not touched on an alleged state deficiency that other scholars have maintained threatens its moral authority to punish.[82] Pervasive social injustice, especially in forms that leave some members of society destitute or otherwise vulnerable has often been seen to call into question the state's right to punish. Simply put—a bit too simply perhaps—how can the state claim the authority to punish in relation to individuals some of whose basic moral rights it consistently does little to secure? More specifically, if legal punishment is to make sense as a morally communicative enterprise, should we not have to ensure that the broader social conditions supportive of citizen responsiveness to moral considerations are sufficiently satisfied? If we do not, then it would seem the coherence of the state's morally communicative efforts is compromised.

Although I am deeply sympathetic to this line of argument, it is one that depends on acceptance of some controversial assumptions about the nature of the just society, in particular, whether and to what extent such a society tolerates inequalities in people's life prospects. I will have more to say about this matter in Chapter 8. In this chapter, I have chosen to highlight moral requirements of criminal justice that I suspect will have broader appeal, including to those whose views about social or distributive justice diverge. Commitments to human dignity, truth-seeking, and equality before the law are ones that most theorists will accept as binding on state officials, at least in some form or other. As that last qualifying phrase implicitly concedes, even with regard to such values, little is simple or obvious.

Notes

1 An important point made by John Rawls in "Two Concepts of Rules," *The Philosophical Review* 64 (1955): 3–32.

2 See Mirjan R. Damaška, *The Faces of Justice and State Authority* (New Haven, CT: Yale University Press, 1986); Larry Laudan, *Truth, Error, and Criminal Law* (Cambridge: Cambridge University Press, 2006); R. A. Duff, Lindsay Farmer, Sandra Marshall, and Victor Tadros, *The Trial on Trial, Vol. 3: Towards a Normative Theory of the Criminal Trial* (Oxford: Hart Publishing, 2007); and Thomas Weigend, "Is the Criminal Process about Truth? A German Perspective," *Harvard Journal of Law and Public Policy* 26 (2003): 157–74 and "Should We Search for the Truth and Who Should Do It?" *North Carolina Journal of International Law and Commercial Regulation* 36 (2011): 389–416.

3 Anonymous, "Note: Restructuring the Plea Bargain," *Yale Law Journal* 82 (1972): 286–312; Richard L. Lippke, *The Ethics of Plea Bargaining* (Oxford: Oxford University Press, 2011); Darryl K. Brown, *Free Market Criminal Justice: How Democracy and Laissez Faire Undermine the Rule of Law* (New York: Oxford University Press, 2016).

4 Frank H. Easterbrook, "Criminal Procedure as a Market System," *Journal of Legal Studies* 12 (1983): 289–332 and "Plea Bargaining as Compromise," *Yale Law Journal* 101 (1992): 1969–78.

5 Weigend, "Should We Search?" 393 and "Is the Criminal Process about Truth?" 168.
6 Weigend, "Is the Criminal Process about Truth?" 169.
7 Alexandra Natapoff, "Underenforcement," *Fordham Law Review* 75 (2006): 1715–76.
8 William J. Stuntz, "Race, Class, and Drugs," *Columbia Law Review* 98 (1998): 1795–842, at 1800.
9 See, among others, Jeremy Waldron, *Dignity, Rank, and Rights* (Oxford: Oxford University Press, 2012); George Kateb, *Human Dignity* (Cambridge, MA: Harvard University Press, 2011); Michael Rosen, *Dignity: Its History and Meaning* (Cambridge, MA: Harvard University Press, 2012); and Charles R. Beitz, "Human Dignity in the Theory of Human Rights: Nothing But a Phrase?" *Philosophy and Public Affairs* 41 (2013): 259–90. For an insightful discussion of dignity in the context of criminal justice see Michael Tonry, *Doing Justice, Preventing Crime* (New York: Oxford University Press, 2020), Chapter 2.
10 Immanuel Kant, *Groundwork of the Metaphysics of Morals*, Mary Gregor (trans.) (Cambridge: Cambridge University Press, 1998), and *Critique of Practical Reason*, Mary Gregor (trans.) (Cambridge: Cambridge University Press, 2015).
11 See, for instance, Jeremy Waldon (ed.), *Theories of Rights* (Oxford: Oxford University Press, 1982) and Will Kymlicka, *Contemporary Political Philosophy: An Introduction* (Oxford: Oxford University Press, 2002).
12 I take no position here on whether the ultimate ground of such constraints is deontological or consequentialist. I originally developed an account of this kind in Richard L. Lippke, *Taming the Presumption of Innocence* (New York: Oxford University Press, 2016), Chapter 6.
13 This is the standard articulated by the US Supreme Court in *Terry v. Ohio*, 392 U. S. 1 (1968). For critical discussion, see, David A. Harris, "Factors for Reasonable Suspicion: Why Black and Poor Means Stopped and Frisked," *Indiana Law Journal* 69 (1994): 659–88.
14 The "reasonable doubt" standard for the adjudication of criminal cases at trial is not uncontroversial. However, most theorists seem unprepared to reduce the standard of proof by very much, in which case the evidence that the state must muster will still be higher than what it must be to justify arrests, searches, or briefly detaining suspects. For critical discussion of the standard, see Larry Laudan, "The Rules of Trial, Political Morality, and the Costs of Error: Or, Is Proof beyond a Reasonable Doubt Doing More Harm than Good?" in L. Green and B. Leiter (eds.), *Oxford Studies in the Philosophy of Law, Vol. 1* (New York: Oxford University Press, 2011): 195–227 and Erik Lillquist, "Recasting Reasonable Doubt: Decision Theory and the Virtues of Variability," *University California-Davis Law Review* 36 (2002): 85–197.
15 Lippke, *Taming the Presumption of Innocence*, Chapter 7.
16 For discussion of parsimony as a sentencing value, see Michael Tonry, "Proportionality, Parsimony, and Interchangeability of Punishment," in R. A. Duff, S. Marshall, and R. Dobash (eds.), *Penal Theory and Practice* (Manchester: Manchester University Press, 1994): 59–83 and Richard S. Frase, *Just Sentencing: Principles and Procedures for a Workable System* (New York: Oxford University Press, 2013): 11 and 32–33.
17 See Lippke, *Taming the Presumption of Innocence*, Chapter 7.
18 See John D. Jackson and Sarah J. Summers, *The Internationlisation of Criminal Evidence: Beyond the Common Law and Civil Law Traditions* (Cambridge: Cambridge University Press, 2012), Chapter 8; Stefan Trechsel and Sarah Summers, *Human Rights in Criminal Proceedings* (Oxford: Oxford University Press, 2006); Albert

W. Alschuler, "A Peculiar Privilege in Historical Perspective," in R. H. Helmholtz, et al. (eds.), *The Privilege against Self-Incrimination: Its Origin and Development* (Chicago: University of Chicago Press, 1997): 181–204. For a more critical perspective on the privilege, see David Dolinko, "Is There a Rationale for the Privilege against Self-Incrimination?" *UCLA Law Review* 33 (1986): 1063–148.

19 See Jeffrie G. Murphy, "Cruel and Unusual Punishments," in M. A. Stewart (ed.), *Law, Morality, and Human Rights* (Dordrecht: D. Reidel, 1979): 373–404.

20 There is debate about whether the torture of individuals suspected of involvement in very serious crimes is ever justified, with special attention to so-called "ticking bomb" kinds of cases. See, for instance, David Luban, "Liberalism, Torture, and the Ticking Bomb," in Stephen P. Lee (ed.), *Intervention, Terrorism, and Torture: Contemporary Challenges to Just War Theory* (Dordrecht, Netherlands: Springer, 2010): 249–62.

21 Tom R. Tyler, *Why People Obey the Law* (Princeton, NJ: Princeton University Press, 2006).

22 Tyler, *Why People Obey*, 108.

23 For an eloquent account of the role of defense attorneys in helping to ensure that accused persons are treated with dignity, see John B. Mitchell, "The Ethics of the Criminal Defense Attorney—New Answers to Old Questions," *Stanford Law Review* 32 (1980): 293–337.

24 The claim that indigent persons should be provided defense attorneys at state expense is more controversial than is sometimes acknowledged by legal scholars. For discussion, see Loren E. Lomasky, "Aid without Egalitarianism: Assisting Indigent Defendants," in William C. Heffernan and John Kleinig (eds.), *From Social Justice to Criminal Justice: Poverty and the Administration of Criminal Law* (New York: Oxford University Press, 2000): 84–97 and Richard L. Lippke, "The Minimal State and Indigent Defense," *Criminal Justice Ethics* 35 (2016): 1–20.

25 However, the right of the accused during the pre-plea stage to information that might impeach the testimony of witnesses against them is limited. See *U. S. v Ruiz* 536 U. S. 622 (2002).

26 See Milton Heumann, *Plea Bargaining: The Experiences of Prosecutors, Judges, and Defense Attorneys* (Chicago: University of Chicago Press, 1978): 69–70. For other failures in obtaining informed consent in US plea bargaining, see Jenia I. Turner, *Plea Bargaining across Borders* (New York: Aspen Publishers, 2009): 40–41, and Darryl K. Brown, *Free Market Justice: How Democracy and Laissez Faire Undermine the Rule of Law* (New York: Oxford University Press, 2016): 107.

27 Turner, *Plea Bargaining across Borders*, 40.

28 See Laudan, *Truth, Error, and the Criminal Law*, especially Chapter 7.

29 See Weigend, "Is the Criminal Process about Truth?"; Mirjan R. Damaška, "Truth in Adjudication," *Hastings Law Journal* 49 (1998): 289–308; and Elisabetta Grande, "Dances of Criminal Justice: Thoughts on Systematic Differences and the Search for the Truth," in John Jackson, Máximo Langer, and Peter Tiller (eds.), *Crime, Procedure, and Evidence in Comparative and International Context: Essays in Honour of Mirjan Damaška* (Oxford: Hart Publishing, 2008): 145–64.

30 See Albert W. Alschuler, "The Changing Plea Bargaining Debate," *California Law Review* 69 (1981): 652–730 and Weigend, "Is the Criminal Process about Truth?" 169.

31 See Keith A. Findlay and Michael S. Scott, "The Multiple Dimensions of Tunnel Vision in Criminal Cases," *Wisconsin Law Review* 2006 (2006): 291–397 and Daniel S. Medwed, "The Zeal Deal: Prosecutorial Resistance to Post-Conviction Claims of Innocence," *Boston University Law Review* 84 (2004): 125–83.

32 Findley and Scott, "Multiple Dimensions," 323–31.

33 Findley and Scott, "Multiple Dimensions," 333–40.

34 Findley and Scott, "Multiple Dimensions," 387–88.
35 Alexandra Natapoff, "Misdemeanors," *Southern California Law Review* 85 (2012): 1313–75 and Jenny Roberts, "Why Misdemeanors Matter: Defining Effective Advocacy in the Lower Criminal Courts," *University of California-Davis Law Review* 45 (2011): 277–372.
36 Josh Bowers, "Punishing the Innocent," *University of Pennsylvania Law Review* 156 (2008): 1117–179, at 1128.
37 Ronald F. Wright, "How Prosecutor Elections Fail Us," *Ohio State Journal of Criminal Law* 6 (2009): 581–610 and Richard L. Lippke, "Prosecutors: Experts or Elected Officials?" in J. Ryberg and J. Roberts (eds.), *Popular Punishment: On the Normative Significance of Public Opinion for Penal Theory* (Oxford: Oxford University Press, 2014): 163–82.
38 Angela J. Davis, *Arbitrary Justice: The Power of the American Prosecutor* (New York: Oxford University Press, 2007): 150–54 and Findley and Scott, "Multiple Dimensions," 351–53.
39 Dan Simon, "The Limited Diagnosticity of Criminal Trials," *Vanderbilt Law Review* 64 (2011): 143–223, at 150–51.
40 Findley and Scott, "Multiple Dimensions," 334–41.
41 See David Luban, *Lawyers and Justice: An Ethical Study* (Princeton, NJ: Princeton University Press, 1988): 68–74 and Weigend, "Is the Criminal Process about Truth?" 159–60.
42 Simon, "Limited Diagnosticity," at 184–89.
43 Weigend, "Is the Criminal Process about Truth?" 165–66.
44 Weigend, "Is the Criminal Process about Truth?" 165–66.
45 Richard L. Lippke, "The Case for Reasoned Criminal Trial Verdicts," *Canadian Journal of Law and Jurisprudence* 22 (2009): 313–30.
46 Weigend, "Is the Criminal Process about Truth?" 166–67.
47 Findley and Scott, "Multiple Dimensions," 348–49.
48 Albert W. Alschuler, "The Prosecutor's Role in Plea Bargaining," *University of Chicago Law Review* 36 (1968): 50–112; Lippke, *The Ethics of Plea Bargaining*; Turner, *Plea Bargaining across Borders*; Brown, *Free Market Criminal Justice*; and Yue Ma, "Prosecutorial Discretion and Plea Bargaining in the United States, France, Germany and Italy: A Comparative Perspective," *International Criminal Justice Review* 12 (2002): 22–52.
49 William J. Stuntz, "The Pathological Politics of Criminal Law," *Michigan Law Review* 100 (2001): 505–600, at 519–23.
50 Stephen J. Schulhofer, "Rethinking Mandatory Minimums," *Wake Forest Law Review* 28 (1993): 199–222.
51 Heumann, *Plea Bargaining*, 127–52; Turner, *Plea Bargaining across Borders*, 23; Bowers, "Punishing the Innocent," 1147.
52 Leanna C. Minix, "Examining Rule 11 (b) (1) (N) Error: Guilty Pleas, Appellate Waiver, and Dominguez Benitez," *Washington and Lee Law Review* 74 (2017): 552–606, at 564–65.
53 Richard S. Frase, "Comparative Criminal Justice as a Guide to American Law Reform: How Do the French Do It, How Can We Find Out, and Why Should We Care?" *California Law Review* 78 (1990): 539–683 and W. T. Pizzi, "Understanding Prosecutorial Discretion in the United States: The Limits of Comparative Criminal Procedure as an Instrument of Reform," *Ohio State Law Journal* 54 (1993): 1325–74.
54 Ma, "Prosecutorial Discretion," 31 and Turner, *Plea Bargaining across Borders*, 73–80.
55 Weigend, "Should We Search for the Truth?" 405.
56 See Thomas W. Church, Jr., "In Defense of 'Bargain Justice'," *Law & Society* 13 (1979): 509–25, at 521.

57 For more on the role that judges might play in overseeing negotiated pleas, see Lippke, *Ethics of Plea Bargaining*, 16–23; Albert W. Alschuler, "The Trial Judge's Role in Plea Bargaining, Part 1," *Columbia Law Review* 76 (1976): 1059–154.
58 Indigent defense provisions in the US are especially deficient. See Stephen B. Bright and Sia M. Sanneh, "Fifty Years of Defiance and Resistance After *Gideon v. Wainwright*," *Yale Law Journal* 122 (2013): 2150–74.
59 England and Wales have adopted limits on the magnitude of the sentence discounts available to accused persons who agree to admit their guilt, although there remains debate about whether they sufficiently reduce the pressures on accused persons to do so. See Andrew Ashworth and Mike Redmayne, *The Criminal Process, Fourth Edition* (Oxford: Oxford University Press, 2010): 310–20.
60 Medwed, "Zeal Deal," 138–47.
61 See Angela J. Davis (ed.), *Policing the Black Man: Arrest, Prosecution, and Imprisonment* (New York: Vintage Books, 2017); Michelle Alexander, *The New Jim Crow: Mass Incarceration in the Age of Colorblindness* (New York: The New Press, 2012); Michael Tonry, *Malign Neglect: Race, Crime, and Punishment in America* (New York: Oxford University Press, 1995); David Cole, *No Equal Justice: Race and Class in the American Criminal Justice System* (New York: The New Press, 1999); and Stuntz, "Race, Class, and Drugs."
62 Michael Tonry, *Punishing Race: A Continuing American Dilemma* (New York: Oxford University Press, 2011): 59–67.
63 Tonry, *Punishing Race*, 73.
64 Natapoff, "Misdemeanors," and Bowers, "Punishing the Innocent." See also Alice Ristroph, "Criminal Law as Public Ordering," *University of Toronto Law Journal* 70 (2020): 64–83 and "An Intellectual History of Mass Incarceration," *Boston College Law Review* 60 (2019): 1949–2010.
65 Natapoff, "Misdemeanors," 1344–45.
66 See Jeffrey Fagan and Tracy L. Meares, "Punishment, Deterrence, and Social Control: The Paradox of Punishment in Minority Communities," *Ohio State Journal of Criminal Law* 6 (2008): 173–229. More generally, see Tyler, *Why People Obey the Law*.
67 See David J. Smith, "Ethnic Origins, Crime, and Criminal Justice in England and Wales," *Crime and Justice: A Review of Research* 21 (1997): 101–82; Roderic Broadhurst, "Aborigines and Crime in Australia," *Crime and Justice: A Review of Research* 21 (1997): 407–68; Liz Fekete, "Europe against the Roma," *Race & Class* 55 (2014): 60–70; and Akwasi Owusu-Bempah and Scot Wortley, "Race, Crime, and Criminal Justice in Canada," in S. Bucerius and M. Tonry (eds.), *The Oxford Handbook of Ethnicity, Crime, and Immigration* (New York: Oxford University Press, 2013): 281–320.
68 Stuntz, "Race, Class, and Drugs," 1802–13.
69 John Braithwaite and Gilbert Geis, "On Theory and Action for Corporate Crime Control," *Crime & Delinquency* 28 (1982): 292–314.
70 Braithwaite and Geis, "On Theory and Action," 298.
71 See, for instance, Jeffrey Reiman, *The Rich Get Richer and the Poor Get Prison: Ideology, Class, and Criminal Justice, Eighth Edition* (Boston, MA: Pearson, 2007): 82–87 and K. Calavita, R. Tillman, and H. N. Pontell, "The Savings and Loan Debacle, Financial Crime, and the State," *Annual Review of Sociology* 23 (1997): 19–38.
72 Barbara Hudson, "Punishing the Poor: Dilemmas of Justice and Difference," in Heffernan and Kleinig, *From Social Justice to Criminal Justice*, 189–216. Still, the increasing imposition of "user fees" on offenders without regard to their abilities to pay such fees suggests that poor offenders are now losing more than their

liberty. On this, see Katherine Beckett and Alexes Harris, "On Cash and Conviction: Monetary Sanctions as Misguided Policy," *Criminology & Public Policy* 10 (2011): 509–37.

73 See Rebecca Campbell, Hannah Feeney, Giannina Fehler-Cabral, Jessica Shaw, and Sheena Horsford, "The National Problem of Untested Rape Kits (SAKS): Scope, Causes, and Future Directions for Research, Policy, and Practice," *Trauma, Violence, and Abuse* 18 (2017): 363–76, and Kevin J. Strom and Matthew J. Hickman, "Unanalyzed Evidence in Law Enforcement Agencies: A National Examination of Forensic Processing in Police Departments," *Criminology & Public Policy* 9 (2010): 381–404.

74 Emily J. Sack, "Battered Women and the State: The Struggle for the Future of Domestic Violence Policy," *Wisconsin Law Review* 2004 (2004): 1657–740; Anna Clark, "Domestic Violence, Past and Present," *Journal of Women's History* 23 (2011): 193–202; and Deborah Epstein, "Effective Intervention in Domestic Violence Cases: Rethinking the Roles of Prosecutors, Judges, and the Court System," *Yale Journal of Law & Feminism* 11 (1999): 3–50. Many countries fail to protect women from domestic violence. See Dorothy Q. Thomas and Michele E. Beasley, Esq., "Domestic Violence as a Human Rights Issue," *Human Rights Quarterly* 15 (1993): 36–62.

75 See "Missing and Murdered Indigenous Women & Girls: A Snapshot of Data from 71 Urban Cities in the United States," Urban Indian Health Institute, at www.uihi.org/wp-content/uploads/2018/11/Missing-and-Murdered-Indigenous-Women-and-Girls-Report.pdf (accessed June 22, 2020) and "Reclaiming Power and Place: The Final Report of the National Inquiry into Missing and Murdered Indigenous Women and Girls, Volume 1a," at www.mmiwg-ffada.ca/wp-content/uploads/2019/06/Final_Report_Vol_1a-1.pdf (accessed June 22, 2020).

76 Natapoff, "Underenforcement," 1719. See also Randall Kennedy, *Race, Crime, and the Law* (New York: Vintage, 1998) and William J. Stuntz, "Unequal Justice," *Harvard Law Review* 121 (2008): 1969–2040.

77 Natapoff, "Underenforcement," 1750.

78 See Shawn Boyne, "Is the Journey from the In-Box to the Out-Box a Straight Line? The Drive for Efficiency and the Prosecution of Low-Level Criminality in Germany," in Erik Luna and Marianne Wade (eds.), *The Prosecutor in Transnational Perspective* (Oxford: Oxford University Press, 2012): 37–53.

79 Turner, *Plea Bargaining across Borders*, 73–127, and Maximo Langer, "From Legal Transplants to Legal Translations: The Globalization of Plea Bargaining and the Americanization Thesis in Criminal Procedure," *Harvard International Law Journal* 45 (2004): 1–64.

80 As Alexander notes in *The New Jim Crow*, at 117, the US Supreme Court, in the case *U.S. v. Armstrong* 517 US 456 (1996), effectively shielded prosecutors from having to reveal the grounds for their charging decisions.

81 Udi Ofer, "Getting it Right: Building Effective Civilian Review Boards to Oversee Police," *Seton Hall Law Review* 46 (2016): 1033–62.

82 See, among others, Jeffrie G. Murphy, "Marxism and Retribution," *Philosophy and Public Affairs* 2 (1973): 217–43; Richard Delgado, "Rotten Social Background: Should the Criminal Law Recognize a Defense of Severe Environmental Deprivation?" *Law & Inequality* 3 (1985): 9–90; Duff, *Punishment, Communication, and Community*, at 183–84; and Göran Duus-Otterström and Erin I. Kelly, "Injustice and the Right to Punish," *Philosophy Compass* 14 (2019), at https://doi.org/10.1111/phc3.12565 (accessed November 27, 2021).

6 A Mixed Theory of Sentencing

In previous chapters, I have developed and defended a mixed theory of legal punishment. It is an account of the institution that puts moral communication in the presumptive lead role, with crime reduction in an important, albeit secondary, role. I have also maintained that the larger criminal justice system of which legal punishment is a part must be structured so that its officials accept and abide by certain principles guiding their practices, principles that furnish the rationale for checking and balancing the considerable power bestowed upon them. All persons suspected of or accused of crimes should be treated with dignity, the methods used to investigate crimes and adjudicate charges should be reliably truth-oriented, and all persons must be treated as equals by and before the law.

Once individuals are convicted of crimes, they must be sentenced. As anyone who has thought about it for very long comes to recognize, the sentencing of individuals for their crimes is a complicated affair. It is important to keep in mind that the majority of individuals facing sentencing will have committed relatively minor criminal offenses.[1] There is some tendency, I believe, in punishment theorizing, to focus on serious criminal offenses and their sentencing, and thus to regard imprisonment as the paradigm of state punishment. Yet many offenders will not be legitimate candidates for custodial sentences, ones that not only curtail liberty but, historically at least, impose numerous other significant losses upon them. In this chapter, as in previous ones, I will avoid such "felony-centric" thinking in my efforts to articulate what a mixed theory of punishment implies about sentencing.

Given the centrality of moral communication in my account, the principle of proportionality, according to which offenders should be punished in accordance with the seriousness of their crimes, will be assigned a central role. Punishment, I have argued, will not communicate accurately if it does not assign offenders sanctions that "appropriately value" and thus reflect, in terms of the burdens they impose, the wrongs done to victims. Those wrongs, following standard retributive logic, should be understood as a complex function of the harms done, threatened, attempted, or risked and the culpability of offenders in acting. The principle of proportionality has been challenged by

DOI: 10.4324/9781032661667-7

scholars who are skeptical about its implications or the useful role it can play in sentencing. In the second section of this chapter, I address several of these challenges. Some are more concerning than others. In the end, I acknowledge that proportionality, as a sentencing principle, cannot be made to yield precise sentencing guidance. There will be a number of available sentencing schemes that satisfy the requirements of relative and absolute (or what Andreas von Hirsch termed "ordinal" and "cardinal") proportionality.[2] However, I contend that this does not make the principle useless for sentencing purposes; far from it. Importantly, the mixed approach to justifying legal punishment that I support provides additional normative resources for devising defensible sentencing schemes.

In the third section, I discuss various ways in which punishment's crime reduction purposes might be utilized to narrow the list of defensible sentencing schemes. Otherwise proportionate schemes that are relatively harsh in the sentences they would yield might be rejected if there is reason to believe they will not serve crime reduction purposes and might actually frustrate them. However, these concessions to crime reduction considerations bring us nowhere near acceptance of a sentencing scheme more robustly based on such considerations. In the first part of that section, I detail why such a scheme is unlikely to be unavailable.

In the fourth section of the chapter, I consider the implications of the account of sentencing I defend for one of the more difficult problems with which sentencing theorists have wrestled. There is ongoing debate about how to sentence recidivists, individuals who persist in offending despite having been caught, convicted, and punished for previous crimes. I contend that the mixed theory I propose offers some useful guidance in thinking about the difficulties posed by such offenders.

In the first part of the chapter, I discuss the value of parsimony in sentencing. With regard to sentencing, I cast parsimony as a framing value. As such, it does not tell us much about the kinds or durations of the sentences that ought to be assigned the numerous types of offenders that criminal justice systems confront. Instead, on the assumption that all persons have certain basic rights that the state must respect, parsimony requires state officials to prefer less intrusive or burdensome penal measures over more intrusive or burdensome ones. We should not view offenders' rights as forfeited or suspended by their criminal convictions. They are retained but can be defensibly intruded upon or curtailed by state officials pursuing legitimate sentencing purposes.

Parsimony in Sentencing

The principle of parsimony, interpreted in a specific way, is one that we have already encountered in Chapter 5, where the implications of the mixed theory of punishment I defend for criminal procedure were discussed. There, I argued that while we should be cognizant of and accepting of the ways in which state officials must be permitted to infringe upon basic rights of individuals as they detect, investigate, and adjudicate criminal offenses, respect for those rights and thus acknowledgement in our criminal justice practices of their importance should guide and constrain those practices. More specifically, we should always prefer to limit such infringements by placing the burden of justifying more rather than fewer of them on state officials. Our basic moral rights ground rebuttable presumptions, of varying strengths, against their infringement. In this way, the power of such officials can be restrained and channeled for legitimate purposes.

In my view, nothing changes once individuals are convicted of crimes.[3] Although the convicted are appropriately held accountable for their crimes, state officials should always be understood as tasked with finding and employing sanctions that do so while least infringing their basic moral rights.[4] For instance, on the plausible assumption that custodial sanctions infringe basic moral rights more than noncustodial ones, the latter ought always to be preferred unless the former can be shown to be necessary for the purposes of validating the interests of victims or the rules of the civil order that limit risk or regulate and coordinate various activities. Among noncustodial sanctions, some (e.g., GPS monitoring) will be more intrusive upon the basic rights of offenders than others (e.g., nonintensive probation). Again, unless we can justify the former kinds of sanctions, the latter, less right-infringing ones, ought to be preferred.

More controversially, parsimony arguably has important implications for custodial sanctions. At a minimum, such sanctions deprive offenders of their liberty of movement in society by confining them in jails or prisons for periods of time.[5] Suppose that this curtailment of the right to liberty is justified in some cases. The problem is that once the right to liberty is curtailed, the enjoyment and exercise of other basic rights is more or less inevitably impacted—rights to privacy, paid labor of one's own choosing, and freedom of association, among them. Yet an argument can be made that although parsimony does not rule out the curtailment of liberty in some cases, it does not permit the loss or infringement of other basic rights, or at least that those losses or infringements should be countered by state efforts to minimize or ameliorate them.[6] For instance, the state could reduce the impact of justifiably diminished liberty by providing prisoners with access to paid labor, by housing them in cells that provide them with some privacy, and by ensuring that prisoners continue to have access (through prison visitation and prisoner furlough policies) to persons in the outside world. Again, if rights are interpreted as placing successive hurdles in the paths of state officials as they proceed against those suspected, accused of, or convicted of crimes, it makes sense to view custodial sentences as consisting of the next gradual step up in severity from the most intrusive noncustodial sentences. Noncustodial sanctions typically permit those assigned them the continued enjoyment and exercise of their basic moral rights. Viewing custody as the next step up in sentence severity in this way provides us with grounds for objecting to the deliberate imposition by state officials of further losses on prisoners, as well as to official complaisance to the inability of the confined to exercise and enjoy other of their basic rights.

Also, if we see parsimony as grounded in the moral requirement to respect the dignity of persons, as was urged in Chapter 5, it follows that we have grounds for insisting that state officials avoid forms of sanctions or penal practices that are unnecessarily cruel or demeaning.[7] Even those who commit serious crimes, and whose confinement is justified in order to stand for victims and assure them and others that the state will not allow rights to be violated with impunity, should not be subjected to malnourishment, lack of proper medical care, extreme cold or heat, constant surveillance, violence or cruelty at the hands of guards or other inmates, or verbal abuse and derision. None of these forms of treatment is necessary to morally communicate with serious offenders about their crimes. Nor are they likely needed to serve effectively the aims of crime reduction, especially if we take into account, as we must, the damaging impact of such harsh treatment on the future willingness of individuals to abide by the dictates of the criminal law. As such, parsimony forbids them. In similar ways, it forbids forms of noncustodial sanctions that belittle offenders or hold them up to ridicule, such as chain gangs or practices wherein offenders are ordered to stand on busy street corners with signs proclaiming their offenses.[8] State officials are under an obligation to find and deploy sanctions that hold offenders accountable in ways that recognize that they are human beings who, though they have made mistakes, have feelings and sensibilities that should not be derided or crushed.

This brings us to an important challenge to the notion of parsimony as I have interpreted it. Some theorists maintain that those who violate the criminal law, and especially do so in serious ways that inflict substantial harms on victims, forfeit their rights.[9] At its simplest, the idea is that those who refuse to abide by the responsibilities toward others that rights entail should not be regarded as entitled to the benefits of rights. If such a position can be made out, then the presumptions against interference that I have argued basic moral rights establish might be understood as waived or lost by some or all of those convicted of crimes. The state would therefore act permissibly in imposing any losses or deprivations on offenders that it deemed useful in punishing them. Parsimony as a value might remain operative in the pre-conviction stage, but not post-conviction.

There are numerous problems with which those who defend the notion of right forfeiture in the penal context must contend. First, they have to explain whether all convicted offenders forfeit their basic rights, or if only some do—perhaps those convicted of serious crimes, however those are defined. It will not be easy to draw this line. If failing to shoulder the responsibilities correlated with rights is the ground for right forfeiture, then minor offenders do this as well as those who commit more serious offenses. Second, forfeiture accounts must address the questions of whether convicted offenders lose all of their basic rights, or only some of them, and which ones. Most forfeiture theorists lean toward the latter kind of account, with some suggesting that offenders forfeit all and only the basic rights that they, through their crimes, violated.[10] Yet such partial forfeiture accounts will have to explain why someone who, for instance, violates the property rights of another person by stealing her bicycle, forfeits her right to property in its entirety (versus some aspect of her right to property). Also, if offenders forfeit only the right or rights they have violated, then some version of parsimony would remain in effect. The state would presumably be justified in infringing only upon the right or rights corresponding to the right or rights offenders violated, not all of their rights. Third, for how long does an offender forfeit whatever rights she is alleged to have forfeited? "Forfeiture" sounds rather permanent, but few of us will be attracted to accounts that suggest that minor offenders, or even more serious ones, forfeit all or some of their basic moral rights in perpetuity. Fourth, if some offenders forfeit all or some of their basic rights, would that mean that just anyone could punish them, or worse, attack them with moral impunity, since those who forfeit rights would appear to have no claim against anyone who attacked them in the relevant respects?[11]

These and other problems with the right forfeiture approach to thinking about crime and punishment have led one recent defender of the view to argue that the right forfeited by (presumably all) criminal offenders is one that we might not ordinarily think of as basic, such as life, physical and psychological integrity, liberty, or property. Instead, Christopher Wellman suggests that offenders forfeit "the right not to be punished."[12] He takes it to be obvious that in the absence of having been convicted of one or more crimes, individuals have such a right.[13] Of course, it might equally be claimed that in the absence of having been convicted of one or more crimes, individuals' basic rights to liberty or property should not be infringed or curtailed. It is apparent, at least to many theorists of human rights, that individuals have such rights. It seems less apparent that they have "the right not to be punished." Such a right does not appear on standard lists of basic human rights. One suspects that few people have ever marched and demanded "the right not to be punished" in ways that they have, rather more often, marched and demanded rights to "life, liberty, and property." It also seems doubtful that anyone has a right not to be punished simpliciter. If one has a right not to be punished, it would make more sense to conceive of it as a qualified right, as in a right not to be punished *if* one is innocent of crime, or, perhaps, *if* one is not provably guilty of one or more crimes. But then the problem is that even those guilty or provably guilty of crimes would not forfeit that right. Most significantly, forfeiture of the right not to be punished seems simply to remove a moral barrier to punishment. It does not tell us how to punish or how much to punish. As Wellman concedes, for that, we need an account of the purpose or purposes of legal punishment.[14] Whatever those turn out to be, it could be argued that offenders should be subject to no more punishment than is needed to serve it or them. Their basic rights to life, liberty, and property might be thought to shield them from more than that by establishing presumptions against their infringement. But that means that Wellman's account is consistent with parsimony, and might be supportive of it, rather than hostile to it in ways that more robust forfeiture accounts appear to be.

Even if we accept the notion that the value of parsimony is relevant to our thinking about the sentencing of those convicted of crimes, it will not get us very far by way of determining what kinds of sentences to impose on the wide variety of criminal offenders. "Do not punish offenders more than is necessary to assure victims and members of the public that the state is prepared to stand by their basic rights" does not tell us much about whether and when to use custodial or noncustodial sanctions, what kinds of the latter to favor, including alternatives to many now in use, or the duration of whatever sanctions are to be employed. Parsimony is, in this way, more of what we might think of as a "framing" value for sentencing—one that generally encourages us to look at justification in sentencing as becoming more burdensome as we ascend the scale of penal severity.[15]

That being said, there is arguably a "bright line" beyond which sentencing should never pass if it is to remain coherent with our understanding of legal punishment as an institution that censures individuals for their failures to act as responsible citizens while treating them with the dignity that all persons deserve.[16] If our liability to legal punishment depends on our being responsive to moral considerations, it seems problematic to employ criminal sanctions that defeat or destroy that responsivity.[17] Surely, while they are being punished, we will want offenders to remain capable of understanding what is happening to them, and why. More than this, as Antony Duff so eloquently demonstrates, we will want offenders to take the moral communication of which legal punishment partly consists to heart, renounce further offending, and work to make themselves into the kinds of beings who can successfully do so.[18] If some offenders remain defiant or cynical about what the state, acting on behalf of all citizens, demands of them, then so be it. We will still want them to be able to grasp the viewpoint being expressed by their sanctioning. If, for some reason, they become incapable of doing so, it no longer seems appropriate to continue to punish them. Consider, for instance, our likely response to prisoners who lose their sanity while incarcerated, or ones who suffer debilitating strokes or other grave health breakdowns that leave them shadows of their former selves. It seems clear, in these kinds of cases, that continuing to confine such individuals in penal institutions would be a dubious enterprise.[19] It might be that they will have to be assigned to other kinds of state institutions, as few good options may exist for them. But to continue "punishing" them when they are no longer capable of understanding what is happening to them and why seems bizarre.

How might legal sanctions degrade offenders? They can do so in a variety of ways. One does not have to look very hard into the history of punishment, or very broadly across the world today, to find forms of it that do so. Suppose that we set to one side things like torture, dismemberment, and beatings as obviously beyond the pale when it comes to state penal sanctions. It is nonetheless apparent that poorly run prisons can degrade. There are prisons in which violence and predation are the norm, or in which inmates' basic needs for nutrition are not satisfied. Such conditions leave inmates so desperate that, over time, their capacities to do anything more than look out for themselves are apt to be fatally compromised. The advent of super-maximum security prisons in some countries, the United States foremost among them, has brought with it a new form of degradation. Inmates in such prisons might have their basic physical needs satisfied, and they may be safe from violence or predation from their fellow inmates, but the isolation and monotony of such facilities tends, over time, to make those who inhabit them deeply uneasy about interacting with their fellow human beings.[20] Worse than this, such facilities engender rage, irrational acting out, or insanity. Although there is room for debate about the impact of supermax prisons on their inhabitants, they certainly appear to be facilities that erode inmates' capacities for moral thinking and acting, even if they do not wholly destroy them. Penal practices that damage or destroy responsiveness to moral considerations in offenders should be rejected as profoundly at odds with the moral communication logic of state punishment.

Proportionality

In the account of punishment's moral communication aim that I defended in Chapter 4, I made clear that the burdens and impositions of legal punishment should be proportional with the seriousness of the crimes they are designed to address. By doing so, punishment can be understood to stand symbolically for the interests of victims, when there are victims, or for the various societal interests at stake in the observation of *mala prohibita*. On standard accounts, crime seriousness is determined by the harms the various types of crimes inflict, threaten, or attempt, modified by the extent and ways in which those who commit them are culpable for bringing about, attempting, or risking such harms. Deliberately planned and inflicted harms are more blameworthy than ones brought about through recklessness or negligence. Indeed, many legal systems tend to relegate negligently inflicted harms to the realm of civil law. Another aspect of culpability consists of the various justifications or excuses that those charged with crimes might invoke in attempts to stave off conviction, along with the aggravating and mitigating circumstances surrounding their crimes that might be considered by judges at sentencing. Crimes, and especially *mala in se* offenses, invade victims' rights in more or less profound ways and thereby undermine their assurance that they will be able to craft and live lives of their own choosing. When they occur, we look to the authorities to act decisively and effectively to apprehend, convict, and punish those who committed them, in ways that appropriately reflect the importance of the interests breached.

In his influential work on the concept of proportionality, Andreas (formerly Andrew) von Hirsch refers to the rankings of crimes according to their seriousness, and the assignment of sanctions that appropriately reflect that ranking, under the heading of "ordinal" proportionality.[21] In thinking about ordinal proportionality, it is useful to draw the distinction between crime types and crime tokens.[22] The former encompass groups of similar criminal acts, things like first-degree homicide, rape, armed robbery, and residential burglary. Crime tokens are the particular instances of the types, such as the armed robbery committed by some individual on a specific day, at a specific time and place. Legislators or sentencing commissions typically set sentence ranges for types of crimes—two to four years in prison for armed robbery, for instance. When individuals commit and are convicted of tokens, they are sentenced within the relevant range for the crime type, where the specific sentence assigned depends on such things as the amount of actual harm threatened or produced and the various aggravating and mitigating factors that affect an offender's level of culpability for threatening or producing those harms. Ordinal proportionality is best interpreted as applying initially to the sentencing regime of crime types. Accordingly, we should strive to rank the crime types and tailor sentence ranges to reflect their relative severity. Yet ordinal proportionality also has implications for the sentencing of tokens. Thus, we should strive, at least presumptively, to sentence criminal actors who have committed similar tokens similarly. Doing so helps us to achieve the element of ordinal proportionality that von Hirsch terms "parity."[23]

There are various complexities to the notion of proportionality that the preceding brief overview obscures. First, we need an account of the seriousness of criminal offenses. We might intuitively believe that armed robbery is worse than shoplifting, that rape is worse than armed robbery, and that homicide is at or near the top of the list of the most serious kinds of offenses. But critics of proportionality are correct in claiming that more than such intuitions are needed and in claiming that there are surprisingly few normative accounts of crime seriousness in the literature.[24] What we find, instead, is evidence cited that there is widespread agreement, both among individuals in a given society, and across various societies, about relative crime seriousness.[25] Most individuals and most modern legal systems have remarkably similar crime seriousness rankings. Saying this is consistent with recognizing that religious or cultural beliefs might, in some cases, lead individuals or societies to rank some crimes differently in terms of their gravity.

Jesper Ryberg points out that this apparent consensus is nothing more than that—a set of overlapping beliefs about the relative severity of crime types.[26] It is an interesting phenomenon, but not a theory about how to rank crime types. Nonetheless, it is not hard to see why such a consensus exists or how a full theory might be developed. If we think about what we need in order to live decent lives on our own terms, then, obviously, a ranking of threats to doing so quickly emerges: Loss of life or threats to life will always rank high on the list of things to be prohibited, followed by injuries to our bodies or minds, and the more debilitating these are, the worse they will be, followed by loss of all or most of the property on which we depend to meet our needs or pursue our projects, and so on. Lots of crimes, as we have already seen, are minor in character. They take relatively small amounts of property from us or injure us slightly or pose risks to us or cause us inconvenience. These kinds of harms are ones from which we will want to be protected, although most of the time we will recover quickly from them and be able to get on with our lives. None of this is meant to suggest that there will not be some room for disagreement about the severity of harms and thus the crimes that cause or threaten them. There will be. But even in the absence of a full-fledged theory of crime severity, the outlines of such an account are discernible.

Critics of proportionality also argue that we need a theory of penal severity, one which will enable us to explain why some kinds of sanctions are more burdensome than others, and perhaps to explain why we should avoid the use of some penal losses or impositions altogether.[27] Again, I would not deny that a fully worked out theory is desirable. However, I suspect that if we think about the array of losses or impositions utilized by modern liberal democratic societies to punish offenders, it is not difficult to discern some rough ordering of their severity. Fines, unless they are quite substantial, will seem the least intrusive to most of us, followed by such things as required community service, restitution, probation (which can be of more or less intense kinds, with the latter nudging it up in severity), GPS monitoring, home detention, and, finally, imprisonment, of shorter or longer durations.[28] Roughly, the losses imposed by sanctions will seem more severe the more they interfere with our abilities to live our lives as we choose and the longer they do so. It seems natural to focus on such things as the ways in which penal sanctions interfere with our abilities to meet our needs or those of others dependent upon us, remain employed, maintain our relationships with family and friends, and engage in the activities and pursuits that give us pleasure. Most sanctions other than imprisonment will allow us to go on about our lives, albeit with some restrictions in place or requirements that we must satisfy. If several noncustodial sanctions are assigned in a given case, this will constitute a more substantial interference with our lives, at least for their duration. Still, imprisonment is a severe sanction because, as we have seen, it deprives us not only of our liberty but threatens to deprive us of other rights, privileges, and goods, ones that most of us value and will profoundly experience the loss of. None of this should be taken to assert that there is no room for debate about which sanctions are more burdensome than others. But again, as with the seriousness of offenses, some plausible ranking of the severity of the losses or impositions utilized by modern states to punish offenders seems available.

The two most vexing challenges that proponents of proportionality in sentencing face, in my view, have to do with "cardinal" or "absolute" proportionality in sentencing and with the question whether, or to what extent, the "subjective experiences" of those being punished should be taken into account in determining the severity of sanctions.[29] Let me put the latter problem aside for the time being and focus, first, on the issues raised by cardinal or absolute proportionality. Even if there is some fairly broad consensus on the rank order of criminal offenses and on the relative severity of sanctions, there seem to be clear differences of opinion across persons and liberal democratic societies about how severe we should let sanctions become, even if we set to one side the debates that exist about extreme sanctions such as the death penalty and the assignment of sentences of life without parole. One criminal justice system might top out with sentences of 15 years imprisonment for the worst offenses, scaling sanctions down from there for lesser offenses. Another might top out with life sentences, with the possibility of release after some minimum time served, and scale sanctions down from there. Both systems might satisfy the requirements of ordinal or relative proportionality—that is, they might punish more serious crimes more harshly than less serious crimes. It is on the matter of what von Hirsch termed "cardinal" proportionality, or what others term "absolute" proportionality, that the two regimes diverge. Supporters of the milder regime might view sentences of more than 15 years in custody as "absolutely" disproportionate, while those in the harsher regime might view 15-year sentences for murderers, and especially multiple murderers, as absolutely too mild. Still, supporters of both regimes presumably view murderers as requiring more punishment than rapists, bank robbers, and shoplifters. Translated into the terms of my moral communication account of punishment, the disagreement is about how much punishment of murderers, and other, lesser offenders, is needed to "properly value" victims and thus appropriately censure offenders. Von Hirsch has wrestled with the question whether there is a best or most defensible way to determine the high (or low) ends of a sentencing regime and thus a solution to the problem posed by cardinal proportionality. At times, he suggested that how societies determine the overall mildness or harshness of their sentencing regimes is mostly a matter of convention. At other times, he worried that such an approach deprives us of the normative resources to declare some sentencing regimes indefensibly harsh or mild.[30]

I am skeptical about the prospect of defending an absolutely proportional sentencing regime, especially one that puts some reasonable cap on the severity of sanctions for the most serious offenses and scales the punishment of lesser offenses down from that cap. I doubt that we will find much consensus about how to punish the gravest crimes, especially in a world in which individuals seem determined to come up with new ways in which to kill or injure lots of people in a single incident or a connected series of them.[31] Also, even if we could defend such a cap, there will likely remain some room for reasonable disagreement among those committed to proportionality about how to deal with certain types of crimes (e.g., the punishment of attempts) and what von Hirsch termed the "spacing" between crimes (that is, now much more or less serious two types of offenses are, even if there is consensus on their rank ordering). However, I do believe that the prospects for defending some measure of proportionality in sentencing are less bleak than some of its most ardent critics contend. Even if we must concede that, for a given crime token, or even for a given crime type, there is no discernible absolutely proportionate sentence or sentence range, it does not follow that we have no normative tools at our disposal to narrow the range of possible sentencing options.

First, proponents of proportionality in sentencing should reiterate the distinction between the sentencing of crime tokens and crime types. The latter are where the action is, so to speak, for once we have defensible sentence ranges for crime types in place, crime tokens will presumptively be assigned sentences within the relevant ranges.[32] My point here is not that sentencing judges cannot reasonably disagree about how to sentence crime tokens, but only that we should not think of their task as plucking some kind of proportionate sentence out of the sky, so to speak. Of course, we might doubt that uncontroversial proportionate sentence ranges for crime types exist or can be discerned, but at least the fact that they will involve ranges (of possibly greater or lesser scope) means that we are not searching for something that is too specific.

Second, and more interestingly, perhaps, is the use that might be made, at this point, of the value of parsimony in limiting, to some extent, the top sentence ranges for the most serious types of offenses, at least for the most typical kinds of worst offenses. Again, on my account of parsimony, it requires the state to justify imposing more in the way of penal burdens and losses on offenders, including serious offenders, rather than fewer of them. In the debate about the death penalty, for instance, Hugo Adam Bedau has argued that as between assigning the death penalty and assigning life sentences to the "worst" murderers, we should prefer the latter on the grounds that it is not apparent that the former advances any defensible penal purpose to a significant extent.[33] In line with this, I would argue that there ought to be a burden on the state to show that in order to properly validate the lives and interests of serious crime victims, longer rather than shorter terms of penal confinement (assuming that is the sanction of choice for such offenders) are needed.

In Chapter 3, I objected to von Hirsch's claim that sentences of longer than five years in prison assigned to those who commit homicide are excessive. Of course, von Hirsch's argument on this point is wholly deterrence-based. He believes that there is little evidence that longer sentences will effectively (all costs and benefits considered, presumably) deter would-be murderers.[34] My point was that such relatively meager sentences will plausibly be seen to undervalue the lives of murder victims. Think about it this way: Jones commits a murder against a wholly innocent victim when he is 25. Upon his conviction, Jones is sentenced to five years in a humane custodial facility and emerges when he is just past 30. He now has the rest of his life to live, more or less as he pleases. To my way of thinking, this seems too mild—if not a slap on the wrist, awfully close to it. But suppose that the sentence range for homicide is set higher, at a minimum of 15 to 20 years in prison. It is not hard to imagine that some people will still react to such sentences with dismay, asserting that they undervalue the lives of murder victims who, after all, have lost everything. Still, I find it harder to think of such a sentence as a slap on the wrist. Fifteen to twenty years in prison is a substantial loss, in my view, constituting, as it likely will, something like a quarter of someone's life. And if we imagine the minimum sentence for homicide set at 25–30 years, especially for first-degree homicide, the claim that this does not appropriately communicate the gravity of the wrong done to the victim becomes harder still to defend, not that some will not persist in defending it. Again, there might be some crimes that are so awful that life sentences, without the prospect of parole, or even the death penalty, seem needed to communicate the extreme gravity of what their perpetrators have done. For instance, I am not sure how to argue that mass murderers or war criminals should be shown much mercy. But it is vital to keep in mind that such wrongdoers are extremely rare cases and that more run-of-the-mill serious offenders should not be viewed or treated like them. In the more typical cases of serious crimes, parsimony might serve as a valuable constraint on how high we are tempted to push custodial sentences.

Third, as I noted in Chapter 3, I believe that it is useful in thinking about proportionality and crime seriousness for us to draw a rough distinction between crimes whose standard impacts on victims are "significantly life-altering" and crimes whose standard impacts are not. Even among those in the former category, there will be a range of such impacts, from the loss of life, at one end of the continuum, to the loss of property upon which individuals depend to meet their basic needs, at the other. It is apparent that many of the crimes of which people are convicted in contemporary societies fall short of being significantly life-altering to victims, if indeed they have any victims.[35] The victims of such crimes might lose some of their property and be temporarily inconvenienced by it, or they might suffer some mild injury from an altercation that went just a bit too far, one from which they will fairly quickly recover. In other cases, individuals will be convicted of violating *mala prohibita*. They ignore or breach various rules and regulations but in ways that put no one seriously at risk. With crimes that are not significantly life-altering in their impact on others, the main point of state punishment, on a morally communicative approach, would seem to be to emphatically remind offenders of their responsibilities under the criminal law, perhaps along with encouraging them to more avidly embrace and live up to those responsibilities. Such communication presumably can be accomplished by employing a variety of relatively mild criminal sanctions, including fines, community service, restitution, and probation. What should be avoided are sanctions that significantly diminish the lives of offenders, given that their crimes did nothing of the sort to their victims, assuming there were any. In other words, even if there is room for reasonable disagreement about what proportionality requires by way of punishment when it comes to significantly life-altering crimes, we should not infer from this that there is bound to be such disagreement across the entire range of offenses. With low-level offenses, almost any mild state penal imposition or loss will tend to suffice for purposes of censure.

With significantly life-altering crimes, the situation is more complicated. The victims of homicide lose everything when they are murdered. The victims of aggravated assault might be left with disabling injuries or trauma that diminish their capacities to enjoy and exercise their basic moral rights in significant ways for the duration of their lives. The victims of rape or other sexual assaults might not suffer physical injuries, but the indignity of what befell them and the emotional trauma that results can affect them for years to come.[36] All of us are likely to view these kinds of crimes with considerably more fear and dread. We will find it easy to imagine ourselves, our loved ones, our neighbors and friends, or other innocent members of the community as the victims of such crimes. We will therefore reasonably seek assurance that the state will stand decisively for the victims of such crimes, imposing sanctions on those who commit them that appropriately value their victims, rather than downplaying the losses they have suffered. We might therefore insist that, presumptively at least, life-altering offenses ought to be met with significantly life-altering sanctions. Imperfect as it might be, imprisonment is such a sanction. By depriving offenders of their liberty, we take something from that that is one of the foundations of their being able to craft and live lives of their own choosing. No one can plausibly view imprisonment—even humane imprisonment that is designed to limit the impact of liberty curtailment on the exercise and enjoyment of other basic rights—as an insubstantial sanction, at least on the assumption that its duration is something other than brief.

Nonetheless, there is no sharp cut-off point on the scale of crime seriousness between minor offenses and more substantial ones. And if the principle of parsimony counsels restraint in the use of penal impositions and losses, as I have argued, then there should be no abrupt change in sentence severity from the mostly mild kinds of losses and impositions appropriate for minor offenses and the more burdensome ones needed to censure serious offenders, stand for the victims of crimes, and remind the public of the obligations of responsible citizenship. Hence, we might reasonably insist that terms of custody for significantly life-altering crimes should be relatively brief unless or until the losses culpably inflicted on victims (or the threat of such losses) seem to warrant more than this. Armed robbery and rape are serious crimes, but it seems hard to imagine why custodial sentence ranges of more than, say, three to five years, would be necessary to demonstrate to offenders and their victims that we mean business, at least in the vast majority of cases. Three to five years in prison cannot plausibly be seen as an insubstantial penal burden, even with regard to crimes whose victims are left injured or traumatized, at least assuming that such victims can be expected, over time, to recover from their injuries or trauma. Even humane forms of imprisonment, assuming we can achieve them, will be difficult to endure and apt, in a variety of more or less subtle ways, to leave their marks on those to whom it is assigned.

Granted, when it comes to crimes that leave their victims dead or gravely and permanently debilitated, we do not have a lot of good options short of more lengthy terms of confinement to staunchly censure offenders and signify to their victims (or those who survive them) that we are serious about what has been done to them. But again, parsimony requires us to offer some convincing justification for choosing longer rather than shorter terms of confinement, especially where the latter can plausibly be cast as doing enough to morally communicate with offenders, their victims, and the public.

Despite all of this, nothing in what I have said here should be taken to suggest that we will find it easy to reach consensus on sentence ranges for the types of serious crimes that merit the use of imprisonment. Nor will it be obvious what the appropriate ranges should be for the more common minor offenses that clog our criminal justice systems, even if it is conceded that the burdens such sentences ought to impose should not be substantial. To this extent, proportionality is, I would submit, an imprecise guide to sentencing, although I do not believe it is as unhelpful as some of its critics make it out to be, for the reasons just adduced. Should we expect some variability across societies or cultures concerning what von Hirsch terms the "anchoring points" of the sentencing scale?[37] Yes, I suspect that we should, although it does not follow from this that any anchoring points, no matter how unmoored from a sober assessment of offense harm and culpability, and unconstrained by considerations of parsimony, are acceptable. Also, ordinal or relative proportionality remains a useful tool in sentencing, especially once we have reached some consensus on the appropriate sentence ranges for at least some types of offenses. Still, all things considered, the most plausible conclusion is that there will be a number of sentencing schemes that can be plausibly cast as both relatively and absolutely proportional, although there will also be quite a few that fail one or both of these tests. Whether considerations of crime reduction can be employed to help us choose among the available proportionate schemes is a question I take up in the next section.

This brings us back to the question of whether and to what extent we should assess the severity of penal sanctions by taking into account their impact on the subjective experience of those on whom they are imposed. Critics of proportionality take it as fairly obvious that we ought to do so, especially since punishment, they assert, involves the deliberate infliction of suffering, pain, or distress on the convicted.[38] If we are to treat like cases alike, they argue, then we should have to investigate and assess the extent and variety of ways in which those punished suffer, taking into account the considerable diversity of offenders in age, physical abilities, mental health, idiosyncratic interests, and other factors. Given that diversity, sentencing like offenders alike will turn out to be a daunting task, one that critics of proportionality believe casts doubt on its plausibility. Yet if we must eschew the principle of relative proportionality, and the prospects for achieving broad consensus on matters of absolute proportionality are slim, there might seem little left to recommend proportionality as a sentencing principle.

In response to this, my view is that we should seek to minimize the extent to which a sentencing scheme inquires into the subjective experiences of those for whom punishment is warranted.[39] I have already indicated my unease with the notion that punishment essentially involves the state seeking to make offenders suffer. Especially when it comes to the variety of sanctions utilized in relation to minor offenders, the notion that the state is doing anything more by imposing burdens of various kinds on them than seeking to gain and hold their attention, however briefly, to remind them of their responsibilities under the criminal law, seems more plausible than the notion that it is striving to make them suffer. Granted, when it comes to penal confinement for shorter or longer periods of time, it might seem more plausible to maintain that the state's aim is to inflict suffering. But it could also be argued that we ought to impose more substantial and noticeable burdens on those who commit serious crimes in order to symbolically capture the gravity of such offenses and thus validate the significance of the victim interests damaged or violated by them. When offenders commit crimes that are significantly life-altering to their victims, the state must do something commensurate to them or its neglect or failure to do so will seem an abandonment of, if not an affront to, their victims.[40]

To the preceding, I would add three points: First, it would be a daunting and arguably unwise course of action for the state to attempt to go very far by way of investigating and taking into account the considerable variation in the subjective experiences of those punished. The kinds and potential intrusiveness of the necessary inquiries into the internal lives of those punished ought to give us pause. So should the resulting evaluative challenges involved in taking subjective experience into account in determining sentences for crime types and crime tokens. Arguably, these are not matters that we should probably feel comfortable about tasking state officials with. And would we also task them with titrating state punishment, after its initiation, so as to ensure that offenders "suffered" as much as their crimes warranted, whatever that means? Instead, it seems preferable to conceive of legal sanctions in more "objective" terms, which requires us to consider how and for how long they standardly interfere with abilities of persons to have decent lives lived on their own terms.[41] Imprisonment is, by this measure, a very burdensome punishment, much more so than fines, community service, or even monitoring and home confinement. Imprisonment deprives individuals of the opportunity to exercise their liberty in most of the ways in which persons typically value doing so. Imprisonment also will be apt to limit the abilities of those punished to exercise and enjoy other basic rights. That some offenders will feel the sting of this more than others is something that, in my view, we should be prepared to live with.

Second, the complexities involved in taking the subjective experience of offenders into account are not ones that those who prefer a consequentialist approach to sentencing could reasonably hope to avoid. The psychological reactions and perceived costs of the penal burdens imposed on those convicted of crimes will vary considerably, and with those variations will go different propensities toward reoffending. For instance, some offenders will strongly dislike the sanctions imposed on them, in ways that are apt to deter them from future offending; others will have come to accept and endure even severe sanctions such as imprisonment. How we sentence the former, if our aim is to reduce future crime, will surely have to be different than how we sentence the latter. Similar points could be made with respect to special deterrence, incapacitation, and rehabilitation, all of which will be affected, it would seem, by the differences among those punished in how they subjectively experience it.

Those who prefer a crime reduction approach to sentencing might concede this point but argue that they will not have to worry so much about treating like offenders alike, a principle to which proportionality theorists give considerably more weight. However, I doubt that crime reductionists can blithely accept sanction regimes that sentence those who commit similar crimes in substantially different ways. Doing so might undermine the legitimacy of such regimes, especially in the eyes of those who tend to receive longer or harsher sentences, in ways that will not bode well for their future desistance from crime. Since it will often be the poor or socially excluded who are more used to difficult lives, and thus who might be better equipped to endure the burdens of penal sanctions, they likely will be the prime candidates for enhanced sentences, especially ones based on special deterrence or incapacitation. Yet those who already perceive themselves to be at a disadvantage will probably not react constructively to the tougher sentencing hands dealt to them, in ways that should give crime reductionists pause.

Third, a plausible case can be made for the proposition that it is not the state upon whom the entire responsibility rests for taking into account the significant variations in the subjective experience of punishment that will occur among those sentenced for crimes. If you are a sensitive type, or a rich person used to enjoying the finer things in life, or someone who will profoundly miss the freedom to travel and see the world or spend time with your spouse and children, then the thing to do is to refrain from forms of criminal offending the punishment of which might have an especially adverse impact on you. Too often, those who emphasize the wide variety of ways in which offenders subjectively experience punishment, and especially the diverse forms of suffering it will cause, make it seem as if responsibility for such suffering is all on the state and not at all on those who make ill-advised choices to offend. Yet those who contemplate offending surely have some idea of what awaits them if they are caught and convicted and the ways in which it might impact them. If they have some reason to suspect that they will find punishment particularly unpleasant, then that is all the more reason for them to refrain from conduct that puts them at risk of experiencing it. After all, most of them have other reasons to refrain from such conduct, at least if they are responsive to moral considerations up to the level that liability to punishment seems to require. Importantly, I am not suggesting that advance warning of penal losses and impositions justifies them no matter how harsh or degrading they turn out to be. Rather, I am claiming that if the state adopts, warns citizens about, and imposes reasonable penal burdens on those duly convicted of offending, it has done most of what it needs to do to act responsibly and fairly in relation to its citizens.

The phrase "most of what it needs to do" is a hedge, of course. Although I believe that the state should employ what some have termed "objective" penal burdens, in the forms of fines, conduct requirements, and loss of freedom, and thus to keep its distance from attempts to read or interpret the subjective reactions of offenders to such burdens, I would admit that a few concessions to penal subjectivism might have to be made. For instance, if those eligible under the law for custodial sanctions given their crimes suffer from forms of mental illness that do not amount to insanity, then we should take this into account. One option, in some cases, might be to opt for noncustodial sanctions in relation to such offenders, especially if their crimes are not too serious and the relevant sentence range permits it (or if a justified exception to the range can be defended). Another option would be to make sure that such offenders receive treatment while serving their custodial sentences. Notice that while this appears to make some concession to the rigors of custody and their impact on certain kinds of offenders, it does not go very far by way of delving into their subjective experiences of punishment or adjusting their sentences to those experiences. Also, other offenders assigned to custody might be given some help in adjusting to it, especially if they are first-time offenders.[42]

Doug Husak discusses another kind of case in which he claims that some ground needs to be ceded to those concerned about offenders' subjective experiences of punishment.[43] It has often been noted that the use of fines as penal sanctions differentially impacts offenders. Rich offenders might be able to pay substantial fines without experiencing much of a burden, whereas poor offenders will likely notice and feel the impact of fines, more or less regardless of their magnitude. Fines will thus in many instances constitute a failure to treat like offenders alike, at least if we focus on the subjective experiences of those on whom they are imposed. In response, European countries have adopted what are known as "day fines," where the amount of the fine imposed on offenders varies depending on their income levels. Presumably, day fines can be made to work to better ensure that like offenders "suffer" alike. I admit that this practice can be plausibly viewed as a concession to penal subjectivism, albeit a limited one. The adjustment of fine levels does not delve very far into the subjective experiences of offenders. After all, there might be some wealthy offenders who are misers, who feel acutely any fine imposed on them by the state for their misconduct, no matter how small. Likewise, there might be poor offenders who view fines as little more than the cost of doing (perhaps illicit) business and so are not bothered much by them. The proponents of day fines do not appear to be suggesting that the state should modify fines to account for these more specific variations in the subjective experience of punishment. Thus, if day fines are a concession to penal subjectivism, they seem a rather crudely crafted one.

Moreover, it could be argued that it is not really the amount of suffering felt by offenders that the practice of day fines is designed to track. Instead, it might be that we worry that the typically modest fines assessed for many minor offenses will hardly be noticed by rich offenders as forms of censure. By contrast, with less affluent offenders, fines will more often communicate what we want them to communicate. Perhaps the practice of day fines is no more than an attempt to make sure that the censure that fines communicate is noticeable to all offenders. If this is correct, then the practice seems even further removed from the more problematic inquiries into the subjective experiences of persons assigned penal sanctions that some penal theorists would have us undertake.

Crime Reduction and Sentencing

Although I have defended proportionality as a central, if not the central, value in sentencing, especially on a morally communicative approach to legal punishment's justification, I have conceded that the guidance it provides in setting sentence ranges for the various crime types is imprecise. Some will continue to regard that guidance as hopelessly vague, despite my efforts to show how, in conjunction with the value of parsimony, it might enable us to narrow the range of defensible sentencing regimes. It is natural to wonder whether the value of crime reduction in my account might be brought into play at this point, and indeed to ask whether it will provide us more guidance than proportionality in setting up a defensible sentencing regime. I believe that crime reduction considerations can play a valuable supplementary role in our thinking about sentencing; more on that subsequently. But first I want to directly take on the proposition that such considerations can be mined to yield a more determinate account of the sentence ranges for the various crime types.[44] It is tempting to believe that if proportionality is either underwhelming as a guide to sentencing, or altogether a failure, we have a readily available alternative in the form of a sentencing scheme grounded in what we know or believe will optimally reduce crime. Oddly, that option has rarely, if ever, been spelled out by critics of proportionality.[45] Perhaps that is because the crime reduction approach seems to supply an abstract formula, of sorts, for sentencing, one the finer details of which have yet to be elaborated. That formula tells us to adopt sentence ranges for the various crimes types that will optimally reduce crime, taking both the positive and negative consequences of legal punishment into account. It is worth pausing here to briefly explain why the prospects of employing that formula to produce a concrete and plausible sentencing regime are, in fact, rather bleak.

The impact of legal punishment on the reduction of crime has been empirically studied for nearly half a century. As we saw in Chapter 1, there are quite a few things that we can plausibly claim to have shown about punishment's effects on crime. Here, I will summarize them very briefly. Legal punishment does seem to tamp down overall crime via general deterrence. However, much to the surprise of many, it does not seem that harsher sanctions are correlated with increases in marginal deterrence.[46] By contrast, it does seem that the perceived certainty of punishment has some impact on general deterrence, although even that conclusion must be embraced with caution.[47] Yet the prospect that the certainty of punishment might be increased does not help us much with discerning what the appropriate sentence ranges should be for the various crime types. Imprisonment clearly has the potential to reduce crime via incapacitation of those prone to it. But as we have seen, many crimes are not apt to be punished by imprisonment because doing so will not be cost-effective, and some crimes for which imprisonment might initially appear cost-effective might turn out not to be so given the "aging out" phenomenon.[48]

Also, some types of offending in communities will not be reduced by punishment's incapacitation effects, since other individuals will be recruited or step forward on their own to take the place of those convicted and sent off to prisons.[49] Most importantly, nothing in the preceding tells us much about the kinds and durations of sentences that are optimally incapacitative.

We have evidence that some types of rehabilitation programs work to reduce offending—in fact, most do although some do so more effectively than others.[50] Yet this evidence also will not enable us to determine sentence ranges for the various crime types, although it might help us to figure out what to do with offenders once they are under the supervision of the state. Special deterrence has not been studied extensively. What has been studied are the seeming criminogenic effects of state punishment, especially custodial sanctions. Here the evidence is disconcerting, with some consensus among researchers that state punishment might be more apt to increase, rather than reduce, recidivism among those who have experienced it.[51] This will especially be true for the socially deprived and excluded offenders who tend to predominate in contemporary criminal justice systems. Most had difficult lives to begin with; the stigma and sanctions they are made to endure for their crimes render more, rather than less, tenuous their prospects for starting or resuming responsible lives.

The preceding points would all need to be qualified and elaborated. What they plausibly show, I believe, is that we have discovered a number of important things about what legal punishment can and cannot be reasonably expected to do by way of reducing crime in communities. However, these vital insights are still a very long way from the more detailed information we would need to set up an optimally crime reductive sentencing scheme. For instance, there seems little in the empirical study of legal punishment that informs us what the optimal sentence range would be for a crime like armed robbery. Would that range start at the low end with noncustodial sanctions, or with modest custodial ones? And what would be the high end of the relevant range? Two years in custody, four, six? I know of nothing in the empirical literature on legal punishment's crime reduction effects that would enable us to answer these questions with any certainty, or even respectable level of probability. Not only is this true for armed robbery, it is true for all of the various other types of criminal offenses. Even if we focus narrowly on general deterrence, we lack the empirical information required to determine optimal sentence ranges for the various crime types. Adding in special deterrence, incapacitation, and rehabilitation would require us to have considerably more information. Further, we could not assume that the various crime reduction modes would all point us in the same direction when it comes to setting up optimal sentence ranges for the various crime types. Sentence ranges that might generally deter armed robbers at optimal levels might or might not suffice to incapacitate or rehabilitate them at optimal levels. Note also that the term "optimal" in my characterization of what we would need to know for each of these crime reduction modes presupposes that we have taken into account the various negative consequences of longer or shorter or different kinds of sentences for the various crime types. That too would require us to have more finely detailed information about legal punishment's effects on offenders, their families, and wider communities than we likely have.

One further point should be made. Even if we had the empirical information regarding how various possible sentence types and ranges would impact crime reduction in its different modes, including the costs and negative consequences of those types and ranges, the task of processing all of that information so as to yield an optimal sentence range for a single crime type, let alone for all of them, would be formidable, to say the least. The crime reduction approach to legal punishment is typically conceived in rather ambitious terms. Accordingly, it is not enough to locate sentence ranges for the various crime types that will produce some net reduction in crime, taking into account the worrisome fact that the effect of some penal sanctions appears to be to increase it. Preventionism is standardly cast as a maximizing or optimizing project, according to which we should strive to identify sentence ranges for crime types that produce the highest levels of good consequences while minimizing bad ones, taking into account all of the available sentencing options. Arguably, such a project is beyond our ken. We might hope that forms of artificial intelligence will be devised to help us weigh and process all of the information that would be needed to accomplish this task, but it seems safe to say that it will be some time before we can reasonably expect to have anything approaching a systematic and well-grounded sentencing scheme designed to optimally reduce crime.

That being said, I believe that there is a significant role for crime reduction considerations to play in sentencing beyond those suggested in the previous chapter with regard to the sentencing of offense tokens. We might not be anywhere close to having a well worked-out sentencing scheme based on what we know about general and special deterrence, incapacitation, rehabilitation, and moral reinforcement. However, we do have quite a bit of information about the impact of sanctions of numerous kinds on offenders, and particularly on their propensities to reoffend or return to lives of responsible citizenship. This information is important because the vast majority of people punished for crimes will at some point return to civil society, sometimes in relatively short order. Indeed, most minor offenders will never leave it, since they will be sanctioned with fines, community service, required restitution payments, or forms of probation. In light of this, it behooves us to employ sanctions that will not make those punished for their crimes more likely to resort to further offending, and especially not worse forms of it. Sanctions that do so will be, in a very real sense, self-defeating.

What I would therefore suggest is this: If considerations of proportionality leave us with an array of sentencing regimes, some more severe in the sentences that they are prepared to mete out to offenders than others, then we might bring in what we know about the ways in which penal sanctions can be self-defeating to argue for some of the milder forms of proportionate sentencing regimes. Doing so will not constitute a break with proportionality, since all of the candidate regimes are assumed to satisfy it. But bringing in crime reduction considerations might enable us to make better choices from among proportionate (or not disproportionate) sanction regimes, avoiding or minimizing the use of ones that, in one way or another, erode the ability or willingness of offenders to respond to the kinds of reasons they have against offending, whether those consist of moral or prudential reasons, or both. Many offenders are already less than reliable about exercising responsibility in their lives. Yet the evidence suggests that harsh, debilitating, socially isolating, and economically crippling sanctions will further diminish their capacities for responsible action.[52]

For instance, suppose that in relation to what I have termed "significantly life-altering crimes," assigning offenders terms of confinement are appropriate ways in which to censure them and thereby communicate with them, their victims, and the public about the gravity of their wrongs. Nonetheless, we should remain cognizant of the fact that most of the more serious offenders sentenced to prison will, one day, complete their sentences and re-enter civil society. If they are to do so successfully, it behooves us not to have confined them for so long or in conditions such that their capacities to function well in civil society are significantly compromised. There is clear evidence that "prisonization" is a real phenomenon; individuals who serve long stretches of time confined will struggle to readjust to normal lives.[53] This fact gives us good reason to prefer sentencing regimes for serious crimes that impose shorter rather than longer terms of custody, at least so long as the former can still be seen as validating the lives and interests of crime victims. It also gives us reason to employ forms of custody that will do less damage to inmates than many current forms do and that, in fact, enable them to develop and maintain social and work skills that will set them up for lives of responsible citizenry. Taking young, often socially deprived serious offenders and locking them up for long periods of time in prisons in which idleness is the norm, meaningful work and education are unavailable, relations with their loved ones are strained if not broken, and in which many of them will be exposed to violence and predation of various kinds, is a recipe for disaster, mostly in the form of high recidivism rates.

It will not be easy to design prisons that, at a minimum, do not make those who inhabit them less responsible, let alone encourage them to become more so. As noted previously, we should look to some of the European or Scandinavian prison systems for guidance.[54] Not only do such countries generally impose shorter terms of confinement on serious offenders, they seek, in various ways, to make imprisonment less harsh or damaging. Again, we should view the purpose of prisons as to deprive inmates of the basic right to liberty, or at least to radically curtail it, while attempting in other ways to facilitate the exercise and enjoyment of their retained rights.[55] Not only should all of the basic welfare needs of prisoners be satisfied, they should be provided opportunities to work and earn income, to receive visitors on a regular basis and, in some cases, go on furloughs from prison. Prisoners should also be able to exercise their religious freedom and political rights, and engage in recreational or leisure activities, within the confines of the prison's walls. Some who write about prisons cast these measures in terms of the "normalization" of prison life, that is, the attempt to model it on ordinary life, with its opportunities and responsibilities, as far as this is feasible.[56] By doing so, it is hoped that those serving time in prisons will not become hardened and institutionalized in ways that do not bode well for their return to society.

As we move away from serious crimes and the sanctions appropriate to them, what we know about crime reduction might also be of use in helping us to devise sentencing regimes for minor offenders that are more helpful than detrimental. Again, with minor criminal offenses, and even with some moderately serious ones, moral communication can usually be effected without assigning offenders custodial sentences, or even sentences that are substantially burdensome in other ways. The point of sanctions in such cases is to forcefully remind offenders of the responsibilities they have in a societally recognized and enforced scheme of basic rights. Fines, required community service, victim restitution, probation, temporary monitoring, or home confinement are all ways of signaling to offenders (and to others) that the conduct they have engaged in is off limits. Yet crime reduction considerations should encourage us to design and administer these milder kinds of sanctions in ways that reduce impediments to the successful exercise of offenders' capacities for responsible action.

By way of illustration, in recent years, drug and mental health courts have sprung up, in recognition of the need to both hold offenders accountable for their misconduct while, at the same time, getting them the help they need to address problems in their lives that are precipitators of their offending.[57] There are hopeful signs that these ways of dealing with mostly minor drug offenders work to reduce their reoffending, although more study of them, and adjustments to their design and implementation, might be needed. Crime reduction logic should be interpreted as supporting such experimentation and study, especially if they help us to discover ways to hold minor offenders accountable without worsening their criminal proclivities.

Other proposals to address minor forms of offending in responsibility-enhancing ways have emerged. Restorative justice scholars urge less direct state involvement in the resolution of many crimes.[58] They would have offenders who are willing to admit their guilt meet with the victims of their crimes, in controlled and mediated settings, in order to work out some way to atone for their wrongs. Some form of apology to the victim, along with making amends for any losses caused by the crime or crimes in question would, these scholars contend, work better to satisfy victims and encourage offenders to recognize and learn from their mistakes. In this way, the restorative justice approach seeks both to hold offenders accountable for their crimes, communicating with them the errors of their ways, while empowering them and their victims to work out some solution to the rift caused by the offender's actions. There is also the hope that keeping the state with its more impersonal and one-size-fits-all sanctioning tendencies at a distance will do less damage to offenders. Again, the jury might still be out on restorative justice's crime reduction tendencies.[59] Yet it is an approach worth considering given the apparent shortcomings of more traditional forms of sanctioning many of the mostly minor offenders who cycle through criminal justice systems.

To reiterate, within the loose constraints set by proportionality considerations, and therefore consistent with accurate moral communication with offenders about the wrongs they have committed, we should look for ways to sanction offenders that hold them accountable while not worsening their criminal proclivities. We might also seek to counter or otherwise address those proclivities, to weaken their influence. Even if we are not in a position to say with any certainty what an optimal crime reduction sentencing scheme would look like, we have considerable evidence about how many existing forms of sanctions impact offenders and the communities from whence they came and to which most of them will return. We should heed that evidence and look for and test new forms of criminal justice intervention, thereby avoiding or minimizing the use of sanctions that weaken the responsiveness of those punished to the moral and prudential reasons they have against offending.

Implications

It will be instructive to use the mixed theory of sentencing I have proposed to examine one of the more vexing problems with which sentencing theorists have wrestled, namely, how to sentence those who repeatedly offend, despite having been convicted and punished for their earlier crimes. Should we assess them what have come to be called "recidivist premiums," that is, added sentence increments in response to their recurring refusals to abide by the criminal law?[60] It might be questioned whether a mixed account of punishment's justification can make much headway with resolving the challenges such offenders pose. After all, there seems little consensus among either retributive or crime reduction theorists about how to deal with recidivists. Some retributivists would have us sentence repeat offenders no differently than first-timers.[61] Assuming that such individuals served their sentences for their earlier crimes, their slates were "wiped clean," as it were. To now assign them longer sentences, in response to their criminal persistence, would be to punish them again for their earlier crimes. Other retributivists argue that persistent offenders demonstrate bad character or at least a refusal to heed the lessons they should have learned from their earlier convictions and sentences.[62] They therefore deem repeat offenders deserving of longer sentences, or at least as forfeiting any sentencing discounts bestowed by judges who might plausibly have viewed their earlier offenses as one-off mistakes.[63] Those who favor a crime reduction approach to sentencing must wrestle with the conflicting directions provided by the various modes of the approach. On special deterrence grounds, we might be tempted to assign repeat offenders longer sentences, to bring home more sternly to them the costs and consequences of their continued offending. Similarly, on incapacitation grounds, we might reasonably worry that the persistence of repeat offenders requires us to assign them longer sentences, including longer custodial terms, to remove them from society and thereby assure the law-abiding that they will not be subject to predation or harm. Yet against considerations such as these, we must weigh the costs and negative consequences of longer or harsher sanctions, including their criminogenic tendencies, their drain on public resources, and the impact on offenders' families and communities. The task of weighing all of these factors is, to say the least, complicated and the implications of doing so seem somewhat murky.

If we focus on the moral communication branch of my mixed account, there seems some reason to sentence at least some repeat offenders differently than most first-time offenders. I say "some" here because there will be cases involving individuals who were convicted of one or more crimes many years ago, who fully served their sentences, and have apparently remained law-abiding for quite some time. It is less clear to me whether viewing and treating such individuals as ordinary recidivists makes sense. At some point, it would seem that those who have committed crimes in the distant past ought to be treated as if they have clean slates for subsequent sentencing purposes. Nonetheless, there will be many individuals who commit crimes, serve their sentences, and in relatively short order, repeat their offenses or commit other ones. In response to such offenders, it seems natural to try to convey a sterner message to them, to get and hold their attention in some more forceful way, given that they did not apparently heed the moral communication conveyed to them by burdensome sanctions the first (or second, or third) time around. On the supposition that considerations of proportionality provide us with no more than sentence ranges for the various crime types, a defensible approach would be to bump repeat offenders up in the relevant sentencing range as compared with how we would sentence them if they were not recidivists.[64] Doing so would convey to repeat offenders sterner messages about their crimes. Yet, so long as we assign them sentences in the appropriate crime type range, it would not communicate with them as if they were offenders of more serious kinds. For instance, we might assign repeat shoplifters higher sentences in the relevant range but decline to assign them sentences that treat them like home burglars or armed robbers. One of the problems with recidivist premiums in some jurisdictions is that they can result in offenders being assigned sentences that would only be appropriate if they were convicted of much more serious crimes.[65] If we value accurate moral communication with offenders, we should eschew such robust recidivist premiums.

Of course, we might be skeptical about whether repeat offenders will listen to or heed the kind of modestly stronger moral communication I am urging. A few will, but many might not. I am willing to live with that. For one thing, my account of moral communication does not assume the success of the state's censure efforts in relation to offenders themselves. There might still be victims who witness and appreciate the moral communication conveyed by the offender's punishment or members of the general public who are assured by seeing the obligations of the criminal law forcefully affirmed. For another, some recidivists will be unmoved by the threat or reality of recidivist premiums almost no matter how burdensome we make them. We might also encounter some individuals who will continue their offending even after they have previously been assigned sentences at the top of the relevant sentencing range for their previous crimes. In general, I would resist proposals to bump them up into a higher sentencing range, as doing so would distort the gravity of their offenses. However, I have allowed that, in a few cases, especially ones involving repeat violent offenders who show few signs of desisting, that special measures, including sentences above the range for their most recent offense of conviction, might be justified. Again, however, such cases should require state officials to go through special procedures in which they would have to demonstrate the heightened risks of such offenders and the lack of alternatives to enhanced sentences to prevent their reoffending.

Generally speaking, crime reduction considerations appear to support some gradual increase in the sentences assigned to repeat offenders within the ranges that demarcate the various kinds of criminal offenses and communicate their seriousness. As we have seen, the evidence supporting marginal deterrence of harsher or longer sentences is unimpressive. Although it has not been studied as much, it seems likely that something similar will be true for special deterrence. Also, repeat offenders seem poor candidates for special deterrence, having experienced punishment first-hand already and, apparently, been unmoved by the prospect of experiencing it again. Of course, we might hope that having to absorb recidivist premiums will make some difference in their future deliberations about whether to offend, but it seems reasonable to have modest expectations in this regard. Further, recidivist premiums of almost any magnitude seem unlikely to play any significant role in rehabilitating repeat offenders, especially all by themselves and in the absence of programs designed to more directly address their criminogenic needs and tendencies. If anything, we might worry that longer sentences will exacerbate offending. Interestingly, when we turn to the moral reinforcement of norms against offending, the case for gradually increasing the sentences of recidivists, but only up to the point where they become disproportionate, seems supported by some empirical evidence. As Julian Roberts has detailed, there is widespread public support for recidivist premiums, but that support wanes once the public believes that the sentences assigned to individuals become disproportionate.[66]

Perhaps the strongest case for recidivist premiums of more robust kinds, ones that might even exceed proportionality limits, is based on the notion of incapacitation, yet even that case must be characterized judiciously and made subject to qualifications. As I have previously noted, violent or predatory offenders of certain kinds pose particularly worrisome threats to us, and perhaps more so as they repeat their offending. In Chapter 4, I held out the possibility that a few such offenders might be appropriately sentenced above the ranges applicable to their crimes, assuming that certain stringent conditions are satisfied. We should always keep in mind the limits on our abilities to predict accurately the behavior of individuals, even those with formidable histories of offending.[67] But I would not rule out the possibility of our having convincing evidence that a few offenders are apt to continue their violent or predatory ways. Against such considerations we must weigh the possibility that repeat offenders will age out. In that case, longer sentences will consume more in the way of scarce societal resources with little ultimate benefit. There are also the criminogenic tendencies of longer or harsher sentences to keep in mind.

To these well-known considerations, I would add one more: There seem to be many repeat offenders who are not terribly violent or predatory, at least not in ways that it makes sense to saddle them with substantial recidivist premiums and especially ones that would push their sentences above the tops of the ranges relevant to the crimes of which they have been convicted. Lots of recidivists remain low-level drug offenders or petty thieves or prone to arrests for being drunk and disorderly. We might, as they appear repeatedly before the courts to be sentenced, gradually push up the sentences assigned to them within the relevant ranges. Still, doing so should suffice for incapacitation purposes, given that there is little about their conduct that poses a substantial threat to others, let alone a grievous one. Only with the worst kinds of repeat offenders might sentences above the relevant ranges for their most recent crimes be contemplated.

Summarizing, the mixed approach to sentencing I have articulated offers some support for recidivist premiums, albeit primarily of kinds that gradually increase the sentences of repeat offenders within the relevant ranges of their offenses of conviction. Although such offenders might trouble or annoy us, their repeat offending does not make it appropriate to communicate that their most recent offenses are of kinds that are substantially more serious. Modest and progressive recidivist premiums should be the norm, not ones that effectively convey that offenders of one kind are akin to those of substantially more serious kinds.

Concluding Remarks

I have attempted, in this chapter, to articulate and defend an account of sentencing in criminal cases based on the mixed theory of punishment elaborated in Chapters 3 and 4. It seems fair to say that theorists of legal punishment have expended considerably more effort identifying and defending a justifying aim of legal punishment than exploring the implications of such abstract accounts for the issues raised by sentencing. Of course, it might be that sentencing, as a somewhat more practical matter, can only be theorized so far. Yes, there are various abstract principles upon which we can reasonably draw, but nothing approaching an exact "science" of sentencing exists or is likely to emerge.

Parsimony and proportionality are both somewhat abstract sentencing values. The former requires us to justify each successive penal imposition or loss, such that imposing fewer of them, or doing so for shorter periods of time, is always to be preferred to imposing more of them or any of them for longer periods of time. Yet this, by itself, does not tell us much about the kinds of sanctions to impose, even if we add the notion that punishment should never be allowed to degrade offenders. Proportionality provides more guidance, although I concede that, at best, it might leave us with a number of defensible sentencing schemes arranged according to both relative and absolute crime seriousness. Crime reduction considerations might enable us to narrow the defensible sentencing options, both by discouraging the use of schemes that employ longer or harsher sentences and by enabling us to find and employ sanctions for crimes, and especially minor offenses, that reduce rather than exacerbate offending. Still, what I have termed "significantly life-altering crimes" merit stern moral communication on the part of the state. As much as we might wish to minimize the use of penal confinement, few options other than it seem available to mark such crimes as grave and to thereby stand by and for their victims. However, we can and should strive to keep imprisonment humane and nondegrading and to prepare those who spend time in custodial institutions for their return to lives of responsible citizenship.

Notes

1 Alexandra Natapoff, "Misdemeanors," *Southern California Law Review* 85 (2012): 1313–75 and Jenny Roberts, "Why Misdemeanors Matter: Defining Effective Advocacy in the Lower Criminal Courts," *University of California-Davis Law Review* 45 (2011): 277–372.

2 Andrew von Hirsch, *Censure and Sanctions* (Oxford: Clarendon Press, 1993): 18–19. See also von Hirsch's "Proportionality in the Philosophy of Punishment," *Crime and Justice: A Review of Research* 16 (1992): 55–98.

3 For discussion of parsimony as a sentencing value, see Michael Tonry, "Proportionality, Parsimony, and Interchangeability of Punishment," in R. A. Duff, S. Marshall, and R. Dobash (eds.), *Penal Theory and Practice* (Manchester: Manchester University Press, 1994): 59–83 and Richard S. Frase, *Just Sentencing: Principles and Procedures for a Workable System* (New York: Oxford University Press, 2013): 11 and 32–33.

4 Frase, *Just Sentencing*, 32.

5 See Richard L. Lippke, *Rethinking Imprisonment* (Oxford: Oxford University Press, 2007): 105–9, where I discuss and defend what I call the "minimum conditions of confinement."

6 Lippke, *Rethinking Imprisonment*, Chapters 5 and 6–9. See also Michael Tonry, "Has the Prison a Future?" in M. Tonry (ed.), *The Future of Imprisonment* (New York: Oxford University Press, 2004): 3–24.

7 John Kleinig, "The Hardness of Hard Treatment," in A. Ashworth and M. Wasik (eds.), *Fundamentals in Sentencing Theory* (Oxford: Clarendon Press, 1998): 273–98 and Michael Tonry, *Doing Justice, Preventing Crime* (New York: Oxford University Press, 2020): 15–42.

8 As described in Dan S. Kahan, "What Do Alternative Sanctions Mean?" *University of Chicago Law Review* 63 (1996): 591–653, at 633.

9 A. John Simmons, *The Lockean Theory of Rights* (Princeton, NJ: Princeton University Press, 1992): 148–61; Christopher W. Morris, "Punishment and Loss of Moral Standing," *Canadian Journal of Philosophy* 21 (1991): 53–79; and Christopher Heath Wellman, *Rights Forfeiture and Punishment* (New York: Oxford University

Press, 2017). For critique of the notion of right forfeiture in accounts of legal punishment, see Warren Quinn, "The Right to Threaten and the Right to Punish," *Philosophy and Public Affairs* 14 (1985): 327–73; Rex Martin, *A System of Rights* (Oxford: Clarendon Press, 1983): 280–84; and Richard L. Lippke, "Criminal Offenders and Right Forfeiture," *Journal of Social Philosophy* 32 (2001): 78–89.

10 See Alan H. Goldman, "The Paradox of Punishment," *Philosophy and Public Affairs* 9 (1979): 42–58, at 45.

11 Quinn, "The Right to Threaten," 332–33.

12 Wellman, *Rights Forfeiture*, 34.

13 Wellman, *Rights Forfeiture*, 25.

14 Wellman, *Rights Forfeiture*, 48.

15 Whether the scale of sentence severity involves a steady incline or is more complex is a matter of some debate. For instance, Michael Tonry and Mary Lynch have raised the question of whether brief custodial sentences are always more harsh than longer sentences involving intensive probation. See their "Intermediate Sanctions," *Crime and Justice: A Review of Research* 20 (1996): 99–144.

16 Richard L. Lippke, "Some Surprising Implications of Negative Retributivism," *Journal of Applied Philosophy* 31 (2014): 49–62, at 55. See also Kleinig, "The Hardness of Hard Treatment," 287–88.

17 von Hirsch, *Censure and Sanctions*, 9–12, and R. A. Duff, *Punishment, Communication, and Community* (Oxford: Oxford University Press, 2001): 79–82.

18 Duff, *Punishment, Communication, and Community*, 107–12. Still, how far we should go by way of attempting to ensure that offenders feel remorse, repent of their crimes, and reform themselves is a matter about which, as we have seen, there is some debate.

19 Duff, *Punishment, Communication, and Community*, 180.

20 See Craig Haney, "Mental Health Issues in Long-Term Solitary and 'Supermax' Confinement," *Crime & Delinquency* 49 (2003): 124–55.

21 von Hirsch, *Censure and Sanctions*, 18. Göran Duus-Otterström suggests the terms "relative" and "absolute" are preferable, in his "Weighing Relative and Absolute Proportionality in Punishment," in Michael Tonry (ed.), *Of One-Eyed and Toothless Miscreants: Making the Punishment Fit the Crime?* (New York: Oxford University Press, 2020): 30–50, at 34. I will use both sets of terms interchangeably.

22 Michael S. Moore, *Act and Crime: The Philosophy of Action and Its Implications for Criminal Law* (Oxford: Oxford University Press, 1993): 80.

23 von Hirsch, *Censure and Sanctions*, 18.

24 Jesper Ryberg, "Proportionality and the Seriousness of Crimes," in Tonry (ed.), *Of One-Eyed and Toothless Miscreants*, 51–75. For an important version of the harm element in crime seriousness, see Andrew von Hirsch and Nils Jareborg, "Gauging Criminal Harm: A Living-Standard Analysis," *Oxford Journal of Legal Studies* 11 (1991): 1–38.

25 Paul H. Robinson and Robert Kurzban, "Concordance and Conflict in Intuitions of Justice," *Minnesota Law Review* 91 (2007): 1829–907.

26 Ryberg, "Proportionality and the Seriousness of Crimes," 54. See also Vincent Chiao, "Proportionality and Its Discontents," *Law and Philosophy* 41 (2022): 193–217.

27 Jesper Ryberg, "Punishment and the Measurement of Severity," in Jesper Ryberg and J. Angelo Corlett (eds.), *Punishment and Ethics: New Perspectives* (Basingstoke: Palgrave Macmillan, 2010): 72–91.

28 I assume here, although I do not demonstrate it, that the death penalty is not justified as a criminal sanction.

29 For discussion of cardinal proportionality, see von Hirsch, *Censure and Sanctions,* 18–19 and "Proportionality in the Philosophy of Punishment," 75–79. See also Duff, *Punishment, Communication, and Community*, 133–35. On the claim

that proportionality theorists must take into account the subjective experiences of those being punished, see Adam J. Kolber, "The Subjective Nature of Punishment," *Columbia Law Review* 109 (2009): 182–236 and "The Comparative Nature of Punishment," *Boston University Law Review* 89 (2009): 1565–608. See also Ryberg, "Punishment and the Measurement of Severity."

30 von Hirsch, "Proportionality," 84. See also von Hirsch and Andrew Ashworth, *Proportionate Sentencing: Exploring the Principles* (Oxford: Oxford University Press, 2005): 141–42.

31 The cases of Anders Breivik killing 77 people in Norway, many of them youths, and Adam Lanza killing 26 people at an elementary school in Sandy Hook, Connecticut, 20 of them children, come to mind.

32 Although, as I noted in Chapter 4, a case might be made for permitting judges to sometimes assign sentences above the sentencing range for the crime type in question if they can offer persuasive reasons for doing so, ones that should have to survive appellate review.

33 Hugo Adam Bedau, "The Minimal Invasion Argument against the Death Penalty," *Criminal Justice Ethics* 21 (2002): 3–8.

34 von Hirsch, *Censure and Sanctions*, 43.

35 Again, approximately 80 percent of the crimes addressed by the US criminal justice system involve misdemeanors. See Natapoff, "Misdemeanors," 1320.

36 See Patricia A. Resick, "The Psychological Impact of Rape," *Journal of Interpersonal Violence* 8 (1993): 223–55.

37 von Hirsch, "Proportionality in the Philosophy of Punishment," 76.

38 Kolber, "Subjective Experience," 197.

39 See Richard L. Lippke, "Penal Severity and the Modern State," in Tonry (ed.), *Of One-Eyed and Toothless Miscreants*, 127–48.

40 Of course, the culpability of offenders in significantly harming victims must also be taken into account in determining the seriousness of a crime token and thus the sentence to be assigned.

41 Here, I follow the lead of von Hirsch and Jareborg in casting the severity of penal sanctions in terms of their impact on "standard" human lives, although their reference to "standardization" is with respect to the harms done by the various kinds of criminal offenses. See their "Gauging Criminal Harm," 4–5. Such standardization seems a staple of human rights theory, whereby we abstract from differences among humans in determining which of their interests are fundamental and thus deserving of the designation of "rights."

42 That those who are new to imprisonment have a difficult time adjusting to it is well-known. See, for instance, Jonathan Masur, John Bronsteen, and Christopher Buccafusco, "Happiness and Punishment," *University of Chicago Law Review* 76 (2009): 1037–81.

43 Douglas Husak, "The Metric of Punishment Severity: A Puzzle about the Principle of Proportionality," in Tonry (ed.), *Of One-Eyed and Toothless Miscreants*, 97–126, at 109–11.

44 I first explored this possibility in Richard L. Lippke, *Rethinking Imprisonment* (Oxford: Oxford University Press, 2007): 40–50.

45 As Douglas Husak notes in "Proportionality in Personal Life," *Criminal Law and Philosophy* 15 (2021): 339–60, at 341.

46 Daniel S. Nagin, "Criminal Deterrence: Research at the Outset of the Twenty-First Century," *Crime and Justice: A Review of Research* 23 (1998): 1–42, and "Deterrence in the Twenty-First Century," *Crime and Justice: A Review of Research* 42 (2013): 199–263; Anthony N. Doob and Cheryl Marie Webster, "Sentence Severity and Crime: Accepting the Null Hypothesis," *Crime and Justice: A Review of Research* 30 (2003): 143–95.

47 For useful discussion, see Nagin, "Deterrence in the Twenty-First Century," 233–42.
48 See, for instance, Jeffrey T. Ulmer and Darrell Steffensmeier, "The Age and Crime Relationship: Social Variation, Social Explanations," in Kevin M. Beaver, J. C. Barnes, and Brian B. Boutwell (eds.), *The Nurture Versus Biosocial Debate in Criminology: On the Origins of Criminal Behavior and Criminality* (Thousand Oaks, CA: Sage, 2015): 377–96.
49 Franklin E. Zimring and Gordon Hawkins, *Incapacitation: Penal Confinement and the Restraint of Crime* (New York: Oxford University Press, 1995): 53–55.
50 Gerald G. Gaes, Timothy J. Flanagan, Laurence L. Motiuk, and Lynn Stewart, "Adult Correctional Treatment," *Crime and Justice: A Review of Research* 26 (1999): 361–426; and Paul Gendreau, "Offender Rehabilitation: What We Know and What Needs to Be Done," *Criminal Justice and Behavior* 23 (1996): 144–61; and Mark W. Lipsey and Frances T. Cullen, "The Effectiveness of Correctional Rehabilitation: A Review of Systematic Reviews," *Annual Review of Law and Social Science* 3 (2007): 297–320.
51 See Daniel S. Nagin, Frances T. Cullen, and Cheryl Lero Jonson, "Imprisonment and Reoffending," *Crime and Justice: A Review of Research* 38 (2009): 115–200, who note (at 115) that "compared with noncustodial sanctions, incarceration appears to have a null or mildly criminogenic effect on future criminal behavior."
52 Craig Haney, *Reforming Punishment: Psychological Limits to the Pains of Imprisonment* (Washington, DC: American Psychological Association, 2006) and Bruce Western, *Punishment and Inequality in America* (New York: Russell Sage, 2006).
53 Haney, *Reforming Punishment*, especially Chapter 6.
54 See Liora Lazarus, *Contrasting Prisoners' Rights: A Comparative Examination of Germany and England* (Oxford: Oxford University Press, 2004) and John Pratt and Anna Erikson, *Contrasts in Punishment: An Explanation of Anglophone Excess and Nordic Exceptionalism* (London: Routledge, 2013).
55 Lippke, *Rethinking Imprisonment*, and Tonry, "Has the Prison a Future?"
56 See, for instance, Ram Subramanian and Alison Shames, *Sentencing and Prison Practices in German and the Netherlands: Implications for the United States*, Vera Institute of Justice (2013), at www.vera.org/downloads/Publications/sentencing-and-prison-practices-in-germany-and-the-netherlands-implications-for-the-united-states/legacy_downloads/european-american-prison-report-v3.pdf (accessed May 7, 2020).
57 Ojmarrh Mitchell, David B. Wilson, Amy Eggers, and Doris L. Mackenzie, "Assessing the Effectiveness of Drug Courts on Recidivism: A Meta-Analytic Review of Traditional and Non-Traditional Drug Courts," *Journal of Criminal Justice* 40 (2012): 60–71 and Allison D. Redlich, Henry J. Steadman, John Monahan, Pamela Clark Robbins, and John Petrila, "Patterns of Practice in Mental Health Courts: A National Survey," *Law and Human Behavior* 30 (2006): 347–62.
58 Heather Strang and Lawrence W. Sherman, "Repairing the Harm: Victims and Restorative Justice," *Utah Law Review* 2003 (2003): 15–42 and John Braithwaite, "Restorative Justice," in Michael Tonry (ed.), *The Handbook of Crime and Punishment* (New York: Oxford University Press, 1998): 323–43.
59 Hennessey Hayes, "Assessing Reoffending in Restorative Justice Conferences," *Australian & New Zealand Journal of Criminology* 38 (2005): 77–101.
60 See, for instance, Julian V. Roberts, "Punishing Persistence: Explaining the Enduring Appeal of the Recidivist Sentencing Premium," *British Journal of Criminology* 48 (2008): 468–81. See also Roberts and Andrew von Hirsch (eds.), *Previous Convictions at Sentencing: Theoretical and Applied Perspectives* (Oxford: Hart Publishing, 2014).
61 Mirko Bagaric, "Double Punishment and Punishing Character: The Unfairness of Prior Convictions," *Criminal Justice Ethics* 19 (2010): 10–28.

62 Youngjae Lee, "Repeat Offenders and the Question of Desert," in Roberts and von Hirsch (eds.), *Previous Convictions at Sentencing*, 49–72 and Benjamin Ewing, "Prior Convictions as Moral Opportunities," *American Journal of Criminal Law* 45 (2019): 252–303.

63 Andrew von Hirsch (sometimes with co-authors) has urged what is known as a "progressive loss of mitigation" approach, according to which first-time offenders might be given a break in sentencing, whereas repeat ones gradually lose any grounds for sentence mitigation. See Martin Wasik and Andrew von Hirsch, "Section 29 Revisited: Previous Convictions in Sentencing," *Criminal Law Review* (1994): 409–18.

64 For a similar approach, see Frase, *Just Sentencing*, 190.

65 The adoption of "three strikes" sentencing provisions in the US are the leading example of recidivist premiums that seem excessive. For discussion, see Michael Tonry, "Sentencing in America: 1975–2025," *Crime and Justice: A Review of Research* 42 (2013): 141–98.

66 Julian V. Roberts, *Punishing Persistent Offenders: Exploring Community and Offender Perspectives* (Oxford: Oxford University Press, 2008).

67 On the limits of our abilities to accurate predict future offending, see Michael Tonry, *Doing Justice, Preventing Crime* (New York: Oxford University Press, 2020), especially Chapter 7.

7 User Fees and Collateral Legal Consequences

We do not live in a world in which individuals convicted of crimes are assigned sentences which are appropriate, serve those sentences, and then attempt to resume normal lives of citizenship and responsibility. Granted, one of the reasons why we do not live in such a world is that there is an enduring stigma of criminal conviction, one that hampers those with criminal records in their efforts to find or keep employment and housing. As we have seen, there is debate about whether and to what extent the criminal histories of individuals should be matters of accessible, public record.[1] But independently of the public "naming and shaming" of offenders that exists in some countries, other steps are increasingly taken to burden offenders as they serve their sentences or, more often, after they do so.

First, there are various fees, or what some call "legal financial obligations," (LFOs) assessed to individuals who are convicted of crimes.[2] These include fees for providing indigent defendants with attorneys, room and board costs charged to individuals kept in pretrial detention or assigned jail sentences upon conviction, fees to register for probation services and to pay for the supervision they provide, and even fees for things like finger-printing, trial transcripts, or failures to appear for trials. As scholars have noted, for many of the mostly minor offenders who cycle through the criminal justice system, the burdens these fees create can collectively outweigh those resulting from their formal sentences.[3] In some jurisdictions, failure to pay LFOs can result in the incarceration of individuals who have committed fairly minor offenses, this in spite of official court disapproval of such outcomes.[4] Making matters worse, some local police and court jurisdictions have become partially dependent for their funding on the collection of such fees, thus heightening their incentives to charge and collect them.[5] If this potential conflict of interest is not worrisome enough, another has emerged: Overburdened local and regional criminal justice agencies have turned to private providers of criminal justice services.[6] These private providers charge a variety of fees to the individuals assigned to them by the courts some portion of which providers hope will furnish them with profits for their services.

DOI: 10.4324/9781032661667-8

Second, once individuals convicted of crimes have served their sentences, many of them are subject to what are known as "collateral legal consequences" (CLCs).[7] CLCs include provisions excluding former offenders from voting, from public housing or low-interest student loans, and from certain occupations. They also include residency restrictions imposed on sex offenders or requirements that they register as such. For the most part, CLCs seem aimed at reducing the risks that former offenders are deemed to pose to the public. However, some of them also appear to be premised on notions that former offenders have forfeited certain of their rights or are undeserving of social welfare benefits which law-abiding citizens receive.[8] Notably, some of these CLCs persist long after individuals convicted of crimes have otherwise served their sentences. Like LFOs, they can aggregately and cumulatively burden offenders in ways that exceed the impositions or losses they are made to endure by their formal sentences.[9]

In the previous chapter, I identified the values that should guide us in crafting sentences for crimes that serve the purposes of moral communication and crime reduction. Those values were parsimony, proportionality, and within broad proportionality constraints, a concern to reduce crime in ways that are not self-defeating. Initially, it might seem unclear whether and to what extent these values ought to inform our thinking about LFOs and CLCs. The courts and some scholars argue that CLCs are "regulative" or "civil" in character, and so not concerned with punishing offenders for their crimes.[10] Also, it might be suggested that LFOs are more in the way of "user fees," requiring those who have participated in crimes to bear some of the costs to the larger community of having to arrest, prosecute, and punish them. As such, LFOs might also seem to have little to do with the formal sentencing of offenders.

I suspect that court and scholarly pronouncements about whether the imposition of these costs and burdens amount to punishment might not matter to the individuals who are made to bear them. They will likely view such impositions as part of their punishment, since they are foisted on them by the state in response to their having been charged with or convicted of crimes. I will have more to say subsequently about the issue of whether LFOs and especially CLCs should be conceived as penal in character. But even if they should not be so conceived, they are troubling for other reasons. In the first section of this chapter, I examine LFOs and argue that the most worrisome feature of their increasing imposition is their unfairness. Those who violate the law and are properly held accountable for doing so should usually be understood as having prepaid such fees, in the form of taxes supporting various government endeavors, the administration of criminal justice among them. Also, the selective enforcement of the criminal law that we identified in Chapter 5 means that only some offenders—disproportionately poor people or poor people of color in many societies—are saddled with user fees. Others who should be punished and assessed such fees tend to escape both. Defenses of LFOs that claim that it is "only fair" that those who drive up criminal justice costs should bear them seem problematic in this light. Then there is underenforcement of the criminal law, such that some members of society who are victimized by crimes seem to receive less support or attention from criminal justice officials when their basic rights are infringed. Arguably, such individuals are not getting what they pay for when they support the state's endeavors through their taxes. Should they therefore receive refunds on their taxes, in keeping with the logic of LFOs? So it might seem. Yet when some of these same individuals commit crimes and are arrested, convicted, and punished for them, LFOs are imposed upon them. Fairness would seem to dictate that they have a credit, of sorts, for the resources their tax payments supplied to the state but which have not been used to secure or stand by their rights.

When it comes to CLCs, my primary focus will be on the possibility that some of them might be defended as purely public safety measures. Following the work of Zachary Hoskins, I outline various conditions that have to be satisfied if such measures are to be justified and distinguished from penal sanctions for crimes. I argue that state officials should have to demonstrate, at special hearings, that CLCs aimed at preventing harms will be effective, narrowly tailored, and no more burdensome than necessary. The permanence of such measures should not be presupposed and if the state is to fully distinguish them from penal impositions, it should undertake ameliorative efforts to limit the burdens they foist on individuals. However, many existing CLCs are imposed on ex-offenders without any pretense of the state satisfying these conditions. Further, even if state officials attempted to satisfy them, there are other challenges to doing so that I outline in the last section of the chapter, ones that cast further doubt on their feasibility or justifiability. I conclude that the prospects of defensible CLCs aimed at protecting public safety are bleak.

The position toward which my analysis points is clear: Although the state is justified in imposing penal sanctions on those duly convicted of crimes, once individuals fully satisfy the requirements of their sentences, they should be presumptively treated as full-fledged members of society with all of the rights and privileges accorded to other citizens. We might wish to permit the state to rebut this presumption in some cases, but the procedural and substantive hurdles to doing so should be formidable. Importantly, the post-punishment lives of many offenders will already be difficult, for a variety of well-known reasons. We should therefore recognize and accept that there is little to gain, and much to risk or lose, by making their lives more challenging.

LFOs as User Fees

LFOs are different from CLCs, in part, because, in theory at least, they can be fully discharged while individuals are serving their court-assigned sentences, or even before they are served. Also, unlike some CLCs, LFOs are not aimed at reducing the risks to society of those deemed dangerous because of their past criminal convictions. Instead, LFOs are "user fees," assigned to those who are alleged to have driven up the costs of maintaining a criminal justice system by committing crimes. It might seem fair to assess them at least some of those costs, since offenders could have avoided generating them by refraining from crimes. Indeed, as imprisonment rates skyrocketed in countries such as the United States during the 1990s and 2000s, demands that offenders pay some of the costs of their punishment became commonplace. Polls indicate widespread support for LFOs in some jurisdictions.[11] The idea behind them—that if you voluntarily participate in legally proscribed activities you should bear some of the costs of punishing them—has considerable intuitive appeal.

Such user fees will impact offenders in widely disparate ways. They might be paid by affluent offenders with ease, or avoided by them altogether if, for instance, they can make bail or do not need court-appointed attorneys. The problem is that offenders who are relatively unburdened by LFOs are apt to be the rarest of rare birds. Not only are most offenders far from financially comfortable, when they are assigned LFOs by the courts, they will struggle to discharge them both while they are serving their formal sentences and after they complete them.[12] In some jurisdictions, offenders who have otherwise completed their sentences will not be allowed to exercise certain civil rights (e.g., the right to vote) until they pay off the debts generated by LFOs.[13] Neither will they be able to invoke bankruptcy provisions in order to ease the burdens of their accumulated LFOs.[14]

Public enthusiasm for imposing LFOs might diminish if there was greater awareness of some of the salient facts about and consequences of them. First, there is evidence that the costs of collecting the fees owed by offenders tend to exceed the total amount of the fees collected.[15] Collecting fees from offenders might sound like a good idea until we consider the burdens and bleak prospects of success at doing so. In response, it might be suggested that fee collections could be improved with more or better efforts by state authorities. But then we run up against the stubborn fact that many of those from whom state agents seek to collect fees are not only poor to begin with, their income-earning prospects will be diminished further by their criminal records. Also, those who have spent significant stretches of time in jail or prison will lack work training or experience.[16] Some of those convicted of crimes will have families to support, which means that they will face difficult choices between feeding and housing their children and paying off their LFOs. One can hardly fault them for wanting to give care for their families higher priority. Collection efforts, we might plausibly surmise, will never be terribly successful in the face of these characteristics of many offenders.

Second, there is the question of what to do about offenders who fail to fulfill their LFOs. Should those who routinely fall short of paying assigned fees be imprisoned for their failures, in which case they might be assessed "room and board" fees, thus compounding their woes? In some jurisdictions, incarceration for failure to pay accumulated fees does occur, although there are supposed to be legal barriers to imprisoning people for debt.[17] If such troublesome measures are eschewed, then how else will we wring LFO payments from those who struggle to pay them or simply refuse to do so? Courts in the United States have been more willing to permit imprisonment of the latter kinds of debtors. Whether doing so is a plausible approach to getting them to pay up is unclear. Imprisonment is costly; assessing inmates the costs of custody is probably a futile endeavor in the absence of state provision of paid labor opportunities for inmates. A better option might be to treat LFO debts like civil debts, with payment schedules worked out so that individuals can pay them off while remaining free to work and thus provide for themselves and their families. Although such an approach seems superior to imprisoning offenders for their user fee debts, required payments will remain a significant burden to many offenders who struggle to make ends meet and support their families. It is apparent that the burdens of a criminal record, along with the myriad ways that time spent in jails or prisons tends to be criminogenic, already make it difficult for ex-offenders to hew to the legal straight and narrow. Burdening them more, with LFOs, seems likely to make many of them more desperate or simply more alienated from society. Scholars who study LFOs routinely quote offenders who lament the ways in which they cannot seem to escape these burdens and humiliations, even when they have otherwise fully served the sentences assigned to them for their crimes.[18] A more potent recipe for recidivism is hard to imagine. Yet this means that the practice conflicts with one of the justifying aims of punishing offenders in the first place, which is to reduce crime.

This brings us to the question of whether we should conceive of LFOs as forms of legal punishment assigned to those convicted of crimes, or as something else—say as adjuncts to it. On the one hand, it seems difficult to deny that LFOs have at least some implicit communicative content and purpose. Not only do they consist of efforts to hold those convicted of crimes accountable for the costs that doing so are deemed to create, LFOs seem to express social disapproval of offenders for having foisted such costs on the law-abiding public. On the other hand, it does not seem that in assigning them we are communicating with offenders about their crimes or the relative or absolute seriousness of their crimes. It is legal sanctions proper that do that or are supposed to do that. Instead, LFOs communicate with offenders about the burdens that their crimes impose on the public born of having to police, investigate, prosecute, and punish them. This makes it seem as if the most plausible way to think about LFOs is in terms of their being adjuncts to criminal sanctions. Bolstering this conclusion is another point: It might not seem to matter to us whether fees burden those on whom they are imposed. As we have seen, a few offenders might be able to pay them with ease. If they do so, we do not trouble ourselves with assigning them further fees, ones that we believe will burden them. If one of the hallmarks of legal punishment is its intended burdensomeness, then fees do not appear to fit the bill.

However, the preceding considerations are not as decisive as they first appear. For one thing, it is foreseeable that many to whom fees are assigned will struggle to pay them, some mightily so. And if it was not immediately apparent that this would be true, it certainly has become so, since efforts to collect them have, as we have seen, been ramped up considerably, although often to little avail. If nothing is done by state officials to ameliorate the burdens fees impose on many offenders, then it becomes harder to resist the inference that state officials intend them as such. Making matters worse, as we have just seen, is the fact that, in some jurisdictions, failures to pay fees can result in individuals being imprisoned or imprisoned for longer periods of time. This complicates the case for distinguishing fees from legal punishment proper. Also, until they are fully paid, individuals who have otherwise served their sentences are sometimes not allowed to exercise or enjoy certain of the basic rights of citizenship. This reluctance to restore their full citizenship status makes it look as if the individuals involved have not yet paid their full penal debts to society.

Admittedly, some of the ways in which fees have been designed and administered might be modified or eliminated. We could and no doubt should refuse to imprison offenders for their LFO debts, instead relying on approaches that treat them like civil debts to be paid off according to some reasonable schedule. Of course, such civil debts will still be burdensome to most who have them. Also, just as those with civil debts enjoy the rights of full citizenship, so might those who have otherwise served the sentences assigned to them for their crimes regain their full rights. This would make it seem that their sentences fully constituted their legal punishment. Nonetheless, I wonder if the effort to distinguish LFOs from punishment proper is not something of an academic parlor game. I suspect that many offenders will view having to endure them as part of their punishment or an extension of their punishment, even if it might seem more theoretically sound to view them as adjuncts to it. This will especially be true if LFO obligations turn out to be more burdensome than the official sentences imposed on the many, mostly minor offenders who circulate through the criminal justice system.

My sense is that the deeper problems with LFOs are ones that have to do with the fairness of their imposition. As we saw in Chapter 5, there are pervasive and long-standing problems with both the skewed enforcement of many criminal provisions and the underenforcement of others. For instance, vice crimes of various kinds are disproportionately policed and prosecuted in poor communities, and especially poor communities with substantial racial or ethnic minority populations.[19] Yet vice crimes are committed by many individuals throughout society, including many who, due to their race, class, or ethnicity, are not the favored targets of law enforcement officials. Such skewed enforcement of the criminal law creates the image—some would say the illusion—that it is poor people of color who predominately commit vice crimes. It is bad enough that they are disproportionately targeted for arrest, investigation, prosecution, and conviction, and likely assigned longer or harsher sentences than their more affluent or racially or ethnically dominant counterparts. LFOs are then piled on to add insult to injury. Supporters of LFOs might comfort themselves with the notion those who are pushing up the costs of law enforcement are being made to pay those costs. Yet this ignores or downplays the ways in which who gets convicted and assigned LFOs is an artifact of questionable policing and prosecution practices.

Add to the preceding the fact that the communities whose members are disproportionately targeted for law enforcement often overlap substantially with the communities in which criminal victimization goes underpoliced or underprosecuted.[20] As we have seen, crimes against poor people of color may be disproportionately ignored or downplayed by the authorities. Such underenforcement of the criminal law not only creates despair in such communities, it alienates many of their members from the social order, making them less likely to cooperate with the authorities when they do investigate crimes in their communities. More to the point, people in such communities are, like all citizens, required to pay their taxes, some portion of which goes to support the operations of the criminal justice system. Yet they appear to receive fewer of the benefits of that system, perhaps many fewer. This makes it seem like they ought to receive refunds for services not provided, although paid for. Worse than this, when people in such communities commit crimes, or are convicted of doing so by police and prosecutors who might be a bit too intent on aggressively fighting crime in their communities, they incur LFOs. Fairness would instead seem to require us to regard them as having criminal justice cost credits that they should be able to "cash in" to cover the costs of their convictions.

As I noted in the preceding paragraph, poor people in communities with substantial racial or ethnic minorities, are expected, like all citizens, to pay their fair share of the taxes needed to support the state's various endeavors, the enforcement of the criminal law among them. Yet this suggests that most members of society, including most criminal offenders, will have "prepaid" some of the costs associated with arresting, convicting, and punishing them. Income, property, sales, and other taxes are levied on all persons in society, or at least all of them who participate, in one way or another, in economic and social life. Given this reality, it seems that LFOs constitute a kind of "double charging."

It might be objected that many of the individuals who engage in criminal offending are unlikely to have "prepaid." Some of them, it might be claimed, will have skirted these burdens by resorting to illegal ways of acquiring income, or by underreporting their income so as to minimize their taxes. I need not deny this, although sorting out who has prepaid and who has not, or worse, who has prepaid their "fair share" and who has not, will be difficult and resource-consuming tasks. The LFOs assigned to many criminal offenders incorporate no requirement by state officials to determine which of the individuals among the convicted have or have not prepaid. Instead, LFOs are assigned without regard to such matters. Also, although some offenders may succeed in concealing all or part of their income from taxes, other kinds of taxes that support state activities will be harder to evade. These will include sales taxes, gasoline taxes, and property taxes. Even renters are likely to contribute to property taxes, since landlords will factor them into the rents they charge. Almost everyone will have prepaid some of the costs of operating the criminal justice system. Given that fact, "user fees," in the form of LFOs, seem to charge offenders for costs they have already paid.

Further, there is a worrisome "us versus them" mentality that underlies the emergence of and surge in LFOs. The user fees of which they consist are often sold to the public with the idea that "we," the law-abiding, should see ourselves as sorely used by "them," the law-defying, such that we should get back at "them" by shifting "our" criminal justice costs to "them." Yet not only have many of "them" prepaid, many of "us" are not innocents with respect to law-breaking. In the United States, for instance, roughly one in three citizens has a criminal record.[21] Many of those with records will, as we have seen, have been convicted of minor offenses. Still, the number of "thems" ought to be a sobering fact to members of the public, perhaps reducing their enthusiasm for the kind of cost-shifting of which LFOs consist. Also, not having a criminal record obviously does not mean that one is innocent of offending. Many of "us" commit misdemeanors that go undetected or unpunished, and some of us commit felonies for which we are never caught. Factor in the ways in which the more affluent or socially advantaged are less subject to police surveillance that produces arrests and convictions, or better resourced to ward off convictions in the event that their legal wrongdoing is detected, and the sharp line between "us" and "them" is muddied further.

That being said, we might be troubled by the prospect of individuals who persist in committing crimes after having been once, or perhaps twice, arrested, charged, convicted, and punished. Those who are first- or second-time offenders might plausibly be thought to have prepaid the costs of full and fair due process in the disposition of any charges filed against them and any sanctions imposed on them. But some individuals continue to commit crimes, lots of them over the course of many years, and wrack up numerous convictions. Even if most or many of their crimes are fairly minor, they nonetheless persist in committing them and this drives up the costs of the criminal justice system. Would it not therefore seem reasonable for us to force them to share the burdens of processing their convictions and carrying out their sentences by assigning them "habitual users fees" in the forms of LFOs?

In response to this, it is important to bear in mind that recidivists will likely be sentenced higher within the sentence ranges pertinent to their most recent offenses of conviction. I have defended such an approach on the grounds of providing more emphatic moral communication with persistent offenders and the desirability, in some cases, of incapacitating them for longer periods of time, with the hope that they will edge closer to "aging out" of offending. Adding LFOs to their already enhanced sentences seems like piling on. Also, the kinds of individuals who rack up numerous convictions do not tend to be living organized, productive lives that provide them with reliable and legally obtained income to support themselves and those who depend upon them. More often than we might like to acknowledge, they are scrambling to make ends meet, and more than a few of them will be hampered in this by such things as alcohol or drug abuse, mental illness, homelessness, and marginal employment prospects.[22] Admittedly, some recidivists are professional criminals, individuals who are dedicated to living outside the law and who are moderately to substantially successful at it. Such offenders might be reasonably assessed the kinds of user fees of which LFOs consist. But many recidivists will not be suitable targets of criminal justice user fees, not if we have any hope of collecting them. Assessing them LFOs seems a bit of a lost cause, in the ways that scholars have thoroughly documented. We would probably do better, in terms of conserving scarce societal resources, to look for ways to help such offenders get their lives back on track. Doing so might involve providing drug or alcohol treatment, mental health treatment, job training, and stable and secure living accommodations. There will be costs to providing these things in the short-term, of course, but they might be less, in the long-term, than doing nothing and enduring the repeat offending that will more or less inevitably result.

I would concede that there might be limited ways in which some offenders could be required to help with the costs of their punishment. For instance, in some European prison systems, prison inmates are encouraged, and sometimes required, to work and they are paid for their work.[23] I have argued elsewhere that we should undertake efforts to provide inmates with access to decently paid labor.[24] If we did this, then it might make sense to assess inmates for some of the costs of their own upkeep, although we should not do so in ways that leave them without income to help support their families or save for their futures. Measures such as these would help to "normalize" prisons, in the sense of making them more like the real world of work and responsibility than they often are. Prisoners would not only be able to support themselves and others, they might also receive job training and work experience that would better set them up for success in civil society once they are released from prison. But the aim of normalizing prisons in this way is very different than the aim of most LFOs, which are too often assessed without regard to whether offenders can pay them or will learn anything from them that will strengthen their commitments to responsibility.

A further way in which LFOs seem unfair should be noted, although defending it would require an extended discussion of contested claims about the nature of social justice that I will not attempt to provide in this context. Here, I will simply note that on some accounts of social justice, the state must do more than shield the members of society from violence, predation, or other interferences with their lives, property, and personal liberty. The state must also provide all members of society with minima of social welfare, in the forms of subsistence, housing, education, medical care, and eldercare.[25] Some theorists defend accounts according to which the minima should be robust, up to the level of guaranteeing that all persons have decent lives that they can live on their own terms. Some existing societies will live up to the terms of such conceptions of social justice, but many will not. Since the United States is a country in which LFOs have proliferated, let us take it as an example of a society that has fallen short of securing the basic moral rights of its citizens. Not surprisingly, perhaps, some of those whose lives are diminished by the state's failure to provide for their social welfare will be more likely to engage in criminal offending, for a variety of well-known reasons. As I have previously noted, some penal theorists argue that state punishment of such individuals is problematic, if not unjust.[26] They have been put in an untenable bind by the state's failure to provide for many of their basic needs; to treat them as if they can be held to the same standards of conduct as other, better off members of society seems unfair. If we do more than this—if we assign them LFOs because of the added costs of having to police, prosecute, and punish their crimes—then that seems to simply pour salt in their wounds. Arguably, the state has failed them in ways that precipitate some of their criminal misconduct. Now it wants to assess them "user fees" for having to deal with their criminal misconduct, at least some of which is born of state failures to live up to its obligations to them to begin with? That seems profoundly unfair.

Still, it is a type of unfairness that seems more controversial than that stemming from skewed enforcement and underenforcement. Some theorists will reject conceptions of social justice that posit a social welfare role for the state. Yet even they will likely endorse the propositions that state officials should strive for impartial enforcement of the criminal law and stand for all victims of crimes, not simply those who tend to be better off or deemed more worthy in other respects.

CLCs and Public Safety

Unlike the "user fees" of which LFOs mostly consist, CLCs have other purposes and are typically imposed post-punishment, that is, after an offender has served his or her sentence. Over the course of the last 40 years, a wide variety of CLCs have been adopted in many legal jurisdictions. They include felon disenfranchisement provisions, sex offender registry and residency restrictions, occupational exclusions, license forfeitures, restrictions on gun ownership, and the loss of social welfare provisions in the forms of access to public housing and low-interest student loans.[27] As a result, those convicted of crimes, and especially of more serious crimes, endure all manner of restrictions on their liberty, along with requirements to register or report their whereabouts, even though they will often have completed the formal sentences handed down to them by the courts.

The rationales offered in support of CLCs vary. Often, more than one of them is put forward in support of a given CLC. As I have already noted, many CLCs seem primarily aimed at reducing the risks that ex-offenders are thought to pose to the public. Such harm reduction or public safety rationales for CLCs will be my main focus in the remainder of the chapter. Before considering them, however, it is useful to pause and consider why other prominent defenses of CLCs are likely to be unconvincing. For instance, although it is possible to cast things like felon disenfranchisement or the loss of social welfare benefits as promoting public safety, my sense is that they are better understood as having different bases. Loss of such basic citizenship rights, or what some might view as citizenship privileges, seems more plausibly understood in terms of notions of right forfeiture or in terms of the notion that persons who have been convicted of certain kinds of crimes are undeserving of the rights or privileges enjoyed by other citizens. Both approaches invite us to regard and treat offenders who might have otherwise fully served the sentences for their crimes as something other than full-fledged members of society.

We have already seen some of the problems encountered by right forfeiture approaches in the criminal justice context. It seems implausible to regard those who have been convicted of crimes as having forfeited all of their basic rights and few attracted to the logic of right forfeiture appear to support such an extreme view.[28] But that means that they must provide some account of which basic rights are forfeited by criminal conviction and for how long. It will be difficult to argue that offenders forfeit rights that are wholly unrelated to the rights violated, if indeed they violated any, by their criminal misconduct. Why, for instance, should those who steal significant amounts of property forfeit the right to vote or to have access to public housing, rather than the right to property? Also, even if it is the right to property that is forfeited by an individual's criminal misconduct, why should it be lost entirely, as opposed to being infringed upon by requirements, say, to pay substantial fines? Most standard legal sanctions do not logically compel us to regard those on whom they are imposed as having forfeited rights in their entirety, only as justifiably having their rights infringed or curtailed. Moreover, parsimony in sentencing requires us to explain and justify each further infringement or curtailment, to demonstrate why ones of less magnitude or duration are not sufficient to hold offenders accountable. Forfeiture approaches seem to take us too far too quickly in justifying incursions upon the rights of offenders.

Those who defend claims to the effect that offenders who have otherwise served the sentences for their crimes are no longer deserving of certain kinds of goods provided as matters of right to other citizens need to explain why these individuals are not at least presumptively entitled to equal status within the social order. Ex-offenders are not usually denied their rights to freedom of speech or the free exercise of religion, for instance, so why should they be denied access to basic social welfare goods? Granted, some will regard things like public housing and low-interest student loans as more in the way of privileges than basic rights. But even if they are so to be regarded, we should require some explanation why ex-offenders should not have the full privileges of citizenship restored to them once they have served the sentences for their crimes, especially if other privileges are typically accorded to them. And we might wonder how any plausible defense of denying them privileges accorded to other members of society could establish that such denials should be permanent. It is at this point, I suspect, that considerations of harm reduction or public safety will surface. It might be claimed that we should be wary of the risks posed by ex-offenders and so grudging in permitting them to have or enjoy the full rights or privileges of citizenship.

A critical empirical and analytical literature has emerged with regard to CLCs and their impact on public safety. I believe it is fair to say that this literature finds fault with many, if not most, CLCs. Some of them are criticized because they appear to increase the risks of further offending, especially by pushing ex-offenders to the margins of society such that they have few viable options to earn income except through crime.[29] Others are faulted because they are applied in ways that are insufficiently discriminating among offenders, some of whom do appear to be dangerous, and others of whom appear to pose no substantial risks to their fellow citizens.[30] CLCs have also been criticized for their duration. Even if it might seem a good idea to restrict the liberty or keep an official eye on ex-offenders for some period of time, at some point, CLCs ought to lapse. For instance, if an offender has not been arrested or charged with a crime for many years, it seems that all CLCs in effect against him or her ought to expire.[31]

The conclusions toward which much of the scholarly literature seem to point are that while some CLCs might be defensible risk-reduction measures, many of them are not. Those that are should be more narrowly crafted and applied to offenders on a case-by-case basis, rather than imposed in blanket fashion on all offenders, or on those who commit certain types of offenses. Also, CLCs should incorporate sunset provisions, such that, at some point, offenders regain the full complement of rights and privileges accorded to other persons in society. My focus in this chapter will not be on evaluating specific CLCs and the arguments for and against them. I am sympathetic with the skeptical conclusions about many CLCs urged by other scholars and agree that, at best, limited forms of them might be defensible in some cases. More on that subsequently.

One point of contention about CLCs concerns whether they should be counted as part of an offender's legal punishment.[32] Some argue that CLCs are mostly civil or regulative in character.[33] They are not condemnatory in the ways that legal punishment is standardly held to be; they are aimed at reducing risks rather than censuring ex-offenders, giving them what they deserve, restoring a fair distribution of societal benefits and burdens, or providing offenders a penance that will spur them to feel remorse, make amends to those they have wronged, and seek to reform their lives. Unfortunately, for those who pursue this line of argument, it should be noted that harm prevention is often held to be a standard aim of legal punishment. This fact would seem to pose a challenge to penal theorists who cast CLCs as non-punitive in character.

Others argue that CLCs, like formal state sanctions, are imposed by the state pursuant to criminal conviction and are at least implicitly condemnatory, since they deny ex-offenders the full exercise and enjoyment of their basic moral rights, which full exercise is accorded to non-offenders.[34] Yet if CLCs are forms of punishment, then sentencing values such as proportionality, parsimony, and the reduction of risk would seem pertinent in evaluating them. In particular, it would seem to follow that the sanctions meted out to offenders for their crimes would have to be adjusted in light of the CLCs that are also imposed on them. A commitment to proportionality in sentencing would, in the face of the indiscriminate heaping on of CLC burdens, seem to require some downward adjustment in the sentence kinds or lengths assigned to those convicted of crimes. However, given the diverse kinds of CLCs and the widely varying ways in which they affect ex-offenders, incorporating their impact into the determination of proportionate sentences would be challenging, to say the least. Some ex-offenders might find the burdens CLCs impose to constitute substantial interferences with their lives; others might barely notice them. Then there is the indefinite duration of many CLCs and how that should be countenanced in efforts to keep the overall bite of penal impositions proportional with the seriousness of crimes.

In previous work, I have sided with those who believe that we should regard and treat CLCs as penal measures.[35] I believe that this especially makes sense in jurisdictions in which they are piled on ex-offenders indiscriminately and without regard to their impact on ex-offenders' lives. As with LFOs, I suspect that most offenders will regard CLCs as part of their punishment, and reasonably so. However, it might be possible to conceive of regimes in which some CLCs would be utilized in defensible ways, ones that arguably keep them distinct from legal punishment. Zachary Hoskins' work on CLCs has done the most to make a case for retaining limited CLCs as harm reduction or public safety measures. The conditions that Hoskins articulates for defensible CLCs are as follows: First, he argues that such measures must be aimed at protecting a "compelling interest."[36] He admits there will be debate about what is or is not such an interest. However, protecting children from predatory sex offenders is one, he thinks, we might all agree is compelling and might be served by a ban on persons convicted of such crimes from employment in schools. Other employment restrictions of various kinds, especially ones imposed on individuals who have, in the past, violated fiduciary relationships or engaged in theft or financial fraud in the course of their work, might likewise be harm reduction measures aimed at protecting compelling interests.

Second, defensible CLCs must be "effective" at securing or protecting the relevant compelling interests.[37] Sex offender residency restrictions, for instance, seem aimed at serving a compelling interest. Yet the empirical study of such restrictions has not shown that they are actually all that effective at reducing sex offender recidivism.[38] Likewise, employment bans and restrictions on access to public housing, while seeming to serve the public interest in safety in some cases, might actually turn out to be somewhat self-defeating if they leave ex-offenders so desperate that they resort to further offending in order to meet their needs for food, clothing, and shelter. As Hoskins notes, "empirical research indicates that the inabilities to secure housing and employment correlate with recidivism."[39]

Third, Hoskins argues that even if some CLCs are effective at serving compelling interests, we ought to consider their broader negative impact on offenders, their families, and communities.[40] The logic of public safety is forward-looking and consequentialist. Yes, we might derive some public benefit from the various restrictions or denials of opportunities imposed on ex-offenders, but that benefit must be weighed against any negative consequences of such measures. For instance, if employment or residency restrictions make it difficult for ex-offenders to earn income or reside with their spouses and children, this will create hardships not only for the ex-offenders but for those who depend on them emotionally and financially.

Fourth, and significantly, we should look for ways to tailor CLCs as narrowly as possible and to have them ease off or lapse entirely once they no longer are needed to protect the public.[41] Hoskins captures this condition in terms of what he calls the "least burdensome alternative," meaning that we should always be on the lookout for ways to craft CLCs so that they are less, rather than more, burdensome to offenders and imposed on ex-offenders only for as long as needed. Not all ex-offenders are at risk of recidivism, although some are. And not all of the worrisome offenders are at risk of indefinite recidivism. Most offenders age out at some point and thus pose significantly reduced risks to the public.[42] Thus, permanent CLCs imposed on all felons, or all felons or certain kinds, will not usually be defensible.

We might agree with Hoskins that there will be some offenders about whom the public is reasonably concerned, such that they appear to warrant continued scrutiny and restriction. This will be most true, perhaps, in cases of predatory or violent recidivists, individuals whose criminal predilections seem to be persistent. We might also agree that if the state undertakes genuine efforts to keep the restrictions and impositions modest and narrowly defined and is prepared to let them lapse at some point when individuals show themselves to have moved on from their earlier lives centered on serious crime, it might be plausible to claim that such impositions and restrictions are not "punishment" proper. Instead, they are entirely forward-looking measures aimed at protecting the public. Of course, those on whom such measures are imposed might regard the continuance of state monitoring and control as punishment for their past crimes. But I am willing to concede that Hoskins is on his way to making a credible case for viewing such restrictions and impositions differently.[43]

I say "on his way," because I believe that there are further limiting or qualifying conditions that we would have to insist upon to more convincingly make the case that we are not simply heaping more censure and hard treatment on offenders. To motivate this contention, consider Hoskins' response to an argument that I put forward several years ago.[44] I argued that the imposition of PS CLCs on convicted offenders, and especially ones that take hold after offenders have otherwise served the formal sentences for their crimes, appears to treat them as if their status in society is diminished. We do not usually impose such targeted PS restrictions on ordinary citizens who have not been convicted of crimes. Granted, we impose some restrictions on all citizens as matters, arguably, of public safety. For instance, we adopt and enforce speed limits on motor vehicles that all citizens are expected to observe. PS CLCs are not like speed limits, however, since the former are not imposed on everyone, but only on individuals convicted of certain kinds of criminal offenses. Yet, if those individuals have otherwise served their formal sentences—and thus on Hoskins' account, have "paid their debts to society"—then it would appear that we are treating them as less than equal citizens if we further restrict their liberties or deny them privileges or opportunities.[45] As I put it, their legal rights are "more fragile and thus susceptible to infringement by the government."[46] Since Hoskins had, in an earlier published paper, defended such PS measures, I maintained that his account did not seem, in this way, to treat ex-offenders as equal members of society.[47]

In his book, Hoskins's strategy is to suggest that we could justifiably impose targeted PS restrictions on individuals who have not been convicted of crimes.[48] He gives us the example of Tom, an individual who lives in a jurisdiction in which dog fighting has not yet been legally prohibited. Tom not only regularly engages in dog fighting, he posts videos of himself doing so, along with videos in which he boasts that he will continue to engage in dog fighting even if the jurisdiction in which he lives prohibits it. Suppose that the jurisdiction in which Tom lives finally gets around to prohibiting dog fighting. Hoskins suggests that, at that point, the jurisdiction might subject Tom to risk assessment and to incapacitative measures designed to limit his ability to engage in the now-prohibited conduct. Thus, in principle at least, Tom, who has not been convicted of any crime, might be singled out for PS restrictions. In this way, the jurisdiction would treat some nonoffenders no differently than ex-offenders on whom it imposed PS restrictions. Hoskins does not make clear what kinds of PS measures might be adopted in relation to Tom or how they would be made to work. But set that point to one side, for Hoskins agrees that PS CLCs have to be effective means to whatever PS (or dog safety) end they are designed to serve.

One thing that Hoskins does not make clear is whether there would have to be some kind of hearing at which the government would bear the burden of proof for making the case that such public safety measures are appropriate and justified.[49] After all, and as he concedes, there should be a presumption against the imposition of such measures, especially when they target specific individuals. At such a hearing, state officials would be obligated to not only put forth convincing evidence of Tom's likely future engagement in dog fighting, they should have to demonstrate that the measures they propose satisfy the various requirements defended by Hoskins. These would include showing that less restrictive measures were not available and that state officials had tailored whatever measures they proposed to Tom's character and circumstances. Also, there is the question of the "standard of proof" that the state would have to satisfy in establishing Tom's predilection to engage in dog fighting and the likely effectiveness of whatever PS measures it proposes. Since such a hearing would not be the equivalent of a criminal trial, perhaps the state should not be required to establish the likelihood of Tom's engaging in dog fighting "beyond a reasonable doubt." Still, we might believe that deference to individual liberty ought to require the state to provide something like "clear and convincing evidence" of Tom's likely future misconduct, as well as of the effectiveness of the PS measures it proposes.[50] I am not sure how often such a standard could be met, especially given the way in which what people have said in the past about what they will do if certain kinds of conduct are, in the future, prohibited might have to be discounted once the conduct in question is actually prohibited and people face criminal prosecution if they are caught engaging in it. But let us suppose that, in some cases, the state could indeed make the case that a person is poised to do harm. Harm here might be construed narrowly, as involving the violation of legally protected rights in some substantial way, or more broadly, as also encompassing actions that would significantly damage or undermine public health, or in Hoskins's dog fighting example, violate widely accepted standards concerning the humane treatment of nonhuman animals.

By way of illustration, consider the adoption and implementation of so-called "red flag" laws in the United States.[51] Such provisions enable the authorities to confiscate firearms temporarily from individuals who they have reason to believe might use them to commit serious crimes against others. The authorities may confiscate the firearms *ex parte*—that is, before hearings at which the defensibility of doing so must be justified by the authorities to a judge—or they might confiscate them after such hearings. But hearings there must be and the state bears the burden of proof in showing that it has or will act reasonably in confiscating the firearms. State laws vary with regard to the standard of proof that must be met. None require proof "beyond a reasonable" doubt that the targeted individuals will commit illegal acts with their guns should they not be confiscated (or that confiscation will, with certainty, prevent those acts). This makes sense since the hearings are not criminal trials at which individuals might be convicted of crimes. Still, many states require state officials to present "clear and convincing" evidence of imminent harm had not the confiscations occurred or if they are not permitted. Importantly, the confiscations are temporary; they lapse unless someone with the authority to urge their extension comes forward and demonstrates (again, at a hearing) that continuing to withhold firearms from the targeted individuals is justified.[52]

Importantly, red flag hearings permit those whose weapons have been or are about to be confiscated by the authorities to speak on their own behalf, typically with the aid of attorneys who have some better understanding of the laws in question, as well as the standards and expectations of the hearings before judges at which their fates will be decided. Some scholars suggest, reasonably it seems to me, that if the targeted individuals cannot afford to hire attorneys, they should be provided, at state expense, to ensure that those targeted are not overwhelmed by the circumstances and formalities of such hearings.[53] Also, attorneys will likely have a better sense of what those targeted must do to convince the hearing judge that they are responsible individuals whose firearms should not be confiscated. Notice that in instances in which the state succeeds in convincing a hearing judge that its officials acted reasonably in confiscating a citizen's firearms, or will do so in confiscating them after the hearing, the targeted individuals might believe that they have been "punished." They might also feel that state interference with their firearm possession stigmatizes them, communicating to the public that they are irresponsible in the ways that those convicted of crimes are thought to be.[54] But keep in mind that the confiscations are temporary and that their firearms are presumptively to be returned to them once a relatively brief "cooling off" period has elapsed. Thus, it might be argued that, at most, what the confiscation "says" is that the authorities have legitimate concerns about gun-owners' responsibility in light of things they have recently said or done, although there is an expectation that their capacities for responsible conduct will soon return to their former levels. Also, the affected individuals will not have been convicted of any crimes and so the durations of the confiscations are determined not by any legal wrongs they have committed but by what the judge (or state law) regards as an appropriate cooling off period. These features of red flag laws serve to distinguish them from criminal convictions and the expressive sentences attendant to them.[55] It therefore seems plausible to construe the purpose of such confiscations as the purely forward-looking one of temporary and narrowly-tailored harm prevention.

Turning, then, to PS CLCs and their implementation, suppose that we believe that those who have fully served their sentences for previous criminal convictions are presumptively to have their full rights of citizenship restored. As such, if the state is intent on imposing PS CLCs on some of them, and such impositions are to be procedurally and symbolically distinguished from the continuation of legal punishment, some sort of hearing at which the state bears the burden of proof for acting to further restrict the liberty (or other rights) of the individuals in question should be required. Not only should the state have to furnish convincing evidence that the individuals pose continued threats to others (or more broadly, defiance of vital legal norms), it should have to demonstrate that such risks are substantial and that the restrictions imposed on the relevant individuals will be effective at preventing the feared outcomes. Further, state officials should have to show that the costs to the individuals whose liberties are to be restricted (as well as those who will be indirectly affected by such burdens) will not be greater than the harms to be averted. And these state claims would have to survive challenges by the individuals on whom the restrictions or requirements are to be imposed and their attorneys (which again, we might reasonably believe should be supplied to them if they cannot afford their own). These will (and should be) burdensome tasks for state officials. For instance, even if the state can prove that some individuals who have served their criminal sentences are at substantial risk of further individually or socially harmful acts, devising PS CLCs that will effectively promote public safety at not too great a cost to the individuals involved (or their loved ones) will be difficult.

Return to Hoskins's dog fighting example. It might be suggested that Tom can be prevented from his cruelty to animals by forbidding him from owning dogs. But such a limitation on his liberty might prove only modestly or minimally successful, since he could simply borrow other peoples' dogs who are willing to let them be used for Tom's nefarious purposes. Alternatively, Tom could have others keep dogs that he actually owns on their property to disguise his ownership. I suppose that the state could forbid him from being around dogs at all, but such an injunction would present significant enforcement challenges. Would he be deemed in violation of it if he took a walk (with his family) in a public park where others were walking and playing with their dogs, or would it forbid him from visiting a friend's house who owned dogs? Presumably not, but how would his problematic proximity to dogs be determined and formulated in the relevant injunction, especially in ways that would not interfere with his doing rather mundane things with his family and friends? And how would it be determined when Tom's restrictions on access to dogs would be allowed to lapse? This is a problem I will come back to in the next section.

Notice that firearm confiscations under red flag laws seem less problematic in some of the preceding ways since they are narrowly focused in the liberty deprivations that they impose and presuppose that after some brief (typically no more than 30 days) cooling off period, firearm ownership is to be restored. Red flag firearm confiscations are made in special, short-term circumstances where the targeted individuals are thought to be at high risk of irresponsible action. Also, those whose firearms are temporarily confiscated remain otherwise free to go about their lives as they see fit.[56] With more standard PS CLCs, it seems less clear what the relevant time-period of risk is and precisely how we are to go about containing or limiting that risk. We might very much want to keep individuals who have been convicted of aggressive sex crimes against children from being around children once they have served their sentences. But how to do this in ways that are effective, not overbroad, temporary, and not too hard on them or others with whom they associate is difficult to envision.

I would not deny that some PS CLCs might be crafted to both satisfy Hoskins' conditions and survive scrutiny at the hearings which I believe are crucial to distinguishing them from legal punishment proper. For instance, supposed that an individual has, on numerous occasions in the past, been convicted of violating legal standards regulating a profession for which there are licensure requirements. In doing so, this individual has harmed others by defrauding them or damaging their health. Suppose she has fully served her sentence for her most recent offense and yet state officials are concerned that she will continue to operate outside the law if she is permitted to return to her profession. They therefore seek, in the interest of public safety, to suspend her license to practice her profession for some period of time. Doing so would deprive her of something she typically needs to do further harm of the relevant kind, much like confiscating a firearm from an individual makes it more difficult for him or her (in what seems an emotionally fraught time) to harm others. State officials might likewise seek to ban those who work in non-licensed occupations from working in them if they have on numerous previous occasions been convicted of crimes related to their work. Granted, one thing licensure does is make the "relevant field" a bit more precisely specifiable. But I would not deny that the state might act appropriately in seeking to limit the liberty of certain individuals to do the kinds of work for which they are trained or experienced for PS purposes. Although the individuals on whom such restrictions are imposed might believe that all of this amounts to further stigmatization and punishment of them, I believe that a case can be made that such PS CLCs are somewhat distinct from it. First, they are not unilaterally or automatically imposed on all offenders or all offenders of certain kinds. Rather, they are imposed only after specialized hearings, entirely for forward-looking PS purposes. Second, we could insist that all such measures must lapse at some point unless state officials successfully petition the courts and demonstrate their continued viability as cost-effective PS measures.[57] Such restrictions would thus not be tailored to the severity of past wrongs, as expressive legal punishment is supposed to be, but to the prevention of future harms. Third, the individuals subject to such restrictions would not face all manner of further post-punishment restrictions and impositions, in the ways that many current ex-offenders do in the United States. Thus, they arguably are not "ex-prisoned."

Beyond the preceding, if PS CLCs are to be distinguished from penal sanctions, then the state might be obligated to do more to clearly mark them out as such. Suppose, for instance, that given an individual's past offenses involving theft or fraud while employed by financial institutions, the state was to justifiably prohibit her from employment by such institutions for some period of time. The individual in question might find herself with few viable employment options, especially if she is specially trained to work for financial institutions and has little experience or skill in performing other jobs. One thing the state might do would be to provide her with financial support while she acquires other employment skills or while she struggles to find other suitable employment. The state might even help her move to some part of the country where whatever skills she has or has subsequently acquired are more in demand. Such ameliorative actions by the state would help to symbolically distinguish the PS impositions from legal punishment.[58] Again, if PS CLCs are not "intended to be burdensome," then we should not care if they are not perceived as such by the individuals on whom they are imposed. Not only would ameliorative measures mark them out as something distinct from legal punishment, they would help with the some of the indirect burdens inflicted on ex-offenders' spouses and families by PS CLCs.

Despite all that we might do to individually tailor PS CLCs and distinguish them from legal punishment by procedures and standards that require courts to be forward-looking and careful in their imposition, it might be objected that such restrictions communicate censure of the individuals on whom they are imposed. I would not deny this but I would argue that what is expressed by their imposition is somewhat different from what is expressed by legal punishment proper. Granted, PS CLCs "say" that the individuals on whom they are imposed are suspect in certain ways as responsible citizens. Yet surely their criminal histories provide some warrant for such a stance, especially if the individuals are recidivists with violent or predatory tendencies. Also, PS CLCs do not censure them for past wrongs and are not supposed to be reflective of (or proportional to) such wrongs in the ways that criminal sentences are. Further, the restrictions will lapse once the individuals in question demonstrate that they are responsible, or at least are not criminally irresponsible in the relevant ways. Finally, those most likely to be subject to such restrictions will no longer be imprisoned for their crimes and thus can, in most other respects, go on about living their lives.

Further Issues

Although I have urged some significant modifications to the scheme for imposing PS CLCs that Hoskins proposes, I have granted that some such liberty restrictions on individuals who have otherwise fully served their sentences for their most recent crimes might be justified. In this section, I raise further questions about the state's use of the kinds of infringements of basic rights of which PS CLCs consist, ones that I conclude cast considerable doubt on their viability in practice, and thus their defensibility.

First, consider what we might term the "risk threshold" problem. The premise of PS CLCs would seem to be that some of the individuals who have been convicted of crimes, or perhaps of certain kinds of crimes, and who have fully served the sentences for those crimes, are nonetheless at heightened risk of committing further crimes. The risks such individuals pose might be deemed to be general or more specific to the kinds of offenses of which they have been convicted. Yet, as we know, not all of the individuals who have been convicted of crimes at some point will go onto commit further ones. Only some of them will, although perhaps more than a few of them will do so. This raises the question to what level must the perceived risk of further offending rise for the state to justify the imposition of PS CLCS in any given case. For instance, even if Smith is perceived to be at some modest level of elevated risk to commit further crimes, thereby constituting a threat to public safety, it seems unlikely that this alone constitutes sufficient grounds for the justified imposition of PS CLCS. It is well-known, for instance, that many individuals in society commit crimes of various kinds and are not detected, arrested, or convicted of having done so.[59] All or perhaps many of us are at *some* risk to offend and perhaps repeatedly. Also, more of us might offend if we found ourselves in the right kinds of circumstances. We may have simply been lucky to avoid the circumstances of desperation, temptation or provocation in which others, who offended and were convicted of doing so, found themselves. Being at "some risk" or "some increased risk" to commit future crimes are, it seems, too low of thresholds for the justified imposition of PS CLCs, unless, perhaps, we are thinking about crimes that would inflict grave harms on others. It does seem plausible to believe that we should adjust the relevant risk threshold to the gravity of the threats to public safety involved. If the harms that someone might cause would be quite profound—say the deaths or severe injuries of one or more people—then even a modestly elevated risk that he or she might act in ways to cause them might suffice to justify the imposition of PS CLCs.

But for less serious harms, it would seem that the state ought to have to demonstrate that ex-offenders are at some substantial risk to produce them before PS measures limiting the basic rights of ex-offenders could be justifiably imposed. What seems clear here is that no simple formula for "risk of harm X gravity of harm" will work or is apt to be available. I am not suggesting that this "risk threshold" problem cannot be practically resolved, only that doing so is something that will be challenging. Importantly, it is a challenge that has likely been wholly unmet by practices that impose PS CLCs on all offenders or on those who commit certain kinds of offenses. Such indiscriminate practices of imposing PS CLCS on large groups of offenders effectively sweep the "risk threshold" problem under the rug.

This brings me to a second point. The PS defense of CLCs is narrow in its focus and logic. It would have us impose restrictions on the basic rights of individuals for entirely forward-looking kinds of reasons, ones focused on the future harms that such restrictions would enable us to avert. Yet it is clear that many CLCs have been defended on grounds that have little to do with public safety (e.g., the loss of voting rights for felons). Again, it might be thought that individuals convicted of crimes, or perhaps of certain kinds of crimes, forfeit basic rights or are undeserving of the freedoms or social welfare benefits to which law-abiding citizens are entitled. Forfeiture, undeservingness, and public safety rationales are, too often, all mushed together in the public defenses of CLCs proffered by politicians or other government officials. However, if we are focused only on public safety, as Hoskins is in his careful and limited defense of CLCs, then we must be conscientious about keeping forfeiture and desert arguments in abeyance. If we are conscientious about doing so, then problems like that of the "risk threshold" cannot be easily disposed of with claims that implicitly rely on logic that is distinct from public safety. It will seem less imperative to produce and defend a formula for what I have termed the "risk threshold" if we can simply assume that offenders have forfeited all or some of their rights or are undeserving of goods to which others in society have access. Forfeiture or undeservingness arguments might be defensible, but they are distinct from PS arguments.

Third, Hoskins sensibly argues that we should want PS CLCs to be "effective," and, more than this, given the consequentialist logic on which his defense is premised, "cost-effective." Again, we might doubt that many of the measures restricting the rights of offenders routinely deployed in the United States and elsewhere satisfy either of these tests. Also, the first test requires us to address the thorny question of "how effective" a measure must be before its imposition is justified. As previously noted, PS CLCs might seem most appropriately imposed upon recidivists, individuals who have shown, through their repeat criminal convictions, that they are at continuing risk of violating the law and, depending on the kinds of offenses to which they are prone, inflicting harms on others. Unfortunately, recidivists appear to be somewhat dubious targets of "effective" PS CLCs, simply because they seem determined to continue defying the law. We might plausibly worry that those committed to deviant lifestyles will simply find "work arounds" to any PS CLCs imposed on them. Nonetheless, suppose that something like "moderately effective" restrictions can be found and imposed and that this is a defensible interpretation of the goal of such restrictions. That still leaves us with the problem of determining and weighing the "costs" of such restrictions and not just for the individuals upon whom they are imposed. Legislators in the United States have seemingly been indifferent to the negative consequences of many of the CLCs they have instituted. Social scientists who study such CLCs have more reliably noted such consequences and the dubious PS benefits of many of them. Hoskins' approach seems best interpreted as supporting more individually tailored PS CLCs than ones adopted by legislators and applied to categories of offenders. Wisely so, perhaps, but that does raise questions about who determines not only their likely effectiveness but also their negative consequences and who weighs the one against the other in efforts to devise defensible restrictions. Suppose that we would have the judges who conduct the required hearings do so. Would they be expected to consult the best available evidence about costs and effectiveness (assuming it exists), perhaps aided by attorneys for those under consideration for the imposition of PS CLCs? Perhaps, but these will be challenging tasks for the hearing judges. Notice that in the red flag cases, things are different. The volatile emotional states of the targets of firearms confiscations are what "trigger" them and those states are presumed to subside after a brief period of time upon which the firearms are presumptively returned. All the hearing judges have to determine is whether there is (or was, in the case of *ex parte* confiscations) substantial evidence of a risk to public safety caused by the target's emotional state. The confiscations might annoy those who endure them but are apt to have few other significant long-term costs to them or others close to or dependent upon them.[60] Things are different when we contemplate restricting what jobs ex-offenders can have or whether they can have drivers' licenses. These kinds of restrictions will have more significant consequences for their and other peoples' lives, thus complicating the work of hearing judges who must determine their defensibility and duration.

Fourth, talk about the "effectiveness" of PS CLCs might lead us to ask the question "effective compared to what?" It is apparent that PS CLCs are focused narrowly on incapacitating individuals in certain limited respects in ways that it is hoped will enhance public safety. Yet this narrow focus might be challenged. Those who favor crime reduction approaches to the justification of legal punishment have long understood that if reducing future crime is our primary if not exclusive aim, standard forms of censure and hard treatment visited upon those convicted of crimes might not be the most effective means to achieving it. If certain kinds of crimes are born of economic desperation or despair, for instance, then we might better reduce them by bolstering state social welfare programs that provide dependable social minimums of housing, income, and decent wages. Or if offending is precipitated by mental illness or addiction, then social programs designed to address these might more effectively reduce offending than penal measures designed more narrowly to simply deter or incapacitate. Scholars have long noted the sometimes weak and often fraught relationship between legal punishment and the reduction of crime through deterrence, incapacitation, and rehabilitation.[61] PS CLCs are a bit too much like penal hard treatment in their approach, whereas it might be claimed that broader social measures of various kinds would serve us better when it comes to the promotion of public safety.

In response, it might be argued that some mix of broader social measures to enhance public safety and more individualized ones, imposed on individuals with troublesome criminal histories of engaging in harmful conduct, is apt to be the most defensible approach overall. I would not deny this, of course, if effective and not-to-collaterally damaging (to offenders and others) individualized measures can be devised and implemented responsibly. My concern is with the too narrow focus of many PS CLCs, or alleged PS CLCs, especially in the context of little else being done, at least in the United States, to promote public safety and reduce crime through progressive social welfare measures. It is mostly poor or socially marginalized individuals who have been caught up in the criminal justice system and upon whom the brunt of PS CLCs falls. It is problematic for state officials to defend such narrow measures in the more or less complete absence of concern with the implementation of broader social measures that many of us suspect would do more to actually reduce offending. In short, there has been too much focus on continued control of mostly poor and marginalized offenders and not enough on addressing the social conditions that many believe precipitate criminal misconduct. Notice also that the adoption and implementation of broader measures to reduce social deprivation would limit the impact on families and communities of PS CLCs. If individuals were disqualified from employment in their fields of education and training due to past criminal misconduct, their family members would be less apt to suffer while those on whom PS CLCs were imposed searched for new forms of employment if a stable and robust social welfare floor was in place.

Fifth, Hoskins sensibly argues that if public safety is the primary focus of certain CLCs, when the threat to it posed by an individual declines sufficiently (although we must address the difficult question of what "sufficiency" consists of here), PS CLCs should ease off or lapse. In particular, as individuals mature, successfully undergo drug or alcohol dependency treatment, or find decently-paying legal work, they often abandon their previous public safety-endangering ways. Intelligently crafted PS CLCs should be responsive to these changes. However, there are complications involved in tailoring PS CLCs to individuals and the "threat levels" they pose. It seems unlikely, for instance, that we should take the absence of recent convictions or arrests as reliable indicators of the relevant changes in the action-dispositions of individuals formerly deemed to be risks to public safety. The absence of further convictions might show only that state officials could not amass sufficient evidence of further offending, although they might strongly and reasonably suspect it has occurred. The absence of arrests is likewise an unreliable indicator of a reduced threat to public safety, since lots of criminal misconduct goes undetected by the authorities. Also, those with the most to lose from such detection, recidivists foremost among them, might take special pains to avoid detection.

Sixth, it should be noted that there is a "catch-22" element to PS CLCs in some cases, especially when they involve restrictions on certain kinds of activities by individuals about whom there is sufficient reason to doubt that they will conduct themselves responsibly. If we ban from driving those who have been caught repeatedly driving while intoxicated, or if we require them to install locking devices on their vehicles that prevent them from starting their vehicles if they register a prohibited blood alcohol level, the problem this creates is that until we allow them to start driving again, or to remove the locking devices, we will not really know whether they will drive responsibly.[62] A similar problem attends occupational bans or restrictions. Whether individuals formerly deemed not reliably responsible while engaged in those occupations can be permitted to return to them seems to depend on whether they will behave responsibly in them when given a chance. Yet we will not know this until we give them that chance. Granted, there might be indirect ways by which state officials could acquire evidence of an individual's newfound sobriety or commitment to occupational ethics. Individuals should be able to document their having sought treatment for alcohol dependency and might be able to show that they have maintained sobriety for substantial periods of time. Or individuals who misused their previous positions of power or authority might be able to show that they have since behaved admirably when exercising new forms of power or authority, such that permitting them to return to their previous occupations or roles should not constitute too great a risk to public safety. Still, those with sufficiently irresponsible pasts might always seem to be at some elevated risk of future misconduct, compared to others in the population. This bring us back to the "risk threshold" issue with which I began this section. For instance, should a slightly elevated element of risk be deemed sufficient, if demonstrated by the relevant authorities, to refuse to lift or let lapse PS CLCs? Or should the state have to show more—perhaps a "moderately" elevated level of risk, whatever that means?

More troubling than the preceding are the ways in which individuals with previous convictions might be targeted by the police for more surveillance and scrutiny, thus making them more subject to arrests and convictions that will then serve as grounds for official resistance to permitting their PS CLCs to lapse or be lifted. For one thing, there is the phenomenon of "usual suspects" policing.[63] When crimes occur and the police lack evidence about who committed them, it is natural for them to focus at least some of their attention on individuals known to have criminal records, and especially ones whose convictions match the kinds of crimes currently under investigation. This heightened scrutiny of known offenders makes sense, in a way, but it can lead to mistaken arrests and even mistaken convictions in some cases. When it does, those ex-offenders burdened with PS CLCs will be less able to escape them, one would presume.

Further, as we have already seen, there is the worrisome tendency of the police (and prosecutors and judges) to focus more of their attention on some people in society than others. In the war on drugs, for instance, the police have tended to disproportionately surveil, conduct buy and busts, and arrest people in poor, minority neighborhoods as compared with people in more affluent, non-minority neighborhoods. Whether these tactics reflect racial or class bias, or are simply strategic decisions based on the relative ease of policing some neighborhoods as opposed to others, has been much-examined and discussed.[64] Whatever its causes, the product of these official practices is pretty clearly a skewed sample of arrested and convicted drug users and dealers given what we know or suspect about drug use and sales.[65] Similar forms of racial, ethnic, or class skewing of arrests and convictions will likely exist with regard to other kinds of criminal offenses. The implications of all of this for determinations of whether PS CLCs imposed on offenders who have otherwise served their sentences should be lifted or allowed to lapse are clear: If arrest or conviction records are used by state officials at hearings to determine whether civil restrictions should, after some period of time, expire, some of the individuals upon whom such measures have been imposed will fare poorly for reasons that should deeply trouble us. Yet it is hard to see how we could prohibit state officials from invoking arrest or conviction records at such hearings, despite their fraught natures.

In fairness to Hoskins, he could readily agree with everything I have said here and, indeed, I suspect he might do so. My purpose in this discussion has been to more fully explicate what we, as a society, must do to distinguish purely forward-looking PS measures from legal punishment, or perhaps the continuation of legal punishment. It has also been to show just how complicated and messy imposing such PS CLCs is apt to be, and thus to raise doubts about whether the state can be trusted to do so in ways that are responsible and effective. Although I believe it is possible, theoretically, to defend the use of narrowly-focused, time-limited, and forward-looking PS CLCs, it seems safe to say that we are nowhere near observing the conditions Hoskins lays out for PS CLCs, let alone in meeting the further challenges that my analysis reveals. We are a long way from having the kinds of careful, individually tailored, adversary hearings for PS CLCs that are needed, ones governed by appropriately developed and nuanced standards of risk, effectiveness, and net social cost. Until we make serious efforts to impose defensible PS CLCs, my sense is that most of them remain little more than the heaping on of additional punishment, whatever state officials might say about them in efforts to distinguish them. As such, their impact on offenders should be incorporated into proportionality analyses of the overall severity of penal sanctions for crimes, such that the formal sentences the courts hand out for convictions should be reduced in anticipation of the further losses and impositions that blunt-force CLCs impose.

Concluding Remarks

The general conclusion that we should draw from my analysis in this chapter is that offenders who have been appropriately sentenced for their crimes and completed their sentences should be regarded and treated as full-fledged members of the social order. This means that they should be accorded the rights and privileges such status entails. There are some cases in which the imposition of limited LFOs that are treated as civil debts and structured to minimize the burdens such debts create might be defensible. Likewise, there might be some cases in which narrowly tailored CLCs aimed at public safety can be justified, although demonstrating that will require us to address numerous difficult challenges. State officials and members of the public who support the blanket and indiscriminate imposition of LFOs and CLCs on all offenders or on certain classes of them have largely failed to address these challenges in serious ways. As a result, the restrictions or impositions of which they consist amount to forms of side-punishment or post-punishment, barely, if at all, distinguishable from the burdens formally imposed on individuals by the courts in response to their crimes. Too often, LFOs and CLCs heap more censorious hard treatment on the mostly disadvantaged individuals who are disproportionately targeted by state officials for their criminal misconduct.

Notes

1 See James B. Jacobs, *The Eternal Criminal Record* (Cambridge, MA: Harvard University Press, 2015) and Richard L. Lippke, "Legal Punishment and the Public Identification of Offenders," *Res Publica* 24 (2018): 199–216.

2 Katherine Beckett and Alexes Harris, "On Cash and Conviction: Monetary Sanctions as Misguided Policy," *Criminology & Public Policy* 10 (2011): 509–37; Mary Fainsod Katzenstein and Mitali Nagrecha, "A New Punishment Regime," *Criminology & Public Policy* 10 (2011): 555–68; Alexes Harris, *A Pound of Flesh: Monetary Sanctions as Punishment for the Poor* (New York: Russell Sage, 2016); Neil L. Sobol, "Charging the Poor: Criminal Justice Debt and Modern-Day Debtors' Prisons," *University of Maryland Law Review* 75 (2016): 486–540; and Alexes Harris, et al., *Monetary Sanctions in the Criminal Justice System*, Arnold Foundation (2017), at www.monetarysanctions.org/wp-content/uploads/2017/04/Monetary-Sanctions-Legal-Review-Final.pdf (accessed July 3, 2020).

3 Sobol, "Charging the Poor," 504.

4 Beckett and Harris, "On Cash and Conviction," 525; Sobol, "Charging the Poor," 508–16.

5 Beckett and Harris, "On Cash and Conviction," 528, and Sobol, "Charging the Poor," 522.

6 Sobol, "Charging the Poor," 523.

7 See Zachary Hoskins, *Beyond Punishment: A Normative Account of the Collateral Legal Consequences of Conviction* (New York: Oxford University Press, 2019); Jeremy Travis, "Invisible Punishment: An Instrument of Social Exclusion," in Marc Mauer and Meda Chesney-Lind (eds.), *Invisible Punishment: The Collateral Consequences of Mass Imprisonment* (New York: The New Press, 2002): 15–36; and Jeffrey M. Brown, "Collateral Legal Consequences of Criminal Convictions in a Society of Equals," *Criminal Law and Philosophy* 15 (2021): 181–205;

8 The disenfranchisement of felons, for example, has been defended on grounds that have more to do with the ways in which the commission of serious crimes are thought to disqualify individuals from eligibility to vote. See Richard L. Lippke, "The Disenfranchisement of Felons," *Law and Philosophy* 20 (2001): 553–80, at

560–61. For useful discussion of the origins of the notion that offenders should be denied access to public welfare benefits, see Travis, "Invisible Punishment," 23–24.

9 Gabriel J. Chin, "The New Civil Death: Rethinking Punishment in the Era of Mass Conviction," *University of Pennsylvania Law Review* 160 (2012): 1789–833, at 1791.

10 On the view of the courts, see Chin, "New Civil Death," 1791. For arguments by scholars that CLCs are more "civil" or "regulatory," than penal in character, see Hoskins, *Beyond Punishment*, 32–67 and Andrew von Hirsch and Martin Wasik, "Civil Disqualifications Attending Conviction: A Suggested Conceptual Framework," *Cambridge Law Journal* 56 (1997): 599–626.

11 Sobol, "Charging the Poor," 526.

12 Beckett and Harris, "On Cash and Conviction," 517–18, and Sobol, "Charging the Poor," 516–21.

13 As Beckett and Harris note, in some jurisdictions, failure to pay LFOs can result in individuals not being permitted to obtain driver's licenses. See "On Cash and Conviction," 518.

14 Beckett and Harris, "On Cash and Conviction," 511.

15 Beckett and Harris, "On Cash and Conviction," 528.

16 See Bruce Western, *Punishment and Inequality in America* (New York: Russell Sage, 2006), Chapter 5.

17 Sobol, "Charging the Poor," 512–15.

18 Harris, *A Pound of Flesh*, see especially Chapter 3.

19 William J. Stuntz, "Race, Class, and Drugs," *Columbia Law Review* 98 (1998): 1795–842; Michael Tonry, *Malign Neglect: Race, Crime, and Punishment in America* (New York: Oxford University Press, 1995); Josh Bowers, "Punishing the Innocent," *University of Pennsylvania Law Review* 156 (2008): 1117–79, at 1124; and Angela J. Davis (ed.), *Policing the Black Man: Arrest, Prosecution, and Imprisonment* (New York: Vintage Books, 2017).

20 See Randall Kennedy, *Race, Crime, and the Law* (New York: Vintage, 1998); Alexandra Natapoff, "Underenforcement," *Fordham Law Review* 75 (2006): 1715–76; and William J. Stuntz, "Unequal Justice," *Harvard Law Review* 121 (2008): 1969–2040.

21 See *Americans with Criminal Records*, The Sentencing Project (2015), at www.sentencingproject.org/wp-content/uploads/2015/11/Americans-with-Criminal-Records-Poverty-and-Opportunity-Profile.pdf (accessed July 4, 2020).

22 See John Corden, "Persistent Petty Offenders: Problems and Patterns of Multiple Disadvantage," *The Howard Journal of Criminal Justice* 23 (1983): 68–90 and Neal Shover, *Great Pretenders: Pursuits and Careers of Persistent Thieves* (Boulder, CO: Westview, 1996).

23 In Germany, prisoners have a duty to work but the courts there have held that they must be properly remunerated for their work. See Liora Lazarus, *Contrasting Prisoners' Rights: A Comparative Examination of Germany and England* (Oxford: Oxford University Press, 2004): 109. See also Dirk van Zyl Smit and Franz Dünkel, *Prison Labour: Salvation or Slavery? International Perspectives* (Aldershot, UK: Ashgate, 1999).

24 Richard L. Lippke, *Rethinking Imprisonment* (Oxford: Oxford University Press, 2007): 158–69.

25 John Rawls, *A Theory of Justice* (Cambridge, MA: Harvard University Press, 1971); Ronald Dworkin, *Sovereign Virtue: Equality in Theory and Practice* (Cambridge, MA: Harvard University Press, 2000); Philippe von Parijs, *Real Freedom for All: What (If Anything) Can Justify Capitalism?* (Oxford: Oxford University Press, 1995); and Bruce Ackerman, *Social Justice in the Liberal State* (New Haven, CT: Yale University Press, 1980).

26 See, among others, Jeffrie G. Murphy, "Marxism and Retribution," *Philosophy and Public Affairs* 2 (1973): 217–43; Richard Delgado, "Rotten Social Background: Should the Criminal Law Recognize a Defense of Severe Environmental Deprivation?" *Law & Inequality* 3 (1985): 9–90; R. A. Duff, *Punishment, Communication, and Community* (Oxford: Oxford University Press, 2001): 183–84; Benjamin Ewing, "Recent Work on Punishment and Criminogenic Disadvantage," *Law and Philosophy* 37 (2018): 29–68; and Göran Duus-Otterström and Erin I. Kelly, "Injustice and the Right to Punish," *Philosophy Compass* 14 (2019), at https://doi.org/10.1111/phc3.12565 (accessed November 27, 2021).
27 Travis, "Invisible Punishment," 22–24.
28 See, for instance, Christopher W. Morris, "Punishment and Loss of Moral Standing," *Canadian Journal of Philosophy* 21 (1991): 53–79. Other defenders of right forfeiture accounts include A. John Simmons, *The Lockean Theory of Rights* (Princeton, NJ: Princeton University Press, 1992): 148–61; and Christopher Heath Wellman, *Rights Forfeiture and Punishment* (New York: Oxford University Press, 2017). For critique of the notion of right forfeiture in accounts of legal punishment, see Warren Quinn, "The Right to Threaten and the Right to Punish," *Philosophy and Public Affairs* 14 (1985): 327–73; Rex Martin, *A System of Rights* (Oxford: Clarendon Press, 1983): 280–84; and Richard L. Lippke, "Criminal Offenders and Right Forfeiture," *Journal of Social Philosophy* 32 (2001): 78–89.
29 von Hirsch and Ashworth, "Civil Disqualifications," 605.
30 Travis, "Invisible Punishment," 35; von Hirsch and Ashworth, "Civil Disqualifications," 607–8.
31 Hoskins, *Beyond Punishment*, 174. There is also, as we have seen, the "aging out" phenomenon, such that most offenders desist from offending in their later twenties or early thirties. If CLCs are premised on reducing the risk of reoffending, then more or less inevitable desistance from offending undercuts the risk reduction rationale at some point.
32 Hoskins, *Beyond Punishment*, Chapter 2; Chin, "New Civil Death," 1826; von Hirsch and Ashworth, "Civil Disqualifications," 615–20; and Richard L. Lippke, *Taming the Presumption of Innocence* (New York: Oxford University Press, 2016): 216–20.
33 Hoskins, Beyond Punishment and von Hirsch and Ashworth, "Civil Disqualifications."
34 Lippke, *Taming the Presumption* and Chin, "The New Civil Death."
35 Lippke, *Taming the Presumption*, 216–20.
36 Hoskins, *Beyond Punishment?* 167.
37 Hoskins, *Beyond Punishment?* 170.
38 For discussion, see J. J. Prescott and Jonah K. Rockoff, "Do Sex Offender Registration and Notification Laws Affect Criminal Behavior," *Journal of Law & Economics* 54 (2011): 161–206 and J. C. Sandler, N. J. Freeman, and K. M. Socia, "Does a Watched Pot Boil? A Time-Series Analysis of New York State's Sex Offender Registration and Notification Law," *Psychology, Public Policy, and Law* 14 (2008): 284–302.
39 Hoskins, *Beyond Punishment?* 170.
40 Hoskins, *Beyond Punishment?* 171–72.
41 Hoskins, *Beyond Punishment?* 173–74.
42 See, for instance, Jeffrey T. Ulmer and Darrell Steffensmeier, "The Age and Crime Relationship: Social Variation, Social Explanations," in Kevin M. Beaver, J. C. Barnes, and Brian B. Boutwell (eds.), *The Nurture Versus Biosocial Debate in Criminology: On the Origins of Criminal Behavior and Criminality* (Thousand Oaks, CA: Sage, 2015): 377–96.
43 In a subsequent chapter, Hoskins argues that prosecutors should be conceived as having an ethical obligation to ensure that individuals charged with crimes have

been made aware of the variety of CLCs that might attend guilty pleas on their part. I would grant that informing those about to plead guilty of what they face over and above their formal sentences is something we should do. However, the discharge of this obligation by prosecutors will not, I would argue, come close to justifying CLCs, let alone distinguishing them from legal punishment. I suspect that Hoskins might agree with me on those points. For Hoskins's argument, see *Beyond Punishment?*, Chapter 8.

44 Lippke, *Taming the Presumption*, 220–21. See also Brown, "Collateral Legal Consequences."

45 For Hoskins's characterization of legal punishment as involving a debt to society, see *Beyond Punishment?* 129–30.

46 Lippke, *Taming the Presumption*, 221.

47 Zachary Hoskins, "Ex-Offender Restrictions," *Journal of Applied Philosophy* 31 (2014): 33–48.

48 Hoskins, *Beyond Punishment?* 182–83.

49 In a subsequent chapter, Hoskins argues that prosecutors should be conceived as having an ethical obligation to ensure that individuals charged with crimes have been made aware of the variety of CLCs that might attend guilty pleas on their part. I would grant that informing those about to plead guilty of what they face over and above their formal sentences is something we should do. However, the discharge of this obligation by prosecutors will not, I would argue, come close to justifying CLCs, let alone distinguishing them from legal punishment. I suspect that Hoskins might agree with me on those points. For Hoskins' argument, see *Beyond Punishment?* Chapter 8.

50 For insightful discussion of the various standards of proof in the law, see Larry Laudan, *Truth, Error, and Criminal Law: An Essay in Legal Epistemology* (Cambridge: Cambridge University Press, 2006).

51 See Joseph Blocher and Jacob D. Charles, "Firearms, Extreme Risk, and Legal Design: 'Red Flag' Laws and Due Process," *Virginia Law Review* 106 (2020): 1285–344, and John R. Richardson, "Red Flag Laws and Procedural Due Process: Analyzing Proposed Utah Legislation," *Utah Law Review* 2021 (2021): 743–65.

52 The targets of such confiscations can also be prohibited temporarily from purchasing firearms.

53 Richardson, "Red Flag Laws," 756.

54 See Hadassa Noorda, "Regulation as Punishment," *Criminal Justice Ethics* 40 (2021): 108–23.

55 On the expressive function of legal punishment, see Joel Feinberg, "The Expressive Dimension of Punishment," *The Monist* 49 (1965): 397–423.

56 The targets of such confiscations thus cannot reasonably be deemed to be "exprisoned," that is, subject to such onerous restrictions outside the prison context that they might as well be imprisoned. On "ex-prisonment," see Hadassa Noorda, "Preventive Deprivations of Liberty: Asset Freezes and Travel Bans," *Criminal Law and Philosophy* 9 (2015): 521–35.

57 My claim that PS CLCs should not be imposed in the absence of a hearing structured in ways to ensure that such measures effectively serve defensible PS purposes might be compared with proposals to permit that state to continue to detain offenders who it deems dangerous but who have fully served their sentences for their most recent crimes. Antony Duff and Stephen Morse have, in somewhat different ways, endorsed what is termed the "preventive detention" of dangerous offenders in a limited number of cases. They both regard the state's doing so as problematic, at best, and if they would license the state to utilize preventive detention, they would only do so under narrowly specified conditions and employing certain procedures. See Stephen J. Morse, "Blame and Danger: An Essay on Preventive Detention," *Boston University Law Review* 76 (1996): 112–55, at 152, and

R. A. Duff, "Dangerousness and Citizenship," in Andrew Ashworth and Martin Wasik (eds.), *Fundamentals of Sentencing Theory: Essays in Honor of Andrew von Hirsch* (Oxford: Clarendon Press, 1998): 141–63.

58 Ferdinand D. Shoeman has argued that we could partially distinguish preventive detention of the dangerous from imprisonment proper by compensating those on whom we impose the former. See his "On Incapacitating the Dangerous," *American Philosophical Quarterly* 16 (1979): 27–35.

59 This seems especially likely if we acknowledge that most criminal activity involves misdemeanors and thus more minor kinds of criminal offending. Scholars have detailed how the majority of cases processed by the criminal justice system are misdemeanors. See Alexandra Natapoff, "Misdemeanors," *Southern California Law Review* 85 (2012): 1313–75 and Jenny Roberts, "Why Misdemeanors Matter: Defining Effective Advocacy in the Lower Criminal Courts," *University of California-Davis Law Review* 45 (2011): 277–372. On the low clearance rates for many criminal offenses, see Paul H. Robinson and John M. Darley, "The Utility of Desert," *Northwestern University Law Review* 91 (1997): 453–99, at 458–64. For anecdotal evidence of the general prevalence of criminal activity, see *We Are All Criminals*, at www.weareallcriminals.org/ (accessed January 26, 2021).

60 Notably, firearms confiscations are sometimes aimed at protecting family members of those targeted by the authorities.

61 Daniel S. Nagin, "Criminal Deterrence: Research at the Outset of the Twenty-First Century," *Crime and Justice: A Review of Research* 23 (1998): 1–42, and "Deterrence in the Twenty-First Century," *Crime and Justice: A Review of Research* 42 (2013): 199–263; Anthony N. Doob and Cheryl Marie Webster, "Sentence Severity and Crime: Accepting the Null Hypothesis," *Crime and Justice: A Review of Research* 30 (2003): 143–95. On the effectiveness of rehabilitation, see Gerald G. Gaes, Timothy J. Flanagan, Laurence L. Motiuk, and Lynn Stewart, "Adult Correctional Treatment," *Crime and Justice: A Review of Research* 26 (1999): 361–426; and Paul Gendreau, "Offender Rehabilitation: What We Know and What Needs to Be Done," *Criminal Justice and Behavior* 23 (1996): 144–61; and Mark W. Lipsey and Frances T. Cullen, "The Effectiveness of Correctional Rehabilitation: A Review of Systematic Reviews," *Annual Review of Law and Social Science* 3 (20007): 297–320.

62 On such locking devices, see Jeffrey H. Coben and Gregory L. Larkin, "Effectiveness of Ignition Interlock Devices in Reducing Drunk Driving Recidivism," *American Journal of Preventive Medicine* 16 (1999): 81–87.

63 See, for instance, Leslie McAra and Susan McVie, "The Usual Suspects? Street Life, Young People, and the Police," *Criminal Justice* 5 (2005): 5–36.

64 Stuntz, "Race, Class, and Drugs" and Tonry, *Malign Neglect*.

65 See Michael Tonry, *Punishing Race* (New York: Oxford University Press, 2011), Chapter 7.

8 Toward Realism about the Prospects of State Punishment

Previous chapters have elaborated and defended a mixed theory of legal punishment, exploring its implications for criminal procedure, sentencing, and the treatment of individuals who have served the sentences for their crimes. Along the way, I noted various shortcomings in the design and operations of contemporary criminal justice systems and sought to explain how my account of legal punishment might be operationalized to produce a more defensible system. Starting with an account of human dignity and the rights it yields, I advanced an approach according to which the state should be conceived as saddled with various burdens of justification as it proceeds to investigate, arrest, detain, charge, convict, and sentence those it deems to have violated defensible criminal prohibitions. In keeping with the priority of moral communication in my account, I insisted that state officials should be focused on getting at the truth about what those they suspect or accuse of crimes have or have not done. Those officials also must be much more concerned with administering equal justice before the law than they have often been in the past. Once individuals are convicted of crimes, they should be assigned sanctions in ways that honor parsimony, proportionality, and do not tend to produce further or worse offending. Most who serve their sentences should be presumptively viewed and treated as full-fledged members of society, entitled to enjoy the rights and privileges this entails.

It is natural, I suspect, in contemplating punishment institutions and their justification to suppose that they can be made at least moderately successful at doing whatever it is we believe that they should do. It would seem odd for penal theorists to invest as much time and energy as they have in thinking about and defending the institution if they believed that, no matter what conclusions they reached, it was unlikely that the institution could be relied upon, very often, to achieve its defensible aims. Yet there is troubling evidence that criminal justice institutions often fail to capture and convict more than a small number of those who commit crimes, including serious crimes. We saw a glimpse of this in Chapter 1, where I noted the low clearance rates for many offenses. Clearance rates measure the percentage of arrests for reported crimes of various kinds. In that chapter, I noted how low clearance rates pose

DOI: 10.4324/9781032661667-9

problems for the general deterrent effects of legal punishment, especially if many would-be offenders have some inkling of such rates. Yet low clearance rates raise problems for retributive accounts of legal punishment as well, including the moral communication version I defend. I detail these problems in the first section below and show how low clearance rates are merely the tip of the proverbial iceberg. For arrests (or "clearances") are not the same as convictions. Also, many crimes are never reported to the authorities, meaning that they are not factored into statistics on clearance rates. It therefore appears that, on average, fewer than 5 percent of crimes result in convictions. With minor offenses, conviction rates are apt to be considerably lower, since they will be less often reported and the authorities will be less inclined to expend their scarce resources on their detection, investigation, or prosecution.

We might hope to improve on this seemingly dismal performance of our punishment institutions with reforms in policing or investigation, or with new forms of surveillance or crime detection technologies, but my hunch is that any improvements will be modest in character. If that is correct, it raises the question of how we should think about the institution of legal punishment. Should we simply have modest expectations for its success, or should we consider options other than legal punishment to address crime and, in particular, to stand by and for the victims of crime?

In the second section, I briefly consider some of the alternatives. They range from various forms of the privatization of punishment to proposals to supplant it with restorative justice practices or offender-supplied restitution. I urge skepticism about these alternatives. The former are likely to be too expensive or impracticable for many members of society or are apt to be more risky than state institutions of legal punishment. There also seems little reason to believe that they will be more successful at capturing and convicting those who harm the vital interests of others than are state efforts to do so. Restorative justice programs and offender-supplied restitution to victims both have defensible roles to play in state punishment regimes. However, they are not really replacements for such regimes; they seem to presuppose its operations in producing arrests and convictions and thus suitable candidates for restorative justice conferences or the assignment of restitution costs. If that is correct, then low conviction rates will plague such alternative approaches as well.

All of this suggests that although we should retain state institutions of legal punishment, we should have modest expectations about them. More than this, we should look beyond them for ways in which to reduce crime and thus the victimization of members of society or to stand by and support victims when we fall short in shielding them from criminal harms. I discuss two such alternatives: First, the adoption of more generous social welfare measures designed to reduce the kinds of desperation or alienation that we have reason to believe precipitates some criminal conduct; second, the implementation of state-sponsored victim compensation programs, ones that do not depend on the successful prosecution of the perpetrators of crimes. Both are controversial measures, but I suggest that they offer partial remedies to the predictable failures of state penal institutions to capture, convict, and punish those who commit crimes.

Reality Check

In Chapter 1, I noted that one of the practical problems encountered by the crime reduction approach to legal punishment is the low "clearance rate" for many criminal offenses. For the most part, clearance rates measure the percentages of crimes of various kinds that have been reported to the authorities for which there has been an arrest.[1] I say "for the most part" because crimes can officially be cleared in other ways—by an arrest warrant being issued, or by the police dealing with a criminal complaint informally, such that nothing further is done about it. However, let us ignore these complications, since they will not much affect the overall conclusion toward which my discussion in this section points.

Taking the United States as an example, in the year 2019, about 46 percent of all violent FBI Index crimes were cleared through an arrest or by other means. For that same year, about 18 percent of FBI Index property crimes were cleared.[2] As Andrew Leipold points out, this means that over half of all reported violent crime victims never see the arrest of a suspect and over 80 percent of reported property crime victims do not see anyone arrested for the crimes against them.[3] These rather desultory figures would no doubt be much lower if non-Index crimes were included. Many of the more minor crimes not covered by the Index probably escape detection by the authorities altogether, or are not reported to them, because the participants in some of them are, for lack of a better term, "willing." Think in this context of small-scale drug possession and sales offenses, or prostitution offenses that occur between consenting adults. Even with minor thefts, assaults, or public disorder offenses, those who are victimized might not wish to notify the authorities or might believe that doing so will not result in anyone's being arrested or prosecuted. Still, let us stick with the clearance rate figures for Index crimes for the time being, knowing that they likely inflate the rates at which the authorities achieve arrests when they become aware of crimes having been committed.

This brings us to a second important point: Many crimes, including many Index crimes, are never reported to the police. How many? Again, those who have analyzed the evidence suggest that roughly half of all the Index crimes committed are never reported.[4] What this means, as Shima Baughman points out citing 2018 figures, is that while the overall clearance rate for Index crimes is about 21 percent, the "true" overall clearance rate (involving both reported and unreported Index crimes) is just over 10 percent.[5] Why would individuals, and specifically the victims of such crimes, decline to report them? After all, these are typically more serious crimes, and sometimes very serious ones. The answers are varied. In the case of crimes involving sexual assault, the victims might be embarrassed by what has been done to them or are convinced that the authorities will do little to investigate or prosecute such crimes or are afraid of retaliation by those who assaulted them. Unfortunately, some of these fears or concerns are often well-founded.[6] In other kinds of cases, the perpetrators of crimes are relatives of the victim, or co-workers, and these factors make some victims reluctant to involve the authorities. More generally, as we have seen in previous chapters, individuals from poor or socially marginalized communities might believe that the authorities will not take seriously crimes committed against them, especially when the crimes consist of thefts or assaults.[7]

The third point to make is the obvious one that "clearances" must be distinguished from "convictions." From the mere fact that the authorities make arrests for Index crimes, it does not follow that they secure convictions in all or most cases. Charges against those arrested might simply be foregone or dropped, outcomes that are far from uncommon. Also, in the relatively few cases that go to trial, the accused might win acquittals. Even when charges produce guilty pleas, prosecutors might drop some of them in exchange for pleas to others or might reduce initial charges to lesser ones to attract pleas. Obviously, in both of these kinds of cases, convictions are obtained. Yet in the former, prosecutors might effectively agree to ignore some of the crimes committed by the accused to gain guilty pleas to others. In the latter, the charge reductions that prosecutors agree to might distort the crimes that the accused actually committed. For instance, the accused might have committed armed robbery but, due to problems with the evidence or with the victim's reluctance to testify, the prosecutor might agree to let the accused plead guilty to larceny. Again, however, let us set to one side these various complications and simply focus on the overall percentage of cases in which those arrested for crimes are convicted. The last year in which convictions were tracked in the United States was 2006. As Baughman reports, conviction rates for homicide typically hover in the 50 percent range. However, convictions for property offenses such as larceny, robbery, burglary, and motor vehicle theft are much lower, often in the 1–2 percent range. Conviction rates for rape and armed robbery hover in the 3–4 percent range. All of this means that true conviction rates overall are in the 1–2 percent range, given that homicide is relatively rare while the various forms of theft are much more common.[8] Factor in what are likely to be lower conviction rates for the more minor kinds of criminal offenses not included in the FBI Index and the implications of all of this are unsettling. Even if these figures are too low, and we imagined that conviction rates are roughly 5 percent on average overall, this would mean that 95 percent of the victims of crimes never see anyone punished for what was done to them.

Finally, the evidence suggests that these figures have not fluctuated much in the United States for the last 40 years.[9] This is true despite increases and decreases in offending, including dramatic ones, and despite increases in funding for the police and the courts, sometimes substantial ones.[10] It is also true despite advances in the technology available to the authorities for detecting and proving crimes.

It seems difficult to avoid the conclusion that the overall performance of the criminal justice system in the United States is rather dismal, despite the hefty resources poured into it. Viewed from the vantage point offered by the mixed theory of legal punishment defended in previous chapters, it is apparent that not much moral communication with offenders occurs, including with many serious offenders. That, in turn, means that few of the victims of their crimes receive the vital assurance that the state takes their interests seriously by acting decisively to hold those who wronged them accountable. Granted, the preceding might overstate the state's shortcomings somewhat, since there will be cases in which state officials do exert considerable effort in trying to hold the perpetrators of serious crimes accountable, only to fall short in doing so for reasons largely beyond their control. Nonetheless, even if, say, 5 percent of the victims of more serious crimes have their interests backed by the successful prosecution of those who wronged them or by conscientious efforts to do so, this can hardly be regarded as an impressive achievement. It seems difficult to avoid the conclusion that the US criminal justice system is a disappointment when it comes to moral communication. It does not follow from this that we should reject moral communication as an aim, and indeed the leading aim of legal punishment. It might be what the institution should strive for, even if it is not often very successful at doing it. Notice, by the way, that little would change if one of the other versions of retributivism was utilized in the mixed theory or was made to stand alone as a justification of legal punishment. If fewer than one in 20 serious offenders get what they deserve or are deprived of the unfair advantages that their crimes create, it will be hard for those who subscribe to these versions of retributivism to view the state's criminal justice endeavors with much enthusiasm.

There is, it should be noted, some reason to believe that the institutions of legal punishment in other societies do somewhat better jobs of convicting those who have committed crimes. There are reports that suggest that across a wide range of countries, conviction rates are just under 20 percent of reported crimes.[11] Of course, "reported" crimes are not the same as actual ones and given what we suspect about the gap between the two in the United States, the 20 percent conviction figure might be closer to 10 percent for actual crimes. It also is not clear whether this figure encompasses only more serious crimes or all crimes. One suspects that, as in the United States, many minor crimes go either unreported or unpunished. In any case, the 20 percent figure, while certainly more encouraging than the US counterpart figure, still means that four out of five offenders are not convicted and so go unpunished. If the 10 percent figure is more accurate, as seems likely, then nine of ten offenders go unpunished. Although this does mean that some criminal justice systems do better jobs at morally communicating with offenders than the US system does, they are still not highly successful at it.

Do the shortcomings of contemporary criminal justice systems in arresting and convicting those who violate the law appear in a better light from the standpoint of the crime reduction element in my account? Not initially, or so it might seem. If the state manages to punish only a small percentage of offenders, then not that many who commit crimes will be viable candidates for special deterrence, incapacitation, or rehabilitation. The majority, and perhaps the vast majority of offenders, will seem to go on about their criminal careers unimpeded by state agents dedicated to detecting, arresting, and prosecuting them. Also, the reinforcement of crucial moral norms that legal punishment is supposed to furnish might appear weak or drowned out if the public is aware of how many of those who commit crimes get away with doing so.

However, in evaluating the efficacy of the criminal justice system in relation to crime reduction, we must be careful to distinguish between criminal offenses and criminal offenders. Many of the former, as we have seen, will likely go unpunished. But many individuals in the United States are punished for crimes, upwards of six million, on average, per year, and this is true even if those same individuals get away with committing many more crimes than they are arrested, convicted, and punished for.[12] The US criminal justice system might not manage to punish the vast majority of crimes committed by those under its purview, but it does, in the aggregate, so to speak, punish many offenders for at least some of their crimes. Notice that this aggregate impact should also extend to the system's moral communication efforts. Even if many or most crimes go unpunished, the large number that are punished presumably serves to reinforce the public rights and responsibilities narrative, at least to some extent.

Still, whether the criminal justice system's punishment of numerous offenders should bolster our confidence in legal punishment's crime reduction impact is hard to assess. If many who are convicted of crimes know that they have gotten away with committing other crimes for which they went unpunished, this might work against special deterrence. They might tell themselves that, sure, they get caught once and awhile, but that they often escape detection, arrest, or conviction. Perhaps this partly explains why recidivism rates are so high. Also, as we saw in Chapter 1, any special deterrence effects that punishment produces must be balanced against the demonstrated tendency of legal punishment to exacerbate offending. Many offenders were poor to begin with. Their criminal convictions will hardly improve their prospects for decently paying jobs and if they spend time in prison for their crimes, this might as much damage their abilities or willingness to abide by the law as improve them.[13]

With respect to incapacitation, the first point to make is that only some who are convicted of crimes will be sentenced to terms in state custody. Those not assigned custodial sentences will not be much hindered from committing further crimes. Admittedly, those offenders who are sentenced to prison will be, for some period, less able to commit further crimes. Let us suppose that is a good thing. Nonetheless, most of them will, at some point, get out of prison and re-enter civil society. Many of them will do so in a relatively impoverished state and face uncertain, if not desultory, futures in the job market. If they know that many crimes go unpunished, as well they might, their incapacitation might do little, in the long-term, to stem their offending. Of course, we might hope that they will have aged out while under the purview of the criminal justice system. Or we might hope that they will have benefitted from well-conceived and appropriately funded rehabilitation programs while imprisoned. How much all of this will reduce future crime, in a society in which the majority of criminal acts go unpunished, is difficult to say. As we noted in Chapter 1, the imprisonment of some kinds of offenders is unlikely to reduce crime in communities, since they will be replaced by other individuals. But we can grant that incapacitation does, in some cases, make some marginal contribution to the reduction of crime.

Turning to moral reinforcement, as we saw in Chapter 1, it seems likely that the criminal justice system is but one of the institutions in society that teaches moral norms against violent or predatory behavior. It may not be the most significant institution in that regard, compared with families, schools, and churches. Nonetheless, if members of society witness a sufficiently large number of people being punished for their crimes, this will presumably remind them of the importance of abiding by the norms the criminal law embodies and strengthen their commitments to doing so. Still, this effect of punishment will seem more plausible if most members of the public are unaware of the substantial number of offenses that escape punishment. Awareness of the inefficacy of the criminal justice system might undermine its credentials as a moral authority. I suspect that public awareness of the extremely modest conviction rates for serious offenses is limited. This means that punishment's moral reinforcement effects depend on public ignorance to some extent. It is not clear whether we should be cheered or disheartened by this.

This brings us to the general deterrence branch of the crime reduction approach. As with the other branches, it might seem that what matters is not so much the percentage of crimes, including serious crimes, successfully punished, but the aggregate workings of the system to punish a large number of offenders. The aggregate workings of the system might suffice to discourage those from offending who lack other motivations to refrain from it. But again, it might do this only so long as they do not grasp the very limited success of the criminal justice system in capturing and punishing the guilty. If those whose internalized norms and commitments are insufficient to keep them from committing crimes have some awareness of the state's shortcomings in punishing the guilty, some of them might convince themselves that they are smart or skilled enough to outwit the authorities. Indeed, many of them, as it turns out, will be. I have embraced the proposition that legal punishment, through its general deterrent effect, serves to keep a lid on offending, even it is less clear how much it works to reduce it. I am not going back on my endorsement of that proposition at this point. Here, I note only that the limited success of legal punishment systems in capturing and convicting offenders might be why we should not expect much from them when it comes to the reduction of crime via general deterrence. As we saw in Chapter 1, it is more the certainty of being punished that deters than the severity of the punishment. In the United States and in other societies, the certainty of punishment is rather low in relation to many crimes, or so it seems.

Could the certainty of punishment be increased? The advent of new surveillance technologies might encourage us to believe that it could be. Alternatively, we could better train police or orient them away from the detection and arrest of those who commit minor offenses and toward the investigation of more serious crimes. I would not deny that changes in technologies or police training and practices might have some salutary effects on conviction rates, especially with regard to more serious kinds of offenses.[14] But suppose that we managed to double or even triple conviction rates for more serious offenses. In the United States, that would mean that approximately 10 to 15 percent of serious offenses would be resolved through legal punishment. Would such a conviction success rate encourage us to regard the criminal justice system as a successful moral communicator? I am not sure that it would and I doubt that further changes in the system are apt to produce conviction rates that would justify our viewing it as a robust backer of the rights of victims.

Again, the low rates at which contemporary criminal justice systems achieve convictions in cases of serious crimes do not show that legal punishment should not aim at moral communication or the reduction of crime. We might hold that it should do so and that these aims are the most plausible candidates for the institution's justification. But low conviction rates do entail that we should have modest expectations about the success of legal punishment at actually achieving moral communication or crime reduction. Legal punishment, as an institution, does not seem a very impressive one in which to invest so many of society's limited resources.

Perhaps we should cheer the relative ineffectiveness of contemporary criminal justice systems at capturing, convicting, and punishing those who commit crimes. As Vincent Chiao has recently noted, countries like the United States already seem to have a problem with overimprisonment.[15] If more of the individuals who commit crimes were convicted of them, that problem would intensify. If all of those who commit crimes were convicted, the problem would be overwhelming. In fairness to Chiao, his target is deontological accounts of legal punishment that seem to eschew consideration of the costs and negative consequences of the institution. For instance, if giving offenders their just deserts is necessary and sufficient to justify the institution, then it seems we should be committed to meting out punishment to the deserving come what may. No amount of aggregate deserved punishment would seem excessive, on such accounts. Chiao's point is that such a view is hard to accept if we already think there is too much punishment, and in particular, too much imprisonment, in countries like the United States.

Chiao is, I believe, too quick to assume that deontological accounts of legal punishment would endorse the high imprisonment rates of some countries. It might be the case that the criminal justice system in such countries set too low a threshold for what qualifies as an imprisonable offense. As we have seen, the majority of crimes in the United States are relatively minor, classified as "misdemeanors."[16] Arguably, such offenses should never, or rarely, be punished with terms of imprisonment, contrary to US practices. Further, the United States employs longer terms of imprisonment than other countries and this plays a role in maintaining its high levels of imprisonment.[17] Think of imprisonment as having a revolving exit door. Longer sentences slow the door and inmates pile up behind it, increasing the prison population. Shorter sentences, which deontologists might support, would speed up the door and reduce the over-crowding. Also, as Chiao concedes, the war on drugs has had a substantial role in increasing the prison population in the United States, despite the critical literature on the merits of that war, one with which deontologists might concur.[18] Finally, even strict deontologists might be concerned about the state efforts that would be required to dramatically increase the percentage of offenders who receive their deserved punishment. The kinds of intense surveillance or other intrusive state actions that would be needed to produce substantially higher conviction rates will have more than financial costs; they might be so over-bearing or intrusive upon citizens' lives that they would reduce the perceived value of their most basic rights.

Despite all of this, I would concede that Chiao has a valid point. We should be prepared to weigh the drain on societal resources and the damaging effects of legal punishment, and especially imprisonment, in our thinking about the justification of the institution. In Chapter 2, I claimed that the value of moral communication by the state gives us only a weighty reason to devise and administer institutions that effect it, not a duty to do so, let alone one that ought to be conceived as overriding all of the other duties that states in liberal democratic societies arguably have. Nonetheless, even if I am doubtful that the institution of legal punishment can be made much more efficient at capturing and convicting offenders at reasonable cost, is Chiao correct in asserting that we should hardly wish it to be?

The answer to that question seems to depend on the kinds of crimes in question. With the majority of crimes, which are relatively non-serious, we might look for other ways to reduce and respond to them besides penal measures. First, we are not ever going to be very successful at capturing and convicting persons for many of them. Second, we should remain somewhat skeptical about whether penal processing of such crimes is apt to reduce them. Later in the chapter, I consider the alternative of enhanced social welfare measures of various kinds to reduce the desperation and alienation that seem to spur many individuals to engage in forms of criminal misconduct. I suggest that there is some hope for such measures, although they are not likely to be a panacea. Importantly, not only might more robust state efforts to guarantee all citizens minima of social welfare and access to well-paying jobs reduce minor forms of offending, they might diminish the number of more serious crimes. More to the point, I would argue that we must be prepared to continue employing penal measures to morally communicate about and attempt to reduce serious crimes. As I argued in earlier chapters, such crimes jeopardize elemental interests of persons and we should prioritize their punishment for that reason. It does not follow that we should automatically imprison all of those who are convicted of them, do so for as lengthy periods of time as have become standard in countries like the United States, or subject offenders to prison conditions that are degrading or will likely incline them toward more or worse kinds of offending, assuming we can devise and administer prisons that avoid such things.

All that being said, it seems unlikely that we will become much more successful, any time soon, at capturing and convicting many of the individuals who commit crimes, including serious ones. A more radical tack would be to urge the abandonment or at least substantial modification of our institutions of legal punishment. After all, if state penal institutions are not very adept at doing the two things that my mixed theory of punishment posits are the dominant theoretical rationales for having them, then perhaps we should look elsewhere for ways of addressing crime. In the next section, I examine some of the alternatives to state punishment that theorists have put forward.

Alternatives to Traditional Forms of Legal Punishment

It might be surprising to discover that state penal institutions are not very adept at doing what it is we believe that they should do. Granted, it is not reasonable to expect such institutions to catch and convict all of those violate the law. But to discover that they manage to convict only one in ten serious offenders—or worse, one in 20 or 30—should be a sobering fact, one that might incline us to take a serious look at alternatives to state punishment, if they exist. There is a substantial history of criticism of retributive and crime reduction approaches to the justification of legal punishment. Some of that criticism urges us to abandon them both and to substitute other ways of dealing with the kinds of violent or predatory behavior that most concern us, as well as with violations of the *mala prohibita* that any viable legal system must enforce.[19] There has also been some, albeit more limited, discussion of alternatives to state legal punishment in any of its forms.[20] Although my responses to these two kinds of proposals will be relatively brief, I believe that it is important to say something about why neither seems promising.

The most prominent alternatives to traditional forms of state-imposed legal sanctions for crimes include proposals to substitute offender restitution for it or to implement restorative justice programs designed to deal with many, if not all, criminal offenses.[21] In earlier chapters, I conceded that requiring offenders to pay restitution to their victims might be a defensible form of legal punishment in some cases. I have also admitted that referring many minor offenders to restorative justice mediation might be a suitable means of addressing their crimes. Both of these approaches will result in the imposition of burdens on those convicted of crimes, which, on my account, is necessary to casting them as forms of legal punishment. In this context, the point worth making about these alternatives to more traditional approaches to state punishment is this: Neither constitutes a complete displacement of the state as the primary agent of the burdens imposed. It is hard to imagine either of them operating except in the context of the state prohibition of an array of acts and state enforcement of those prohibitions. Such enforcement would presumably require the policing of apparent violations of the prohibitions and the prosecution, or at least threatened prosecution, of those violations.

Consider proposals to substitute "pure restitution" for more traditional criminal sanctions. How are we to determine who is required to pay such restitution independent of the operations of the police and the courts? Unless proponents of the pure restitution approach are prepared to implement some version of Robert Nozick's "private protection associations," ones that not only police violations of our basic rights but determine who will be subject to requirements to pay restitution, the answers are not clear.[22] Yet if state officials must be involved in determining who is to pay restitution, then the problems we noted in the previous section concerning low conviction rates will plague pure restitution approaches as much as they plague moral communication and crime reduction approaches. Very few of the individuals whose crimes should require them to pay restitution to victims will be caught and convicted, or so it would seem. Granted, it might be claimed that more victims of crimes will report them to the authorities if they believe that they might thereby gain some compensation for whatever losses or injuries they suffered. If the authorities become aware of more of the crimes that have victimized citizens, they might act to catch and convict the perpetrators. But the authorities might also be overwhelmed by increases in the volume of crimes on their dockets or disinclined to expend many resources on ones that do not reach some level of seriousness. Even if we imagine the doubling or tripling of the victims of crimes afforded some restitution under such a scheme, this will still constitute a relatively small portion of the victimized members of the public. More to the point, state officials will still have to be the primary agents responsible for capturing and convicting those deemed appropriate providers of compensation to their victims.

The same problem will plague restorative justice approaches which preserve some state role in policing and prosecuting crimes, or at least in threatening to prosecute them if the accused refuse to attend or take seriously restorative justice conferences at which remedies to their misconduct are worked out with the aid of mediators. Even if we believe that it makes sense with many offenses to reduce the state's role in determining how violations of the law are to be addressed, there must, it seems, be some authoritative procedure for determining who is subject to restorative justice mediation.[23] If, as seems most plausible, it is the state whose policing and prosecutorial functions determine eligibility for restorative justice mediation, then the low arrest and conviction rates for many criminal offenses will mean that most of the individuals who should be referred to such mediation will not be. It is not apparent why supporters of restorative justice should be happy about or content with that result, even if they are skeptical of traditional state sanctions or critical of state domination of the resolution of many criminal disputes. The fact is that the vast majority of those who violate the law will evade the kinds of negotiated responsibility for their acts that restorative justice theorists prize.

If the alternatives to more standard forms of state involvement in punishing those who violate the law seem as much frustrated or undermined by low arrest and conviction rates as retributive or crime reduction approaches, then what?[24] It might be claimed that we should consider more radical alternatives to state involvement in efforts to secure the rights of persons. One such alternative would be to rely on something like self-enforcement of our basic moral rights.[25] Accordingly, the idea would be that each of us should be prepared to defend our own rights, vigilant about doing so, and reasonably competent to the task. Such an approach would permit, and might encourage, us to band together with family members, friends, and other trusted allies to enhance the prospects of warding off incursions against our lives, liberty, and property, or to respond to such incursions with appropriate measures, whatever those might turn out to be.

Such an alternative to state penal institutions seems deeply unattractive, for a variety of reasons. The self-enforcement of basic moral rights might seem a mildly plausible endeavor if we imagine ourselves as young, able-bodied, fearless, well-resourced, and comfortable with employing violence. It will seem much less plausible if we think about the many individuals in society who do not fit this description. A subset of adult or near-adult males might fit parts of this description, but many males will not, along with many females, who are generally less prone to or comfortable with violence at any age.[26] Also, many in society will be either too young to self-enforce (infants or adolescents) or too old. Others will be disabled, or struggling with mental or physical illnesses, pregnant, responsible for rearing children, or simply timid by temperament. They will have to rely on partisans to secure their rights, hoping that there will be family or friends willing to do so, ones who will not take advantage of them or be indifferent to their welfare. Bluntly stated, existence in or return to a mythical "state of nature" would be a nightmare for many people.

More to the point, the self-enforcement of rights seems, at times to presuppose a view about violent or predatory behavior that is, well, quaint. It will be possible to self-enforce only if we know who victimized us and where they are. Yet in geographically dispersed societies, or even in ones in which many of the people who live in close proximity to us are relative strangers, knowing who did or might victimize you, or where they have gone off to, will often be matters concerning which individuals, or their protectors, will be quite helpless. One signal advantage of state enforcement of rights is that it has the resources and expertise to investigate crimes and discover the whereabouts of those who committed them. Even then, it is disconcertingly unsuccessful at doing so. If we imagine the state removed from the enterprise of right protection or enforcement, and individual victims or their partisans having to take on these tasks, it is hard to believe that they would be anywhere near as successful as the state is—which is, after all, not very successful. It is misleading to think of criminal victimization as mostly involving known victimizers who are easily found and dealt with by non-state actors. And this was true even before the advent of the digital age and the new opportunities it affords to steal the property of others or otherwise exploit them.

In addition, limited resources will pose problems for self or partisan-enforcement of basic moral rights in other ways. Even if alleged violators can be caught and made to face their alleged victims, not all cases will permit easy resolution. Some alleged right violators will deny that they victimized others or claim that they had justifications or excuses for doing so. These are familiar features of criminal cases for which states have developed elaborate procedures. Will self or partisan enforcers bother with trials or other means of getting at the truth of what actually occurred? Doing so would require the expenditure of what will likely be a fairly limited supply of resources. One suspects that "rough justice" will more often be the chosen outcome in cases in which there is some doubt about who did what to whom and why.

An alternative to self or partisan enforcement of basic moral rights involves the privatization of criminal justice. Again, Nozick once floated the possibility of private protection associations in place of state punishment institutions.[27] He quickly abandoned it with the realization that someone (and who, in the absence of the state?) would have to police these associations, to keep them from fighting among themselves, armed and dangerous as they would have to be. Yet this only partially captures the likely deficiencies of private protection associations. Other problems would include the probable fact that some persons would be unable to afford their services. The poor, the disabled, and the ill, for instance, might find themselves having to mostly self-enforce, or hope that others will just leave them alone. Also, what would prevent the private protection associations from turning into organized extortion rackets, ones that forced "customers" to sign on for their services or exploited existing customers ruthlessly? Further, why believe that private protection associations would observe anything like due process constraints in their investigation of attacks on the rights of their customers and in the prosecution of those alleged to have committed such attacks? Due process would be more costly, it seems, so why not cut corners by coercing suspects to confess or by precipitously declaring them guilty and dispatching them? Finally, what incentives would such associations have to employ humane or proportionate sanctions if the use of less comely ones would maximize their profits? Imprisonment is hugely expensive, as we have come to discover. It would be much cheaper to kill or maim known or suspected offenders so that they did not pose continuing threats.

Setting aside all of these objections, a further one comes to the fore in the current context. Why think that private protection agencies would do a better job than state institutions at detecting crimes, identifying perpetrators, arresting them, and dealing with them (whatever dealing with them turns out to mean)? State officials involved in enforcing the criminal law inevitably have limited resources with which to do their jobs. But at least they do not have to concern themselves with making a profit on top of this. Private protection associations would have to keep an eye on the bottom line. Assuming (perhaps inaccurately) that they would not be inclined to keep raising the prices of their services (as they will be in competition with other providers), such associations might be tempted to focus more of their resources on crimes that are easier to resolve. Yet such crimes will not reliably overlap with the more serious kinds of offenses, the resolution of which are often more resource-demanding.

It might be suggested that private associations would be more adept at investigating and proving crimes than state agencies, especially if by doing so they can attract more customers. Perhaps, but would private associations be prepared to invest the resources in training their employees to do so skillfully and carefully, or would they cut corners in a variety of predictable ways (thus imperiling the innocent) or rely on elaborate advertising campaigns aimed at convincing old and new customers that they offer the best criminal justice services around (regardless of the facts)? I suspect it is hard to say. But this means that their customers might not be any better off when it comes to either the protection of their rights or effective action when their rights were violated than are those who rely on more traditional state schemes of criminal law enforcement. Indeed, some members of society might wind up worse off because they cannot afford to pay for private protection or can afford only the lowest-tier provider.

If none of the alternative forms of state action in response to crime or private responses to it are likely to be more successful at securing the basic rights of most members of society, then what? Must we simply be determined to "grin and bear it," in the sense that we retain state involvement, perhaps hoping to improve it in certain respects, but with limited expectations about the chances of doing so? Or should we consider options for reducing crime that lie largely outside of the criminal justice system, as well as measures designed to help those victimized by it that are independent of the punishment of those who wronged them? In the remainder of this chapter, I discuss these two options. To be clear, I do not conceive of them as replacements for the institution of legal punishment. I assume that we must retain the institution and continue to shape and improve it in accordance with the values of accurate moral communication and crime reduction as I have elaborated them in previous chapters. But given the likely limited efficacy of the institution, we should consider other steps to reduce victimization and ameliorate it when it occurs.

Enhanced Social Welfare Measures

One plausible thing we might do to reduce crime is see to it that all members of society are provided minima of social welfare, in the forms of adequate housing, nutrition, education, healthcare, and, as far as this is possible, stable access to decently paying jobs. In the absence of such access, or for individuals who are too young, disabled, or elderly and cannot work, we should see to it that their basic needs are provided for. We have seen glimmers of the ways in which poverty and social exclusion foster crime in previous chapters. Despite this, it will be useful to provide a brief overview of what we might term the "social deprivation narrative" with respect to criminal offending.

First, depending on the extent to which individuals are impoverished and their prospects for meeting their most basic needs for food and shelter, not to mention other goods such as healthcare or education, they may be reduced to desperate measures of various kinds to acquire income, some of which may be prohibited by the criminal law. Selling drugs or sexual services, or engaging in forms of theft or fraud are common forms of crime to which those with few other meaningful options resort, especially when they live in areas that, for one reason or another, do not afford them decent work opportunities.[28] Second, many of the poor are homeless, or occasionally so, which not only exposes them to risks of various kinds and exacerbates their desperation, it also subjects them to routine surveillance and harassment by the police, with attendant arrests and convictions more than merely possible outcomes.[29] The poor have often been subject to arrest for conduct that is dubiously criminal, such as vagrancy or loitering, in part because they lack acceptable accommodations.[30] Third, combine poverty or homelessness with drug or alcohol abuse, and the limited supply of treatment options available to the destitute for such conditions, and the prospects for disorder and crime are enhanced. Fourth, factor in mental illness and the dearth of treatment options for the disadvantaged in society. The criminal justice system is often the "first responder" to the poor who exhibit mental illness symptoms, yet the arrest and confinement of such individuals rarely results in their treatment and is apt to worsen their conditions.[31] The outcomes, when they are released back into communities, are sadly predictable. Fifth, poor parents will not only face challenges in feeding and housing their children, but also in monitoring and shaping their conduct. If they are able to find work, poor parents may lack affordable and decent childcare options. They also might have to work two or three jobs to make ends meet, which will leave their children insufficiently cared for and supervised for significant stretches of time. The kinds of impoverished neighborhoods they are likely to inhabit will tend to be marked by forms of social disorder and violence that pose both temptations and risks of various kinds to children.[32] Teens are by nature more impulsive than adults and thus are at enhanced risk of offending, even before peer pressure is factored in. Street gangs will offer young people forms of social acceptance and solidarity in a harsh world, although they might also encourage or require them to engage in forms of criminal offending.[33] Further, children from impoverished families will not have the kinds of more positive opportunities that middle class or privileged children have in greater abundance—in the forms of nurturing and challenging schools and sports or other recreational activities. Public schools in socially deprived neighborhoods are notoriously underfunded and decrepit.[34] Those who emerge from them will lack basic reading, writing, and other skills, which will limit their job prospects going forward. Sixth, the impoverished and socially excluded will not be unaware of their lots in life, relative to other, better off or more privileged members of society.[35] More than a few will both understand and feel their limited life-chances and resent their predicaments. The resulting alienation from the larger society and the government that sustains it will play some understandable role in their willingness to breach criminal prohibitions. Seventh, and overlaying the preceding, factor in the myriad ways in which, as we have seen, forms of systemic racism, as well as both subtle and unsubtle forms of gender, ethnic, and sexual orientation bias further limit the options individuals have available to them, and the result is a potent mixture of criminogenic forces that push the socially deprived and excluded toward offending.[36]

As I have previously acknowledged, the social deprivation narrative need not be interpreted as denying that the poor or socially excluded have some responsibility for how their lives go. Obviously, some persons born or raised in pockets of severe social deprivation manage to hew to the legal straight and narrow and carve out responsible lives of work, family, and civic participation. But many will struggle to do so. It is helpful to think of social deprivation as perching individuals on a somewhat steeply inclined walkway, with the pitch of the walkway varying somewhat to reflect the range of diminished opportunities and other obstacles that individuals face. The goal is to get to the top of the inclined walkway, at which point one will enjoy a decent, responsible life. Some of the severely socially deprived will make it there, despite the steep incline; more than a few will be defeated by it, succumbing to temptations to depart the walkway or having their abilities to stay upright and keep moving forward gradually defeated by the rigors and disappointments of their lives. The temptations and frustrations that the socially deprived or marginalized endure should be conceived as chronic rather than one-off or occasional.[37] Their lives are marked by ongoing hardships that challenge and often defeat even the most honest and steadfast among them. By contrast, individuals who grow up in the middle classes or above find themselves on a much flatter walkway, or one that is sloped downwards. They too can make choices that lead them to fall off, but getting to the end is considerably less fraught and challenging for them.

Set to one side, for the time being, the question of whether and by how far ensuring minima of social welfare will actually work to reduce offending. The deeper challenges to such an approach will come from those who favor conceptions of social justice that assign the state a modest role, mostly in the form of securing or protecting moral rights to life, liberty, and property, where these rights are construed negatively as rights against interference. Those who subscribe to libertarian or neoliberal views tend to regard individuals as largely responsible for their own lots in life, regardless of the circumstances in which they began their lives or the obstacles they faced or had to overcome.[38] Alternatively, those inclined toward such views might simply be more wary of enlisting the state to limit or ameliorate inequalities in peoples' life prospects. They will prefer to rely on private, charitable efforts to do so, rather than state coercion in the form of taxation and redistribution. Even among social justice theorists who assign the state some social welfare role, there will be differences of opinion about how far it should go in "raising the floor" or trying to see to it that the members of society have equal life-chances.

I will not pretend to dive very far into the numerous and complex issues that competing accounts of social justice raise. However, since those inclined toward libertarian or neo-liberal views are among those most likely to resist proposals for enhanced state social welfare measures as a non-penal strategy to reduce crime, I believe some response to them is needed. First, those who favor a minimal state cannot simply ignore the ways in which past injustices—consisting of violations of the basic moral rights of individuals which their own accounts endorse—have some bearing on the impoverishment and social marginality of many people in existing societies. Robert Nozick and other such theorists have conceded that past injustices that deprived individuals of their rightful property, or denied them property altogether, which losses left them and their heirs substantially worse off than they would have been, ought to be rectified in some way.[39] Yet I think it is fair to say that libertarian and neoliberal theorists have struggled to explain the form such rectification should take or have tended to dismiss its need or feasibility too quickly.[40]

Also, the scale of the rectification problem has not always been appreciated by theorists who favor austere accounts of basic moral rights and a minimal state. It will, in many cases, be a mistake to view the past wrongs in need of rectification as isolated or occasional, as minor blemishes in the evolution of current property holdings that are otherwise substantially just. Too see why, consider the history of African Americans in the United States. The historical progression from institutionalized slavery, to Jim Crow (with both its legal-formal and informal means of enforcement), to forms of legal segregation and discrimination in living arrangements and employment opportunities, to lingering forms of systemic racial exclusion or prejudice of both explicit and implicit kinds has had devastating effects on the life-prospects of African Americans.[41] No sober assessment of the countless ways in which the basic moral rights of African Americans to life, physical and psychological integrity, liberty, and property have been systematically violated for hundreds of years can simply be dismissed by rational and thoughtful libertarian or neoliberals.[42] Sadly, Native Americans and Hispanics in the United States have their own histories of basic rights abuse which, although somewhat distinct, are similar enough that they too ought to be deeply troubling to those inclined toward libertarian or neoliberal accounts of social justice.[43] Throw in the historical mistreatment of individuals of Asian descent, and other groups too numerous to mention, and the profile of contemporary property holdings, along with the life prospects those holdings either facilitate or impede, appears profoundly morally tainted.[44]

It is not only the United States that has a disturbing history of human rights abuses. Many contemporary societies have histories of systemic racism, ethnic exclusion, and religious or class oppression that infect their current distributions of property holdings.[45] Nozick might have been wise to throw up his hands in the face of the rectification problem and concede that a more Rawlsian social welfare state that redistributes property would have to be accepted, at least in the short term, to achieve fair starting points after which the operations of a minimal state might be defensible.[46] Unfortunately, we are, at this point, nowhere near such a hypothetical fair starting point for many members of existing societies.

Second, unless libertarians and neo-liberals are inclined to reject the social deprivation narrative in its entirety, they face a bit of a dilemma. Either they must be prepared to rely on what is apt to be a not-very-successful institution of legal punishment to address violations of the basic rights of individuals of the kinds that their own theories would presumably legally proscribe, or they should consider measures that might more effectively reduce the number and kinds of such violations. Admittedly, such theorists might argue that the minimal state would have more limited criminal justice ambitions. Vice crimes would be cut back or eliminated from the state's repertoire of policing and prosecution tasks, as would regulatory crimes of various kinds that states less committed to laissez faire forms of capitalism have adopted. Yet even if we concede these points, there would still be plenty of other crimes for the authorities to deal with, some of which would flow rather inevitably from the inequality in people's life prospects that libertarians and neoliberals seem prepared to tolerate. Even if such theorists remain reluctant to regard things like subsistence, housing, education, and health care as basic moral rights, they could view providing them up to some minimal level as an effective strategy to reduce the pressures toward crime and thus the violation of the rights of persons that they do recognize.[47] Whether private sources of the funds needed to diminish such threats would be sufficient is not clear. A society committed to libertarian or neoliberal principles might strongly encourage its better off members to contribute to the cause, so to speak. Perhaps they would respond. If they do not, then they will reap what they sow, as we sometimes say, and probably should not expect the institution of legal punishment to do much by way of protecting their rights or responding to violations of them. Of course, the better off might reasonably hope that the poor and disenfranchised will mostly prey on those like themselves, as, sadly, so often appears to be the case.

By contrast, those who support welfare liberal or egalitarian accounts of social justice will be more inclined to endorse the kinds of social welfare provisions that seem likely to diminish the attractions of crime or the frustrations that give rise to it.[48] Still, proponents of these views will disagree about how far in or what ways the state should act to reduce inequalities in individuals' life prospects.

It is worth noting that not only will substantial social welfare provisions reduce social deprivation and all that goes with it generally, they will help the families of those sentenced to imprisonment to keep their heads above water. Such provisions will also support offenders who have served their sentences while they look for work or stable work, a process that often takes considerable time and effort.[49] Ex-offenders who are desperate because they cannot find well-paying jobs might be more inclined to return to offending to make ends meet in the absence of adequate social supports.

Despite the plausibility of the claim that social welfare provisions of various kinds will staunch criminal offending, the evidence about whether, how, and by how much they do so is not unequivocal. For instance, it is not always the case that when social welfare measures have been on the increase, crime has decreased, and vice-versa. As Paul Knepper points out, social welfare increased in the United States in the 1960s and 1970s, yet crime also was on the increase. In the 1990s, by contrast, social welfare was being cut back and yet crime fell during the second half of the decade.[50] This at the very least suggests that crime rates are affected by a variety of factors and that strengthened social welfare measures are no magic bullet when it comes to decreasing them. Broader economic conditions, and in particular, an overall increase or decrease in employment opportunities might also play a crucial role in determining crime rates. Crime persists and fluctuates even in countries which seem more committed than others to providing at least minimally good lives for all of their citizens.[51] Even scholars who express confidence in the link between more extensive social welfare measures and decreases in crime admit that more precision is needed in order to determine which such measures have crime-curbing effects.[52] Also, there is some reason to believe that social welfare measures will only reduce offending up to a point, beyond which they will have diminishing impact.[53]

Hence, although it makes abundant good sense to believe that stemming the desperation and alienation that social deprivation tends to bring in its wake will likely do as much if not more to reduce crime than standard penal measures, we should probably admit that the evidence in support of such intuitions is less decisive than we might like it to be. It has long been understood by criminologists that the determinants of crime are complex. How best to reduce it in ways other than by legal punishment is apt to be complicated as well.

Victim Compensation

This brings us to a second supplement to legal punishment, one which involves state efforts to compensate the victims of crimes for their losses and thereby demonstrate society's support of them through efforts to restore them to their former lives. Crucially, we should not make the compensation of victims dependent upon the conviction of those who harmed them. Doing so would leave the majority of victims to deal, on their own, with the losses or injuries unfairly inflicted upon them. If the state cannot stand by and for victims by holding those who wronged them accountable, then at least it ought to do so by attempting to restore their property and functioning to them. Moreover, victim compensation provisions ought to be less controversial than social welfare measures. The latter, as we have seen, will be resisted by those with views inimical to the welfare state in any but its most minimal forms. But the wrongs suffered by crime victims will often be ones that moral rights theorists of different stripes will see as properly prohibited by the criminal law. Those who are unjustly deprived, through criminal wrongdoing, of things to which they are entitled might be seen as deserving of state help in putting their lives back together, especially if the state has failed to prevent crime against them or hold accountable those who committed them.

That being said, it should be noted that the provision of adequate social welfare would likely reduce some of the need to compensate victims for the losses or injuries caused by crimes against them. For instance, if victims have all or most of their property stolen, social welfare provisions will ensure that they do not simply fall into homelessness or abject poverty. Likewise, if victims are traumatized by the violence done to them or injured, the provision of health-care services to all citizens would help them to recover. Still, there might be some victims whose losses or injuries exceed what even robust social welfare provisions will provide. Individuals who are relatively well-off but who had all or most of their property stolen from them will not be restored to their former lives by social welfare measures that provide a floor below which no one in society is allowed to fall. Likewise, individuals who are severely injured by the crimes committed against them might require expensive medical treatment or high levels of ongoing material or other support in their lives that exceed what more standard social welfare measures provide. In such cases, timely and well-funded victim compensation programs might enable individuals to resume their former lives, or at least come as close to doing so as is feasible.[54] Also, where social welfare provisions are minimal, or spotty, state compensation of victims will be the primary means through which their losses or injuries can be at least partially redressed.

There are important arguments against state-sponsored victim compensation programs that must be addressed. Most prominent among them will be the contention that it is not the state that should compensate crime victims but those who criminally harmed them. At most, it might be argued, the state should facilitate such compensation by seeing to it that restitution requirements are aspects of or added to criminal sentences. Alternatively, the state could take a less active role in helping crime victims obtain compensation in a different way, one that involves leaving it to victims to initiate civil suits to recover damages for some or all of their losses. Both of these arguments suggest that it is offenders, rather than law-abiding taxpayers, who should be the ones to help victims recover from their undeserved injuries or losses.

Though initially persuasive, the problems with these approaches to victim compensation are, I believe, sufficient to raise serious doubts about them. First, it is well-known that many criminal offenders are relatively impoverished, as are their victims.[55] If the state shifts victim compensation to such offenders, then the prospects of many victims receiving adequate or timely compensation will be, in many cases, bleak. This will especially be true if offenders are also assigned terms of imprisonment. Granted, such offenders might be permitted to work off their compensation debts over time. Their abilities to do so will vary, depending on the length of their imprisonment, the opportunities for work available to them during their imprisonment (often quite limited and poorly paying), and the opportunities for work available to them after they are released from prison (also apt to be limited and poorly paying).[56] In fact, many offenders who are not sent to prison will struggle mightily to pay their victim compensation debts if those debts turn out to be significant. All of this means that many victims who have been harmed significantly will never, one suspects, receive anything like full compensation for their losses. Similar problems attend the suggestion of tort suits, by victims, as means to gain compensation against those who have harmed them. Added to those problems will be the costs, uncertainties, and delays that will invariably attend successful tort suits in the civil courts.

Second, offender compensation of victims, if it occurs over relatively extended periods of time, will have the effect of increasing the harms that many victims suffer. Suppose, for instance, that an elderly person is bilked out of her life savings by some sophisticated bit of thieving. The courts might force the bilker to pay her full and fair restitution—though how long this will take and whether it will ever occur are both dependent on numerous contingencies. Nonetheless, until it occurs, the victim might have to endure months or years of living at whatever minimal level of state welfare is guaranteed to all members of society. In addition to the short, sharp shock of initial victimization, many victims' losses will be compounded by the pace at which the criminal justice process moves, including the full completion of any requirements that offenders pay restitution (which in many cases they will be ill-suited to do at all or quickly). If, however, the state stepped in and quickly and fully compensated victims for their undeserved losses, this would staunch them, perhaps significantly. Also, the state could then assume the burden of going after the offenders who caused the harms, seeking to claw back from them at least some of the costs of providing compensation.

Third, in the absence of state efforts to compensate crime victims, it should be clear, by now, that most of them of them will never receive compensation because their victimizers will not be identified, apprehended, or convicted of the crimes that they committed. Again, in the United States, upwards of 95 percent of victims will not see those who wronged them convicted. State-sponsored compensation programs would ensure that many more victims received some help in dealing with the harms they have suffered. If the concern is that state-sponsored compensation in the absence of criminal convictions would lead some citizens to falsely claim criminal victimization, then solutions to this are not hard to find. We could require candidates for compensation to file police reports as a precondition of receiving compensation.[57] False reports would then be subject to prosecution, just as falsely reporting crimes is.

Finally, some weight ought to be given to the likely effects of forcing offenders to pay compensation to their victims. Again, many offenders, just like their victims, come from relatively impoverished backgrounds and their convictions make it more likely that they will remain impoverished. This is bad enough for them, and probably criminogenic in many cases, but it is worse for those who depend on them for shelter, food, education, health care, and other goods. Many who commit and are convicted of crimes have dependent children.[58] Requiring them to pay restitution to the victims of their crimes will leave them with fewer resources to expend on their children or other loved ones. In addition to increasing misery, there is some reason to believe this will have criminogenic effects.[59] State compensation of victims, by contrast, is much less likely to have such effects.

In short, if crime victim compensation is to be timely, adequate, and assured, then it ought to be provided, in the first instance, by the state, which has the resources to do so. The state could then go after criminal offenders to seek reimbursement of the funds it has expended on victim compensation, though whether it should do so might depend on complex judgments about its feasibility and consequences.

Concluding Remarks

We began this chapter on a desultory note: It does not appear that contemporary criminal justice systems are more than modestly successful at holding offenders accountable for many of the crimes that they commit. This means that moral communication with those offenders, their victims, and the broader community will not occur anywhere near as often as it should. Add to this the limited success of legal punishment at reducing crime and its credentials as a successful institution appear suspect. In light of this, we considered partial and more complete alternatives to state penal institutions. Yet the prospects of these alternatives were not brighter and, in some cases, seemed considerably dimmer. All of this led me to suggest that if we want to reduce crime and stand for the victims of it, we need to supplement legal punishment with state measures of different kinds, in the forms of social welfare provisions and victim compensation programs.

I have, throughout the discussion in this chapter, said little about the ways in which the operations of many contemporary criminal justice systems are skewed along class, racial, ethnic, gender, and other lines. As we saw in Chapter 5, the police often engage in overenforcement of the criminal law in poor neighborhoods with racial or ethnic minorities, perhaps most often when it comes to arrests for vice crimes or public disorder offenses.[60] More to the point given my concerns in this chapter, there is underenforcement of the criminal law in such neighborhoods when it comes to the authorities taking seriously crimes against their inhabitants.[61] There is also underenforcement of the criminal law with regard to crimes of sexual assault or domestic violence against women and especially women from racial or ethnic minorities.[62] What this skewing of law enforcement means is that not only will many victims of crimes not see those who wronged them held accountable, some in society will see this less often than others, perhaps much less often.

In light of this, it is useful to note that one potential additional benefit of state-supplied victim compensation would be that poor victims of crimes who are more often underserved by the criminal justice system might at least receive some help in recovering from their losses or injuries. Granted, poor or minority or female crime victims might find the police less willing to arrest and charge perpetrators of crimes against them. But the choice to seek compensation would be in the hands of victims, not the authorities. This means that victims willing to report crimes would receive compensation for their injuries and losses. Of course, we cannot dismiss the possibility that eligibility for victim compensation might be overseen or enforced in ways that discriminate against the poor or socially excluded. Still, decisions about eligibility presumably would not be made by the police, whose track records when it comes to treating all citizens as equals before the law are less than encouraging.

Further, enhanced social welfare measures might help indirectly to address some of the problems posed by underenforcement. If such measures had the effect of reducing the desperation or alienation of the poor or socially excluded, they might be less inclined to criminally victimize others, including those who live in their communities.

Still, the general conclusion toward which this and other chapters point is a sobering one: We should have limited expectations about the institution of legal punishment. It is not apt to be highly successful in doing the things that it seems most defensible to hope it will do. But it equally is not clear that we should be prepared to abolish it or radically transform it into something else. Obviously, we should take steps to reduce offending in ways that have little to do with punishing those who engage in crime. And we should be prepared to substantially reform the institution of legal punishment in societies in which its operations and outcomes flout the very purposes for which, in its most defensible forms, it exists. Nonetheless, crime, including serious crime, is likely to persist and the punishment of those who engage in it will likewise have to continue, troubling as that prospect might in certain respects seem to be.

Notes

1 Shima Baughman, "How Effective Are Police? The Problem of Clearance Rates and Criminal Accountability," *Alabama Law Review* 72 (2020): 48–130 and Andrew D. Leipold, "The Puzzle of Clearance Rates, and What They Can Tell Us about Crime, Police Reform, and Criminal Justice," *Wake Forest Law Review* 56 (2021): 47–95.

2 Leipold, "The Puzzle of Clearance Rates," 61–62. FBI Index crimes are divided into "violent" and "property" crimes. The former include murder, aggravated assault, forcible rape, and robbery. The latter include arson, burglary, larceny-theft, and motor vehicle theft.

3 Leipold, "The Puzzle of Clearance Rates," 62.

4 Leipold, "The Puzzle of Clearance Rates," 62–63.

5 Baughman, "How Effective Are Police?" 90. The 21 percent reflects the fact that there are many more property index crimes cleared than violent ones, presumably because there are many more of the former than the latter.

6 See, for instance, Rebecca Campbell, et al., "The National Problem of Untested Sexual Assault Kits (SAKs): Scope, Causes, and Future Directions for Research, Policy, and Practice," *Trauma and Violence* 18 (2017): 363–76.

7 See Alexandra Natapoff, "Underenforcement," *Fordham Law Review* 75 (2006): 1715–76.
8 Baughman, "How Effective Are Police?" 94.
9 Leipold, "The Puzzle of Clearance Rates," 67.
10 Leipold, "The Puzzle of Clearance Rates," 64.
11 Paul Smit and Stefan Harrendorf, "Responses of the Criminal Justice System," in Stefan Harrendorf, Markuu Heiskanen, and Steven Malby (eds.), *International Statistics on Crime and Justice* (Helsinki: HEINU Publication Series, 2010): 87–112, at 95.
12 Estimates are that close to seven million people in the United States are on probation, in jail, or in prison in an average year. See *Incarceration and Reentry*, Office of the Assistant Secretary for Planning and Evaluation, U. S. Department of Health and Human Services, at https://aspe.hhs.gov/topics/human-services/incarceration-reentry-0 (accessed January 10, 2022).
13 See Bruce Western, *Punishment and Inequality in America* (New York: Russell Sage Foundation, 2006), especially Chapter 5.
14 For skepticism about increasing the certainty of punishment, see Todd R. Clear, *Imprisoning Communities: How Mass Incarceration Makes Disadvantaged Neighborhoods Worse* (New York: Oxford University Press, 2007): 22–23.
15 Vincent Chiao, "Mass Incarceration and the Theory of Punishment," *Criminal Law and Philosophy* 11 (2017): 431–52. See also his *Criminal Law in the Age of the Administrative State* (Oxford: Oxford University Press, 2018).
16 Alexandra Natapoff, "Misdemeanors," *Southern California Law Review* 85 (2012): 1313–75 and Jenny Roberts, "Why Misdemeanors Matter: Defining Effective Advocacy in the Lower Criminal Courts," *University of California-Davis Law Review* 45 (2011): 277–372.
17 Michael Tonry, "Sentencing in America, 1975–2025," *Crime and Justice: A Review of Research* 42 (2013): 141–98.
18 Chiao, "Mass Incarceration," 440.
19 Randy E. Barnett, "Restitution: A New Paradigm of Criminal Justice," *Ethics* 87 (1977): 279–301 and *The Structure of Liberty: Justice and the Rule of Law* (Oxford: Oxford University Press, 1998), especially Chapter 11; Daniel Boonin, *The Problem of Punishment* (Cambridge: Cambridge University Press, 2008); and Deidre Golash, *The Case against Punishment* (New York: New York University Press, 2005).
20 Robert Nozick, *Anarchy, State, and Utopia* (New York: Basic Books, 1974): 12–15.
21 On substituting offender restitution payments for state punishment, see Barnett, "Restitution," 393 and *The Structure of Liberty*, 233. For useful overviews of the restorative justice approach, see Heather Strang and Lawrence W. Sherman, "Repairing the Harm: Victims and Restorative Justice," *Utah Law Review* 2003 (2003): 15–42; and John Braithwaite, "Restorative Justice," in Michael Tonry (ed.), *The Handbook of Crime and Punishment* (New York: Oxford University Press, 1998): 323–43.
22 Nozick, *Anarchy, State, and Utopia*, 12.
23 There will also be the need for the state to serve in a back-up role if those accused of crimes refuse to participate in restorative justice conferences or fail to live up to what they pledge to do during such conferences to make amends to the victims of their crimes.
24 Similar problems would seem to plague a preventive detention alternative to legal punishment discussed by Steven P. Garvey. See his "Alternatives to Punishment," in John Deigh and David Dolinko (eds.), *The Oxford Handbook of Criminal Law* (Oxford: Oxford University Press, 2011): 493–513.

25 To be fair to those who broach this view, they often do so to argue for the view that the state derives its authority to punish from the moral right of individuals to punish in the state of nature. The idea of such a natural executive right to punish in the state of nature comes from John Locke in *Two Treatises of Government*, P. Laslett (ed.) (Cambridge: Cambridge University Press, 1963). For more on the Lockean view and the debate about it, see A. John Simmons, *The Lockean Theory of Rights* (Princeton, NJ: Princeton University Press, 1992), especially Chapter 3. See also Daniel M. Farrell, "Punishment Without the State," *Noûs* 22 (1988): 437–53, and Nozick, *Anarchy, State, and Utopia*, 10–12.

26 Darrell Steffensmeier, Hua Zhong, Jeff Ackerman, Jennifer Schwartz, and Suzanne Agha, "Gender Gap Trends for Violent Crimes, 1980 to 2003," *Feminist Criminology* 1 (2006): 72–98.

27 Nozick, *Anarchy, State, and Utopia*, 12–15.

28 See, for instance, Richard B. Freeman, "Why Do So Many Young American Men Commit Crimes and What Might We Do about It?" *Journal of Economic Perspectives* 10 (1996): 25–42. As Freeman notes (at 34–35), many of the poor commit crimes to supplement sources of legal income, and thus do not engage in offending continuously but more episodically.

29 Kevin M. Fitzpatrick and Brad Myrstol, "The Jailing of America's Homeless: Evaluating the Rabble Management Hypothesis," *Crime & Delinquency* 57 (2011): 271–97.

30 Natapoff, "Misdemeanors," 1333.

31 See *Mentally Ill Offenders in the Criminal Justice System: An Analysis and Prescription*, The Sentencing Project (2002), at www.sentencingproject.org/wp-content/uploads/2016/01/Mentally-Ill-Offenders-in-the-Criminal-Justice-System.pdf (accessed July 10, 2020).

32 See Clear, *Imprisoning Communities.*

33 Irving A. Spergel, "Youth Gangs: Continuity and Change," *Crime and Justice: A Review of Research* 12 (1990): 171–275.

34 Johnathan Kozol, *Savage Inequalities: Children in America's Schools* (New York: Harper Perennial, 1988).

35 See Jennifer L. Hochschild, "The Politics of the Estranged Poor," *Ethics* 101 (1991): 560–78.

36 For a provocative recent account that strongly emphasizes preventive justice measures over legal punishment, see Allegra M. McLeod, "Prison Abolition and Grounded Justice," *UCLA Law Review* 62 (2015): 1156–239.

37 See Richard L. Lippke, "Chronic Temptation, Reasonable Firmness, and the Criminal Law," *Oxford Journal of Legal Studies* 34 (2014): 75–96. See also Benjamin Ewing, "Recent Work on Punishment and Criminogenic Disadvantage," *Law and Philosophy* 37 (2018): 29–68

38 See, among others, Nozick, *Anarchy, State, and Utopia;* Jan Narveson, *The Libertarian Idea* (Philadelphia: Temple University Press, 1988); Loren E. Lomasky, *Persons, Rights, and the Moral Community* (New York: Oxford University Press, 1987); Barnett, *The Structure of Liberty;* and Richard A. Epstein, *Principles for a Free Society: Reconciling Individual Liberty with the Common Good* (New York: Basic Books, 2002).

39 Nozick, *Anarchy, State, and Utopia*, at 152–53. See Epstein, *Simple Rules*, at 59–64, and Jan Narveson, "Present Payments, Past Wrongs: Correcting Loose Talk about Nozick and Rectification," *Libertarian Papers: A Journal of Philosophy, Politics, and Economics* 1 (2009), at http://libertarianpapers.org/wp-content/uploads/article/2009/lp-1-1.pdf (accessed July 13, 2020).

40 See Nahshon Perez, "Libertarianism, Rectification, and Property Rights: A Reevaluation," *Canadian Journal of Law and Jurisprudence* 27 (2014): 123–43.

41 See, for instance, Loïc Wacquant, "Deadly Symbiosis: When Ghetto and Prison Meet and Mesh," *Punishment & Society* 3 (2001): 95–133.
42 Recent figures suggest that the white families have ten times the wealth of black families. See *Examining the Black-white Wealth Gap*, The Brookings Institution (2020), at www.brookings.edu/blog/up-front/2020/02/27/examining-the-black-white-wealth-gap/ (accessed July 13, 2020).
43 See, for instance, David Lyons, "The New Indian Claims and Original Rights to Land," *Social Theory and Practice* 4 (1977): 249–72 and J. Angelo Corlett, *Race, Racism, and Reparations* (Ithaca, NY: Cornell University Press, 2003).
44 See, for instance, Adrian De Leon, "The Long History of US Racism against Asian Americans, from 'Yellow Peril' to 'Model Minority' to the 'Chinese Virus'," *The Conversation*, at https://theconversation.com/the-long-history-of-us-racism-against-asian-americans-from-yellow-peril-to-model-minority-to-the-chinese-virus-135793 (accessed July 13, 2020).
45 See, for instance, Richard Gott, "Let's End the Myths of Britain's Imperial Past," *The Guardian*, October 19, 2011, at www.theguardian.com/books/2011/oct/19/end-myths-britains-imperial-past (accessed January 10, 2022).
46 Nozick, *Anarchy, State, and Utopia*, 230–31.
47 See Lomasky, *Persons, Rights and the Moral Community*, 126–28.
48 Contemporary welfare liberals, some of whom verge over towards egalitarianism, include John Rawls, *A Theory of Justice* (Cambridge, MA: Harvard University Press, 1971); Ronald Dworkin, *Sovereign Virtue: Equality in Theory and Practice* (Cambridge, MA: Harvard University Press, 2000); Philippe von Parijs, *Real Freedom for All: What (If Anything) Can Justify Capitalism?* (Oxford: Oxford University Press, 1995); and Bruce Ackerman, *Social Justice in the Liberal State* (New Haven, CT: Yale University Press, 1980). Egalitarians include Kai Nielsen, *Equality and Liberty: A Defense of Radical Egalitarianism* (Totowa, NJ: Rowman and Allanheld, 1985); G. A. Cohen, *Rescuing Justice and Equality* (Cambridge, MA: Harvard University Press, 2008); Amartya Sen, *Inequality Reexamined* (Cambridge, MA: Harvard University Press, 1992); and John E. Roemer, *Equality of Opportunity* (Cambridge, MA: Harvard University Press, 2000).
49 See Western, *Punishment and Inequality*, Chapter 5.
50 Paul Knepper, "An International Crime Decline: Lessons for Social Welfare Crime Policy?" *Social Policy & Administration* 46 (2012): 359–76, at 361–62.
51 Tapio Lappi-Seppälä and Michael Tonry, "Crime, Criminal Justice, and Criminology in the Nordic Countries," *Crime and Justice: A Review of Research* 40 (2011): 1–32.
52 Maximilian Rudolph and Peter Starke, "How Does the Welfare State Reduce Crime? The Effect of Program Characteristics and Decommodification Across 18 OECD-Countries," *Journal of Criminal Justice* 68 (2020): 1–12.
53 Joanne Savage, Richard R. Bennett, and Mona Danner, "Economic Assistance and Crime," *European Journal of Criminology* 5 (2008): 217–38.
54 Many countries have state-sponsored victim compensation schemes. Even in the United States, which has meager social welfare provisions, most jurisdictions have various kinds of state-sponsored victim compensation. See *U. S. Resource Map of Crime Victim Services and Information*, Office for Victims of Crime, at www.ovc.gov/map.html (accessed December 24, 2021).
55 Clear, *Imprisoning Communities*, 61.
56 On the desultory earnings of inmates in US prisons, see Asatar P. Bair, *Prison Labor in the United States: An Economic Analysis* (New York: Routledge, 2008). For the impact of imprisonment on offenders' earning capacities, see Western, *Punishment and Inequality in America*.

57 This is a requirement in many legal jurisdictions in the United States and elsewhere.
58 Christopher J. Mumola, "Incarcerated Parents and Their Children," *Bureau of Justice Statistics Special Report* (Washington, DC: Bureau of Justice Statistics, 2000).
59 There is some evidence that children whose parents are incarcerated are themselves more at risk for incarceration, perhaps due to the poverty parental incarceration generates, the stigma attached to parental incarceration, the absence in the childrens' lives of a significant care-giver, or other factors. On this see John Hagan and Ronet Dinovitzer, "Collateral Consequences of Imprisonment for Children, Communities, and Prisoners," in *Prisons* (Michael Tonry and Joan Petersilia, eds.), a special volume of *Crime and Justice: A Review of Research* 36 (1999): 121–62. Added victim restitution requirements might further exacerbate family poverty or cause parents to be absent because they must work longer hours to make ends meet and satisfy their legal obligations.
60 See Angela J. Davis (ed.), *Policing the Black Man: Arrest, Prosecution, and Imprisonment* (New York: Vintage Books, 2017); Michelle Alexander, *The New Jim Crow: Mass Incarceration in the Age of Colorblindness* (New York: The New Press, 2012); Michael Tonry, *Malign Neglect: Race, Crime, and Punishment in America* (New York: Oxford University Press, 1995); David Cole, *No Equal Justice: Race and Class in the American Criminal Justice System* (New York: The New Press, 1999); and William J. Stuntz, "Race, Class, and Drugs," *Columbia Law Review* 98 (1998): 1795–842.
61 Alexandra Natapoff, "Underenforcement," *Fordham Law Review* 75 (2006): 1715–76. See also Randall Kennedy, *Race, Crime, and the Law* (New York: Vintage, 1998) and William J. Stuntz, "Unequal Justice," *Harvard Law Review* 121 (2008): 1969–2040.
62 See Campbell, et al., "The National Problem" and Kevin J. Strom and Matthew J. Hickman, "Unanalyzed Evidence in Law Enforcement Agencies: A National Examination of Forensic Processing in Police Departments," *Criminology & Public Policy* 9 (2010): 381–404. On the failure to protect women from domestic violence, see Emily J. Sack, "Battered Women and the State: The Struggle for the Future of Domestic Violence Policy," *Wisconsin Law Review* 2004 (2004): 1657–740; Anna Clark, "Domestic Violence, Past and Present," *Journal of Women's History* 23 (2011): 193–202; and Deborah Epstein, "Effective Intervention in Domestic Violence Cases: Rethinking the Roles of Prosecutors, Judges, and the Court System," *Yale Journal of Law & Feminism* 11 (1999): 3–50.

Bibliography

Ackerman, Bruce. *Social Justice in the Liberal State* (New Haven, CT: Yale University Press, 1980).

Alexander, Michelle. *The New Jim Crow: Mass Incarceration in the Age of Colorblindness* (New York: The New Press, 2012).

Allsop, Cheryl. *Cold Case Reviews: DNA, Detective Work, and Unsolved Major Crimes* (New York: Oxford University Press, 2018).

Alper, Mariel, Durose, Matthew R. and Markman, Joshua. *2018 Update on Prisoner Recidivism: A 9-Year Follow-up Period (2005–2014)*, Bureau of Justice Statistics. At www.bjs.gov/index.cfm?ty=pbdetail&iid=6266 (accessed May 11, 2020).

Alschuler, Albert W. "The Prosecutor's Role in Plea Bargaining," *University of Chicago Law Review* 36 (1968): 50–112.

———. "The Trial Judge's Role in Plea Bargaining, Part 1," *Columbia Law Review* 76 (1976): 1059–154.

———. "The Changing Plea Bargaining Debate," *California Law Review* 69 (1981): 652–730.

———. "A Peculiar Privilege in Historical Perspective," in R. H. Helmholtz, et al. (eds.), *The Privilege against Self-Incrimination: Its Origin and Development* (Chicago: University of Chicago Press, 1997): 181–204.

Altman, Matthew C. *A Theory of Legal Punishment: Deterrence, Retribution, and the Aims of the State* (London: Routledge, 2021).

Americans with Criminal Records. The Sentencing Project (2015). At www.sentencingproject.org/wp-content/uploads/2015/11/Americans-with-Criminal-Records-Poverty-and-Opportunity-Profile.pdf (accessed July 4, 2020).

Andenaes, Johannes. "The General Preventive Effects of Punishment," *University of Pennsylvania Law Review* 114 (1966): 949–83.

Anonymous. "Note: Restructuring the Plea Bargain," *Yale Law Journal* 82 (1972): 286–312.

Arenella, Peter. "Convicting the Morally Blameless: Reassessing the Relationship between Legal and Moral Accountability," *UCLA Law Review* 39 (1992): 1511–622.

Ashworth, Andrew and Redmayne, Mike. *The Criminal Process, Fourth Edition* (Oxford: Oxford University Press, 2010).

Bagaric, Mirko. "Double Punishment and Punishing Character: The Unfairness of Prior Convictions," *Criminal Justice Ethics* 19 (2010): 10–28.

Bair, Asatar P. *Prison Labor in the United States: An Economic Analysis* (New York: Routledge, 2008).

Barnett, Randy E. "Restitution: A New Paradigm of Criminal Justice," *Ethics* 87 (1977): 279–301.

———. *The Structure of Liberty: Justice and the Rule of Law* (Oxford: Oxford University Press, 2000).

Baughman, Shima. "How Effective Are Police? The Problem of Clearance Rates and Criminal Accountability," *Alabama Law Review* 72 (2020): 48–130.

Beckett, Katherine and Harris, Alexes. "On Cash and Conviction: Monetary Sanctions as Misguided Policy," *Criminology & Public Policy* 10 (2011): 509–37.

Bedau, Hugo Adam. "The Minimal Invasion Argument against the Death Penalty," *Criminal Justice Ethics* 21 (2002): 3–8.

Beitz, Charles R. "Human Dignity in the Theory of Human Rights: Nothing but a Phrase?" *Philosophy and Public Affairs* 41 (2013): 259–90.

Bennett, Christopher. *The Apology Ritual: A Philosophical Theory of Punishment* (Cambridge: Cambridge University Press, 2008).

Bennett, Steven C. "The 'Right to Be Forgotten': Reconciling EU and US Perspectives," *Berkeley Journal of International Law* 30 (2012): 161–95.

Bentham, Jeremy. *The Works of Jeremy Bentham*, Vol IV. J. Bowring (ed.) (London: Edinburgh, Simpkin, and Marshall, 1843).

Berman, Mitchell N. "Modest Retributivism," in Kimberly Kessler Ferzan and Stephen J. Morse (eds.), *Legal, Moral, and Metaphysical Truths: The Philosophy of M. S. Moore* (Oxford: Oxford University Press, 2016): 35–47.

Bernburg, Jön Gunnar, Krohn, Marvin D. and Rivera, Craig J. "Official Labeling, Criminal Embeddedness, and Subsequent Delinquency: A Longitudinal Test of Labeling Theory," *Journal of Research in Crime and Delinquency* 43 (2006): 67–88.

Blocher, Joseph and Charles, Jacob D. "Firearms, Extreme Risk, and Legal Design: 'Red Flag' Laws and Due Process," *Virginia Law Review* 106 (2020): 1285–344.

Boonin, David. *The Problem of Punishment* (Cambridge: Cambridge University Press, 2008).

Bowers, Josh. "Punishing the Innocent," *University of Pennsylvania Law Review* 156 (2008): 1117–179.

Boyne, Shawn. "Is the Journey from the In-Box to the Out-Box a Straight Line? The Drive for Efficiency and the Prosecution of Low-Level Criminality in Germany," in Erik Luna and Marianne Wade (eds.), *The Prosecutor in Transnational Perspective* (Oxford: Oxford University Press, 2012): 37–53.

Bradley, Ben. "Two Concepts of Intrinsic Value," *Ethical Theory and Moral Practice* 9 (2006): 111–30.

Braithwaite, John. "Restorative Justice," in Michael Tonry (ed.), *The Handbook of Crime and Punishment* (New York: Oxford University Press, 1998): 323–43.

Braithwaite, John and Geis, Gilbert. "On Theory and Action for Corporate Crime Control," *Crime & Delinquency* 28 (1982): 292–314.

Braithwaite, John and Pettit, Philip. *Not Just Deserts: A Republican Theory of Criminal Justice* (Oxford: Clarendon Press, 1990).

Brandt, Richard. "A Utilitarian Theory of Excuses," *The Philosophical Review* 78 (1969): 337–61.

Bright, Stephen B. and Sanneh, Sia M. "Fifty Years of Defiance and Resistance after *Gideon v. Wainwright*," *Yale Law Journal* 122 (2013): 2150–74.

Broadhurst, Roderic. "Aborigines and Crime in Australia," *Crime and Justice: A Review of Research* 21 (1997): 407–68.

Bronsteen, John, Buccafusco, Christopher and Masur, Jonathan S. "Happiness and Punishment," *University of Chicago Law Review* 76 (2009): 1037–81.

Brooks, Thom. *Punishment, Second Edition* (London: Routledge, 2020).

Brown, Darryl K. *Free Market Criminal Justice: How Democracy and Laissez Faire Undermine the Rule of Law* (Oxford: Oxford University Press, 2016).

Brown, Jeffrey M. "Collateral Legal Consequences of Criminal Convictions in a Society of Equals," *Criminal Law and Philosophy* 15 (2021): 181–205.

Brudner, Alan. *Punishment and Freedom: A Liberal Theory of Penal Justice* (Oxford: Oxford University Press, 2009).

Burgh, Richard. "Do the Guilty Deserve Punishment?" *Journal of Philosophy* 79 (1982): 193–210.

Burnett, Ros and Maruna, Shadd. "So 'Prison Works', Does It? The Criminal Careers of 130 Men Under Release from Prison under Home Secretary, Michael Howard," *The Howard Journal* 43 (2004): 390–404.

Cahill, Michael. "Retributive Justice in the Real World," *Washington University Law Review* 85 (2007): 815–70.

———. "Punishment Pluralism," in Mark D. White (ed.), *Retributivism: Essays on Theory and Practice* (New York: Oxford University Press, 2011): 25–48.

Calavita, K., Tillman, R. and Pontell, H. N. "The Savings and Loan Debacle, Financial Crime, and the State," *Annual Review of Sociology* 23 (1997): 19–38.

Campbell, Rebecca, Feeney, Hannah, Fehler-Cabral, Giannina, Shaw, Jessica and Horsford, Sheena. "The National Problem of Untested Rape Kits (SAKS): Scope, Causes, and Future Directions for Research, Policy, and Practice," *Trauma, Violence, and Abuse* 18 (2017): 363–76.

Chiao, Vincent. "Mass Incarceration and the Theory of Punishment," *Criminal Law and Philosophy* 11 (2017): 431–52.

———. *Criminal Law in the Age of the Administrative State* (Oxford: Oxford University Press, 2018).

———. "Proportionality and Its Discontents," *Law and Philosophy* 41 (2022): 193–217.

Chin, Gabriel J. "The New Civil Death: Rethinking Punishment in the Era of Mass Conviction," *University of Pennsylvania Law Review* 160 (2012): 1789–833.

Church, Jr. Thomas W. "In Defense of 'Bargain Justice'," *Law & Society* 13 (1979): 509–25.

Clark, Anna. "Domestic Violence, Past and Present," *Journal of Women's History* 23 (2011): 193–202.

Clear, Todd R. *Imprisoning Communities: How Mass Incarceration Makes Disadvantaged Neighborhoods Worse* (New York: Oxford University Press, 2007).

Coben, Jeffrey H. and Larkin, Gregory L. "Effectiveness of Ignition Interlock Devices in Reducing Drunk Driving Recidivism," *American Journal of Preventive Medicine* 16 (1999): 81–87.

Cohen, G. A. *Rescuing Justice and Equality* (Cambridge, MA: Harvard University Press, 2008).

Cole, David. *No Equal Justice: Race and Class in the American Criminal Justice System* (New York: The New Press, 1999).

Corden, John. "Persistent Petty Offenders: Problems and Patterns of Multiple Disadvantage," *The Howard Journal of Criminal Justice* 23 (1983): 68–90.

Corlett, J. Angelo. *Race, Racism, and Reparations* (Ithaca, NY: Cornell University Press, 2003).

Cottingham, John. "Varieties of Retributivism," *Philosophical Quarterly* 29 (1979): 238–46.

Cruft, Rowan, Liao, S. Matthew and Renzo, Massimo. *Philosophical Foundations of Human Rights* (Oxford: Oxford University Press, 2015).

Cullen, Frances T. "Rehabilitation: Beyond Nothing Works," *Crime and Justice: A Review of Research* 42 (2013): 299–376.

Dagger, Richard. *Playing Fair: Political Obligation and the Problems of Punishment* (Oxford: Oxford University Press, 2018).

Damaška, Mirjan R. *The Faces of Justice and State Authority* (New Haven, CT: Yale University Press, 1986).

———. "Truth in Adjudication," *Hastings Law Journal* 49 (1998): 289–308.

Davis, Angela J. *Arbitrary Justice: The Power of the American Prosecutor* (Oxford: Oxford University Press, 2007).

——— (ed.). *Policing the Black Man: Arrest, Prosecution, and Imprisonment* (New York: Vintage Books, 2017).

Davis, Lawrence. "They Deserve to Suffer," *Analysis* 32 (1972): 136–40.

De Leon, Adrian. "The Long History of US Racism against Asian Americans, from 'Yellow Peril' to 'Model Minority' to the 'Chinese Virus'," *The Conversation* 2020. At https://theconversation.com/the-long-history-of-us-racism-against-asian-americans-from-yellow-peril-to-model-minority-to-the-chinese-virus-135793 (accessed July 13, 2020).

Delgado, Richard. "Rotten Social Background: Should the Criminal Law Recognize a Defense of Severe Environmental Deprivation?" *Law & Inequality* 3 (1985): 9–90.

Dolinko, David. "Is There a Rationale for the Privilege against Self-Incrimination?" *UCLA Law Review* 33 (1986): 1063–148.

———. "Some Thoughts about Retributivism," *Ethics* 101 (1991): 537–59.

———. "Retributivism, Consequentialism, and the Intrinsic Goodness of Punishment," *Law and Philosophy* 16 (1997): 507–28.

Doob, Anthony N. and Webster, Cheryl Marie. "Sentence Severity and Crime: Accepting the Null Hypothesis," *Crime and Justice: A Review of Research* 30 (2003): 143–95.

Dressier, Joshua. *Understanding Criminal Law, Fourth Edition* (Newark, NJ: Lexis-Nexis, 2006).

Duff, R. A. "Psychopathy and Moral Understanding," *American Philosophical Quarterly* 14 (1977): 189–200.

———. *Trials and Punishments* (Cambridge: Cambridge University Press, 1986).

———. "Penal Communications: Recent Work on the Philosophy of Punishment," *Crime and Justice: A Review of Research* 20 (1996): 1–96.

———. "Dangerousness and Citizenship," in A. Ashworth and M. Wasik (eds.), *Fundamentals of Sentencing Theory: Essays in Honour of Andrew von Hirsch* (Oxford: Clarendon Press, 1998): 173–201.

———. *Punishment, Communication, and Community* (Oxford: Oxford University Press, 2001).

———. *The Realm of Criminal Law* (Oxford: Oxford University Press, 2018).

———. Farmer, Lindsay, Marshall, Sandra and Tadros, Victor. *The Trial on Trial, Vol. 3: Towards a Normative Theory of the Criminal Trial* (Oxford: Hart Publishing, 2007).

Duus-Otterström, Göran. "Weighing Relative and Absolute Proportionality in Punishment," in Tonry (ed.), *Of One-Eyed and Toothless Miscreants* (2020): 30–50.

Duus-Otterström, Göran and Kelly, Erin I. "Injustice and the Right to Punish," *Philosophy Compass* 14 (2019). At https://doi.org/10.1111/phc3.12565 (accessed November 27, 2021).

Dworkin, Ronald. *Sovereign Virtue: Equality in Theory and Practice* (Cambridge, MA: Harvard University Press, 2000).

Easterbrook, Frank H. "Criminal Procedure as a Market System," *Journal of Legal Studies* 12 (1983): 289–332.

———. "Plea Bargaining as Compromise," *Yale Law Journal* 101 (1992): 1969–78.

Epstein, Deborah. "Effective Intervention in Domestic Violence Cases: Rethinking the Roles of Prosecutors, Judges, and the Court System," *Yale Journal of Law & Feminism* 11 (1999): 3–50.

Epstein, Richard A. *Principles for a Free Society: Reconciling Individual Liberty with the Common Good* (New York: Basic Books, 2000).

Ewing, Benjamin. "Recent Work on Punishment and Criminogenic Disadvantage," *Law and Philosophy* 37 (2018): 29–68.

———. "Prior Convictions as Moral Opportunities," *American Journal of Criminal Law* 45 (2019): 252–303.

Examining the Black-white Wealth Gap. The Brookings Institution, 2020. At www.brookings.edu/blog/up-front/2020/02/27/examining-the-black-white-wealth-gap/ (accessed July 13, 2020).

Fagan, Jeffrey and Meares, Tracy L. "Punishment, Deterrence, and Social Control: The Paradox of Punishment in Minority Communities," *Ohio State Journal of Criminal Law* 6 (2008): 173–229.

Farrell, Daniel M. "Punishment without the State," *Noûs* 22 (1988): 437–53.

Fazel, Seena and Wolf, Achim. "A Systematic Review of Criminal Recidivism Rates Worldwide: Current Difficulties and Recommendations for Best Practices," *PloS One* (2015). At https://doi.org/10.1371/journal.pone.0130390 (accessed January 30, 2022).

Feeley, Malcolm M. *The Process Is the Punishment: Handling Cases in a Lower Criminal Court* (New York: Russell Sage, 1979).

Feinberg, Joel. "The Expressive Function of Punishment," *The Monist* 49 (1965): 397–423.

———. *Harm to Others* (New York: Oxford University Press, 1984).

———. *Offense to Others* (New York: Oxford University Press, 1985).

———. *Harm to Self* (New York: Oxford University Press, 1986).

———. *Harmless Wrongdoing* (New York: Oxford University Press, 1990).

Fekete, Liz. "Europe against the Roma," *Race & Class* 55 (2014): 60–70.

Feld, Barry C. "A Slower Form of Death: Implications of *Roper v. Simmons* for Juveniles Sentenced to Life Without Parole," *Notre Dame Journal of Law, Ethics, and Public Policy* 9 (2008): 9–65.

Findlay, Keith A. and Scott, Michael S. "The Multiple Dimensions of Tunnel Vision in Criminal Cases," *Wisconsin Law Review* (2006): 291–397.

Fine, Cordelia and Kennett, Jeanette. "Mental Impairment, Moral Understanding, and Criminal Responsibility: Psychopathy and the Purposes of Punishment," *International Journal of Law and Psychiatry* 27 (2004): 425–43.

Finkelstein, Claire O. "Duress: A Philosophical Account of the Defense in Law," *Arizona Law Review* 37 (1995): 251–83.

Fischer, J. Martin and Ravizza, Mark. *Responsibility and Control: A Theory of Moral Responsibility* (Cambridge: Cambridge University Press, 1988).

Fitzpatrick, Kevin M. and Myrstol, Brad. "The Jailing of America's Homeless: Evaluating the Rabble Management Hypothesis," *Crime & Delinquency* 57 (2011): 271–97.

Fox, Adam R., Kvaran, Trevor H. and Fontaine, Reid Griffith. "Psychopathy and Culpability: How Responsible Is the Psychopath for Criminal Wrongdoing?" *Law & Social Inquiry* 38 (2013): 1–26.

Frase, Richard S. "Comparative Criminal Justice as a Guide to American Law Reform: How Do the French Do It, How Can We Find Out, and Why Should We Care?" *California Law Review* 78 (1990): 539–683.

———. "Punishment Purposes," *Stanford Law Review* 58 (2005): 67–83.

———. *Just Sentencing: Principles and Procedures for a Workable System* (New York: Oxford University Press, 2013).

Freeman, Richard. "Why Do So Many Young American Men Commit Crimes and What Might We Do about It?" *Journal of Economic Perspectives* 10 (1996): 25–42.

Gaes, Gerald G., Flanagan, Timothy J., Motiuk, Laurence L. and Stewart, Lynn. "Adult Correctional Treatment," *Crime and Justice: A Review of Research* 26 (1999): 361–426.

Garvey, Stephen P. "Alternatives to Punishment," in John Deigh and David Dolinko (eds.), *The Oxford Handbook of Criminal Law* (Oxford: Oxford University Press, 2011): 493–513.

Gendreau, Paul. "Offender Rehabilitation: What We Know and What Needs to Be Done," *Criminal Justice and Behavior* 23 (1996): 144–61.

Gert, Heather, Radzik, Linda and Hand, Michael. "Hampton on the Expressive Power of Punishment," *Journal of Social Philosophy* 35 (2004): 79–90.

Gewirth, Alan. *Reason and Morality* (Chicago: University of Chicago Press, 1978).

Glannon, Walter. "Moral Responsibility and the Psychopath," *Neuroethics* 1 (2008): 158–66.

Golash, Deidre. *The Case against Punishment* (New York: New York University Press, 2005).

Goldman, Alan H. "The Paradox of Punishment," *Philosophy and Public Affairs* 9 (1979): 42–58.

Gonzalez, Richard. "Sentence in Stanford Sexual Assault Case Sparks Outrage," 2016. At www.npr.org/sections/thetwo-way/2016/06/06/481010919/california-rape-case-sentence-sparks-outrage (accessed October 13, 2021).

Gott, Richard. "Let's End the Myths of Britain's Imperial Past," *The Guardian*, October 19, 2011. At www.theguardian.com/books/2011/oct/19/end-myths-britains-imperial-past (accessed January 10, 2022).

Grande, Elisabetta. "Dances of Criminal Justice: Thoughts on Systematic Differences and the Search for the Truth," in John Jackson, Máximo Langer, and Peter Tiller (eds.), *Crime, Procedure, and Evidence in Comparative and International Context: Essays in Honour of Mirjan Damaška* (Oxford: Hart Publishing, 2008): 145–64.

Gray, David. "Punishment as Suffering," *Vanderbilt Law Review* 63 (2010): 1617–93.

Hagan, John and Dinovitzer, Ronet. "Collateral Consequences of Imprisonment for Children, Communities, and Prisoners," in *Prisons* (Michael Tonry and Joan Petersilia, eds.), a special volume of *Crime and Justice: A Review of Research* 36 (1999): 121–62.

Hampton, Jean. "The Moral Education Theory of Punishment," *Philosophy and Public Affairs* 13 (1984): 208–38.

———. "The Retributive Idea," in Jean Hampton and Jeffrie Murphy (eds.), *Forgiveness and Mercy* (Cambridge: Cambridge University Press, 1988): Chapter 4.

———. "A New Theory of Retribution," in R. G. Frey and C. W. Morris (eds.), *Liability and Responsibility: Essays in Law and Morals* (Cambridge: Cambridge University Press, 1991): 377–414.

———. "An Expressive Theory of Retribution," in Wesley Craig (ed.), *Retributivism and Its Critics* (Stuttgart: V. Steiner Verlag, 1992): 1–21.

———. "Correcting Harms Versus Righting Wrongs: The Goal of Retribution," *UCLA Law Review* 39 (1992): 1659–702.

Haney, Craig. "Mental Health Issues in Long-Term Solitary and 'Supermax' Confinement," *Crime & Delinquency* 49 (2003): 124–55.

———. *Reforming Punishment: Psychological Limits to the Pains of Imprisonment* (Washington, DC: American Psychological Association, 2006).

Hanna, Nathan. "Say What? A Critique of Expressive Retributivism," *Law & Philosophy* 27 (2008): 123–50.

———. "Retributivism Revisited," *Philosophical Studies* 167 (2014): 473–84.

Harris, Alexes. *A Pound of Flesh: Monetary Sanctions as Punishment for the Poor* (New York: Russell Sage, 2016).

——— et al. *Monetary Sanctions in the Criminal Justice System* (Arnold Foundation, 2017). At www.monetarysanctions.org/wp-content/uploads/2017/04/Monetary-Sanctions-Legal-Review-Final.pdf (accessed July 3, 2020).

Harris, David A. "Factors for Reasonable Suspicion: Why Black and Poor Means Stopped and Frisked," *Indiana Law Journal* 69 (1994): 659–88.

Hart, H. L. A. *Law, Liberty, and Morality* (Stanford: Stanford University Press, 1963).

———. *Punishment and Responsibility: Essays in the Philosophy of Law* (Oxford: Clarendon Press, 1968).

Hayes, Hennessey. "Assessing Reoffending in Restorative Justice Conferences," *Australian & New Zealand Journal of Criminology* 38 (2005): 77–101.

Heffernan, William C. and Kleinig, John (eds.). *From Social Justice to Criminal Justice: Poverty and the Administration of Criminal Law* (New York: Oxford University Press, 2000).

Hegel, G. F. W. *Philosophy of Right*, T. M. Knox (trans.) (Oxford: Oxford University Press, 1965).

Heumann, Milton. *Plea Bargaining: The Experiences of Prosecutors, Judges, and Defense Attorneys* (Chicago: University of Chicago Press, 1978).

Hirschi, Travis and Gottfredson, Michael. "Age and the Explanation of Crime," *American Journal of Sociology* 89 (1983): 552–84.

Hochschild, Jennifer L. "The Politics of the Estranged Poor," *Ethics* 101 (1991): 560–78.

Hoskins, Zachary. *Beyond Punishment: A Normative Account of the Collateral Legal Consequences of Conviction* (New York: Oxford University Press, 2019).

———. "Hybrid Theories of Punishment," in Bruce Waller, Elizabeth Shaw, and Farah Focquaert (eds.), *The Routledge Handbook of the Philosophy and Science of Punishment* (New York: Routledge, 2021): 37–48.

Hudson, Barbara. "Punishing the Poor: Dilemmas of Justice and Difference," in Heffernan and Kleinig (eds.), *From Social Justice to Criminal Justice*, 189–216.

Husak, Douglas N. *Drugs and Rights* (Cambridge: Cambridge University Press, 1992).

———. "Why Punish the Deserving?" *Noûs* 26 (1992): 447–64.

———. "The Metric of Punishment Severity: A Puzzle about the Principle of Proportionality," in Tonry (ed.), *Of One-Eyed and Toothless Miscreants* (2020): 97–126.

———. "Proportionality in Personal Life," *Criminal Law and Philosophy* 15 (2021): 339–60.

Incarceration and Reentry, Office of the Assistant Secretary for Planning and Evaluation, U. S. Department of Health and Human Services. At https://aspe.hhs.gov/topics/human-services/incarceration-reentry-0 (accessed January 10, 2022).

"Incarceration Nation," *Monitor on Psychology* 45 (2014). American Psychological Association. At www.apa.org/monitor/2014/10/incarceration (accessed June 1, 2023).

"Indicators of Mental Health Problems Reported By Prisoners and Jail Inmates," (2017). Bureau of Justice, U. S. Department of Justice. At www.bjs.gov/index.cfm?ty=pbdetail&iid=5946.

Jackson, John D. and Summers, Sarah J. *The Internationlisation of Criminal Evidence: Beyond the Common Law and Civil Law Traditions* (Cambridge: Cambridge University Press, 2012).

Jacobs, James B. *The Eternal Criminal Record* (Cambridge, MA: Harvard University Press, 2015).

Jacobs, James B. and Larrauri, Elena. "European Criminal Records and Ex-Offender Employment," *Oxford Handbooks Online* (2015). At https://doi.org/10.1093/oxfordhb/9780199935383.013.157 (accessed January 15, 2021).

Johnson, Robert and Dobrzanska, Ania. "Mature Coping among Life-Sentenced Inmates: An Exploratory Study of Adjustment Dynamics," *Corrections Compendium* 30 (2005): 8–9, 36–38.

Kahan, Dan S. "What Do Alternative Sanctions Mean?" *University of Chicago Law Review* 63 (1996): 591–653.

Kant, Immanuel. *Groundwork of the Metaphysics of Morals*, Mary Gregor (trans.) (Cambridge: Cambridge University Press, 1998).

———. *Critique of Practical Reason*, Mary Gregor (trans.) (Cambridge: Cambridge University Press, 2015).

Kaplow, Louis and Shavell, Steven. *Fairness Versus Welfare* (Cambridge, MA: Harvard University Press, 2002).

Kateb, George. *Human Dignity* (Cambridge, MA: Harvard University Press, 2011).

Katzenstein, Mary Fainsod and Nagrecha, Mitali. "A New Punishment Regime," *Criminology & Public Policy* 10 (2011): 555–68.

Kelly, Erin. *The Limits of Blame: Rethinking Punishment and Responsibility* (Cambridge, MA: Harvard University Press, 2018).

Kennedy, Randall. *Race, Crime, and the Law* (New York: Vintage, 1998).

Kleinig, John. "The Concept of Desert," *American Philosophical Quarterly* 8 (1971): 71–78.

———. *Punishment and Desert* (The Hague: Martinus Nijhoff, 1973).

———. "Punishment and Moral Seriousness," *Israel Law Review* 25 (1991): 401–21.

———. "The Hardness of Hard Treatment," in A. Ashworth and M. Wasik (eds.), *Fundamentals in Sentencing Theory: Essays in Honour of Andrew von Hirsch* (Oxford: Clarendon Press, 1998): 273–98.

Knepper, Paul. "An International Crime Decline: Lessons for Social Welfare Crime Policy?" *Social Policy & Administration* 46 (2012): 359–76.

Kolber, Adam J. "The Comparative Nature of Punishment," *Boston University Law Review* 89 (2009): 1565–608.

———. "The Subjective Experience of Punishment," *Columbia Law Review* 109 (2009): 182–236.

Kozol, Jonathan. *Savage Inequalities: Children in America's Schools* (New York: Harper Perennial, 1988).

Kymlicka, Will. *Contemporary Political Philosophy: An Introduction* (Oxford: Oxford University Press, 2002).

Langer, Màximo. "From Legal Transplants to Legal Translations: The Globalization of Plea Bargaining and the Americanization Thesis in Criminal Procedure," *Harvard International Law Journal* 45 (2004): 1–64.

Lappi-Seppälä, Tapio and Tonry, Michael. "Crime, Criminal Justice, and Criminology in the Nordic Countries," *Crime and Justice: A Review of Research* 40 (2011): 1–32.

Laub, John H., Nagin, Daniel S. and Sampson, Robert J. "Trajectories of Change in Criminal Offending: Good Marriages and the Desistance Process," *American Sociological Review* 63 (1998): 225–38.

Laudan, Larry. *Truth, Error, and Criminal Law* (Cambridge: Cambridge University Press, 2006).

———. "The Rules of Trial, Political Morality, and the Costs of Error: Or, Is Proof beyond a Reasonable Doubt Causing More Harm than Good?" in L. Green and B. Leiter (eds.), *Oxford Studies in Philosophy of Law, Volume 1* (Oxford: Oxford University Press, 2011): 195–223.

Lazarus, Liora. *Contrasting Prisoners' Rights: A Comparative Examination of England and Germany* (Oxford: Oxford University Press, 2004).

Lee, Youngjae. "Repeat Offenders and the Question of Desert," in Roberts and von Hirsch, *Previous Convictions at Sentencing* (2014): 49–72.

Leigey, Margaret E. "For the Longest Time: The Adjustment of Inmates to a Sentence of Life Without Parole," *The Prison Journal* 90 (2010): 247–68.

Leipold, Andrew D. "The Puzzle of Clearance Rates, and What They Can Tell Us about Crime, Police Reform, and Criminal Justice," *Wake Forest Law Review* 56 (2021): 47–95.

Lillquist, Erik. "Recasting Reasonable Doubt: Decision Theory and the Virtues of Variability," *University California-Davis Law Review* 36 (2002): 85–197.

Lippke, Richard L. "Criminal Offenders and Right Forfeiture," *Journal of Social Philosophy* 32 (2001): 78–89.

———. "The Disenfranchisement of Felons," *Law and Philosophy* 20 (2001): 553–80.

———. *Rethinking Imprisonment* (Oxford: Oxford University Press, 2007).

———. "No Easy Way Out: Dangerous Offenders and Preventive Detention," *Law and Philosophy* 27 (2008): 383–414.

———. "The Case for Reasoned Criminal Trial Verdicts," *Canadian Journal of Law and Jurisprudence* 22 (2009): 313–30.

———. "Rewarding Cooperation: The Moral Complexities of Procuring Accomplice Testimony," *New Criminal Law Review* 13 (2010): 90–118.

———. *The Ethics of Plea Bargaining* (Oxford: Oxford University Press, 2011).

———. "Chronic Temptation, Reasonable Firmness, and the Criminal Law," *Oxford Journal of Legal Studies* 34 (2014): 75–96.

———. "Prosecutors: Experts or Elected Officials?" in J. Ryberg and J. Roberts (eds.), *Popular Punishment: On the Normative Significance of Public Opinion for Penal Theory* (Oxford: Oxford University Press, 2014): 163–82.

———. "Some Surprising Implications of Negative Retributivism," *Journal of Applied Philosophy* 31 (2014): 49–62.

———. *Taming the Presumption of Innocence* (New York: Oxford University Press, 2016).

———. "The Minimal State and Indigent Defense," *Criminal Justice Ethics* 35 (2016): 1–20.

———. "Punishment Drift: The Spread of Penal Harm and What We Should Do about It," *Criminal Law and Philosophy* 11 (2017): 629–46.

———. "Legal Punishment and the Public Identification of Offenders," *Res Publica* 24 (2018): 199–216.

———. "Penal Severity and the Modern State," in Tonry (ed.), *Of One-Eyed and Toothless Miscreants: Making the Punishment Fit the Crime* (2020): 127–48.

Lipsey, Mark W. and Cullen, Frances T. "The Effectiveness of Correctional Rehabilitation: A Review of Systematic Reviews," *Annual Review of Law and Social Science* 3 (2007): 297–320.

Locke, John. *Two Treatises of Government.* P. Laslett (ed.) (Cambridge: Cambridge University Press, 1963).

Lomasky, Loren E. *Persons, Rights, and the Moral Community* (New York: Oxford University Press, 1987).

———. "Aid without Egalitarianism: Assisting Indigent Defendants," in Heffernan and Kleinig (eds.), *From Social Justice to Criminal Justice* (2000): 84–97.

Luban, David. *Lawyers and Justice: An Ethical Study* (Princeton, NJ: Princeton University Press, 1988).

———. "Liberalism, Torture, and the Ticking Bomb," in Stephen P. Lee (ed.), *Intervention, Terrorism, and Torture: Contemporary Challenges to Just War Theory* (Dordrecht, Netherlands: Springer, 2010): 249–62.

Lyons, David. "The New Indian Claims and Original Rights to Land," *Social Theory and Practice* 4 (1977): 249–72.

Ma, Yue. "Prosecutorial Discretion and Plea Bargaining in the United States, France, Germany and Italy: A Comparative Perspective," *International Criminal Justice Review* 12 (2002): 22–52.

Mackie, J. L. "Morality and the Retributive Emotions," *Criminal Justice Ethics* 1 (1982): 3–10.

———. "Retributivism: A Test Case for Ethical Objectivity" reprinted in J. Feinberg and H. Gross, *Philosophy of Law, Fourth Edition* (Belmont, CA: Wadsworth, 1991): 677–84.

Markel, Dan and Flanders, Chad. "Bentham on Stilts: The Bare Relevance of Subjectivity to Retributive Justice," *California Law Review* 98 (2010): 907–88.

Martin, Rex. *A System of Rights* (Oxford: Clarendon Press, 1983).

McLeod, Allegra M. "Prison Abolition and Grounded Justice," *UCLA Law Review* 62 (2015): 1156–239.

Medwed, Daniel S. "The Zeal Deal: Prosecutorial Resistance to Post-Conviction Claims of Innocence," *Boston University Law Review* 84 (2004): 125–83.

Mentally Ill Offenders in the Criminal Justice System: An Analysis and Prescription. 2002. The Sentencing Project. At www.sentencingproject.org/wp-content/uploads/2016/01/Mentally-Ill-Offenders-in-the-Criminal-Justice-System.pdf (accessed July 10, 2020).

Metz, Thaddeus. "Censure Theory and Intuitions About Punishment," *Law & Philosophy* 19 (2000): 491–512.

Mill, John Stuart. *On Liberty* (Indianapolis, IN: Hackett Publishing, 1978).

Minix, Leanna C. "Examining Rule 11 (b) (1) (N) Error: Guilty Pleas, Appellate Waiver, and Dominguez Benitez," *Washington and Lee Law Review* 74 (2017): 552–606.

"Missing and Murdered Indigenous Women & Girls: A Snapshot of Data from 71 Urban Cities in the United States" (2018). Urban Indian Health Institute. At www.uihi.org/wp-content/uploads/2018/11/Missing-and-Murdered-Indigenous-Women-and-Girls-Report.pdf (accessed June 22, 2020).

Mitchell, John B. "The Ethics of the Criminal Defense Attorney—New Answers to Old Questions," *Stanford Law Review* 32 (1980): 293–337.

Mitchell, Ojmarrh, Wilson, David, Eggers, Amy and MacKenzie, Doris L. "Assessing the Effectiveness of Drug Courts on Recidivism: A Meta-Analytical Review of Traditional and Non-Traditional Drug Courts," *Journal of Criminal Justice* 40 (2012): 60–71.

Moore, Michael. *Act and Crime: The Philosophy of Action and Its Implications for Criminal Law* (Oxford: Oxford University Press, 1993).

———. *Placing Blame: A General Theory of the Criminal Law* (Oxford: Clarendon Press, 1997).

———. "Responses and Appreciations," in Kimberly Kessler Ferzan and Stephen J. Morse (eds.), *Legal, Moral and Metaphysical Truths: The Philosophy of Michael S. Moore* (New York: Oxford University Press, 2016): 343–427.

Morris, Christopher W. "Punishment and Loss of Moral Standing," *Canadian Journal of Philosophy* 21 (1991): 53–79.

Morris, Herbert. "Persons and Punishment," *The Monist* 52 (1968): 475–501.

Morris, Norval. *The Future of Imprisonment* (Chicago: University of Chicago Press, 1974).

———. *Madness and the Criminal Law* (Chicago: University of Chicago Press, 1982).

Morse, Stephen J. "Culpability and Control," *University of Pennsylvania Law Review* 142 (1994): 1587–660.

———. "Blame and Danger: An Essay on Preventive Detention," *Boston University Law Review* 76 (1996): 113–55.

———. "Delinquency and Desert," *The Annals of the American Academy of Political and Social Science* 564 (1999): 56–80.

———. "Psychopathy and Criminal Responsibility," *Neuroethics* 1 (2008): 205–12.

Mumola, Christopher J. "Incarcerated Parents and Their Children," *Bureau of Justice Statistics Special Report* (Washington, DC: Bureau of Justice Statistics, 2000).

Murphy, Jeffrie G. "Moral Death: A Kantian Essay on Psychopathy," *Ethics* 82 (1972): 284–98.

———. "Marxism and Retribution," *Philosophy and Public Affairs* 2 (1973): 217–43.

———. "Cruel and Unusual Punishments," in M. A. Stewart (ed.), *Law, Morality, and Human Rights* (Dordrecht: D. Reidel, 1979): 373–404.

Mustard, David B. "Racial, Ethnic, and Gender Disparities in Sentencing: Evidence from the U. S. Federal Courts," *The Journal of Law & Economics* 44 (2001): 285–314.

Nagin, Daniel S. "Criminal Deterrence: Research at the Outset of the Twenty-First Century," *Crime and Justice: A Review of Research* 23 (1998): 1–42.

———. "Deterrence and Incapacitation," in Michael Tonry (ed.), *The Handbook of Crime and Punishment* (New York: Oxford University Press, 1998): 345–68.

———. "Deterrence in the Twenty-First Century," *Crime and Justice: A Review of Research* 42 (2013): 199–263.

Nagin, Daniel S., Cullen, Frances T. and Jonson, Cheryl Lero. "Imprisonment and Reoffending," *Crime and Justice: A Review of Research* 38 (2009): 115–200.

Narayan, Uma. "Appropriate Responses and Preventive Benefits: Justifying Censure and Hard Treatment in Legal Punishment," *Oxford Journal of Legal Studies* 13 (1993): 166–82.

Narveson, Jan. *The Libertarian Idea* (Philadelphia: Temple University Press, 1988).

———. "Present Payments, Past Wrongs: Correcting Loose Talk about Nozick and Rectification," *Libertarian Papers: A Journal of Philosophy, Politics, and Economics* 1 (2009). At http://libertarianpapers.org/wp-content/uploads/article/2009/lp-1-1.pdf (accessed July 13, 2020).

Natapoff, Alexandra. "Underenforcement," *Fordham Law Review* 75 (2006): 1715–76.

———. "Misdemeanors," *Southern California Law Review* 85 (2012): 1313–75.

Nielsen, Kai. *Equality and Liberty: A Defense of Radical Egalitarianism* (Totowa, NJ: Rowman and Allanheld, 1985).

Noorda, Hadassa. "Regulation as Punishment," *Criminal Justice Ethics* 40 (2021): 108–23.

Nozick, Robert. *Anarchy, State, and Utopia* (New York: Basic Books, 1974).

Ofer, Udi. "Getting it Right: Building Effective Civilian Review Boards to Oversee Police," *Seton Hall Law Review* 46 (2016): 1033–62.

Orth, Uli. "Punishment Goals of Crime Victims," *Law and Human Behavior* 27 (2003): 173–86.

Owusu-Bempah, Akwasi and Wortley, Scot. "Race, Crime, and Criminal Justice in Canada," in S. Bucerius and M. Tonry (eds.), *The Oxford Handbook of Ethnicity, Crime, and Immigration* (New York: Oxford University Press, 2013): 281–320.

Pager, Devah. "The Mark of a Criminal Record," *American Journal of Sociology* 108 (2003): 937–75.

Perez, Nahshon. "Libertarianism, Rectification, and Property Rights: A Re-evaluation," *Canadian Journal of Law and Jurisprudence* 27 (2014): 123–43.

Pizzi, W. T. "Understanding Prosecutorial Discretion in the United States: The Limits of Comparative Criminal Procedure as an Instrument of Reform," *Ohio State Law Journal* 54 (1993): 1325–74.

Pratt, John and Eriksson, Anna. *Contrasts in Punishment: An Explanation of Anglophone Excess and Nordic Exceptionalism* (New York: Routledge, 2013).

Prescott, J. J. and Rockoff, Jonah K. "Do Sex Offender Registration and Notification Laws Affect Criminal Behavior," *Journal of Law & Economics* 54 (2011): 161–206.

Primoratz, Igor. "Punishment as Language," *Philosophy* 64 (1989): 187–205.

Pyrooz, David, Decker, Scott H. and Fleisher, Mark. "From the Street to the Prison, from the Prison to the Street: Understanding and Responding to Prison Gangs," *Journal of Aggression, Conflict, and Peace Research* 3 (2011): 12–24.

Quinn, Warren. "The Right to Threaten and the Right to Punish," *Philosophy and Public Affairs* 14 (1985): 327–73.

Rachels, James. "What People Deserve," in J. Rachels, *Can Ethics Provide Answers?* (Totowa, NJ: Rowman and Littlefield, 1996): 175–98.

Ratcliffe, Jerry A., Taniguchi, Travis and Taylor, Ralph B. "The Crime Reduction Effects of CCTV Cameras: A Multi-Method Spatial Approach," *Justice Quarterly* 26 (2009): 746–70.

Rawls, John. "Two Concepts of Rules," *The Philosophical Review* 64 (1955): 3–32.

———. *A Theory of Justice* (Cambridge, MA: Harvard University Press, 1971).

"Recidivism," National Institute of Justice, U. S. Department of Justice (2008). At https://nij.ojp.gov/topics/articles/recidivism-core-criminal-justice-concern (accessed June 2, 2023).

"Recidivism Rates by Country 2021," World Population Review, 2021. At https://worldpopulationreview.com/country-rankings/recidivism-rates-by-country (accessed October 14, 2022).

"Reclaiming Power and Place: The Final Report of the National Inquiry into Missing and Murdered Indigenous Women and Girls, Volume 1a," 2019. At www.mmiwg-ffada.ca/wp-content/uploads/2019/06/Final_Report_Vol_1a-1.pdf (accessed June 22, 2023).

Redlich, Allison D., Steadman, Henry J., Monahan, John, Robbins, Pamela Clark and Petrila, John. "Patterns of Practice in Mental Health Courts: A National Survey," *Law and Human Behavior* 30 (2006): 347–62.

Reiman, Jeffrey. *The Rich Get Richer and the Poor Get Prison: Ideology, Class, and Criminal Justice, Eighth Edition* (Boston, MA: Pearson, 2007).

Resick, Patricia A. "The Psychological Impact of Rape," *Journal of Interpersonal Violence* 8 (1993): 223–55.

Richardson, John R. "Red Flag Laws and Procedural Due Process: Analyzing Proposed Utah Legislation," *Utah Law Review* (2021): 743–65.

Richman, Daniel C. "Cooperating Defendants: The Costs and Benefits of Purchasing Information from Scoundrels," *Federal Sentencing Reporter* 8 (1996): 292–95.

Ristroph, Alice. "An Intellectual History of Mass Incarceration," *Boston College Law Review* 60 (2019): 1949–2010.

———. "Criminal Law as Public Ordering," *University of Toronto Law Journal* 70 (2020): 64–83.

Roberts, Dorothy E. "The Social and Moral Costs of Mass Incarceration in African-American Communities," *Stanford Law Review* 56 (2004): 1272–305.

Roberts, Jenny. "Why Misdemeanors Matter: Defining Effective Advocacy in the Lower Criminal Courts," *University of California-Davis Law Review* 45 (2011): 277–372.

Roberts, Julian V. "Punishing Persistence: Explaining the Enduring Appeal of the Recidivist Sentencing Premium," *British Journal of Criminology* 48 (2008): 468–81.

———. *Punishing Persistent Offenders: Exploring Community and Offender Perspectives* (Oxford: Oxford University Press, 2008).

Roberts, Julian V. and von Hirsch, Andrew (eds.). *Previous Convictions at Sentencing: Theoretical and Applied Perspectives* (Oxford: Hart Publishing, 2014).

Robinson, Paul H. *Intuitions of Justice and the Utility of Desert* (Oxford: Oxford University Press, 2013).

Robinson, Paul H. and Darley, John M. "The Utility of Desert," *Northwestern University Law Review* 91 (1997): 453–99.

Robinson, Paul H. and Kurzban, Robert. "Concordance and Conflict in Intuitions of Justice," *Minnesota Law Review* 91 (2007): 1829–907.

Robinson, Paul H., Goodwin, Geoffrey P. and Reisig, Michael. "The Disutility of Injustice," *New York University Law Review* 85 (2010): 1940–2033.

Roemer, John E. *Equality of Opportunity* (Cambridge, MA: Harvard University Press, 2000).

Rosen, Michael. *Dignity: Its History and Meaning* (Cambridge, MA: Harvard University Press, 2012).

Rudolph, Maximilian and Starke, Peter. "How Does the Welfare State Reduce Crime? The Effect of Program Characteristics and Decommodification across 18 OECD-Countries," *Journal of Criminal Justice* 68 (2020): 1–12.

Ryberg, Jesper. "Punishment and the Measurement of Severity," in Jesper Ryberg and J. Angelo Corlett (eds.), *Punishment and Ethics: New Perspectives* (Basingstoke: Palgrave Macmillan, 2010): 72–91.

———. "Proportionality and the Seriousness of Crimes," in Tonry (ed.), *Of One-Eyed and Toothless Miscreants* (2020): 51–75.

———. "Retributivism and the (Lack of) Justification of Proportionality," *Criminal Law and Philosophy* 15 (2021): 447–62.

Sack, Emily J. "Battered Women and the State: The Struggle for the Future of Domestic Violence Policy," *Wisconsin Law Review* 2004 (2004): 1657–740.

Sadurski, Wojciech. *Giving Desert Its Due* (Dordrecht, Netherlands: D. Reidel, 1985).

Sandler, J. C., Freeman, N. J. and Socia, K. M. "Does a Watched Pot Boil? A Time-Series Analysis of New York State's Sex Offender Registration and Notification Law," *Psychology, Public Policy, and Law* 14 (2008): 284–302.

Sarteschi, Christine M., Vaughn, Michael G. and Kim, Kevin. "Assessing the Effectiveness of Mental Health Courts: A Quantitative Review," *Journal of Criminal Justice* 39 (2011): 12–20.

Savage, Joanne., Bennett, Richard R. and Danner, Mona. "Economic Assistance and Crime," *European Journal of Criminology* 5 (2008): 217–38.

Schulhofer, Stephen J. "Rethinking Mandatory Minimums," *Wake Forest Law Review* 28 (1993): 199–222.

Seiter, Richard P. and Kadela, Karen R. "Prisoner Reentry: What Works, What Does Not, and What Is Promising," *Crime & Delinquency* 49 (2003): 360–88.

Sen, Amartya. *Inequality Reexamined* (Cambridge, MA: Harvard University Press, 1992).

Sher, George. *Desert* (Princeton, NJ: Princeton University Press, 1987).

Shoeman, Ferdinand D. "On Incapacitating the Dangerous," *American Philosophical Quarterly* 16 (1979): 27–35.

Shover, Neal. *Great Pretenders: Pursuits and Careers of Persistent Thieves* (Boulder, CO: Westview, 1996).

Sieh, Edward W. "Less Eligibility: The Upper Limits of Penal Policy," *Criminal Justice Policy Review* 3 (1989): 159–83.

Simmons, A. John. *The Lockean Theory of Rights* (Princeton, NJ: Princeton University Press, 1992).

Simon, Dan. "The Limited Diagnosticity of Criminal Trials," *Vanderbilt Law Review* 64 (2011): 143–223.

Smit, Paul and Harrendorf, Stefan. "Responses of the Criminal Justice System," in Stefan Harrendorf, Markuu Heiskanen, and Steven Malby (eds.), *International Statistics on Crime and Justice* (Helsinki: HEINU Publication Series, 2010): 87–112.

Smith, David J. "Ethnic Origins, Crime, and Criminal Justice in England and Wales," *Crime and Justice: A Review of Research* 21 (1997): 101–82.

Sobol, Neil L. "Charging the Poor: Criminal Justice Debt and Modern-Day Debtors' Prisons," *University of Maryland Law Review* 75 (2016): 486–540.

Spergel, Irving A. "Youth Gangs: Continuity and Change," *Crime and Justice: A Review of Research* 12 (1990): 171–275.

Steadman, Henry J., Osher, Fred C., Robbins, Pamela Clark, Case, Brian and Samuels, Steven. "Prevalence of Serious Mental Illness Among Jail Inmates," *Psychiatric Services* 60 (2009): 761–65.

Steffensmeier, Darrell, Zhong, Hua, Ackerman, Jeff, Schwartz, Jennifer and Agha, Suzanne. "Gender Gap Trends for Violent Crimes, 1980 to 2003," *Feminist Criminology* 1 (2006): 72–98.

Strang, Heather and Sherman, Lawrence W. "Repairing the Harm: Victims and Restorative Justice," *Utah Law Review* 2003 (2003): 15–42.

Strom, Kevin J. and Hickman, Matthew J. "Unanalyzed Evidence in Law Enforcement Agencies: A National Examination of Forensic Processing in Police Departments," *Criminology & Public Policy* 9 (2010): 381–404.

Stuntz, William J. "Race, Class, and Drugs," *Columbia Law Review* 98 (1998): 1795–842.

———. "The Pathological Politics of Criminal Law," *Michigan Law Review* 100 (2001): 505–600.

———. "Unequal Justice," *Harvard Law Review* 121 (2008): 1969–2040.

Subramanian, Ram and Shames, Alison. *Sentencing and Prison Practices in German and the Netherlands: Implications for the United States*, Vera Institute of Justice (2013). At www.vera.org/downloads/Publications/sentencing-and-prison-practices-in-germany-and-the-netherlands-implications-for-the-united-states/legacy_downloads/european-american-prison-report-v3.pdf (accessed May 7, 2020).

Tadros, Victor. *The Ends of Harm: The Moral Foundations of Criminal Law* (Oxford: Oxford University Press, 2011.

Ten, C. L. *Crime, Guilt, and Punishment: A Philosophical Introduction* (Oxford: Clarendon Press, 1987).

Thomas, Dorothy Q. and Beasley, Michele E., Esq. "Domestic Violence as a Human Rights Issue," *Human Rights Quarterly* 15 (1993): 36–62.

Tonry, Michael. "Sentencing Commissions and Their Guidelines," *Crime and Justice: A Review of Research* 17 (1993): 137–95.

———. "Proportionality, Parsimony, and Interchangeability of Punishment," in R. A. Duff, S. Marshall, and R. Dobash (eds.), *Penal Theory and Practice* (Manchester: Manchester University Press, 1994): 59–83.

———. *Malign Neglect: Race, Crime, and Punishment in America* (New York: Oxford University Press, 1995).

———. "Has the Prison a Future?" in M. Tonry (ed.), *The Future of Imprisonment* (New York: Oxford University Press, 2004): 3–24.

———. *Punishing Race: A Continuing American Dilemma* (Oxford: Oxford University Press, 2011).

———. *Doing Justice, Preventing Crime* (New York: Oxford University Press, 2020).

———. *Of One-Eyed and Toothless Miscreants: Making the Punishment Fit the Crime?* (New York: Oxford University Press, 2020).

Tonry, Michael and Lynch, Mary. "Intermediate Sanctions," *Crime and Justice: A Review of Research* 20 (1996): 99–144.

Travis, Jeremy. "Invisible Punishment: An Instrument of Social Exclusion," in Marc Mauer and Meda Chesney-Lind (eds.), *Invisible Punishment: The Collateral Consequences of Mass Imprisonment* (New York: The New Press, 2002): 15–36.

Trechsel, Stefan and Summers, Sarah. *Human Rights in Criminal Proceedings* (Oxford: Oxford University Press, 2006).

Turner, Jenia I. *Plea Bargaining across Borders* (New York: Aspen Publishers, 2009).

Tyler, Tom R. *Why People Obey the Law* (Princeton, NJ: Princeton University Press, 2006).

Uggen, Christopher. "Work As a Turning Point in the Life Course of Criminals: A Duration Model of Age, Employment, and Recidivism," *American Sociological Review* 65 (2000): 529–46.

Ulmer, Jeffrey T. and Steffensmeier, Darrell. "The Age and Crime Relationship: Social Variation, Social Explanations," in Kevin M. Beaver, J. C. Barnes, and Brian B.

Boutwell (eds.), *The Nurture Versus Biosocial Debate in Criminology: On the Origins of Criminal Behavior and Criminality* (Thousand Oaks, CA: Sage, 2015): 377–96.

U.S. Resource Map of Crime Victim Services and Information, Office for Victims of Crime (2020). At www.ovc.gov/map.html (accessed October 14, 2021).

van Zyl Smit, Dirk and Dünkel, Franz. *Prison Labour: Salvation or Slavery? International Perspectives* (Aldershot, UK: Ashgate, 1999).

von Hirsch, Andrew. "Proportionality in the Philosophy of Punishment," *Crime and Justice: A Review of Research* 16 (1992): 55–98.

———. *Censure and Sanctions* (Oxford: Clarendon Press, 1993).

von Hirsch, Andrew and Jareborg, Nils. "Gauging Criminal Harm: A Living-Standard Analysis," *Oxford Journal of Legal Studies* 11 (1991): 1–38.

von Hirsch, Andrew and Shearing, Clifford. "Restorative Justice: A 'Making Amends' Model," in Andrew von Hirsh and Andrew Ashworth (eds.), *Proportionate Sentencing: Exploring the Principles* (Oxford: Oxford University Press, 2005): 110–30.

von Hirsch, Andrew and Wasik, Martin. "Civil Disqualifications Attending Conviction: A Suggested Conceptual Framework," *Cambridge Law Journal* 56 (1997): 599–626.

von Parijs, Philippe. *Real Freedom for All: What (If Anything) Can Justify Capitalism?* (Oxford: Oxford University Press, 1995).

Wacquant, Loïc. "Deadly Symbiosis: When Ghetto and Prison Meet and Mesh," *Punishment & Society* 3 (2001): 95–133.

———. *Prisons of Poverty* (Minneapolis, MN: University of Minnesota Press, 2009).

Waldron, Jeremy. *Theories of Rights* (Oxford: Oxford University Press, 1982).

———. *Dignity, Rank, and Rights* (Oxford: Oxford University Press, 2012).

Walker, Nigel. "Even More Varieties of Retributivism," *Philosophy* 74 (1999): 595–605.

Wallace, R. Jay. *Responsibility and the Moral Sentiments* (Cambridge, MA: Harvard University Press, 1998).

Wasik, Martin and von Hirsch, Andrew. "Section 29 Revisited: Previous Convictions in Sentencing," *Criminal Law Review* (1994): 409–18.

We Are All Criminals (2023). At www.weareallcriminals.org/ (accessed July 2, 2023).

Weigend, Thomas. "Is the Criminal Process about Truth? A German Perspective," *Harvard Journal of Law and Public Policy* 26 (2003): 157–74.

———. "Should We Search for the Truth and Who Should Do It?" *North Carolina Journal of International Law and Commercial Regulation* 36 (2011): 389–416.

Weinstein, Ian. "Regulating the Market for Snitches," *Buffalo Law Review* 47 (1999): 563–643.

Wellman, Christopher Heath. *Rights Forfeiture and Punishment* (New York: Oxford University Press, 2017).

Welsh, Brandon C. and Farrington, David P. "Public Area CCTV and Crime Prevention: An Updated and Systematic Review and Meta-Analysis," *Justice Quarterly* 26 (2009): 716–45.

Western, Bruce. *Punishment and Inequality in America* (New York: Russell Sage Foundation, 2006).

Western, Bruce and Pettit, Becky. "Incarceration and Social Inequality," *Daedelus* (Summer 2010): 8–19.

Wikström, Per-Olof H. "Explaining Crime as Moral Actions," in Steven Hitlin and Stephen Vaisey (eds.), *Handbook of the Sociology of Morality* (New York: Springer, 2010): 211–39.

Wood, David. "Retribution, Crime Reduction, and the Justification of Punishment," *Oxford Journal of Legal Studies* 22 (2002): 301–21.

Wright, Ronald F. "How Prosecutor Elections Fail Us," *Ohio State Journal of Criminal Law* 6 (2009): 581–610.

Wringe, Bill. *An Expressive Theory of Punishment* (London: Palgrave Macmillan, 2016).

Zaibert, Leo. *Punishment and Retribution* (Hants, England: Ashgate, 2006).

Zaitchik, Alan. "Deserving to Deserve," *Philosophy and Public Affairs* 6 (1977): 370–88.

Zimring, Franklin E. and Hawkins, Gordon. *Incapacitation: Penal Confinement and the Restraint of Crime* (New York: Oxford University Press, 1995).

Index

Made in the USA
Monee, IL
14 September 2026

62978585R00144